LIBRARY OF HEBREW BIBLE/ OLD TESTAMENT STUDIES

451

Formerly Journal for the Study of the Old Testament Supplement Series

COLLECTIONS, CODES, AND TORAH

The Re-characterization of Israel's Written Law

Michael LeFebvre

t&t clark

NEW YORK • LONDON

Copyright © 2006 by Michael LeFebvre

T & T Clark International, 80 Maiden Lane, New York, NY 10038

T & T Clark International, The Tower Building, 11 York Road, London SE1 7NX

T & T Clark International is a Continuum imprint.

Library of Congress Cataloging-in-Publication Data
LeFebvre, Michael.
    Collections, codes, and Torah : the re-characterization of Israel's written law / Michael LeFebvre.
        p. cm. -- (Library of Hebrew Bible/Old Testament studies ; 451)
    Includes bibliographical references and index.
    ISBN-13: 978-0-567-02882-2 (hardcover)
    ISBN-10: 0-567-02882-8 (hardcover)
    1. Jewish law--Codification. 2. Customary law (Jewish law) 3. Tradition (Judaism) I. Title. II. Series.

    BM521.L38 2006
    296.1'8--dc22

                                        2006022092

06 07 08 09 10   10 9 8 7 6 5 4 3 2 1

Printed and bound in Great Britain by Biddles Ltd., King's Lynn, Norfolk

to Ken

my older brother

CONTENTS

ACKNOWLEDGMENTS

My interest in biblical law began in the Psalms. Through both academic and devotional attention to those ancient hymns, I became intrigued at the professions of love for God's law sown throughout them. That love proved contagious. This book, based on my Ph.D. dissertation, represents my pursuit of that fascination.

As I think about those whose influence and support has aided me in the preparation of this book, it is, therefore, for King David and his heirs that I owe first thanks. Those ancient hymnists cast the charm which drew me into this study. It was also the Psalms which provided personal inspiration for me throughout this project. I am grateful for so rich a source of stimulation.

But of course, ancient songs cannot provide the practical support needed for a project like this. For such support I must acknowledge the judicious oversight of my dissertation supervisors, Edward D. Herbert and Kenneth T. Aitken, as well as the critical insights of my dissertation examiners, Lester L. Grabbe and Joachim Schaper. I am indebted to these scholars for their interest in my work, their encouragement, and their wise guidance. I am also grateful for other faculty at International Christian College (Glasgow) and the University of Aberdeen, as well as my fellow postgraduate students. Other scholars, for whose labors I am indebted, are indicated by the many footnotes throughout this volume.

I also want to give special recognition to my wife, Heather, for her immense contributions to make this work a reality. Heather not only upheld me with her devoted care through months of dusty books and a husband's thoughts in "another world," but she even took interest to join me in "my world" by reading every one of my papers and discussing my work with me. And all this while helping raise our three children and reckoning with health constraints. My wife has truly shown herself "an excellent wife far more precious than jewels," and it is only right that "her husband rise up and praise her" (Prov 31:10–31).

I am also thankful for my children (Rachel, Andrew, and James) who daily reminded me of other books worth reading, like *Frog and Toad* and *Postman Pat*. Our Scottish church family (Reverend S. Andrew Quigley and the Airdrie Reformed Presbyterian Church) and our American church family (Dr. Roy Blackwood and Second Reformed Presbyterian Church of Indianapolis) surrounded us with their love, prayers, and practical support throughout the duration of my studies—as did various other individuals and organizations not recounted here by name. Without this circle of support, I would have had to close my books and pack my bags without finishing this project.

For whatever benefit others may find in the pages which follow, I would invite you to join in my thanks for these who aided me in producing them. This book is my own work, with all the responsibility remaining with me which that entails. Nonetheless, I am mindful of the many to whom I am indebted for making this work possible.

In one final word of gratitude: although it was David's heritage of Psalms that "cast the bait" for this project, it was the master compositions of the ancient lawgivers themselves which "set the hook." What a wonderful source of marvel these ancient legists—Moses, Hammurabi, and their like—have left for us! Whatever their reasons for inscribing these great compositions, it is the fact such brilliant rulers *did* inscribe their laws that we have such a repository to explore. For those labors I confess my deepest respect.

It is to such great minds and great hearts, both ancient and modern, that I want to give tribute and express my sincere gratitude.

Michael LeFebvre
May, 2006

"I count myself one of the number of those
who write as they learn and learn as they write."
—Augustine

ABBREVIATIONS AND TRANSLATIONS

AB	Anchor Bible
ABD	*The Anchor Bible Dictionary*. Edited by D. N. Freedman. 6 vols. New York: Doubleday, 1992
Aeg	*Aegyptus*
AfO	*Archiv für Orientforschung*
AGJU	Arbeiten zur Geschichte des antiken Judentums und des Urchristentums
AJA	*American Journal of Archaeology*
AnBib	Analecta biblica
ArOr	*Archiv orientální*
AS	*Assyriological Studies*
BBB	Bonner Biblische Beiträge
BETL	Bibliotheca ephemeridum theologicarum lovaniensium
BibInt	Biblical Interpretation Series
BJS	Brown Judaic Studies
BN	*Biblische Notizen*
BO	*Bibliotheca orientalis*
BS	*Bibliotheca Sacra*
BZAW	Beihefte zur Zeitschrift für die alttestamentliche Wissenschaft
CahRB	Cahiers de la Revue biblique
CBQ	*Catholic Biblical Quarterly*
CJ	*Classical Journal*
CPJ	*Corpus papyrorum judaicarum*. Edited by V. Tcherikover. 3 vols. Cambridge, Mass.: Harvard University Press
CurBS	*Currents in Research: Biblical Studies*
CRAI	*Comptes rendus de l'Académie des inscriptions et belles-lettres*
CRINT	Compendia rerum iudaicarum ad Novum Testamentum
DJD	Discoveries in the Judaean Desert
DtrH	Deuteronom(ist)ic History
EV	English Bible verse numbering
EvQ	*Evangelical Quarterly*
FOTL	The Forms of the Old Testament Literature
GRBS	*Greek, Roman, and Byzantine Studies*
HAR	*Hebrew Annual Review*
HO	Handbuch der Orientalistik
HTR	*Harvard Theological Review*
IBC	Interpretation, a Bible commentary for teaching and preaching
IEJ	*Israel Exploration Journal*
ITC	International Theological Commentary
JAOS	*Journal of the American Oriental Society*
JBL	*Journal of Biblical Literature*
JEA	*Journal of Egyptian Archaeology*

JETS	*Journal of the Evangelical Theological Society*
JHS	*Journal of Hellenic Studies*
JJS	*Journal of Jewish Studies*
JLR	*Journal of Law and Religion*
JNES	*Journal of Near Eastern Studies*
JQR	*Jewish Quarterly Review*
JSHRZ	Jüdische Schriften aus hellenistisch-römischer Zeit
JSJ	*Journal for the Study of Judaism in the Persian, Hellenistic and Roman Period*
JSJSup	Journal for the Study of Judaism in the Persian, Hellenistic and Roman Period: Supplement Series
JSOT	*Journal for the Study of the Old Testament*
JSOTSup	Journal for the Study of the Old Testament: Supplement Series
JSPSup	Journal for the Study of the Pseudepigrapha: Supplement Series
JSS	*Journal of Semitic Studies*
HL	Hittite Laws
LCL	Loeb Classical Library
LE	Laws of Eshnunna
LH	Laws of Hammurabi
LL	Laws of Lipit-Ishtar
LU	Laws of Ur-Namma
MAL	Middle Assyrian Laws
MBPF	Münchener Beiträge zur Papyrusforschung und antiken Rechtsgeschichte
NAC	New American Commentary
NCB	New Century Bible
NCBC	New Century Bible Commentary
NIBC	New International Bible Commentary
NIDOTTE	*New International Dictionary of Old Testament Theology and Exegesis.* Edited by Willem A. VanGemeren. 5 vols. Grand Rapids: Zondervan, 1997
OBO	Orbis biblicus et orientalis
Or	*Orientalia*
OrAnt	*Oriens antiquus*
OTL	Old Testament Library
OTP	*The Old Testament Pseudepigrapha*, vol. 2. Edited by J. H. Charlesworth. London: Darton, Longman & Todd, 1983
OTS	*Oudtestamentische Studiën*
PEQ	*Palestine Exploration Quarterly*
P. Hal. 1	Graeca Halensis. *Dikaiomata: Auszüge aus alexandrinischen Gesetzen und Verordnungen, in einem Papyrus des Philologischen Seminars der Universität Halle (Pap. Hal. 1): mit einem Anhang weiterer Papyri derselben Sammlung.* Graeca Halensis. Berlin: Weidmennsche, 1913
P. Oxy.	*The Oxyrhyncus Papyrus.* Edited by E. Loebel et al. London: Egyptian Exploration Society, 1941
P. Tebt.	*The Tebtunis Papyri*, vol. 1. Edited by B. P. Grenfell et al. London: Henry Frowde, 1902
PTMS	Pittsburgh Theological Monograph Series
PW	Pauly, A. F. *Paulys Realencyclopädie der classischen Altertumswissenschaft.* New edition G. Wissowa. 49 vols. Munich, 1980
RB	*Revue biblique*
RHA	*Revue Hittite et asianique*

RIDA	*Revue internationale des droits de l'antiquité*
RSO	*Rivista degli studi orientali*
SBLDS	Society of Biblical Literature Dissertation Series
SBLPS	Society of Biblical Literature Pseudepigrapha Series
SBLSBS	Society of Biblical Literature Sources for Biblical Study
SBLTT	Society of Biblical Literature Texts and Translations
SBLWAW	Society of Biblical Literature Writings from the Ancient World
Schol	*Scholastik*
SJLA	Studies in Judaism in Late Antiquity
STDJ	Studies on the Texts of the Deserts of Judah
TSAJ	Texte und Studien zum antiken Judentum
TynBul	*Tyndale Bulletin*
UM	University Museum of Pennsylvania
VT	*Vetus Testamentum*
VTSup	Vetus Testamentum Supplements
WBC	Word Biblical Commentary
WMANT	Wissenschaftliche Monographien zum Alten und Neuen Testament
YOS	Yale Oriental Series, Texts
ZA	*Zeitschrift für Assyriologie*
ZABR	*Zeitschrift für altorientalische und biblische Rechtgeschichte*
ZAW	*Zeitschrift für die alttestamentliche Wissenschaft*
ZNW	*Zeitschrift für die neutestamentliche Wissenschaft und die Kunde der älteren Kirche*

Translations from cuneiform law collections are taken from Martha T. Roth, *Law Collections from Mesopotamia and Asia Minor* (SBLWAW 6; Atlanta: Scholars Press, 1995). Translations from biblical texts (canonical and deutero-canonical), as well as translations of scholarly works cited in languages other than English, are my own. Where applicable, other translation sources are indicated in the footnotes.

Chapter 1

INTRODUCTION:
COLLECTIONS, CODES, AND TORAH

At the turn of the twentieth century, archaeologists uncovered a seven-foot, black stele engraved with cuneiform laws. The text, ascribed to Hammurabi, was promptly dubbed "the Code of Hammurabi" (LH). Archaeologists have turned up law collections ascribed to other ancient kings, as well: the Laws of Ur-Namma (LU), Lipit-Ishtar (LL), Eshnunna (LE), and so forth. Over half-a-dozen such law compilations have been identified.

The spade of archaeology has also unearthed thousands of law-*practice* documents from the same societies. Documents such as land-transfer agreements, financial contracts, and court rulings record instances where law was applied to actual situations.

A curious problem emerges, however, when these practice documents are compared to the law collections. The law *as practiced* in those societies often differed from, even contradicted, the laws *as stated* in the collections. Penalties dictated in court decisions are repeatedly inconsistent with the penalties inscribed in the collections. Prices established in contracts do not match those given in the law collections. This realization has raised important questions about the purpose of the cuneiform law collections. Whatever their purposes were, they do not appear to have dictated actual legal practice. Instead, scholars (with minority exceptions) have come to regard these law collections as academic or monumental collections, but not *sources* of law.[1]

Changing understandings of the cuneiform law collections have not gone unnoticed in biblical scholarship. The problem of inconsistencies between the biblical "codes" and the norms practiced in the biblical narratives is well known. Indeed, contradictions between one biblical "code" and another are much discussed. In light of these cuneiform finds, it has

---

1. These trends will be discussed further, below.

become necessary to inquire into the nature of the biblical law collections. Was law-*writing* employed by ancient Israel for regulatory purposes,[2] or were Hebrew laws written down for purposes that were not regulatory?[3]

The scarcity of legal material from ancient Israel has made the answer difficult to resolve, and consensus elusive. Nevertheless, it has become increasingly common to view the law writings preserved in the Pentateuch as literary works, and not legal codes. Such writings may offer an idyllic commentary or description of Hebrew law, but these texts were not themselves the source of actual law practice in Israel. Much debate continues to surround the question; nevertheless, consensus does seem to be growing for the non-statutory character of the Hebrew law writings. But to draw this conclusion raises another problem.

Whereas the various cuneiform law collections can be connected to certain societies within certain periods of time, the Hebrew law writings have enjoyed continuous attention in varying conditions over many centuries. Although the Hebrew law writings may have been compiled for non-prescriptive purposes, they later came to be regarded as statutory legislation for Israel. Philip Davies has recently highlighted the problem in this way:

> Now, if, as I have suggested, the law codes in Exodus, Deuteronomy, and Leviticus were not originally descriptive of "Israelite law" nor intended to operate as such, how and why, having been edited into a Mosaic Torah, did they come to serve as the inspiration for an educated and pious Jewish lifestyle? When did "Judaism" come to be defined (if only by certain groups at first) as a way of life, obedient to written laws?[4]

Supposing that the law writings preserved in the Pentateuch were not drafted to regulate Hebrew society but for some other purpose (a supposition which will be more carefully established in Chapter 2, below), what process brought about their reconceptualization as legal prescriptions? How and when did Israel's *descriptive* law writings come to be regarded as *prescriptive* legislation? Several scholars have made contributions to this quest, but important gaps remain to be addressed.

---

2. The following terms will be used in the present study to indicate *regulatory* law writings: legislation, legalistic, law code, codified, statutory law, prescriptivism/ prescriptive law, regulatory law, and "rule of law."

3. The following terms will be used in the present study to indicate *non-regulatory* law writings: non-legislative, law collection, descriptivism/descriptive law, not regulatory, and literary or academic exercises.

4. Philip R. Davies, "'Law' in Early Judaism," in *Judaism in Late Antiquity III. Where we Stand: Issues and Debates in Ancient Judaism* (ed. Jacob Neusner and A. J. Avery-Peck; HO 40; Leiden: Brill, 1999), 3–33 (18).

Dale Patrick, for instance, has argued that Israel's written law came to be viewed prescriptively beginning with the seventh-century, Deuteronomic reforms of Josiah. Although the law collection in Deuteronomy itself reflects a descriptive purpose, Patrick sees in Josiah's *use* of Deuteronomy a prescriptive appropriation emerging. He writes:

> I contend that, for the period during which the legal tradition was in formation, the law of God was unwritten Law... The precepts and judgments of the codes were not prescriptions with statutory force but testimony to God's just and righteous will... A shift in the understanding of God's law can be detected in the literature bearing the stamp of the Deuteronomic school and sustaining the impact of Josiah's reform. The new understanding comes to expression in statements exhorting the addressee to adhere strictly to the words of the legal text and praising persons for doing so.[5]

There are two kinds of "statements exhorting the addressee to adhere strictly to the words of the legal text" which Patrick sees as significant: (1) certain Josiah-era additions (as Patrick explains them) made to Deuteronomy itself, such as the injunction, "everything that I command you, you shall give heed to do. You shall not add to it or take from it" (Deut 13:1 [EV 12:32]); and (2) statements in the Josiah reforms (and subsequent prophets) exhorting and praising obedience "according to that which is written in the book of the law" (e.g. 2 Kgs 23:3, 24). These kinds of expressions are interpreted by Patrick to demonstrate a prescriptive attitude toward the written law emerging with the Deuteronomic reforms of Josiah.

It is not supposed by Patrick that the transition was sudden and "complete" at that time. The Josiah reforms first introduced the prescriptive use of law writings; however:

> The shift in the understanding of divine law did not immediately take hold in all segments of the religious community. The Holiness Code and Priestly Law do not have statements identifying the divine law with the written rules of law, and it may be that this stream of tradition remained untouched by the thought of the Deuteronomic school.[6]

It was only in post-exilic Judaism, according to Patrick, that the written law became *generally* acknowledged as itself "the law" (prescriptive).[7] Patrick, therefore, centers the Torah shift in the seventh century BCE, but allows that it only reached full bloom in the Persian era. However, he does not continue the project to consider how that further blooming of legislative thinking about Torah occurred. Nor, indeed, does he examine

5. Dale Patrick, *Old Testament Law* (London: SCM Press, 1986), 189–90, 200.
6. Ibid., 202–3.
7. Ibid., 204.

the evidence of Josiah's reforms as implemented (i.e. the narrated "practice record") to test whether the emphasis on "the book of the law" in that reform does indeed indicate prescriptivism.

A scholar employing arguments differing from those of Patrick, but who reaches similar conclusions, is Raymond Westbrook. Westbrook is an authority on cuneiform law as well as Hebrew law, and thus brings a breadth of insight to the issue. Westbrook has yet to develop a thorough explanation of how Israel came to understand its law collections prescriptively—his primary concerns lie with the earliest periods of legal development rather than later appropriation. Nevertheless, Westbrook has made contributions to the reconceptualization question.

Westbrook, like Patrick, regards Deuteronomy as "an intermediate stage...between the cuneiform and classical [i.e. descriptive and prescriptive] systems of law."[8] Most striking for Westbrook is the *prospective* nature of the Jubilee debt release in Deuteronomy (ch. 15). Debt-release edicts in the ancient Near East were retrospective in outlook (i.e. debts incurred prior to the edict were remitted). Deuteronomy, in contrast, regularizes debt release prospectively (i.e. debts incurred in the future are already "scheduled" for remittance). This, for Westbrook, is a significant intellectual shift toward a prescriptive use of law writing.[9] Westbrook draws further support from coincident developments in Athens: "The later biblical codes—the Deuteronomic and Priestly Codes—share something of the intellectual ferment of contemporary Greek sources and thus some taste also of their new legal conceptions."[10] Westbrook's reference to Greece's "new legal conceptions" has to do with the Draconian and Solonic reforms where legislative ideas were forming.[11] He suspects these Athenian developments parallel, and may even have influenced, Deuteronomic legal thought. No evidence of pre-exilic, Greek–Hebrew legal contact has been offered, however. Furthermore, the actual ways in which this Deuteronomy sabbath-year law on release was used (i.e. practice records) need to be examined to test whether it was indeed statutory.

In any case, by the time of Ezra, per Westbrook, "the jurisprudential foundations of Jewish Law" are in place, so that "the legal system became

---

8. Raymond Westbrook, "Cuneiform Law Codes and the Origins of Legislation," *ZA* 79 (1989): 201–22 (222).

9. Ibid., 220.

10. Raymond Westbrook, "What is the Covenant Code?," in *Theory and Method in Biblical and Cuneiform Law: Revision, Interpolations and Development* (ed. Bernard M. Levinson; JSOTSup 181; Sheffield: Sheffield Academic Press, 1994), 28; cf. his "Origins of Legislation," 222.

11. Westbrook, "Origins of Legislation," 220; Aristotle, *Ath. pol.* 6.1.

based upon the idea of a written code of law…"[12] Westbrook, like other scholars shortly to be noted, sees something in Ezra's use of "the book of the law" which indicates a legislative conception of Torah in full bloom by that era. It is in Josiah's Deuteronomic reforms that Westbrook sees that legislative use of law writing beginning to emerge, achieving full implementation in the Persian-era reforms of Ezra.

Peter Frei has formulated an influential argument for identifying the prescriptive status of Pentateuchal law with the Persian restoration of Yehud.[13] Using a federal model of government as his point of departure, Frei speaks of the ancient empire as a two-level hierarchy: imperial government and local government. In the Persian empire, local peoples were granted a certain amount of autonomy so long as imperial interests were not violated. Local governments established local law, while the imperial government concerned itself with taxation, expansion, quashing rebellion, and such. However, on occasion a local law could be raised to the level of imperial law. When this took place, according to Frei, the written form of that local custom received imperial enforcement. In the case of Yehud, the Persian decree for Ezra to teach "the law of your God and the law of the king" (Ezra 7:26) is said by Frei to indicate that Ezra's law book received such imperial status—it became also the "law of the king." Persian authorization transformed the Torah of Israel into a normative "constitution" for Yehud.[14]

Frei does not actually frame his argument in terms of a "descriptive to prescriptive" transition for Torah. Nevertheless, his thesis has been cited in support of placing such a transition within the Persian era.[15] One significant problem with this solution is that noted by Anne Fitzpatrick-McKinley: "Persian notions of 'law' were similar to those found throughout the ancient Near East."[16] It would be remarkable for Persia to impose a new use of law writings for Yehud when there is no evidence Persia itself observed such a use of law writings. Furthermore, if indeed

12. Raymond Westbrook, "Biblical Law," in *An Introduction to the History and Sources of Jewish Law* (ed. N. S. Hecht et al.; Oxford: Clarendon, 1996), 3–4.

13. Peter Frei, "Die persische Reichsautorisation: Ein Überblick," *ZABR* 1 (1995): 1–35, a reprint of "Persian Imperial Authorization: A Summary," in *Persia and Torah: The Theory of Imperial Authorization of the Pentateuch* (ed. James W. Watts; SBLSymS 17; Atlanta: Society of Biblical Literature, 2001), 5–40.

14. Frei, "Persian Authorization," 38.

15. E.g. Frank Crüsemann, *The Torah: Theology and Social History of Old Testament Law* (trans. A. W. Mahnke; Edinburgh: T. & T. Clark, 1996), 351; Bernard S. Jackson, *Studies in the Semiotics of Biblical Law* (JSOTSup 314; Sheffield: Sheffield Academic Press, 2000), 141–43.

16. Anne Fitzpatrick-McKinley, *The Transformation of Torah from Scribal Advice to Law* (JSOTSup 287; Sheffield: Sheffield Academic Press, 1999), 148.

the written Torah became a regulative body of law for Yehud, the practice narratives of the period should reflect this. In other words, an examination of the law-practice evidence of Persian Yehud is needed to test this conclusion.

Michael Fishbane's influential study on "innerbiblical exegesis" has offered one widely accepted approach to Torah's use in the Persian era.[17] However, Fishbane presupposes that law writing in Israel was legislative. According to Fishbane, not only in the Persian era but from Israel's hoary past, law writing (and re-writing) in Israel was a legislative activity, distinct from the rest of the ancient Near East.[18] His study presupposes that law writings were regarded legislatively in the Persian era. His examination shows how Torah *would* have been used if it was regarded as the source of regulation for Yehud, but it remains to assess *whether* the practice narratives indicate this to have been the case in fact. Fishbane's arguments are insightful, but the evidence requires assessment without a legislative presupposition.

Other scholars who regard the Persian period as the point at which written law came to be regarded as legislation for Israel include Bernard Jackson and Anne Fitzpatrick-McKinley.

Jackson's work on the non-regulatory nature of law writing in pre-exilic Israel is compelling.[19] Facing the question of Torah's later reception as legislative, Jackson offers two possibilities. In one place, he lends an agreeable nod to Frei's argument for imperial authorization under Persia transforming Torah into a statute book for Yehud.[20] Elsewhere, Jackson speaks of a gradual, Hebrew identification of royal law (which would have addressed immediate matters) with divine law (which was enduring). This coalescence led to records of what were once *ad hoc* royal laws being regarded by later generations as enduring legislation. Jackson finds the evidence for this new legalism in Ezra's reforms "according to the book of the law."[21] Of course, Jackson's salutatory use of Frei's work depends on the validity of Frei's hypothesis. Jackson's further argument presupposes that the integration of divine and royal

17. Michael Fishbane, *Biblical Interpretation in Ancient Israel* (Oxford: Clarendon, 1985).

18. Ibid., 96.

19. Especially Jackson, *Studies*, 70–92. Jackson's long-awaited work, *Wisdom-Laws: A Study of the* Mishpatim *of* Exodus 21:1–22:16 (Oxford: Oxford University Press, 2006) appeared too recently to be included in the present study, but this work promises to be an important addition to Jackson's presentation of Israel's law writings (at least the oldest layers) as non-regulatory "wisdom laws."

20. Ibid., 141–43.

21. Ibid., 144–70.

ideologies would produce, not just an exaltation of status for royal law writings, but a fundamental change in their manner of employment. Whether this was, in fact, the case rides on the Ezra-reform evidence Jackson cites. A closer look at the Torah-practice records of Persian-era Yehud is required.

Fitzpatrick-McKinley draws upon aspects of Jackson's work for her own studies.[22] In particular, she takes a cue from one of Jackson's articles comparing legal transition in Israel with the transition of Brahmin *dharma* into legislation in British occupied India.[23] Fitzpatrick-McKinley develops the *dharma* model as an evolutionary comparison for Torah, producing a fresh approach to the problem. Its ultimate success, of course, depends on whether the Hebrew material itself bears the model. When it comes to demonstrating her posited transformation from the Hebrew records, Fitzpatrick-McKinley relies on Fishbane's assessment of Ezra's exegetical practice in the Persian era.[24] As already noted, these materials require further assessment.

As the foregoing makes evident, many scholars look to the Persian era (and the Ezra–Nehemiah narrative) as a fertile moment for the reconceptualization of Torah. However, little has been done to test this thesis. An important focus of the present study, therefore, will be upon the Ezra–Nehemiah (and Josiah) Torah-application materials. Furthermore, if the Persian-era reforms are not found to provide the sufficient impetus for the legislative reconceptualization of Torah, then the question remains wide open as to how that shift came about.

The present study seeks to address these gaps. It is the aim of this project to develop a model for the re-characterization of Israel's (idyllic) law collections as a (legislative) law code. One issue which emerges from the evidence, as will here be examined, is the generally overlooked complexity of Israel's developing perception of its Torah. Generally, scholars treating the transition question assume a singular change to be at work, a change often connected with Israel's development from an "oral society" into a "written society."[25] In this study, a more nuanced model

22. Fitzpatrick-McKinley, *Transformation*.

23. Bernard S. Jackson, "From Dharma to Law," *American Journal of Comparative Law* 23 (1975): 490–512. Jackson has since retracted some of the views in that article on which Fitzpatrick-McKinley leaned for her book (Bernard S. Jackson, review of Anne Fitzpatrick-McKinley, *The Transformation of Torah from Scribal Advice to Law*, *JSS* 47, no. 2 [2002]: 332).

24. Fitzpatrick-McKinley, *Transformation*, 166–77.

25. E.g. ibid., 152–55; Bernard S. Jackson, "Models in Legal History: The Case of Biblical Law," *JLR* 18, no. 1 (2002): 8–10. Cf. Susan Niditch, *Oral World and Written Word: Ancient Israelite Literature* (Library of Ancient Israel; London: SPCK, 1997).

of transition will be developed, recognizing concurrent but distinct developments. On the one hand, it will be seen that Israel's view of its law writings underwent a change of importance, or increased esteem. Torah became a revered, even authoritative, standard of the Hebrew faith. This is one kind of development, but not necessarily the same thing as Torah's reconceptualization as a text of the *legislative* variety. The former development reflects a new emphasis *that* the ancient law collections be used; the second involves a new way *how* those law collections came to be used. It is this latter transition which realized Torah's movement from a law collection into a law code.

It is the thesis of this project that ancient Israel's law collections underwent several distinct kinds of development: change in the *content* of Israel's ideal law book; an evolving *esteem* for Israel's historic law writings; and a radical *re-characterization* of these law writings as legislative codes. Conceptually distinguishing and chronologically relating these distinct lines of legal development is important for the assessment of biblical law and its function in various contexts.

Although this project will focus primarily on matters of Hebrew law, two other fields of ancient law are relevant and ought to be indicated up front. First, as already noted, it is the developments arising from the study of cuneiform law writings that have provided the particular impetus for recent questions about the Hebrew law writings. A review of the relevant developments in Assyriology will give a useful reference point for approaching the Hebrew law writings. Such a review will also provide a helpful introduction to the whole idea of law writing for non-regulatory purposes (an idea difficult to grasp in modern democracies, thoroughly conditioned by "rule of law" expectations).

Second, legal developments in classical Greece are relevant for the present project. It was in sixth/fifth-century Athens that the western Mediterranean world devised the use of law writing for social regulation. Some scholars, as already noted, have seen in ancient Israel an anticipation of what Athens independently developed, or even an actual contact between the two. Such matters make a review of legal developments in Athens pertinent to this project. Furthermore, such a review will provide a helpful introduction to the idea of law writing becoming used for regulatory purposes in contrast to the "cuneiform pattern."

I. *The Cuneiform Law Writings*

The question of how cuneiform law collections were used in the ancient Near East emerged (as already noted) from the realization that law as practiced in those societies was not consistent with the laws as written in their respective collections. Samuel Meier summarizes the evidence (here with particular reference to LH): "The relevance for society in general of the collection and standardization of Hammurapi's laws is perplexing. Prices, fines, and penalties do not always correspond with actual data from the same period; and records of actual court cases do not cite the collection of laws as a basis or rationale for adjudication."[26]

Josef Klíma argued that this absence of citation simply shows that ancient court procedure did not require such references in the written records.[27] However, Westbrook has shown that royal edicts *were* cited in the records. While royal edicts held legislative force in Mesopotamian courts (and were cited), the written law collections evidently did not.[28] Furthermore, as noted above by Meier, the problem is not merely a lack of citation, but "prices, fines, and penalties" are also frequently fixed differently than indicated in the collections.

In the early 1960s, F. R. Kraus and J. J. Finkelstein published seminal studies questioning the assumed legislative nature of the cuneiform collections.[29] Since that time, scholars have widely concurred that ancient law was practiced, not based on written prescriptions, but based on unwritten customs.[30] The written collections may reflect legal ideals of a given period, but they were not themselves "the law." Legal examples

26. Samuel A. Meier, "Hammurapi," in *ABD* 3:41. Cf. G. R. Driver and J. C. Miles, *The Babylonian Laws* (2 vols.; Oxford: Clarendon, 1952), 1:53, 401.

27. Josef Klíma, "La perspective historique des lois hammourabiennes," *CRAI* 308.

28. Westbrook, "Origins of Legislation," 215. Cf. Jean Bottéro, "Le 'Code' de Hammurabi," *Annali della Scoula Normale Superiore di Pisa classe di lettere e filosofia* 12, no. 3 (1982): 409–44; also *Mesopotamia: Writing, Reasoning, and the Gods* (trans. Zainab Bahrani and Marc van de Mieroop; London: University of Chicago, 1992), 163.

29. F. R. Kraus, "Ein zentrales Problem des altmesopotamischen Rechtes: Was ist der Codex Hammu-rabi?," *Aspects du contact suméro-akkadien, Geneva* NS 8 (1960): 283–96; J. J. Finkelstein, "Ammi-Ṣaduqa's Edict and the Babylonian 'Law Codes,'" *JCS* 15 (1961): 91–104.

30. Bottéro, *Mesopotamia*, 169–79; Raymond Westbrook, "Biblical and Cuneiform Law Codes," *RB* 92, no. 2 (1985): 247–64; idem, "Codification and Canonization," in *La codification des lois dans l'antiquité: actes du colloque de Strasbourg 27–29 novembre 1997* (ed. Edmond Lévy; Travaux du centre de recherche sur le Proche-Orient et la Grèce antiques 16; Paris: De Boccard), 37–41; idem, "The Character of Ancient Near Eastern Law," in *A History of Ancient Near Eastern Law* (ed. Raymond Westbrook; 2 vols.; Leiden: Brill, 2003), especially 1:12–24; Martha T. Roth, *Law Collections from Mesopotamia and Asia Minor* (SBLWAW 6; Atlanta: Scholars Press, 1995), 4–7; idem, "The Law Collection of King Hammurabi: Toward an Understanding of Codification and Text," in Lévy, ed., *Codification*, 9–31.

were compiled into written collections for some purposes other than
social regulation. It is the identification of those purposes that has
become the subject of much debate, with three alternatives commonly
advanced: (1) the law collections as literary exercises; (2) the law collections as royal *apologia*; (3) the law collections as juridical training
texts.

1. *Literary Exercises*

Perhaps the most common view of the ancient Near Eastern law collections is that they represent literary exercises. They are the product of
scribal elite, compiling idyllic collections of problems and solutions,
sometimes reflecting real problems and sometimes reflecting purely
hypothetical problems. Among the most compelling evidence for this
view is the frequent "goring ox" and "induced miscarriage" laws. These
two examples are particularly significant because they exist in remarkable similarity across numerous cuneiform traditions (and, in fact, in
Hebrew law collections as well).

Law provisions dealing with a "goring ox" can be found in LH
(§§250–52), LE (§§53–55), and in the Book of the Covenant (BC) (Exod
21:28–36). According to the view advanced by Adrianus Van Selms, the
frequency of the "goring ox" theme reflects the common use of oxen in
the various societies: there is no necessary connection between these
texts; they reflect the common problem of goring incidents.[31] Meir Malul,
however, has criticized Van Selms' explanation on the basis that the
latter assumes that ox-goring was an actual problem in society when it
probably was not (or at least was not a common one). Malul notes that
among the vast collections of cuneiform practice documents uncovered
to date, no evidence exists of an actual ox-goring dispute.[32] For so celebrated a case in the various legal collections, its lack of reflection in actual
law practice is probably significant. Scholars such as Malul question
whether ox-goring really was a problem, or whether this is instead an
indication of hypothetical exercise in the law collections.

31. Adrianus Van Selms, "The Goring Ox in Babylonian and Biblical Law,"
ArOr 18, no. 4 (1950): 321–30.
32. Meir Malul, *The Comparative Method in Ancient Near Eastern and Biblical
Legal Studies* (AOAT 227; Kevelaer: Butzon & Bercker, 1990), 125–29. Malul does
acknowledge a few possible exceptions in Nuzian legal documents which he believes
are adequately explained by Finkelstein (p. 127 n. 20; cf. J. J. Finkelstein, *The Ox
That Gored* [Transactions of the American Philosophical Society 71/2; Philadelphia:
American Philosophical Society, 1981], 21 n. 5).

This argument is further advanced through another broadly treated case of the cuneiform collections: various scenarios of a pregnant woman being struck and miscarrying (e.g. LH §§209–14; MAL A §§21, 50–53; YOS 1.28 §§1–2; UM 55.21.71 §§4–6; HL §§17–18, XVI–XVII; cf. Exod 21:22–25). Finkelstein has shown that there is no documentary evidence to indicate the actual treatment of such disputes. Furthermore, medical testimony has been produced to contest the likelihood of miscarriage actually occurring in such instances (except in extreme rarity).[33] Here is another instance of a legal provision seeming to deal with a hypothetical problem, not a real problem, yet being widely represented in the ancient law writings.

Malul writes, "[a] significant conclusion emerging from the foregoing discussion is that we are dealing here with a *literary tradition* rather than with a *practical legal tradition*."[34] Not only were these law writings composed as literary (sometimes hypothetical) exercises, but they appear to have been copied and adapted across the ancient Near East.[35]

2. *Royal* Apologia

A second view is that cuneiform law writing was employed for monumental purposes—to extol the justice of great kings. Finkelstein advanced this view by noting a common "royal *apologia* genre": a law collection framed by a prolog/epilog extolling the king. Finkelstein argued, "Their primary purpose was to lay before the public, posterity, future kings, and, above all, the gods, evidence of the king's execution of his divinely ordained mandate: to have been 'the Faithful Shepherd' and the *šār mīšarim*...."[36]

In those instances where such prologs/epilogs exist, the propagandistic (rather than regulatory) purpose of the collection is hardly contested. It is difficult to deny that the LH stele found at Susa, for example, is essentially a tribute to Hammurabi; even Klíma (a proponent of LH's legislative nature) admits *this* rendition of LH was monumental.[37] However, not

---

33. Finkelstein, *Ox That Gored*, 19 n. 11.

34. Malul, *Comparative Method*, 129 (emphasis original). Cf. Fitzpatrick-McKinley, *Transformation*, 91–92, 144–45; John Van Seters, *A Law Book for the Diaspora: Revision in the Study of the Covenant Code* (Oxford: Oxford University Press, 2003), 110–11, 121–22.

35. Malul even posits that the peculiar occurrence of נגף (rather than נגח) in Exod 21:35 indicates the Hebrew scribe had an Akkadian law collection before him: "...by some careless accidence the Akkadian root [*nakāpu*] was left in v. 35..." (Malul, *Comparative Method*, 140–43; cf. Westbrook, "Law Codes," 257).

36. Finkelstein, "Ammi-Ṣaduqa," 103.

37. Klíma, "Lois hammourabiennes," 312–13.

all the cuneiform collections include such framing materials, so that some doubt whether royal *apologia* can be regarded as the "primary purpose" for such law writing (even if it was an important adaptation of the phenomenon). Westbrook, for example, answers Finkelstein:

> If the activity of writing law-codes could be engaged in without the addition of a prologue and epilogue to the legal corpus, it suggests that a royal *apologia* was not the primary purpose in the composition of the latter. This is confirmed by the remarkable dichotomy in style between the Mesopotamian codes' prologues and epilogues and their central legal corpus... It seems to us evidence rather that the legal corpus already existed as an independent unit with an independent purpose and was sometimes inserted into a frame, as in Codex Hammurabi, in order to be applied to a new purpose, that of the royal *apologia*.[38]

Westbrook advances a third interpretation of the cuneiform law-writing phenomenon.

3. *Juridical Treatise*

Westbrook, following Kraus,[39] notes that the law provisions reflect a well-known ancient Near Eastern genre: the "scientific list." Mesopotamian treatises on medicine and divination employ the same form as that found in the law collections: "If the circumstances are X, the diagnosis/treatment is Y." This similarity of form across fields (medicine, divination, and law) suggests, according to Westbrook, a common genre—and a common, professional, didactic use.[40]

Although the cuneiform law collections were not legislative (that is, they did not themselves regulate laws and penalties), neither were they primarily royal *apologia* or literary exercises unconnected to legal practice. Westbrook argues that the collections did have a practical function for legists as idyllic collections of real or hypothetical situations. As the other "scientific list" collections served for the instruction of physicians and diviners, the law collections were "a reference work for consultation by judges"—the king as supreme judge most especially.[41]

An unexpected word of support for Westbrook's comparison might be found in the work of Aristotle, who observed ancient Near Eastern law practices as a contemporary. Apparently, Aristotle also saw a degree of comparability between the law writings and medical writings of

---

38. Westbrook, "Law Codes," 250–51.

39. Kraus, "Codex Hammu-rabi," 283–96.

40. Westbrook: "Law Codes"; idem, *Studies in Biblical and Cuneiform Law* (CahRB 26; Paris: Gabalda), 2. Cf. Bottéro, *Mesopotamia*, 169–79.

41. Westbrook, "Law Codes," 254. Cf. his *Studies*, 76–77.

ancient Near Eastern peoples. In his *Politics*, Aristotle described the lack of prescriptive authority behind ancient Near Eastern law writings with this analogy:

> [In those lands] laws enunciate only general principles but do not give directions for dealing with circumstances as they arise; so that in an art (τέχνη) of any kind it is foolish to govern procedure by written rules (and indeed in Egypt physicians have the right to alter their prescription after four days, although if one of them alters it before he does so at his own risk); it is clear therefore that [in those lands] government according to written rules, that is laws, is not [deemed] the best, for the same reason. (Aristotle, *Pol.* 3.10.4)

Aristotle saw a comparability between the "barbarian" doctor's freedom to vary from medical "prescriptions" and that of a "barbarian" king's variance with written laws. His choice of comparison might be regarded as supporting Westbrook's categorizing ancient Near Eastern law writings within the broader "scientific list" genre.

That certain of the provisions in the law collections were more hypothetical than real need not undermine this position, as theoretical development is evident in the medical and omen catalogs as well. Jean Bottéro notes, for example, the surely hypothetical provision in an omen treatise for interpreting the meaning of a woman birthing 7, 8, or 9 children together! Such fantastic inclusions are not much different from unrealistic measures in the law lists, such as at LH §§268–70 where goats and donkeys are said to be used for threshing.[42] Westbrook concurs that it was a regular practice of the "scientific list" genre to develop hypothetical variations on cases to "fill out" a given paradigm.[43] Whether such hypothetical *extrapolations* (i.e. real problems hypothetically varied) also explains the development of, what Malul and others assert to be, *completely* hypothetical dilemmas (i.e. unreal problems like ox-goring and indirect miscarriage) needs to be determined before the law writings can be conclusively identified as practical treatises.[44]

For archaeological support for his position, Westbrook points to the discovery of the Middle Assyrian Law (MAL) tablets. Most of the extant collection, discovered in Kültepe (Anatolia), was found in a gatehouse identified as the "Gate of *Šamaš*" (the Mesopotamian god of justice).

42. Bottéro, *Mesopotamia*, 175, 177.
43. Westbrook, *Studies*, 3–4.
44. Westbrook considers the ox-goring case "a classic school case of homicide by indirect causation" (*Studies*, 57). It is, in other words, a case through which a *real* dilemma (indirect causation) is illustrated, even if hypothetically (cf. p. 77 n. 156). Cf. Eckart Otto, "Town and Rural Countryside in Ancient Israelite Law: Reception and Redaction in Cuneiform and Israelite Law," *JSOT* 57, no. 3 (1993): 17–18 n. 45.

Ernst Weidner concluded that these law tablets comprised a legal reference library—"eine kleine 'juristische Bibliothek'"—a conclusion which
Westbrook approvingly cites as indication of the precedential value of
such law lists.[45]

Finally, Westbrook points out a distinction between the way Hittite
law collections were copied in contrast with certain copies of the
Hammurabi collection. Hammurabi's collection did become a school
text, many extant copies having been found in scribal schools. These
scribal exercise copies of LH remained unchanged over centuries of
transmission. None of the Hittite law collections, however, can be associated with scribal schools, although extant copies of this corpus likewise
span several centuries. In the case of the Hittite law-copying, modifica-
tion took place, and in some cases explicit amendment.[46] Westbrook
highlights this distinction as illustrating the difference between literary
texts and practical treatises, the former being a secondary use of law
collections in scribal centers (without need of development) and the
latter reflecting a living relationship between written law and legal practice (even if that relationship is academic rather than regulatory). In other
words, some copies of the cuneiform collections were indeed literary
exercises, but the genre belongs in its origin to circles of legal practice
and reflection.[47]

Martha Roth has added to Westbrook's case for at least some practical
relationship existing between the written laws and applied justice—
though she hesitates to define that relationship. Roth observes:

> There is...one Old Babylonian letter which does make reference to a
> "stela" (Akkadian *narû*) upon which wages were inscribed, reminding us
> of the provisions in LH ¶¶273–74, which establish daily wages for
> several categories of workmen... Another piece of evidence from the
> same period, but from outside of Mesopotamia, also refers to a stela that
> publicized prices and wages. This is an early nineteenth century B.C.E.
> stamped mudbrick from Susa, the Elamite capital...[48]

Roth is hesitant to venture an answer to the question of how the law collections were used in the cuneiform world: "Ultimately, such questions

---

45. Westbrook, "Law Codes," 255; E. F. Weidner, "Das Alter der mittelassyrischen Gesetzestexte: Studien im Anschluss an Driver and Miles, *The Assyrian
Laws*," *AfO* 12 (1937): 48.

46. E.g. HL §94: "If a free man burglarizes a house, he shall pay in full.
Formerly they paid 40 shekels of silver as fine for the theft, but now [he shall pay]
12 shekels of silver...."

47. Westbrook, "Law Codes," 255–56; idem, "Origins of Legislation," 205.

48. Roth, *Law Collections*, 5–7. Cf. his "King Hammurabi," 22–28.

as[,] Is there any concord between the formal law collections and the transactional contracts?[,]...are not really answerable..."[49] Nevertheless, she rejects the supposition "that the law collections had little or no impact on the daily operation of legal affairs."[50] Even if not *regulating* law-practice, the law-collections might still be related to legal practice.[51]

*   *   *

Most scholars seem to regard the cuneiform law writings as a more literary than practical phenomenon, and royal propaganda as a prominent reason for writing down laws. Nevertheless, persuasive arguments can be mounted for all three views summarized above. It, however, remains to be demonstrated conclusively whether the cuneiform law collections were at first a literary, monumental, or juridical-training phenomenon, later adapted to the other uses. What should be acknowledged is that all three uses did in fact occur; none is actually exclusive of the other. (Indeed, most scholars in the field could probably be better described as drawing in various ways upon all these views, rather than espousing one or another.) For the present purposes, it is not necessary to establish conclusively which of these is "the primary purpose" for writing laws. What is significant to note, however, is that the debate over how the cuneiform law collections were used is no longer dominated by a legislative model. The broad consensus of Assyriologists is that laws were written down for purposes other than actual regulation. The law writings, while perhaps *reflective* of social customs (description), were not the *source* of legal practice (prescription). Unwritten customs continued to be the source for legal practice.

Some scholars, however, have resisted this consensus. Sophie Démare-Lafont, for example, has agreed that unwritten custom, not codified legislation, governed court operation in oriental society. However, she has defended the claim that ancient kings also wrote down statutory laws to supplement unwritten custom. LH, for instance, she has argued, was published to overturn customs (especially of conquered regions) in order to unify Hammurabi's domain.[52] Law collections were therefore statutory codes though of limited scope. In response to the finding that law-practice documents frequently contradict the collections, Lafont wrote:

49. Roth, *Law Collections,* 7. Cf. his "King Hammurabi," 30–31.
50. Roth, *Law Collections,* 5.
51. Cf. Bottéro, *Mesopotamia,* 167; Eckart Otto, "Aspects of Legal Reforms and Reformulations in Ancient Cuneiform and Israelite Law," in Levinson, ed., *Theory and Method,* 160–63.
52. Sophie Démare, "La valeur de la loi dans les droits cunéiformes," *Archives des philosophie du droit* 32 (1987): 345–46.

> Those texts which deviate from royal legislation attest to the power of custom and the hesitancy of judges and populace to observe principles which are not familiar to them. Such an attitude does not detract anything from the intrinsic force of the laws. Their promulgation does not bring about the inevitable adherence of all. The legislator claims, nonetheless, to make them compulsory. They have, therefore, a normative purpose, regardless of the resistance which they arouse.[53]

What Lafont fails to demonstrate, however, is that the law collections actually do impose themselves as binding. To establish this argument, Lafont relies on the assumption that, if Hammurabi invokes curses (in the LH epilog) against successors who might violate his stele, "…[H]e *a fortiori* wishes to impose his regulations on the judges. This hypothesis is confirmed in the preceding lines, where [his] subjects are encouraged to come and consult the stele to resolve their disputes."[54]

The "preceding lines" to which Lafont refers is the much discussed "wronged man" paragraph (LH §§48.3–19). In that paragraph, the victim of injustice (*awīlum ḫablum*) is urged to search Hammurabi's law stele as a source of consolation and to pray for Hammurabi. Roth, in her exposition of this passage, concludes: "The language of the epilogue is *not* urging him to bring his matter before King Hammurabi [i.e. the royal court], but to Hammurabi's stela. There he can find solace only through prayer and by offering blessings to (the memory of) King Hammurabi."[55]

There is, in fact, no "*a fortiori* imposition" of the LH laws by the stele epilog. The fact that practice documents contradict the collections can hardly be said, therefore, to indicate local resistance to LH. The lack of legal impact by LH seems rather to reflect the non-regulatory nature of LH. Hammurabi's stele was a portrait, not a law code. Furthermore, Westbrook has shown that there is no evidence of an effort on Hammurabi's part to unify the law of the empire. In fact, within Hammurabi's dominion: "The only clear [legal] difference between regions known to

53. Démare, "La valeur de la loi," 344–45: "Les textes s'écartant des législations royales attestent la puissance de la coutume, et la réticence des juges et des sujets à observer des principes qui ne leur sont pas familiers. Une telle attitude ne retire rien à la valeur intrinsèque des lois. Leur promulgation n'entraîne pas forcément l'adhésion de tous. Le législateur prétend néanmoins les rendre obligatoires. Elles ont donc une vocation normative, indépendamment des résistances qu'elles suscitent." Cf. Sophie Lafont, "Ancient Near Eastern Laws: Continuity and Pluralism," in Levinson, ed., *Theory and Method*, 96).

54. Démare, "La valeur de la loi," 345: "…*a fortiori* souhaite-t-il imposer ses prescriptions aux juges. Cette hypothèse est confirmée dans les lignes précédentes, où les justiciables sont incités à venir consulter la stèle pour résoudre leurs litiges."

55. Martha T. Roth, "Hammurabi's Wronged Man," *JAOS* 122, no. 1 (2002): 45.

us is the first-born son's right to ten percent of the total estate in Southern Mesopotamia but to the equivalent of one ordinary heir's share in the North and in peripheral areas. The issue is not dealt with at all in CH."[56]

More recently, Lafont has adapted her argument by identifying LH as a *subsidiary* law code. Lafont points to current European Union doctrine to illustrate. The 1992 Treaty of Maastricht established specific areas for European Union authority; in matters outside these areas, "...the Community shall take action, in accordance with the principle of subsidiarity, only if and in so far as the objectives of the proposed action cannot be sufficiently achieved by the Member States and can therefore...be better achieved by the Community."[57]

Lafont suspects that this same principle operated in the ancient Near East: "The substantive law enacted in the codes, or the normative texts produced from the king, is subsidiary."[58] Consequently, "In the hierarchy of the legal provisions, the written standard is placed after local practice... The chronic ineffectiveness of the codes is thus explained by their supplementary character, but does not indicate anything concerning their legal authenticity."[59]

The reason the practice documents contradict the law collections is because royal law was subsidiary to local custom. Victims of injustice had to work through their local courts (with their own customs) first. Appeal to royal intervention only took place in limited instances. To establish this adaptation of her position, however, Lafont continues to depend upon her reading of the "wronged man" passage as describing a judicial appeals process. The "wronged man," Lafont recently proposed, is one whose case has been poorly handled by local custom and he is appealing for royal intervention.[60] Lafont's reading of the "wronged man" passage has been adequately answered by Roth, as previously noted. Roth points out that the only recourse which LH actually offers to the "wronged man" is the "moral victory" of finding the gods (and Hammurabi) sympathetic to his plight: "The idiom *libbam nuppušum* carries only an

56. Westbrook, "Origins of Legislation," 204. Cf. Roth, "King Hammurabi," 29.

57. Richard Corbett, *The Treaty of Maastrich—From Conception to Ratification: A Comprehensive Reference Guide* (Essex: Longman, 1994), 388.

58. Sophie Lafont, "Codification et subsidiarité dans les droits du Proche-Orient ancien," in Lévy, ed., *Codification*, 49–60 (50): "le droit positif édicté dans les codes ou dans les textes normatifs émanant de la royauté est subsidiaire."

59. Lafont, "Subsidiarité," 58: "Dans la hiérarchie des règles de droit, la norme écrite est placée après les usages locaux et même... L'ineffectivité chronique des codes s'explique ainsi par leur caractère complémentaire, mais ne touche en rien leur valeur juridique."

60. Ibid., 53–55.

emotional or psychological element of appeasement and ease; there is no concrete (or here legal) measure implied."[61] Lafont's earlier views, and her recent adaptations, require that the "wronged man" passage describes an appeal in process—a reading it does not seem to bear.

Lafont's are not the only arguments for a legislative reading of the cuneiform law writings.[62] Nonetheless, Lafont's arguments highlight the importance of the inconsistency problem for any analysis of the ancient Near Eastern law collections. If the law collections were legislative, some explanation needs to be offered for their failure actually to regulate practice. Neither the theory of an imperial reform resisted from beneath, nor the invocation of subsidiarity, seem to satisfy the problem of inconsistency between law collections and law-practice documents. At present, the dominant consensus among scholars of ancient Near Eastern law is that legal practice operated based on custom, not texts. When laws were written down, they were written for literary, monumental, or juridical instruction purposes. It does not appear that laws were written down to regulate society.

But what about *Hebrew* law writing? Were the law compilations of ancient Israel put into writing for regulatory or literary/monumental purposes? It certainly cannot be supposed that, simply because other ancient Near Eastern societies did not perceive of written laws as regulatory, Israel likewise wrote laws for reasons other than legal practice. The trends of scholarship in Assyriology do open up important questions for the examination of the Hebrew evidence, but they do not themselves dictate answers. An examination of the early employments of law writing in Israel has to rely on Hebrew evidence. The Hebrew evidence will be taken up in Chapter 2.

II. *The Athenian Law Writings*

A second field of ancient law bears noting: namely, the legal developments of Athens. Classical Athens offers the clearest demonstration of an ancient society devising a legislative use for law writing. This aspect of Athenian history is relevant to the present study for two reasons. First, it

61. Roth, "Wronged Man," 41.
62. Klíma, "Lois hammourabiennes"; H. P. H. Petschow, "Die §§45 und 46 des Codex Hammurapi Ein Beitrag zum altbabylonischen Bodenpachtrecht und zum Problem: Was ist der Codex Hammurapi?," *ZA* 74 (1984): 181–212; W. F. Leemans, "Quelques considerations a propos d'une etude recente du droit du Proche-Orient ancien," *BO* 48 (1991): 409–37; Klaus R. Veenhof, "'In Accordance with the Words of the Stele': Evidence for Old Assyrian Legislation," *Chicago-Kent Law Review* 70 (1995): 1717–44.

provides a known example of the kind of transition being inquired after in ancient Hebrew law. Second, Athens is a known *source* for the concept of regulatory law writing in the ancient world. A number of scholars specializing in biblical law suspect, in one way or another, that Greek contact may have played a role in Hebrew adaptations of law writing. For these reasons, the legal innovations of classical Athens deserve preliminary review. According to the classicist Martin Ostwald, this legal innovation of Athens can be understood as a roughly two-stage movement, beginning with the attainment of popular sovereignty (i.e. pure democracy) and culminating with the sovereignty of written law (i.e. "rule of law" democracy).[63]

Like many ancient societies, Greek Athens was long ruled by absolute monarchs. Traditional monarchy was replaced by aristocratic rule in Athens around 700 BCE. Various instabilities in succeeding centuries led to further, periodic reforms. The reforms of Draco (ca. 620) "may have been the result of tensions within the upper classes of Athens" after a failed coup attempt.[64] A generation later (in 594), Solon was granted powers for further reforms. Aristotle speaks of three measures by Solon which laid the foundation of Greek democracy (*Ath. pol.* 9.1). These are summarized by Ostwald as follows:

> The first, the prohibition against giving loans on the security of the debtor, created the minimal social and economic prerequisite for the common man's exercise of citizenship. The second populist measure, the extension to any person of the right to take legal action in behalf of an injured party [e.g., when the community as a whole was endangered], constituted a major step toward the advancement of popular power… [Third,] the institution of an appeals procedure…provided—at least theoretically—a check against the arbitrary administration of justice on the part of the aristocratic establishment.[65]

In other words, with Solon's reforms, the poorest classes were recognized as citizens with guaranteed rights and recourse for wrongs, and the ruling elite became judicially accountable. It was roughly a century later, however, before the potential of the newly empowered δῆμος as a political force was fully realized.

63. Martin Ostwald, *From Popular Sovereignty to the Sovereignty of Law: Law, Society, and Politics in Fifth-Century Athens* (Berkley: University of California Press, 1986).

64. Josiah Ober, *Mass and Elite in Democratic Athens: Rhetoric, Ideology, and the Power of the People* (Princeton: Princeton University Press, 1989), 59.

65. Ostwald, *Sovereignty*, 14–15. Cf. Josiah Ober, *The Athenian Revolution: Essays on Ancient Greek Democracy and Political Theory* (Princeton: Princeton University Press, 1996), 38.

In 546, one Pisistratus acquired the powers of tyrant. He was later succeeded by his son Hippias. In 510, opposing aristocratic families (principally the Alcmaeonids) obtained help from the Spartans to depose Hippias. In the subsequent vacuum, Cleisthenes (an Alcmaeonid) vied with one Isagoras (who had Spartan backing) for principal authority. Cleisthenes appears to have had popular appeal due to the Alcmaeonid family's leadership in the overthrow of the Pisistratids; however, Isagoras achieved initial superiority with his Spartan backing. Isagoras' victory was short-lived, however. Cleisthenes soon after achieved authority in Athens. While scholars differ in their reconstruction of the forces leading to Cleisthenes' rise,[66] there is agreement that Cleisthenes found it necessary to enlarge the powers of the public Assembly (ἡ ἐκκλησία) as part of his bid for office. Herodotus famously recounts how Cleisthenes "completely attracted to his faction the Athenian commons (δῆμος), which had previously been rejected" (*Hist.* 5.69).[67]

Although the major offices of government remained in the hands of the elite, Cleisthenes' reforms gave the δῆμος significant complementary authority. "No major decision or legislation [could now] be made or implemented," Ostwald sums up the situation, "without the approval of the [representative] Council and [popular] Assembly."[68] The momentum of popular rule (δημοκρατία) had begun with Cleisthenes, so that ancient authors frequently call him the giver of democracy.[69] It was only with a further set of reforms by Ephialtes in 462/1, however, that Athens achieved its high point of "popular sovereignty." Under Ephialtes, the political powers of the elite Areopagus were transferred to the popular organs of government: the Assembly, the Council of Five Hundred, and the recently formed popular law court (δικαστήρια). "Only after Ephialtes removed from the Areopagus those powers that had given it guardianship over the state," notes Ostwald, "can we fairly call Athens a democracy."[70]

Nevertheless, there were problems with early Athenian democracy, and these problems were made painfully evident under the strain of the

66. E.g. Ostwald emphasizes *Cleisthenes'* masterful maneuvering (Martin Ostwald, *Nomos and the Beginnings of the Athenian Democracy* [London: Oxford University Press, 1969], 148–60; *Sovereignty*, 15–28), while Ober emphasizes *the people's* riot (*Mass and Elite*, 65–69; *Athenian Revolution*, 32–52) as the transforming impetus.

67. Translation from Ostwald, *Sovereignty*, 16.

68. Ostwald, *Sovereignty*, 26. Cf. Ober, *Mass and Elite*, 72.

69. E.g. Herodotus, *Hist.* 6.131.1; Aristotle, *Ath. pol.* 29.3.

70. Ostwald, *Sovereignty*, 78. Cf. Christian Meier, *The Greek Discovery of Politics* (trans. David McLintock; Cambridge, Mass.: Harvard University Press, 1990), 82–89; Aristotle, *Ath. pol.* 41.2.

Peloponnesian War. Running a war by majority vote proved disastrous. A number of severe debacles resulted in loss of the war. Ostwald writes:

> The disastrous end of the Sicilian expedition in the autumn of 413 B.C. showed that popular sovereignty was vulnerable... The major blame for the fiasco fell upon the institutions of the Athenian democracy. The Assembly had spurned Nicias's cautions...after letting Alcibiades arouse its enthusiasm for the expedition... And again, when common sense demanded a withdrawal from Sicily, the *dēmos* had opted for sending reinforcements...; these served only to increase the magnitude of the defeat.[71]

Mass rule, it seems, was too prone to emotion. Pure democracy gave the inexperienced majority too much authority to overrule the minority voice of wisdom.[72] The war ended with Athenian surrender to Sparta. Out of the turmoil that followed, an oligarchic body—"the Thirty"—achieved control. Democracy was lost under the repressive Thirty. An uprising under Thrasybulus in 403, however, brought the overthrow of the Thirty. Democracy was restored, but it was evident that the previous form of democracy needed significant reforms. In the restoration that followed, "A new social and political order was created that retained the characteristic institutions of the Athenian democracy while subordinating the principle of popular sovereignty to the principle of the sovereignty of [written] law."[73]

Although some scholars question whether the "new order" had quite so dramatic a social and political impact as often portrayed,[74] a series of developments in the Athenian use of written law—the issue of present importance—are well attested. First of all, a single collection of laws was compiled and inscribed in the Royal Stoa. Previously, law writing had been employed in Athens for declaratory, mnemonic, and perhaps religious purposes.[75] Numerous tablets, boards, and other media were posted

---

71. Ostwald, *Sovereignty*, 337.

72. Hence Plato's famous tongue-in-cheek description of democracy: "...a delightful form of government...assigning a kind of equality indiscriminately to equals and unequals alike!" (Plato, *Rep.* 8.558C).

73. Ostwald, *Sovereignty*, 497. Cf. Whitehead: "...403/2, the great watershed in Athenian constitutional development..." (David Whitehead, *The Demes of Attica— 508/7–ca. 250 B.C.: A Political and Social Study* [Princeton: Princeton University Press, 1986], 287); Garner: "...the new democratic city-state was not merely a continuation of the old one. The present was radically...cut off from the past" (Richard Garner, *Law and Society in Classical Athens* [London: Croom Helm, 1987], 131–32).

74. E.g. Ober, *Mass and Elite*, 95–103.

75. Especially Rosalind Thomas, "Written in Stone? Liberty, Equality, Orality and the Codification of Law," in *Greek Law in its Political Setting: Justifications not Justice* (ed. L. Foxhall and A. D. E. Lewis; Oxford: Clarendon, 1996), 9–31. Cf. Henry S. Maine, *Ancient Law: Its Connection with the Early History of Society and*

in scattered locations around the city. As part of the 403 reforms, a project lasting several years to compile and harmonize the ancestral law writings began. The result was inscribed into a single, consistent code on the wall of the Royal Stoa.

Second, recognizing the inadequacy of this compilation, a procedure was established for drafting new laws (νόμοι). A board of legislators (νομοθέται), probably filled by lot from the ἐκκλησία, was created for this purpose. Third, a distinction was now drawn between the decrees (ψηφίσματα) of the Assembly and the written laws (νόμοι). Laws passed through the more complicated νομοθέται boards were given superiority over ἐκκλησία decrees, thereby subjecting the Assembly itself to the written law. Finally then, an act was passed denying any further legal force to unwritten custom, thereby subjecting the courts, as well, to the written law: "In no circumstances shall magistrates enforce a law which has not been inscribed (ἀγράφω). No decree (ψήφισμα), whether of the Council or Assembly, shall override a law (νόμος)…" (Andocides, *Myst.* 1.87).

It was with these revisions that the Greeks had arrived at a legal model that is well known to the modern world but was revolutionary in the ancient world: the "rule of (written) law."[76]

Some scholars have questioned whether unwritten law was actually completely supplanted at this time, or whether written law and custom operated in tandem for a period.[77] Others have argued that the frequently

---

its Relation to Modern Ideas (The World Classics; London: Oxford University Press, 1950), 3–7; J. W. Jones, *The Law and Legal Theory of the Greeks: An Introduction* (London: Oxford University Press, 1956), 102–3; Martin Ostwald, "Was There a Concept of ἄγραφος νόμος in Classical Greece?," in *Exegesis and Argument: Studies in Greek Philosophy Presented to Gregory Vlastos* (ed. E. N. Lee et al.; Phronesis Supplement 1; Assen: Van Gorcum, 1973), 83–86; idem, *Sovereignty*, 153–54; Michael Gagarin, *Early Greek Law* (Berkeley: University of California Press, 1986), 131–32, 143–44.

76. Mogens Herman Hansen, "*Nomos* and *Psephisma* in Fourth-Century Athens," in *The Athenian Ecclesia: A Collection of Articles 1976–1983* (*Opuscula Graecolatina* 26; Copenhagen: Museum Tusculanum Press, 1983), 161–77; idem, "Did the Athenian *Ecclesia* Legislate after 403/2?," in *Athenian Ecclesia*, 179–206; A. R. W. Harrison, "Law-Making at Athens at the End of the Fifth Century B.C.," *JHS* 75 (1955): 26–35; Douglas M. MacDowell, *The Law in Classical Athens: Aspects of Greek and Roman Life* (London: Thames & Hudson, 1978), 46–49; Ostwald, *Sovereignty*, 85–108; Gagarin, *Greek Law*, 143–46; Ober, *Mass and Elite*, 299–304; C. Meier, *Greek Discovery*, 173–76; Raphael Sealey, *The Athenian Republic: Democracy or the Rule of Law?* (London: Pennsylvania State University Press, 1987), 45–50.

77. Kevin Clinton, "The Nature of the Late Fifth-Century Revision of the Athenian Law Code," in *Studies in Attic Epigraphy, History and Topography:*

supposed "two part" sequence—sovereignty of the δῆμος followed by sovereignty of written νόμοι—is problematic. Josiah Ober notes that the rule of written laws was probably conceived as a continuation of popular sovereignty rather than its replacement: "the will of the people was still sovereign, but now that will was defined in broader chronological terms."[78] On the other hand, Raphael Sealey claims that the νόμοι of Solon were always regarded as of greater authority than the Assembly's decrees (ψηφίσματα), so that the "rule of law" was perfected in the 403/2 restoration, but had been operative much earlier.[79] These controversies are not unimportant; but notwithstanding these, there is agreement that classical Athens devised a new use for its practice of law writing, with the fifth century as a focal point for that development. Athens had discovered how a law collection could become a political institution in itself and serve as a *source* for social regulation.

Whether Israel independently anticipated a similar possibility for law writings, or whether Hebrew law writers shared a common impetus with Athens at some early point, are among the questions to be encountered in the present study. These Athenian developments, therefore, are important background for the present study.

III. *Methodology and Approach*

In the preceding pages, two paradigms for writing law have been represented: non-legislative and legislative. Certainly, there are many variations possible within these two basic paradigms. (At least three kinds of non-legislative reasons for law writing were noted in connection with the cuneiform evidence.) Nevertheless, a fundamental distinction can be discerned between essentially legislative (e.g. classical Athens) and essentially non-legislative (e.g. the cuneiform literature) law writings.

In the society which views law writings non-legislatively, a conceptual separation exists between actual law and written law. That is, what is written may be a *description* of what law looks like, but what is written is not viewed as *being* "the law." When judges in a non-legislative society hear a case, they appeal to an abstract (generally religious) sense of righteousness to support their rulings; they do not look to texts to authorize their rulings. Whatever law writings are used for, they are not used to

Presented to Eugene Vanderpool (Hesperia Supplement 19; Princeton: American School of Classical Studies in Athens, 1982), 27–37.

78. Ober, *Mass and Elite*, 302.

79. Raphael Sealey, "On the Athenian Concept of Law," *CJ* 77 (1982): 289–302; *Athenian Republic*, 45–50.

prescribe judicial decisions. The idea of law, in these cultures, is abstract, like the ideas of justice, truth, and righteousness. All of these ideas can be *discussed* in writings, but none of them are ever supposed to be *embodied* by a text.[80] For instance, a written text about righteousness points beyond itself to the unwritable, abstract ideal that is righteousness, without that text itself becoming perceived as being "the righteousness." Likewise, a written text about law may be useful for describing divine law, but it is not itself supposed to be "the law." There is a distinction between actual law and law writings in the non-legislative society.

Within the legislative society, actual law is *identified* with written law. A law writing is more than a portrait of law: it is law. Actual law and written law are one and the same. Law is written down and becomes a *source* for legal practice. As in the Athenian decree earlier noted (p. 22), courts are expected to use written compilations as the source of their decisions. The magistrate's task is no longer to discern justice, but to apply what the law writings prescribe for a certain kind of case. In such a system, law is by definition a text. Law is no longer an abstract reality like justice, righteousness, and truth, but is textual by nature. Legal practice in such a society appeals to texts as the source of rulings.

These two concepts of law and law writing might be presented in the following manner:

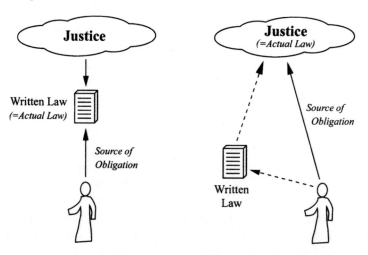

Law Code (i.e. Legislation)   Law Collection (i.e. Not Legislation)

---

80. Cf. the Babylonian ideas of *kittum* and *mīšarum* (S. M. Paul, *Studies in the Book of the Covenant in the Light of Cuneiform and Biblical Law* [VTSup 18; Leiden: Brill, 1970], 5).

Whereas the legislative paradigm expects a written text to serve as the source of legal practice (left diagram), the non-legislative paradigm looks to a cultural (often religious) perception of justice as the source of legal practice (right diagram). In the latter instance, certain customs (or *opposition* to certain customs) might be written down for literary, monumental, or educational purposes. They are not, however, written down for the purpose of regulation.

Scholars generally recognize this basic distinction, although demonstrating when one or the other paradigm is operative is not always straightforward. Toward making such assessments, Westbrook has helpfully identified four characteristics indicative of a society's use of law writings. Westbrook's outline can be regarded as generally representative of those also advanced by other scholars:[81]

The Characteristics of Law Codes	*The Characteristics of Law Collections*
1. The written law is itself authoritative; it is itself "the law."	1. The written law describes the law but is not itself "the law."
2. The norm written originated with its publication.	2. The norm written merely documents a norm already operating.
3. The exact wording of the written law is binding.	3. The wording of the written law is illustrative, but not binding.
4. The written law's publication overrides previous norms on the same subject.	[4. The written law's promulgation may add to, rather than replace, earlier variations on the same norm.][82]

These four attitudes toward law writings distinguish a legislative society on the one hand, and a custom-law society on the other. One scholar, Lafont, has raised a particular challenge to Westbrook's "tests." Although her criticism does not undermine their validity, she does raise an important cautionary issue. According to Lafont, Westbrook's codes/collections distinction "mistakes the effects and the nature of the law."[83] The

81. Westbrook, "Origins of Legislation," 202. Cf. Hans J. Boecker, *Law and the Administration of Justice in the Old Testament and Ancient East* (trans. J. Moiser; London: SPCK, 1980), 55–56; Bottéro, *Mesopotamia*, 161–64; Fitzpatrick-McKinley, *Transformation*, 16–19, 72–78; Jackson, *Studies*, 70–71, 117–18.

82. Point 4 under "Law Collections" is inferred but not explicit in Westbrook, "Origins of Legislation," 202. He explicitly develops this point, nonetheless, in his "Covenant Code."

83. Lafont, "Ancient Near Eastern Laws," 94. Lafont is responding directly to Westbrook's "Covenant Code," and indirectly (see p. 94 n. 7) to his similar arguments in "Origins of Legislation."

first point above is a true statement of the *natural* distinction between law codes and collections. Points 2–4, however, are *effects* which are not so reliable a gauge of a law text's nature as, according to Lafont, Westbrook makes them out to be.

Westbrook's first point is, according to Lafont, an accurate statement of the *natural* distinction between a legislative and non-legislative law text. Westbrook writes: "Legislation is an authoritative source of law; the courts are bound to obey its precepts... An academic treatise on the law may be good evidence of what the law is, but it is not an authoritative source."[84]

Lafont accepts the validity of this first distinction: legislation is "a text proceeding from an institution vested with legislative power, enforceable for everybody and for an unlimited time."[85] Legislation is that which *is itself* the law—the source of regulation and enforcement. It is in Westbrook's other points that he strays, in Lafont's view, from a discussion of a law writing's *nature* to over-mechanical conclusions based on a law writing's *effects*.

For instance, Lafont takes issue with Westbrook's second distinction (as outlined above) that legislation introduces a law, whereas a law treatise documents existing law. Under that distinction, Lafont deduces, "Westbrook's reasoning identifies legislation with innovation. The law [to be legislation] must necessarily be reformatory."[86] Lafont counters by noting the Code of Napoleon: Napoleon's Code was certainly drafted as legislation; however, it was not innovative. "Napoleon's masterpiece," Lafont recalls, "is primarily a synthesis of the adductions of Roman, Common, and Canon laws, as well as royal and revolutionary legislations."[87] It was essentially a drawing together of pre-existing norms and therefore, under Westbrook's innovation test, would look more like a law collection than a law code.

Lafont's criticism raises a valid caution, although it does not neutralize Westbrook's distinctions. Such criticism rightly cautions against drawing too mechanical a conclusion about a text's *nature* from a certain list of *effects*. In this instance: the innovation of new norms might be a frequent effect of legislation, but its absence does not automatically indicate the opposite. Just because a law composition (e.g. Napoleon's Code) is not innovative does not mean it is not legislative. Actually, Westbrook was more sensitive to this matter than Lafont recognized. She

84. Westbrook, "Origins of Legislation," 202. Cf. his "Codification," 33–34.
85. Lafont, "Ancient Near Eastern Laws," 96.
86. Ibid., 94.
87. Ibid., 94.

appears to have overlooked Westbrook's statement that, "Even if the legislation does not change the existing law but merely codifies it, the effect is to exclude reliance on the earlier sources."[88] In other words, Westbrook recognizes that a code like Napoleon's can be legislation without innovating. Legislation is not *always* reformatory and innovative (Point 2, above); but Westbrook notes that when such a law compilation does replace other sources of law once it is promulgated (Point 4, above), it is legislative rather than academic. Thus Westbrook recognizes that, while certain effects are good indicators of a law writing's nature, it is the cumulative evidence of a text's effects (rather than the mechanical notation of one or two of them) that is persuasive. Lafont's criticism raises a valid caution against over-mechanical deductions from certain effects, but does not negate the importance of observing these effects. After all, it is only through observing the effects of a law text on its society that deductions about its nature are possible. Ancient Near Eastern societies did not leave behind philosophical texts explaining their legal institutions. More specifically, there are no texts from ancient Near Eastern societies explicating their philosophies of law writing. It is only through study of the law writings themselves, and their effects (or non-effects) on society, that deductions about their nature are possible. Lafont would appear to desire that all such examination be disqualified and that, instead, any law text originating from the king be automatically regarded as legislative: "…ancient Near Eastern law codes contain true legal rules [because they were] set forth by the king in accordance with the prerogatives he was given by the gods, valid for all his subjects and designed to remain in force permanently, as is shown by the curses uttered in the epilogue of the codes."[89]

Such a presumption is problematic for most scholars. The question of a law collection's effect (e.g. in the law-practice records) remains an important, even if complex, indicator of that text's nature. Consequently, examination of a law writing's effects cannot be overlooked if one would discover (rather than presume) its legislative or non-legislative nature.

Westbrook's outline of distinctive effects, even if not to be applied mechanically, are nonetheless generally acceptable and will be used in the present project. Point 3 (as outlined above) is particularly noteworthy: in Westbrook's words, because a legislative text is "the source of law," therefore, "the courts must pay great attention to the wording of

---

88. Westbrook, "Origins of Legislation," 202. In a later article ("Covenant Code," 24), to which Lafont is more directly responding, Westbrook did not repeat this qualification, which may explain Lafont's oversight.
89. Lafont, "Ancient Near Eastern Laws," 96.

the text" and "interpret its meaning..."[90] When a text is itself the law, legal practice will derive from the provisions written. The sanctions as written will be the sanctions applied. Furthermore, where sanctions other than those written are deemed preferable, some process of exegetical interpretation (or textual amendment) would become necessary in order to justify variation from the text's stipulation.[91] It has been generally allowable, in comparing cuneiform law writings with practice documents, that contradictions between the stated stipulations of the former and the practice of the latter are indicative of the law collections' failure actually to regulate practice (i.e. to be legislation). "Besides," to quote Bottéro on the matter, "what law is it if it is not compelling in itself...?"[92] This same distinctive operative in cuneiform law studies will be observed in the present review of Israel's law writings and their function.

The present study will focus on discerning the nature of law writing in consecutive periods of Israel's history—whether law writings are employed as a source of law, or as an idyllic text not ascribed with regulatory force. The particular interest of this project is to model Israel's transition from a non-legislative to a legislative conception of its law writings.

Such a project is obviously ambitious. The scope of examination which would be necessary to complete such a project, were it to be comprehensive, would be mammoth. There are, however, ways to limit the selection of materials to be addressed by this study. First of all, as earlier observed (pp. 3–7, above), there are key periods in Israel's history which scholars have already identified as important windows into Hebrew legal development. A viable outline of Israel's uses of its law writings can be compiled through attention to these key periods.

There will be five periods, in all, which will be surveyed in this book. Patrick and Westbrook have advanced arguments for legal development during the Deuteronomic reforms of seventh-century Judah. Chapter 3 will engage with the work of these scholars as an entry point into the use of law writings in that period. A number of scholars have also offered arguments in support of legislative activity in the Persian era. These will be addressed in Chapter 4. A particular contribution of this project will be its examination of Hellenistic-era evidence. Scholars have frequently alluded to Greek "rule of law" innovations in relation to Israel's adoption

90. Westbrook, "Origins of Legislation," 202. Cf. Boecker, *Law and Justice*, 56; Bottéro, *Mesopotamia*, 163–64; Fitzpatrick-McKinley, *Transformation*, 16–17, 72–78; Jackson, *Studies*, 70, 117–18.
91. Cf. Fishbane, *Biblical Interpretation*, 3.
92. Bottéro, *Mesopotamia*, 163.

of legislative ideas, but little work has been done to test and explain that relationship. Chapters 5 and 6 will identify two Hellenistic influences and their specific relationship to the development of Hebrew legislative ideas. In addition to these three prominent periods of legal foment, analyses of early Israel's non-legislative uses of law writings (in Chapter 2) and Roman-era, legislative uses of Torah (in Chapter 7) will provide framing *termini* for the transition here being modeled.

It is recognized that study in other periods will be necessary to qualify and fill out the findings here produced. Nevertheless, there is already a scholarly consensus surrounding these five periods and the importance of their witness to the development of Hebrew law. The present project will use these periods as a framework for modeling Israel's shifting attitudes toward law writings—specifically the shift from non-legislative to legislative uses.

It is also recognized that the resulting model only identifies general mechanics for that transition. As will be seen from the sampling of Roman-era Jewish sects in Chapter 7, the practical ramifications of Torah's reconceptualization as a legislative code are manifold and complex. There will need to be sect-by-sect studies to define the exact manner in which various strands of postbiblical Judaism "worked out" the new, legislative approach to the Torah. In other words, this project provides a general outline of the basic transition from non-legislative to legislative thinking, but leaves the door opened for more detailed assessments of how certain Judaic sects appropriated (or perhaps, in cases, resisted) those developments.

In addition to this focus on certain periods of legal development, it will also be appropriate in this project to focus on a limited circle of texts for each period. It is important, first of all, to focus in this study on the indigenous Hebrew literature. This is in distinction from biblical law studies which begin with comparative or evolutionary models and then look to Hebrew texts to validate those models.[93] Such approaches are certainly valid and productive—indeed, the present study makes frequent use of insights produced by such evolutionary/comparative models. Nevertheless, it is ultimately necessary to construct an understanding of Hebrew law from Hebrew evidence. The present project will accept the heuristic value of comparative evidence but will concentrate on the analysis of Hebrew literature for drawing conclusions about Hebrew attitudes towards law and law writings.

93. E.g. Westbrook, *Studies*; Fitzpatrick-McKinley, *Transformation*; Jackson, *Studies*.

Furthermore, as observed earlier (pp. 1–2, above), there are certain kinds of texts which scholars have generally accepted as indicators of a society's attitude toward its law writings—namely, *law practice* records. It is the comparison of cuneiform law collections (like LH) on the one hand, with cuneiform law-practice materials (such as property deeds, contracts, courtroom verdicts, and the like) on the other, that has been central to the study of Mesopotamian attitudes toward law writing. A similar method is expected for the study of biblical law,[94] and will be the focus of the present study. It must be noted up front, however, that archaeology has not recovered Hebrew law-practice records to match the wealth of contractual materials exhumed from the cuneiform traditions. Nevertheless, despite this lack of *actual* law-practice records, there is much useful evidence of Hebrew law practice in the extant Hebrew literature. Trial narratives, court forms, and legal reforms are represented in the biblical and extrabiblical writings in forms that can be used profitably for the present project. Such materials are, of course, reshaped for narrative purposes, and this fact will need to be taken into consideration. Nonetheless, the witnesses to law practice (and law book uses) in the Hebrew literature afford insights which deserve to be examined.

Through a focus on the aforementioned periods, and specifically on Hebrew law-practice evidence in those periods, a measured study can be conducted that will produce a viable model of Israel's transition from non-legislative to legislative ways of using law writings.

In recent decades, important advances have been made in the study of biblical law. Many studies have focused on Hebrew law in the monarchical period, or in Second Temple Yehud, or in other periods. In light of the insights produced by such studies—and particularly the significant differences in the ways in which law writings were perceived in different periods—it has now become a pressing need of biblical law studies to develop a model of Israel's transition from a non-legislative society to one which viewed its law writings legislatively. This book offers an outline of just such a model.

94. Henry McKeating, "Sanctions Against Adultery in Ancient Israelite Society, with Some Reflections on Methodology in the Study of Old Testament Ethics," *JSOT* 11 (1979): 66; Jackson, *Studies*, 114–17; Pamela Barmash, "The Narrative Quandry: Cases of Law in Literature," *VT* 54, no. 1 (2004): 1–16.

Chapter 2

WRITTEN LAW IN ANCIENT ISRAEL

As new understandings of the cuneiform law writings emerged, questions about the nature of Hebrew law writings were certain to follow. The similar forms employed (e.g. the much discussed casuistic form), as well as similarities in content (e.g. ox-goring laws), certainly invite comparisons. Some scholars view these similarities as adequate grounds for presuming a shared, cuneiform/Hebrew legal culture (including common uses for law writing).[1] Most scholars are wary of over-comparison, however. Despite the similarities, there are marked differences between the traditions as well. One cannot assume the uses of cuneiform law writings automatically apply to Hebrew law writings.[2]

Nevertheless, it is no longer permissible to assume Hebrew law writings were legislation. This was long the dominant view, but it was the dominant view by assumption. With the heuristic offerings of cuneiform studies, reassessment of the Hebrew law writings has become necessary. Such reassessment has brought a growing consensus that ancient Israel's law collections, also, were not legislation. Even if Hebrew law does differ in marked ways from Mesopotamian law, nonetheless in this respect there are similarities. Law writings in ancient Israel were idyllic, not legislative. One is still apt to encounter scholarship treating the Hebrew law writings as though they were statutory. "The [legislative] assumption is still all to[o] easy to slide into," Philip Davies aptly notes. Notwithstanding, the legislative view "is probably now regarded by most scholars as naive and obsolete."[3] The general consensus is that Israel wrote laws for idyllic, not regulatory, purposes.

1. E.g. S. Paul, *Studies*, 104–5; Finkelstein, *Ox That Gored*, 20; Westbrook, *Studies*, 1–8; idem, "Ancient Near Eastern Law," 24.

2. Albrecht Alt, *Essays in Old Testament History and Religion* (Oxford: Blackwell, 1966), 97; Boecker, *Law and Justice*, 154–55; Malul, *Comparative Method*, 99–112; Samuel Greengus, "Some Issues Relating to the Comparability of Laws and the Coherence of the Legal Tradition," in Levinson, ed., *Theory and Method*, 60–62, 86–87 (cf. p. 72 n. 34); Jackson, *Studies*, 16–17; Van Seters, *Diaspora*, 30–31.

3. P. Davies, "'Law' in Judaism," 7.

The present chapter will set forth the arguments for this consensus. The trend is already moving in this direction, but not without controversy. One particular problem is that scholarship in the field has generally embraced this view based on negative evidence: for instance, that the Hebrew law writings are nowhere said to be used by Israel's judges or enforced in judicial settings. Though the position is not completely based in arguments from silence, that is sometimes the impression.[4] The present chapter will review these (primarily) negative arguments, and will also seek to advance the present consensus through introduction of a further, positive argument. Thus the chapter here will offer more than a review of the current trend, but will seek to strengthen that trend by contributing toward filling one of its weak points: namely, the need for positive arguments. By doing so, a beginning point will be fixed for the inquiry of the present study into the later prescriptivization of the Hebrew law writings.

I. *Current Scholarship on Hebrew Law Writing*

As noted in the previous chapter, reassessment of the cuneiform law collections has been facilitated by contemporaneous contracts and trial documents. It has been the comparison of the laws as stated (in the collections) with the laws as practiced (in praxis materials) that led to non-legislative explanations for the cuneiform collections. It is through a similar method that the function of law collections in ancient Israel needs to be assessed. The situation is more complicated, however, when one turns to the Hebrew material. There are no extant stashes of Hebrew court dockets. Instead, one must examine the Hebrew narrative, wisdom, and prophetic writings for Hebrew attitudes toward law writing.[5] It is generally admitted that BC is the earliest biblical law compilation. It is of "uncertain" dating, but "considered of great antiquity" (perhaps as early as the tenth–twelfth centuries).[6] How do the Hebrew writings show such early law collections being used?

Raymond Westbrook posits a "juridical treatise" function for BC—similar to that use which he ascribes to the cuneiform laws. In one article, Westbrook cites five biblical trial accounts to establish this position.[7] The appeal of the daughters of Zelophehad (Num 27:1–11) is typical of these examples. Since Zelophehad died without sons, his daughters are

---

4. Westbrook, "Codification," 37–38.

5. Jackson, *Studies*, 114; Barmash, "Narrative Quandry."

6. Westbrook, "Biblical Law," 5 (contra Van Seters, *Diaspora*, 4–7).

7. Westbrook, "Law Codes," 261–64. Westbrook's five biblical trial accounts are Num 15:32–36; Num 31/1 Sam 30; Num 9:6–14; 27:1–11; and Lev 24:10–23.

said to have sought inheritance rights. The case was brought to Moses who inquired of the Lord. The decision which Yahweh gave Moses is recorded as follows:

> The words of the daughters of Zelophehad are right. You shall give…their father's inheritance to them. And you shall speak to the sons of Israel, saying, "If a man dies and has no son, then you shall transfer his inheritance to his daughter. And if he has no daughter, then…to his brothers. And if he has no brother, then…to his father's brothers. And if his father has no brothers, then…to his nearest kinsman… It shall be a statute and a judgment for the sons of Israel, as Yahweh commanded Moses. (Num 27:7–11)

For Westbrook, this record illustrates the way a specific precedent was extrapolated for ongoing instruction. The case here was about a certain man (Zelophehad) and certain heirs (his daughters). The resulting "statute and judgment" is cast in anonymous terms ("if a man dies and has no son"); the variables of the case are expanded to cover more circumstances than the initial case ("and if he has no daughter…"); and the judgment is verbally preserved ("it shall be a statute and a judgment").[8] Israel's law collections, Westbrook avers, arose from actual cases and were recast for judicial education[9]—or, at least, that was the expectation. Westbrook suspects the Zelophehad story is artificial; this inheritance custom may actually derive from ancient Sumer.[10] The Zelophehad account may be a Hebrew construct to explain a borrowed custom. Even so, this construct shows that Israel *expected* such a precept to emerge from an actual case. If the real case was not known, a new one could be invented. Each of the biblical accounts examined by Westbrook similarly suggest a Hebrew expectation that casuistic laws arise from seminal cases. Westbrook's arguments on this point are helpful.

In another facet of Westbrook's argument, however, he steps beyond the evidence of Hebrew writings and bases a further conclusion on cuneiform evidence. It is here that his conclusions are more tenuous. Because the "scientific list" form was employed for juridical reference in other ancient Near Eastern societies,[11] Westbrook allows the same for Israel. This assumption is not unreasonable,[12] but it is not actually supported by

8. Ibid., 262–63. Cf. idem, *Studies*, 4.

9. Ibid., 253–58; idem, *Studies*, 1–8; idem, "Origins of Legislation," 202. Cf. Otto, "Town and Countryside," 20–22.

10. Westbrook, "Law Codes," 262 (citing Miguel Civil, "New Sumerian Law Fragments," in Hans Gustav Güterbock, "Mursili's Accounts of Suppiluliuma's Dealings with Egypt," *RHA* 18.66 [1960]: 4–5).

11. See pp. 12–15, above.

12. Greengus, "Comparability of Laws," 79.

the texts Westbrook develops. It was, after all, "to the sons of Israel" (not to the elders or judges) that Moses was said to address the precepts noted by Westbrook. It might actually be suspected that these statements of law were composed for *popular* instruction rather than judicial education. Westbrook's insights into the *formulation* of Hebrew rulings (i.e. they often derived from seminal cases) is supported by indigenous evidence; his projected *use* for the law writings (i.e. they were for judicial instruction) actually lacks indigenous support and must therefore be regarded as hypothetical.

Two other scholars have helped address this use question from the Hebrew material: Dale Patrick and Bernard Jackson. Patrick focuses, first of all, on biblical judge commissions. In the body of BC, the following instructions to judges and court witnesses appear:

> You shall not bear a false report. You shall not conspire with a wicked man to be a malicious witness. You shall not follow the multitude to do evil; you shall neither answer in a dispute, siding with the multitude, to pervert justice, nor shall you favor the poor in his suit… You shall keep far from a false charge, and shall not execute the innocent or the righteous, for I will not acquit the wicked. Also, you shall not take a bribe, for a bribe blinds the eyesight and distorts the cause of the righteous. (Exod 23:1–3, 7–8)

Other charges specifically addressed to judges appear elsewhere in the literature (Exod 18:21; Lev 19:15–16; Deut 1:16–17; 16:19–20; 25:1; cf. 2 Chr 19:9–11). In each of these instances, judges are exhorted to decide cases honestly, righteously, and without succumbing to bribes. However,

> It is noteworthy that none of these catalogs have a commandment to consult the lawbooks or adhere to the letter of the law. However judicial decisions were argued and rendered, it is evident that conformity to rules of law was not itself a value to be inculcated… From this silence one may surmise that Israelite judges were not expected to consult the legal codes to find the rule that applied to the case before the bar.[13]

To test this "surmise from silence," Patrick then moves to an examination of seven court descriptions in the Hebrew narratives: Gen 18:23–25; Num 27:1–11; 2 Sam 14:5–17; 1 Kgs 21:8–13, 19–24; 2 Kgs 8:1–6; Jer 26:8–24.[14] In each of these, Patrick further notes the absence of appeal to written norms when rendering decisions. In fact, in some instances rulings are proffered which contradict Israel's written stipulations. In the case of the woman of Tekoa (2 Sam 14:5–17), for example,

13. Patrick, *Old Testament Law*, 191–93.
14. Ibid., 193–98.

the king gives a ruling contrary to every law and principle in Scripture governing murder. In the [written] laws, murder *must* be answered by the execution of the perpetrator... (Num. 35:31, 33). Thus, not only does David's judgment [to excuse a murderer] not appeal to a rule of law, it is diametrically opposed to a known rule... [Nonetheless, according to the account] David, "is like the angel of God to discern good and evil" (vs. 17).[15]

Not only are written laws absent, but they are at times contradicted, and that with the narrator's full approbation.[16]

Another biblical court scene can also be noted: the trial of Jeremiah (Jer 26). This case is significant because the arguments of both plaintiffs and defense are recorded; it is "the most detailed description of a trial in the Old Testament."[17] The recorded charge against Jeremiah is that he is preaching against the temple. It is a charge for which no written law is known. He is defended based on a precedent—that another prophet once did the same. In this unusually full trial narrative, the arguments advanced by both sides of the case are offered on theological and precedential grounds; no law writings are cited.[18] These examples are typical of the juridical narratives in the Hebrew scriptures. Law writings are never cited as decisive in a court of law, and at times cases are decided in contradiction to what is written.

One further example from Patrick's study should be noted: the trial against Naboth (1 Kgs 21:19–24).[19] This is one case in which Patrick discerns an actual appeal to BC. In the account, Jezebel manufactures a case against Naboth in order to seize his vineyard. The charge devised by the queen is stated thus: "You have cursed God and the king" (1 Kgs 21:10). According to Patrick, this is "a virtual citation of Exodus 22:28 [MT v. 27]."[20] Patrick sees this as an indication that BC was extant at the time, and that Jezebel designed her case to fit a known, legal paradigm that would ensure a death sentence for Naboth. In other words, one might see Jezebel's charge as indicating an expectation the judges would rule according to BC. Notwithstanding this initial suspicion, there are

15. Ibid., 195.

16. Other "irregularities" between the laws-as-stated and law-as-practiced are widely discussed. For example, McKeating ("Sanctions," 57–72) compares the penalties for adultery in the law writings with its penalties in the narrative, wisdom, and prophetic literature.

17. Boecker, *Law and Justice*, 44. Cf. Gerald C. Keown et al., eds., *Jeremiah 26–52* (WBC 27; Waco, Tex.: Word, 1995), 7–8.

18. Patrick, *Old Testament Law*, 197.

19. Ibid., 195–96.

20. Ibid., 195.

irregularities in the punishment handed down. Not only was Naboth executed, all his heirs were also killed (cf. 2 Kgs 9.26) and his property was ascribed to the crown. "The court's judgment," observes Patrick, "diverges from any known Israelite law or practice."[21] Even though BC might have been *influential upon* court jurisprudence, it was not *the basis for* court decisions. Patrick deduces from this example that BC was an academic text known to the judiciary, but not legislation. The court at Jezreel decided the case against Naboth according to the ideals in BC, but they were not actually ruling according to BC. Thus Patrick arrives at a "use" position similar to Westbrook's (though Patrick has argued from the Hebrew evidence):

> the lawbooks [of Moses] were intended not for judicial application but for instruction in the values, principles, concepts, and procedures of the unwritten divine Law... One might term them exercises in legal thinking. By means of examples, the legal experts of the community inculcated the legal concepts, principles, and judicial procedures that they held to have standing in the legal tradition...of Israelite society.[22]

Whether Jezebel made a "virtual citation" from BC is debatable, however. That is, one can certainly see that Jezebel's charge and Exod 22:27 (EV v. 28) both point to a common custom; whether Jezebel can therefore be said to have used BC specifically is doubtful. Jezebel's charge against Naboth uses the verb ברך; BC uses אֹרֹר...קלל. Jezebel charges Naboth with cursing אלהים ומלך; BC warns not to curse אלהים or a נשׂיא בעמך. It can hardly be concluded that Jezebel made a "virtual citation" of BC if, by saying so, Patrick means that Jezebel used that text to form her charge. In fact, that Jezebel did not actually quote BC might be said to infer the opposite: although she cited a custom which BC also records, she was not consulting BC itself. The evidence is not clear that BC was a judicial treatise consulted by Jezebel, even though the Naboth case shows that Exod 22:27 (EV 28) is a realistic description of period custom. It remains uncertain whether Israel's law writings were employed as professional reference works.

Apart from this point, Patrick mounts a persuasive argument. In addition to his arguments from silence (i.e. that law writings are not assigned to judges and are not consulted in court narratives), Patrick demonstrates actual contradictions between law-as-practiced and law-as-stated. Whatever the law writings were, they do not appear to have been legislative. But what *were* they used for? Thus far, the case has been primarily

21. Ibid., 196.
22. Ibid., 198–200.

negative: law writings were *not* used where they should be expected if they were legislative. For what uses, positively, were laws written down in ancient Israel?

It is Jackson who has helped to open the positive argument. To begin with, Jackson shares Patrick's interest in biblical judge commissions. He is particularly interested in the judicial commissions in Deut 1:16–17 and 2 Chr 19:9–11, because both these books also contain numerous references to the law book. Both of these judicial commissions "record that the instructions to the judges are of an entirely general character [e.g. to avoid partiality and bribes, and to judge in the fear of the Lord]... No mention of a written source of law is found..."[23] Yet elsewhere, "both Deuteronomy and 2 Chronicles also provide explicit information about the use of a written text of law."[24] That is, the "book of the law" *is* an important theme in both these corpora, with instructions to *priests* (e.g. 2 Chr 17:9) and *kings* (e.g. Deut 17:18) on law book use. That Deuteronomy and 2 Chronicles evince a thematic concern for the law book, but that their *judicial* charges do not share in its use, is, for Jackson, remarkable: "In both sources, written law has a didactic function...[but] it is not the basis of adjudication."[25] Thus Jackson takes Patrick's argument on the judge commissions a step further: because the law book is mentioned where it is applicable in these works, its non-mention in judicial settings can be regarded as real evidence of their non-application to courts.

This argument requires, however, that the applications which are explicit for the law book be cataloged. Jackson offers four categories of use for written law that can be demonstrated in the biblical literature. They can be summarized thus:[26]

1.   *Monumental uses*—When Joshua led Israel into the land, he inscribed the law on stone at Mount Ebal (Josh 8:32). From such examples, Jackson concludes, "The inscription of laws on stone serves a primarily monumental purpose, as has been recognized in the case of the Laws of Hammurabi."[27]

23.   Jackson, *Studies*, 118–20.
24.   Ibid., 121.
25.   Ibid., 121.
26.   Ibid., 121–41. (Though Östborn does not distinguish between written and unwritten law; cf. Gunnar Östborn, *Tōrā in the Old Testament: A Semantic Study* [Lund: Håkan Ohlssons Boktryckeri, 1945].)
27.   Jackson, *Studies*, 126. For other applications of the monumental nature of ancient Near Eastern law writings to Israel, see S. Paul, *Studies*, 27–29; John H. Sailhamer, *The Pentateuch as Narrative: A Biblical-Theological Commentary* (Grand Rapids: Zondervan, 1992), 64–65; Fitzpatrick-McKinley, *Transformation*, 165–66.

2. *Archival uses*—At the end of his life, Moses instructed the Levites to place his "book of the law" beside the ark (Deut 31:26). Similarly, Jackson notes that Samuel "writes a *mishpat hamelukhah*, and—significantly—deposits it in a sanctuary."[28] In such instances, Jackson sees the law book as archival.

3. *Didactic uses*—A further use for written law, which Jackson notes, is educational. Deuteronomy expects the king to study (under Levitical oversight) from a law book (Deut 17:18–20); Joshua is instructed to meditate in the law book (Josh 1:8); Jehoshaphat sent princes and Levites throughout the land with the law book to teach the people (2 Chr 17:7–9). Jackson places particular emphasis on the didactic uses of Hebrew law writings.[29]

4. *Ritual Uses*—Finally, Jackson notes that the law book was used for ritual reading. Moses appointed the reading of his law book every seven years at the Feast of Booths (Deut 31:9–13). Moses himself led a ritual reading of a law book after the initial events at Sinai (Exod 24:3–8). Joshua (Josh 8:34) and Josiah (2 Kgs 23:1–3) are similarly recorded as having led in ritual reading from a law book. Laws were thus written down for ritual uses.

These are the only four functions for written law—notably not including any judicial uses—that the Hebrew narratives document.[30] Jackson's study also points the didactic use toward *public* instruction, rather than the judicial education posited by Patrick and Westbrook. The latter is plausible, but Hebrew evidence for it is lacking.

Such studies as those reviewed above are significant. Combined, insights such as Westbrook's handling of law formulation, Patrick's evidence on court practice, and Jackson's demonstrable functions for law texts (along with the overall more-literary-than-legal character of the law

---

28. Jackson, *Studies*, 130 (citing 1 Sam 10).

29. Especially ibid., 70–92. For another "didactic" approach to the law writings, see Calum Carmichael, *The Spirit of the Law* (Athens, Ga.: University of Georgia Press, 1996), 52, and the particular example of his approach in *Law and Narrative in the Bible: The Evidence of the Deuteronomic Laws and the Decalogue* (London: Cornell University Press, 1985), 142–45 (cf. Jackson, *Studies*, 228–30). For criticism of Carmichael's approach, see Bernard Levinson, "Calum M. Carmichael's Approach to the Laws of Deuteronomy," *HTR* 83.3 (1990): 227–57, and the response by Carmichael, "Laws of Leviticus 19," *HTR* 87.3 (1994): 239–56.

30. Jackson does perceive "the transformation of the biblical legal collections into 'statutory' texts, binding upon the courts and subject to verbal interpretation," during the time of Ezra (Jackson, *Studies*, 142).

texts themselves[31]) have proven compelling. "Many of the characteristic features of Biblical drafting," Jackson summarizes, "illustrate not the religious nature of Israel's law, but rather the non-statutory nature of Israel's chief religious document."[32] At least these two points can be confidently accepted: (1) a legislative use of law writings cannot be demonstrated from the Hebrew literature; and, (2) non-legislative uses of law writings can be demonstrated from the Hebrew literature. It is in view of such evidence that the field of biblical law is moving away from the legislative model.[33]

The state of scholarship might therefore be displayed, as follows:

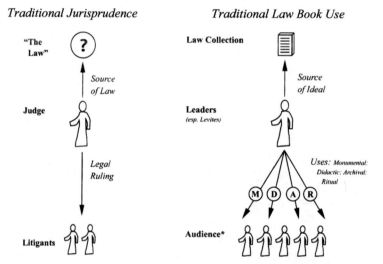

Traditional Jurisprudence	*Traditional Law Book Use*

"*Negatively*": The law writings are not being used as the source of law in Hebrew court narratives.

"*Positively*": The law writings are being used as idyllic texts in monumental, didactic, archival, and ritual roles. *(*The audience in such uses is not always human, but may be divine.)*

The picture would be more complete if something positive could also be said about the *source of law* for traditional jurisprudence in Israel: If not law writings, what *was* the source of legal decisions in ancient Israel? It is toward filling this gap that the following section will be focused.

31. Bernard S. Jackson, *Essays in Jewish and Comparative Legal History* (SJLA 10; Leiden: Brill, 1975), 29 n. 27: "E.g., the first and second person formulations, the common absence of sanctions, and many (but not all) motive clauses."

32. Ibid., 29.

33. For discussion of those still endorsing a legislative view of biblical law, see pp. 48–53, below.

II. *Source Law in the Pentateuchal Judiciary*

Scholars generally speak of "custom," or "the sense of justice and right shared by the legal community,"[34] as the actual source for justice in ancient Israel. Without completely denying this, it would seem that more can be said. It will here be asserted that Israel's prescriptive law-source was not so much custom but divine oracle. Dynamic oracle, not static texts, was perceived as the source of jurisprudence for Israel's court system.[35]

This conclusion arises from the Pentateuchal descriptions of Israel's court system. The Pentateuch preserves three traditions concerning Israel's court system: (1) Exod 18:13–27; (2) Num 11:16–25; and (3) Deut 1:9–17; 17:8–13. It is broadly recognized that these texts are related, although their exact relationship remains unsettled.[36] It is also generally admitted that they represent monarchic-era traditions retrojected to Moses. (Some find connections as early as David or as late as Josiah, with Jehoshaphat being perhaps the most frequently mentioned.[37]) Exodus 18 is generally accepted as the oldest of them and will serve as a launch point for this examination, with the parallel texts compared.

Exodus 18 describes a Hebrew court system via a narrative about Jethro (Moses' father-in-law). Jethro, it is said, watched all day while Moses "sat to judge" the people (v. 13). At the end of the day, Jethro asked Moses to explain his practice. Moses responded, "…the people come to me to inquire of God (לדרש אלהים); for when a dispute arises between them, they come to me, and I judge (שפטתי) between a man and his fellow, and I teach (הודעתי) the statutes of God and his laws" (18:15–16).

There are three aspects of Moses' court procedure here indicated: (1) divine inquiry (דרש); (2) dispute resolution (שפט); and (3) teaching law (ידע). Jethro recommends an amendment to this court protocol. His recommendation only alters one aspect of the three, however: the burden of dispute resolution (#2) should now be shared with others. Divine inquiry (#1) and teaching law (#3) continue to be Moses' peculiar responsibilities:[38]

---

34. Patrick, *Old Testament Law*, 189.

35. Jackson has pointed this direction (see pp. 45–46, below).

36. Hanoch Reviv, "The Traditions Concerning the Inception of the Legal System in Israel: Significance and Dating," *ZAW* 94 (1982): 566–67.

37. For a review and critique of the opinions, see Axel Graupner, "Exodus 18,13–27—Ätiologie einer Justizreform in Israel?," in *Recht und Ethos im Alten Testament—Gestalt und Wirkung: Festschrift für Horst Seebass zum 65 Geburstag* (ed. Stefan Beyerle et al.; Neukirchen–Vluyn: Neukirchener Verlag, 1999), 11–26.

38. Crüsemann, *The Torah*, 83.

...You will (continue to) represent the people before God and bring their cases to God [#1], and you will (continue to) warn them about the statutes and the laws and teach them the way in which they should walk and the deeds they should do [#3]. Moreover, search out from all the people capable men who fear God... They will judge the people at all times, and the great matters they will bring to you, but all the small matters they will judge themselves [#2]. (Exod 18:19–22)

It is the first of these three features (divine inquiry) which is of immediate concern. It seems remarkable to find inquiry (דרשׁ)—a practice normally connected with personal distress or religious concern[39]—employed for dispute resolution. Several alternative explanations for this use of דרשׁ have been offered.

Some consider Exod 18 to integrate three *distinct* traditions of the Mosaic office: inquiring, teaching, and judging. Even if this is the case, these traditions have here been combined in what is explicitly (and only) a courtroom scene: "Moses sat to judge..." (v. 13).[40] The text intends Mosaic inquiry to be included among his judicial activities.[41] Brevard Childs has suggested that the term lost its usual import as divine consultation in this context. Verse 16 indicates that it was actually Moses himself who rendered decisions: "they come to me and I judge." Childs concludes that Moses was, in fact, judging himself (not by inquiry). Nonetheless, "because God continued to be regarded as the ultimate judge of all of Israel's laws, the retention of the old vocabulary was not inappropriate," even though technically imprecise.[42] Childs is likely correct to note that Moses rendered decisions in many cases without inquiry. Oracle may not have been routine in Moses' court. Nevertheless, v. 19 confirms that דרשׁ, in this setting, does retain its technical reference to divine consultation: "you will be before God...and bring their cases to God." The choice of the often cultic terms חק and תורה in v. 16 also supports the cultic idea of דרשׁ here.[43] In fact, divine inquiry is a frequent

39. E.g. Gen 25:22; 1 Sam 9:9; 2 Kgs 22:18; Jer 37:7.
40. Brevard S. Childs, *Exodus: A Commentary* (OTL; London: SCM Press, 1974), 330–31; John Van Seters, *The Life of Moses: The Yahwist as Historian in Exodus–Numbers* (Louisville, Ky.: Westminster John Knox, 1994), 212–14.
41. The literary unity of the text does not permit the attribution of this combination to divergent sources; see John I. Durham, *Exodus* (WBC 3; Waco, Tex.: Word, 1987), 241; Cornelis Houtman, *Exodus: Volume 2 (Chapters 7:14–19:25)* (trans. S. Woudstra; Historical Commentary on the Old Testament; Kampen: Kok, 1996), 396.
42. Childs, *Exodus*, 330.
43. Richard Hentschke, *Satzung und Setzender: Ein Beitrag zur israelitischen Rechtsterminologie* (BWANT 83/3; Stuttgart: Kohlhammer, 1963), 30–31. Cf. Durham, *Exodus*, 251.

enough facet of Mosaic judgment elsewhere in the Pentateuchal traditions that it need not be otherwise explained in Exod 18.[44] In other words,
the court system endorsed here depends on dynamic inquiry (דרש) as the
ultimate source for law.[45]

It is this cultic law source that led to logistical problems. Rather than
consulting their own family and tribal elders (the primitive norm),[46] the
people were now coming *en mass* to Moses because of their preference
for mantic law: "the people come to me to inquire of God…when a dispute arises between them" (v. 15). Even though Moses did not necessarily inquire for every decision, his divine access was what made his court
more authoritative than that of the local elders.[47]

The genius of Jethro was his design of a hierarchy whereby local
judges could share in Moses' divine access. Moses evidently saw no
alternative to handling all the disputes himself, since he alone had the
divine access that the people expected for just rulings.[48] It was not that
Moses was unaware of the possibility of delegation; rather, it was the
case that his capacity for divine inquiry could not be delegated. Jethro's
genius was to establish a system whereby lower judges could operate
under the auspices of, and with access to, Mosaic inquiry.[49] Under Jethro's
system, those cases which did not require inquiry (the קטן cases; vv. 22,
26) would be delegated to other judges. Moses would handle only the
"difficult" cases (the גדל or קשה cases; vv. 22, 26) which required mantic
rulings. That the "difficult" cases were those needing divine inquiry is
confirmed by v. 19, where Jethro says Moses will resolve these "hard
cases" by "represent[ing] the people before God, and bring[ing] their
[hard] cases to God."[50] The parallel account in Deut 17 also indicates that

44.   E.g. Exod 33:7–11; Lev 24:10–16; Num 9:6–14; 15:32–36; 27:1–11; 36:1–12.
45.   Durham, *Exodus*, 250; J. Hoftijzer, "Description or Categorical Rule? Some
Remarks on Ex. 18:16," in *Veenhof Anniversary Volume: Studies Presented to Klaas
R. Veenhof on the Occasion of his Sixty-Fifth Birthday* (ed. W. H. Van Soldt et al.;
Leiden: Nederlands Instituut voor het Nabije Oosten, 2001), 193; Jackson, "Legal
Models," 15. (Note the use of oracle for the identification of guilt in BC: Exod
22:8–11.)
46.   Boecker, *Law and Justice*, 26, 29–40.
47.   W. H. C. Propp, *Exodus 1–18* (AB 2; New York: Doubleday, 1999), 631.
Contrast Exod 2:13–14: "Who made you a prince and a judge over us?"
48.   Durham, *Exodus*, 250. Cf. Num 11:29.
49.   George W. Coats, *Exodus 1–18* (FOTL 2A; Grand Rapids: Eerdmans, 1999),
147; Hoftijzer, "Ex. 18:16," 195–96.
50.   Perhaps the immediately preceding phrase, ויהי אלהים עמך, is not a word of
assurance to a doubtful Moses, or a suggestion that this plan needs to be confirmed,
as traditionally supposed. Rather, it is a statement of Moses' unique relationship
with God in Jethro's system: "*But let God be with you*—you will represent the

the difficult cases (פלא, v. 8) are those requiring inquiry (דרש, v. 9) at the shrine.[51]

The key of Jethro's solution, then, was the hierarchical integration of the whole judicial system, so that lower magistrates could bring their difficult matters to Moses for inquiry. It was not litigants who appealed to Moses. *It was the lower magistrates* who now had the option of deciding a case or consulting the Mosaic high court: "*They* will judge the people at all times, and the great matters *they* [i.e. the judges] will bring to you, but all the small matters *they* [i.e. the judges] will judge themselves" (v. 22).[52] Those making the decision in the small cases are also the ones who consult at the Mosaic court in hard cases. As a result of Jethro's system, *every judge in Israel could now effectively consult Yahweh in difficult matters.* The people could once again take their disputes to local leaders yet now with the assurance that divine oracle was accessible if negotiations proved difficult.[53]

The parallel accounts in Numbers and Deuteronomy, despite important differences, are harmonious in this point. In Num 11, the crucial need for inspiration is again emphasized. It is an ecstatic outpouring of Yahweh's Spirit—already on Moses, now on the elders also (v. 17)—that makes it possible to share the load.[54] This general outpouring is emphatically identified as a one-time event (v. 25), however. As desirable as it would be for all Israel to have such inspiration (v. 29), it is only Moses who enjoys continual access to divine revelation (12:1–9). Nonetheless,

---

people before God and bring their [hard] cases to God…"). The traditional rendering of this phrase (as a word of assurance or need for confirmation) may be unduly influenced by v. 23, where וצוך אלהים *does* express divine approbation for the system. Cf. Propp, *Exodus 1–18*, 632; Houtman, *Exodus*, 2:416.

51. This interpretation of the "great"/"difficult" cases in Exod 18 is a refinement on Noth's position. Noth sensed the cultic/non-cultic distinction behind hard/simple cases, but mistakenly expressed it in terms of content. That is, Noth thought the difficult cases were cases *about cultic matters*, and simple cases were those *about non-cultic matters*. See Martin Noth, *Exodus: A Commentary* (OTL; London: SCM Press, 1962), 150. Scholars have generally dismissed such a distinction between sacred and secular cases. It would seem, however, that Noth was right in his basic intuition, but the distinction is a matter of method, not content. The difficult cases are those *requiring cultic resolution*; simple cases are those which *do not require cultic inquiry*.

52. Cf. Deut 1:17; 17:8–10. See also n. 56, below.

53. Bearing in mind that "the purpose of a Hebrew trial was to settle a dispute between members of the community" (Boecker, *Law and Justice*, 37): an *easy case* was probably one where all parties are satisfied with the judge's negotiated solution; a *hard case* was likely one where the judge could not negotiate a solution satisfactory to all and thus needed to invoke a divine ultimatum.

54. Philip J. Budd, *Numbers* (WBC 5; Waco, Tex.: Word, 1984), 127.

lower administrators must also be party to inspiration: manifestly in their initial prophetic utterance; procedurally in their operational hierarchy (vv. 16–17). For Num 11 also, inspiration is the source of administrative prescript.

Deuteronomy reflects the post-Mosaic continuation of this "oracular judgeship" through the establishment of a central court in Jerusalem (Deut 17:8–13). Both judges and priests sat together in that court (v. 9). Difficult (פלא) cases—those "requir[ing] priestly intervention"[55]—could be brought to that court by lower magistrates (v. 8). There, expert consultation and divine inquiry (דרש, v. 9, 12) could be made. In situations requiring an ordeal to establish the guilty party, it seems that litigants also came to Jerusalem (cf. 19:15–21). In matters where the difficulty was one of knowing the right law to apply (v. 8), it was only the judge who inquired at the central court.[56] But once the judge made the decision to consult, *he was strictly bound to exact the ruling received at the shrine-court.* Deuteronomy 17 goes to lengths to underscore the prescriptive nature of the verdict pronounced through the high court, and that this authority derived from its cultic position "before Yahweh":

> If a matter is too perplexing (פלא) for you to judge…then you shall arise and go up to the place which Yahweh your God will choose. And you shall come to the Levitical priests, and to the judge which shall be (in office) in those days, and you shall inquire (דרש), and they will declare to you the judgment of the matter. Then you shall do according to the terms of the verdict (על־פי הדבר) which they declare to you from that place which Yahweh will choose; and you shall listen to do according to all that they instruct you. According to the terms of the instruction (על־פי התורה) which they instruct you, and according to the judgment which they pronounce to you, you shall do. You shall not turn from the verdict which they declare to the right or left. But the man who acts presumptuously by not listening to the priest who stands to serve there, before Yahweh your God, or to the judge—that man shall die. So you shall purge the evil from Israel, and all the people will hear and fear, and they will not act presumptuously again. (vv. 8–13)

55. Richard D. Nelson, *Deuteronomy: A Commentary* (OTL; Louisville, Ky.: Westminster John Knox, 2002), 221.

56. Gerhard von Rad, *Deuteronomy: A Commentary* (trans. D. Barton; OTL; London: SCM Press), 118; Alexander Rofé, "The Organization of the Judiciary in Deuteronomy (Deut. 16.18–20; 17.8–13; 19.15; 21.22–23; 24.16; 25.1–3)" (trans. H. N. Bock), in *The World of the Arameans*. Vol. 1, *Biblical Studies in Honour of Paul-Eugène Dion* (ed. P. M. M. Daviau et al.; JSOTSup 324; Sheffield: Sheffield Academic Press, 2001), 100; J. G. McConville, *Deuteronomy* (Apollos Old Testament Commentary 5; Leicester: Apollos, 2002), 291.

When a local judge does consult the central court (with its oracular access), he is obliged to enforce their decision. He cannot simply "get a second opinion"; the determination deriving from "the priest who stands…before Yahweh your God, and the judge [with him]" is obliging.

In the three Pentateuchal court etiologies, cultic inquiry is the (ultimate) source of law. Although many cases (the "easy" ones) would be handled by custom, it was the possibility of divine inquiry for the "hard" cases that validated the system.[57] This finding offers an important contribution to the overall argument concerning written law in ancient Israel. Not only can it be discerned that written law was not the source of jurisprudence for ancient Israel's courts, something else can be demonstrated to have filled that place—namely oracles.

Rather than assuming that "unwritten custom" provided the source of law for ancient Israel, it should now be recognized that cultic oracle was the perceived law source for all Israel's courts. Even if, in practice, judges negotiated resolutions based on custom more often than not, it was oracle which was appealed to when "the law" needed to be consulted.[58] Jackson has also pointed in this direction, though he has not developed the way in which oracle could be said to be sourced by all Hebrew courts as here shown. Instead, he has suggested that all Israel's judges were held to be personally inspired.[59] The evidence does not warrant this expectation, however. The (royal) court at the central shrine is uniquely connected with inspiration.[60] Moreover, precisely because all Israel's judges needed

57.   "An oracle (קֶסֶם) is on the lips of a king; his mouth does not sin in judgment" (Prov 16:10; cf. 21:10; Deut 1:17; 2 Chr 19:6). Note also the judicial inspiration of: Joshua (Exod 28:30; Num 27:21; Josh 7:6–15); the Judges (e.g. Judg 4:4); Samuel (1 Sam 3:20–21; 7:6, 15–17); Saul (1 Sam 8; 10:1–13; 11:6; 12:5); David (1 Sam 16:13–14; 2 Sam 14:17, 20; 21:1–10); Solomon (1 Kgs 3:9, 28; 10:6–9). In fact, Whitelam sees the rise of the monarchy in Israel as connected with the king's "encroaching" on the priestly claim to divine access and subordinating "priestly judicial authority" (Keith W. Whitelam, *The Just King: Monarchical Judicial Authority in Ancient Israel* [JSOTSup 12; Sheffield: JSOT Press, 1979], 45–46).

58.   If the delineation between "hard" and "easy" cases drawn in n. 51, above, is correct: it might be said that the "judge" was not really a judge, proper, so long as the court operated according to custom. He was a wise *negotiator* helping the parties *come to agreement* as to what was (socially) right. This negotiator only took on the force of a *judge*, proper, when no clear solution could be negotiated from custom. In such cases, "the law" (i.e. divine oracle) had to be sought and applied. In this sense, custom is really not a source of law at all but a grounds for negotiation. Only divine oracle is a source of law, properly speaking.

59.   Bernard S. Jackson, " 'Law' and 'Justice' in the Bible," *JJS* 49 (1998): 225–26; *Studies*, 90–92; "Legal Models," 15 n. 37.

60.   In addition to the court descriptions just discussed, see 2 Sam 14:5–7; 1 Kgs 3:28; Prov 16:10.

access to cultic inquiry *but lacked inspiration*, an elaborate hierarchy was devised. If local judges too were inspired, they would presumably not need to consult the central court in difficult matters (and there would have been no reason for the people's coming to Moses instead of their local elders). In Jethro's system, every magistrate could now claim access to cultic inquiry despite a lack of personal inspiration. Although Jackson has rightly suspected the importance of inspiration for the Hebrew court's authority, he has not developed the argument and thus overstated the case. Every court did have access to divine oracle as the source of law, but not through direct inspiration of all judges.

Examination of the Exod 18 court system need not stop with the above results. Having discerned the place of inquiry in Exod 18, the place of written law in that same system can also be discerned and bears drawing out. It will be recalled that the third aspect of the Mosaic practice was to *teach* law. After (1) inquiring and (2) judging, Moses told Jethro, (3) "I make them know (הודעתי) the statutes of God and his laws" (v. 16). Jethro's counsel urged continuation of this practice: "...You will represent the people before God and bring their cases to God, and you will warn them about the statutes and the laws and teach them the way in which they should walk, and the deeds they should do" (vv. 19–20).

It is here that the formulation of "statutes and laws" for publication (oral or written?) enters into view. Yet the activity here is not, as some have represented it, a court "arbitrating legal issues between parties *based on* the standard of 'God's decrees and laws' (v. 16)."[61] Rather the reverse: the teaching of "God's decrees and laws" (v. 16) *follows* inquiry and arbitration.[62] Law publication arises out of—and procedurally follows—inquiry and adjudication. This is consistent with Westbrook's finding that law precepts generally arise from seminal cases (p. 33, above); but contrary to Westbrook, this text further indicates that such texts were often published for *popular* instruction.

It is not for judicial guidance that Moses formulates these law teachings; it is for the guidance of the public: "You will warn *them* [i.e. the people] about the statutes and the laws and teach *them* the way in which they should walk..." (v. 20). Only subsequently does Jethro speak about appointing judges (vv. 21–23). Several standards are ascribed for these judges ("men who fear God, honest...hating a bribe") like those elsewhere

61. Peter E. Enns, *Exodus* (NIVAC; Grand Rapids: Zondervan, 2000), 371 (emphasis added).

62. Cf. Lev 24:10–16; Num 9:6–14; 15:32–36; 27:1–11; 36:1–12. Cf. also Jackson, *Studies*, 59–60.

discussed by Patrick and Jackson.[63] In Exod 18, law texts are appointed for public exhortation (v. 20) in virtually the same breath as a judicial charge is given to magistrates (vv. 21–23). Exodus 18 thus shows similar evidence to that which Jackson has offered from Deuteronomy and 2 Chronicles (p. 37, above), but within a much tighter context. Laws are published for national exhortation, but are not assigned to the court as legislation.

Overlooking these carefully defined roles for oracle and law publication, some have mistakenly read Exod 18 as an introduction of Mosaic legislation proper. Cornelis Houtman, for instance, draws this picture from Exod 18: Moses ruled from an extant law code; he inquired of God for cases not mentioned in the law code; the divine verdict in those cases was added into the law code; thus Israel's legislation grew. Thereafter, judges would "render their judgements guided by and in accordance with the body of law put together by Moses (18:19f.)."[64] This description sounds sensible to modern ears, but it allows modern presuppositions about law to intrude and fails to observe what is actually taking place in the text. The published laws of Moses are not addressed to the judges at all. They are propagated for national exhortation.[65]

Ancient Israel's courts, in the period epitomized by the Mosaic etiologies, observed dynamic sources of law: custom for negotiating simple cases and oracle for ruling on the difficult cases. Static law writings had no apparent place within the system of justice, but arose out of legal wisdom for (Levitical) instruction of the people.[66]

63. See pp. 34, 37, above.
64. Houtman, *Exodus*, 2:420 (cf. p. 415). Cf. Propp, *Exodus 1–18*, 634–35.
65. Note also the BC announcement: "Now these are the judgments that you shall set *before them*" (i.e. before the people; Exod 21:1). Cf. S. Paul, *Studies*, 38–39.
66. These findings may offer insight into the legal thought of the Pentateuch's final form. In the MT Pentateuch, Moses is *already* judging according to divine law prior to the Sinai revelation (Exod 18:13–16; cf. 16:26). Furthermore, it is noteworthy that the extended Sinai narrative is framed by Exod 18 and Num 11 (two of the law teaching and oracular administration etiologies here examined). Did the Pentateuch's editors place these etiologies to frame the Sinai revelation as popular teaching on law, while fully expecting oracles to provide actual rulings (i.e. in hard cases)? The question can only here be raised. Cf. Eugene E. Carpenter, "Exodus 18: Its Structure, Style, Motifs and Function in the Book of Exodus," in *A Biblical Itinerary: In Search of Method, Form and Content; Essays in Honor of George W. Coats* (ed. Eugene E. Carpenter; JSOTSup 240; Sheffield: Sheffield Academic Press, 1997), 91–108; M. R. Hauge, *The Descent from the Mountain: Narrative Patterns in Exodus 19–40* (JSOTSup 323; Sheffield: Sheffield Academic Press, 2001), 258–78.

III. *Proponents of the Legislative Model*

In the face of comparative evidence from cuneiform law, and indigenous evidence from the Hebrew literature, the legislative model is now
regarded as inappropriate for biblical law. Nonetheless, some scholars
continue to advance biblical law as legislation. Two prominent defendants of the position are Michael Fishbane and Anthony Phillips.

While admitting that the cuneiform collections (e.g. LH) were "literary and non-legislative," Fishbane argues that, *"the internal traditions of
the Hebrew Bible present and regard the covenantal laws as legislative
texts."*[67] There are three "internal traditions of the Hebrew Bible" which
Fishbane has in view: (1) the biblical presentation of law as divine revelation; (2) the assignment of the law books to official uses; and, (3) the
presence of law book citations in the Hebrew literature. The first and
second of these are not so decisive as Fishbane purports, however; and
the third requires closer attention before drawing conclusions.

The first of these—that Israel conceived of its laws as divine revelation—is somewhat distinctive from the situation known from the texts of
other ancient Near Eastern nations. It is not wholly distinctive, however.
Even Hammurabi identified *Šamaš* as the source of his legal insight.[68]
That Israel went "one step further" and identified the very pronouncement
of their laws as from Yahweh is noteworthy. This does not, however,
indicate Hebrew law writings were legislation, any more than Hammurabi's claim to inspiration made his collection legislation.[69]

Fishbane's second point is that the law writings were enforced by
priests, judges, kings, and prophets in Israel: "The priests must teach
these laws (e.g. Lev. 10:10–11; Mal. 2:7); the judges are enjoined to
follow them (e.g. Deut. 16:18–20; 2 Chron. 19:6–10); the kings are held
accountable to their enforcement; and the prophets repeatedly exhort
their observance."[70] Fishbane thus notes that priests are called to teach
the law writings. It has already been seen, however, that *popular* instruction from the law book points toward the book's idyllic (not regulatory)
function (p. 38, above). Fishbane further notes that "judges are enjoined
to follow them." As already seen, however, although judges are called to
judge justly, they are actually never charged to judge according to law
writings (pp. 34, 37, above). The judge commissions cited by Fishbane

67. Fishbane, *Biblical Interpretation*, 95–96 (emphasis original).
68. Visually in the crowning image, and textually in, for instance, LH §§48.95–
49.17. Cf. S. Paul, *Studies*, 7–8.
69. P. Davies, "'Law' in Judaism," 10.
70. Fishbane, *Biblical Interpretation*, 96.

actually say nothing about law writings. Fishbane also notes that "kings are held accountable for their enforcement." Kings are indeed called *to study* the law book (especially Deut 17:18–20); it is not evident, however, that kings were *to rule* according to a law book. (Further discussion of Hebrew kings and their use of the law book will follow in Chapter 3.) As for Fishbane's claim that "the prophets repeatedly exhort their observance," the cry of the prophets is for justice and righteousness (e.g. Mic 6:8) not for the "rule of written law." The law book is rarely (if ever) mentioned by the prophets.[71] In each of these Hebrew offices, Fishbane confuses what is emphasized (i.e. the duty to enforce justice) and what actually is not indicated (i.e. a purported duty to enforce law writings). The official duties of Hebrew priests, judges, kings, and prophets do not seem to have included the enforcement of legislation.

Fishbane's third point—that there is a preponderance of law book citations in the Hebrew literature—is the most important. He notes that the presence (or absence) of citation has been a decisive issue in the assessment of the cuneiform law collections: "Neither the Laws of Hammurapi nor the other [cuneiform] legal corpora are cited as precedents in the many legal dockets and protocols which have been preserved."[72] The Torah, however, is cited in biblical narratives. Fishbane regards this as indicating a different approach to law on Israel's part. This assumption overlooks a crucial difference, however, between the relevant cuneiform and Hebrew materials.

---

71. The absence of reference to written law in the prophetic literature is well known. This insight was decisive for Wellhausen's dating the bulk of Israel's legal material *after* the prophets (Julius Wellhausen, *Prolegomena to the History of Israel* [Edinburgh: A. & C. Black, 1885], 124). In those few instances in the prophets where reference is made to law *writings*, either they are explicitly identified as wisdom texts (e.g. Jer 8:7–9; Hos 8:12), or their reference is too imprecise to determine their nature (e.g. Isa 10:1–2, which looks more like a written court verdict than legislation). In his essay on "Prophecy and Law," Phillips (who regards the Decalogue and BC as legislative), admits the absence of statutory reference to law writings in the prophets. He explains this absence by suggesting that Israel was basically law-abiding and that the prophets were not confronting legal violations. Rather, the social injustice of Israel was exclusively *moral* injustice achieved by abusing *legitimate* institutions. Hence the prophets appealed to humanitarian rather than legal obligations (Anthony Phillips, "Prophecy and Law," in *Essays on Biblical Law* [JSOTSup 334; London: Sheffield Academic Press, 2002], 164–78; repr. from *Israel's Prophetic Tradition: Essays in Honour of Peter Ackroyd* [ed. Richard Coggins et al.; Cambridge: Cambridge University Press, 1982], 217–32). Actually, Phillips' essay helps to demonstrate that law writings were not appealed to by the prophets in their polemics against impure worship and social injustice.

72. Fishbane, *Biblical Interpretation*, 96.

The reason the question of citation has been so decisive in cuneiform studies is because the materials lacking citations are *law-practice records*: "legal dockets and protocols." The presence or absence of references to the law collections in such court-practice records automatically addresses the question of legislative force. The situation is different in the Hebrew materials: there are no actual law-practice documents available. The presence of references to the law collection in Hebrew *narratives* is not necessarily so automatic an indication of prescriptivism. Whereas the cuneiform court records are manifestly regulatory, the Hebrew narratives include much didactic and religious material. It therefore must be established whether the citations show the law collections to be authoritative for regulation (legislation), or in fact if those citations confirm their use for didactic and ritual purposes (non-legislative). Fishbane rightly notes the importance of the law book citations for the question of law writing in Israel, but he too hastily assumes their implications.

The law citations in the biblical literature require examination. It is necessary to assess how the law book is being used when it is cited: Is it being cited as legislation for social regulation? Is it being referenced as an eminent didactic guide? Or is it being held up as a ritual symbol? Furthermore, if cited in places as legislation, is that legislative use indication of an emerging approach to law or a long-standing practice? Fishbane is not negligent of the need for such examination; his book on "innerbiblical exegesis" does much to explore the possible implications of these citations. Fishbane will be an important discussion partner for some of the "law-book citation" studies in later sections of this project (especially Chapter 4). Nonetheless, Fishbane allows the mere presence of these citations to establish a legislative presupposition up front. His presupposition that Israel wrote legislation is, therefore, problematic.

Phillips' legislative argument is more qualified than that of Fishbane. For Phillips it is only the Decalogue and the מֹשְׁפֵּטִים (Exod 21:12–22:16) that were true legislation.[73] Other law writings in the Hebrew Bible are "not so much instructions to the judiciary as sermons to the nation."[74] Most of the extant law writings of Israel, Phillips therefore accepts, are didactic rather than legislative. It is only in the Decalogue, and particularly in the מֹשְׁפֵטִים that a record "of actual statutes and precedents to be put into effect by Israel's judges" is preserved.[75]

The view of the Decalogue as a legislative code has not been widely persuasive. Phillips' work on the individual commands of the Decalogue

73. The מֹשְׁפֵטִים, according to Phillips, are the integration of the Decalogue (Israel's native criminal law code) with Canaanite law (Phillips, *Essays*, 53).

74. Ibid., 13.

75. Ibid., 52–53.

is insightful, but his efforts to show the whole to be a court-enforceable law code seem unconvincing. The criticisms of others need not be repeated in full here.[76] It will be sufficient to outline two problems. First, Phillips overcomes the lack of sanctions in the Decalogue by asserting the whole to be a *suzerainty treaty*. As part of a suzerainty covenant treaty, the Decalogue commands had "implied" death penalties.[77] Scholars now regard the suzerainty treaty form as a rubric applied to the re-publication of the Decalogue (especially in Deuteronomy), but not its original framework.[78] The lack of sanctions remains an obstacle to the Decalogue's purported function as a law code.

Second, the contents of the Decalogue are imprecise: they are more like moral ideals than enforceable offenses. In order to derive actual statutes, Phillips has found it necessary to interpret them in new ways. For instance, the command against taking God's name in vain is interpreted as a law against magic,[79] the command to honor parents as a law against repudiating the ancestral religion,[80] and the command not to covet as condemning property seizure leading to a city elder's loss of status.[81] Moshe Greenberg has accused Phillips of conducting "exegetical acrobatics" in order to transform the Decalogue into a statutory code.[82]

Phillips also regards the מִשְׁפָּטִים as Hebrew legislation. Responding to the insights derived from other ancient Near Eastern law collections, Phillips states:

> It appears that the Babylonian law collections were primarily apologia to the gods to vindicate the king in the exercise of the mandate which they had given him. What actual influence the provisions of a collection such as Hammurabi's had on the day-to-day administration of justice remains very uncertain...
>
> But because of the theological basis of biblical law, it would still seem that the possibility of establishing a distinctive principle of Israelite law

76. See the reviews of Anthony Phillips' book, *Ancient Israel's Criminal Law: A New Approach to the Decalogue* (Oxford: Blackwell, 1970) by Moshe Greenberg (*JBL* 91, no. 4 [1972]: 535–38); J. W. Rogerson (*PEQ* 104 [1972]: 157); Ernest W. Nicholson (*Theology* 75 [1972]: 154–55), and S. A. Kaufman (*JNES* 32, no. 1–2 [1971]: 279). Cf. also the critiques of Jackson (*Essays*, 25–63) and Henry McKeating ("A Response to Dr Phillips by Henry McKeating," *JSOT* 20 [1981]: 25–26). For Phillips' reply to his critics, see Phillips, *Essays*, 2–24.
77. Phillips, *Israel's Criminal Law*, 4–5.
78. G. E. Mendenhall and G. A. Herion, "Covenant," in *ABD* 1:1183–4. Cf. Phillips, *Essays*, 3.
79. Phillips, *Israel's Criminal Law*, 53–63.
80. Ibid., 80–82.
81. Ibid., 149–52.
82. Greenberg, review of Phillips, 538. Cf. Kaufman, review of Phillips, 279.

over against other ancient Near Eastern law cannot be entirely ruled out…
It does seem that the collection of *mišpāṭîm* contained in Exod. 21.12–
22.16 are intended as a statement of actual statutes and precedents to be
put into effect by Israel's judges. All the laws specify sanctions which can
be enforced, whether it is execution or damages…[83]

Like Fishbane, Phillips accepts the non-legislative character of the cuneiform law writings. At the same time, however, he perceives a different
attitude toward the משפטים in Israel. There are two grounds which he
offers for this distinction: (1) the "theological basis" of biblical law; and
(2) the legislative appearance of the משפטים.

Phillips' first point is actually the same as Fishbane's, noted above.
Both scholars rightly recognize a more prominent integration of cultic
concerns into the Hebrew law writings than is the case in extant cuneiform collections. Direct ascription to Yahweh is also unique. It is not
obvious, however, why this religious bent to Israel's law writings should
lead one to regard the משפטים as legislation. As earlier noted, Hammurabi claimed divine inspiration in his law-writings, so that the religious
cast is not completely unique or automatically indicative of prescriptivism. Divine dictation by Yahweh might raise the question whether
Israel's law writings were differently received than, say, Hammurabi's.
But the answer would have to be established from Hebrew court narratives and texts about the law book's use; it cannot be assumed.

Phillips' second point again raises a possibility for, but does not itself
establish, the presence of legislation. He notes that the משפטים "specify
sanctions which can be enforced." The same might as readily be said of
LH or the other cuneiform law collections, however. The "if–then" nature
of the Hebrew (and cuneiform) law writings certainly makes it *possible*
they could be employed legislatively. The question turns, however, on
whether evidence exists to show that they *were* used in this manner. In
the case of the cuneiform law writings, contradictions between those
collections and actual practice records have shown that the presence of
sanctions cannot be assumed to mean they were judicially enforced. That
similar contradictions exist in the Hebrew literature leads one to a similar
conclusion in respect to Israel's law writings.[84]

Henry McKeating has been particularly forthright in his criticism of
Phillips. McKeating's criticisms, and Phillips' responses, provide an
important window into Phillips' work. McKeating wrote concerning
Phillips' legislative views:

83. Phillips, *Essays*, 51–52.
84. Phillips (ibid., 74–95) recognizes such inconsistencies and attempts to harmonize them, as in his response to McKeating's treatment of adultery law "irregularities" (see n. 16, above).

The main issue is certainly a methodological one. Dr Phillips…takes it for granted that we know how Israelite law "worked"; how it functioned in society. Now this is exactly what we do not know. The law itself contains very little to indicate how it was applied; how seriously the various laws were taken; which ones were realistic law and which were theoretical principles. Our only hope of answering such questions is to examine the other literature, narrative, prophecy and wisdom writing.[85]

Phillips does not accept McKeating's caricature of himself as one who "takes it for granted that we know how Israelite law 'worked.'" "On the contrary," he responds, "I fully recognize that…much remains uncertain" about biblical law.[86] On this point, at least, Phillips disowns McKeating's representation. On the matter of methodology, however, Phillips actually seems to affirm what McKeating has noted, albeit maintaining its viability. Whereas McKeating prefers to determine from the Hebrew literature how written law was used, Phillips affirms his presuppositional approach. It is indeed his *a priori* claim that the מֹשְׁפָּטִים were "instructions to the judiciary" and "legal codes." Phillips' approach to other Hebrew materials is advanced "to show that [my postulates]…*can be established*, even if much of my case must of necessity rest on the argument from silence."[87] Thus Phillips accepts McKeating's description of his method, though he denies it is inappropriate. It is Phillips' stated intention, not *to deduce* whether Israel's law writings were legislation, but to begin with that presupposition *and support it.*

Phillips has actually been forthright about this presuppositional agenda all along. In his original book, for instance, Phillips wrote concerning the Decalogue commandment on theft: "If the contention that this [the Decalogue] was ancient Israel's criminal law code is to be maintained, it must be shown that there was a category of theft in pre-exilic Israel for which, on conviction, the offender would suffer the criminal law penalty of execution. This is the crime of manstealing."[88]

Phillips' approach has been, from the beginning, an effort to show *the viability* of reading the Decalogue and מֹשְׁפָּטִים as ancient Israel's criminal law code. To the extent that his presupposition "works," his postulates can be regarded as persuasive. At least that has been Phillips' method—a method with which other scholars, including McKeating, are not necessarily comfortable. Phillips has built an internally coherent system for reading these law collections as legislation; he has not actually demonstrated that this was the case.

85. McKeating, "Response to Phillips," 26. Cf. "Sanctions," 65–67.
86. Phillips, *Essays*, 13.
87. Ibid., 13 (emphasis added). Cf. ibid., 76 n. 14, 94–95.
88. Phillips, *Israel's Criminal Law*, 130.

IV. *Conclusions*

Ancient Israel's reasons for writing laws, and the uses to which those law writings were put, cannot be equated to the reasons for and uses of modern law codes. Scholars today generally recognize monumental and didactic functions for law collections of the ancient Near East—including ancient Israel. Whatever changes in Israel's attitude toward its inherited law writings may have developed over time, there does not appear to have been any perception of law writing as a regulatory activity for ancient Israel.

This conclusion is not dependant on comparative evidence from the cuneiform writings. Although it was the wealth of cuneiform law materials which offered the heuristic models for re-assessing the biblical literature, the internal evidence of the Hebrew materials themselves produce the conclusion. A legislative use of law writing cannot be shown for ancient Israel. Non-legislative uses for law writings can. Furthermore, certain court narratives show rulings which are contrary to what is written, thus indicating that the law writings did not regulate court decisions. What, then, did regulate court decisions? Hebrew judges observed a dynamic concept of law, where custom provided a basis for negotiating simple cases and cultic oracle provided the source of law in difficult cases. Static law texts served many functions, but they were not part of early Israel's court system.

Ancient Israel's law writings were, in other words, idyllic descriptions of law, but they were not themselves binding as "the law."

Chapter 3

WRITTEN LAW IN THE DEUTERONOMIC SCHOOL

In the preceding chapter, the descriptive nature of Israel's early law writings was defended. It is certain that early Israel employed its law writings for ritual, didactic, and other non-juridical purposes. It also appears that law writings were not used as a source of courtroom justice. Law was a metaphysical reality accessed through oracle; it was not a text accessed through reading (or recitation) and exegesis. In this and subsequent chapters, attention turns to the examination of later developments in Israel's perception of law and law writings.

Scholars have long noted a new attitude toward law writings arising in connection with the seventh-century reforms of King Josiah and the Deuteronomic school.[1] Dale Patrick writes:

> A shift in the understanding of God's law can be detected in the literature bearing the stamp of the Deuteronomic school and sustaining the impact of Josiah's reform. The new understanding comes to expression in statements exhorting the addressee to adhere strictly to the words of the legal text and praising persons for doing so.[2]

Statements esteeming "the book of the law" are generally recognized as belonging to the Deuteronomic pen.[3] Several scholars regard this Deuteronomic fascination with law writings as the origin of Hebrew prescriptivism. Patrick argues that, even though Deuteronomy itself is sermonic (not legislative), it came to be regarded as legislation in the seventh-century reforms of Josiah. Raymond Westbrook also ascribes

---

1. Person has suggested that the distinct terms Deuteronomic and Deuteronomistic are no longer helpful. Accepting his reasoning, the present study will use only the term *Deuteronomic*, except where other scholars are being quoted (Raymond F. Person, *The Deuteronomic School: History, Social Setting, and Literature* [SBL Studies in Biblical Literature 2; Atlanta: Society of Biblical Literature, 2002], 4–7).

2. Patrick, *Old Testament Law*, 200.

3. Moshe Weinfeld, *Deuteronomy and the Deuteronomic School* (Oxford: Oxford University Press, 1983), 1, 332–41.

incipient prescriptivism to the seventh century. For Westbrook, it is Deuteronomy's incorporation of a debt-release edict into a seven-year cycle (Deut 15:1–11) that marks the beginning of statutory law in Israel.

In the present chapter, the Deuteronomic attitude toward law writings will be assessed. This assessment will begin through examination of the issues raised by Patrick and Westbrook. In several respects, the points raised by these scholars will be sustained; however, the implications they draw will be re-interpreted through critical re-examination of the evidence. Following the finds adduced from these discussions with Patrick and Westbrook, further evidence on the Deuteronomic attitudes toward law writings will be offered and conclusions drawn.

A few preliminary issues should be noted. It has long been held that Deuteronomy (and the rise of the Deuteronomic school) belongs to the seventh century. This view derives, in part, from the account of Deuteronomy's discovery at the time of Josiah (2 Kgs 22:8). This identification (Josiah's "law book" = Deuteronomy) has been a pillar of critical scholarship since W. M. L. de Wette first popularized the view in 1805.[4] Now, however, scholars question this conclusion on several points.[5] First, scholars question whether the "law book" was in fact Deuteronomy. Alternate proposals include: some form of BC;[6] the "Song of Moses" (Deut 32);[7] or inscriptions from the renovations begun by Joash (2 Kgs 12:3–16

---

4. W. M. L. de Wette, "Dissertatio critica qua a prioribus Deuteronomium Pentateuchi Libris Diversum alius cuiusdam recentioris auctoris opus esse monstratur" (Thesis, 1805). For de Wette's predecessors on this view, see Eberhard Nestle, "Das Deuteronomium und 2 Könige 22," *ZAW* 22 (1902): 170–71, 312–13; M. J. Paul, "Hilkiah and the Law (2 Kings 22) in the 17th and 18th Centuries: Some Influences on W.M.L. de Wette," in *Das Deuteronomium: Entstehung, Gestalt und Botschaft* (ed. Norbert Lohfink; BETL 68; Leuven: Uitgeverij Peeters, 1985), 9–12.

5. For a history of this criticism, see Lohfink, "Zur neueren Diskussion über 2 Kön 22–23," in his *Deuteronomium*, 24–48 (English trans. "Recent Discussion on 2 Kings 22–23: The State of the Question," in *A Song of Power and the Power of Song: Essays on the Book of Deuteronomy* [ed. Duane Christensen; Sources for Biblical and Theological Study 3; Winona Lake, Ind.: Eisenbrauns, 1993], 36–61); Erik Eynikel, *The Reform of King Josiah and the Composition of the Deuteronomistic History* (OtSt 33; Leiden: Brill, 1996), 7–31.

6. Exod 20:22–23:33 per E. Reuter, *Kultzentralisation: Zur Entstehung und Theologie von Dtn 12* (BBB 87; Frankfurt am Main: Anton Hain, 1993), 244–50. Cf. G. J. Venema, *Reading Scripture in the Old Testament: Deuteronomy 9–10; 31— 2 Kings 22–23—Jeremiah 36—Nehemiah 8* (OtSt 48; Leiden: Brill, 2004), 84.

7. So Jack R. Lundbom, "The Lawbook of the Josianic Reform," *CBQ* 38 (1976): 293–302; idem, *Jeremiah 1–20: A New Translation with Introduction and Commentary* (AB 21A; New York: Doubleday, 1999), 105–6, 109–17.

[EV 2–15]).[8] Second, scholars question whether the Josiah story is real history. Being "composed of stereotypical elements" more legend-like than historical,[9] many doubt the event occurred. And if there was a Josianic reform, it is doubted that 2 Kings preserves an accurate report of it.[10] Finally (and in consequence of the previous two points), fresh questions have arisen as to whether either text (2 Kgs 22–23 or Deuteronomy) reflects seventh-century ideals at all. The Josiah story (and the Deuteronomic History [DtrH] in general) is often perceived as addressing conditions of a period long after Josiah's reign,[11] and dates for Deuteronomy are also under review now that the Josianic anchor has come loose.[12]

In regard to the last of these points: despite the recent rise in arguments to the contrary, it is still generally accepted that *Urdeuteronomium* belongs to the seventh century. Even without reference to Josiah, the employment of Assyrian "loyalty oath" language (cf. the 672 BCE Vassal Treaties of Esarhaddon) and the book's awareness of seventh-century concerns point to this dating.[13] A seventh-century date for Deuteronomy, though not certain, remains the general consensus and can be allowed for the present project.

In regard to the other questions noted above: it can no longer be assumed that the *historical* Josiah conducted a reform based on Deuteronomy. Nevertheless, scholars still agree that *the story* of Josiah's reforms has Deuteronomy in view.[14] The expression "book of the law" is

8. So Nadav Na'aman, "Royal Inscriptions and the Histories of Joash and Ahaz, Kings of Judah," *VT* 48 (1998): 119–32. Cf. also L. B. Paton, "The Case for the Post-Exilic Origin of Deuteronomy," *JBL* 47 (1928): 340–41.

9. Lowell K. Handy, "Historical Probability and the Narrative of Josiah's Reform in 2 Kings," in *The Pitcher is Broken: Memorial Essays for Gösta W. Ahlström* (ed. Steven W. Holloway and Lowell K. Handy; JSOTSup 190; Sheffield: Sheffield Academic Press, 1995), 275.

10. Mark A. O'Brien, "The Book of Deuteronomy," *CurBS* 3 (1995): 98–99; Venema, *Reading Scripture*, 69; Lohfink, "2 Kön 22–23," 47–48.

11. Burke O. Long, *2 Kings* (FOTL 10; Grand Rapids: Eerdmans, 1991), 257.

12. O'Brien, "Deuteronomy," 103–4; Philip R. Davies, *In Search of "Ancient Israel"* (JSOTSup 148; Sheffield: Sheffield Academic Press, 1992), 40–41.

13. Ernest W. Nicholson, *Deuteronomy and Tradition* (Oxford: Blackwell, 1967), 1–17; O'Brien, "Deuteronomy," 102; Nelson, *Deuteronomy*, 6–8.

14. Paton, "Origin of Deuteronomy," 326; Nicholson, *Tradition*, 15; O'Brien, "Deuteronomy," 98–99; T. R. Hobbs, *2 Kings* (WBC 13; Waco, Tex.: Word, 1985), 323; Mordechai Cogan and Hayim Tadmor, *II Kings: A New Translation with Introduction and Commentary* (AB 11; Garden City, N.Y.: Doubleday, 1988), 294; Volkmar Fritz, *1 & 2 Kings* (trans. Anselm Hagedorn; Continental Commentary; Minneapolis: Fortress, 2003), 398; Richard D. Nelson, *First and Second Kings* (Int; Louisville, Ky.: Westminster John Knox, 2002), 255; John Gray, *I & II Kings: A Commentary* (OTL; London: SCM Press), 229.

used self-referentially within Deuteronomy (17:18; 28:58, 61; 29:20, 26 [EV vv. 21, 27]; 30:10; 31:24, 26) and likely intends the same book elsewhere in DtrH (Josh 1:8; 8:31, 34; 23:6; 2 Kgs 14:6; 22:8, 11; 23:24). Whatever the historical reality of Josiah, the 2 Kings story expects the reader to link his reform to Deuteronomy. Thus, despite historical questions, the Josiah *account* remains an important witness to the Deuteronomic attitude toward Deuteronomy—and it is that Deuteronomic attitude toward law writings which is of present interest.

I. *Patrick on Deuteronomic Law Writings*

Patrick advances two kinds of evidence on Deuteronomic legal attitudes. The first comes from DtrH, where Josiah discovers "the book of the law" and follows its regulations (2 Kgs 22–23). The second comes from Deuteronomy itself, where a new spirit of legalism is discerned in certain editorial expansions.

1. *Josiah's Reformation (2 Kgs 22–23)*

According to 2 Kgs 22–23, the high priest Hilkiah discovered the lost "book of the law" in the temple and brought it to King Josiah. The king subsequently conducted a series of reforms "according to the book of the law." The centrality of the law book in Josiah's reform reveals, according to Patrick, a "new attitude" toward law writings not evident in older materials.[15]

What has been seen earlier (especially in the previous chapter regarding the Mosaic court system) affirms the likelihood of a "new" attitude here present. For the Deuteronomic Josiah, the law book is a basis for official action. Even the king is found swearing "to uphold the words of this covenant, the ones written in this book" (2 Kgs 23:3). This appears to go beyond the *popular* instruction previously ascribed to law writings. The Deuteronomic vision of the law book includes some sort of official role not previously attested. Nevertheless, this fact does not, on its own, justify Patrick's conclusion that "the will of God is now fixed in [written] rules. It may not be going too far to see incipient 'statutes' in this understanding of the rules of the lawbook… Law [is now perceived] as a body of written rules…the identification of divine law with the body of rules in the book…[a] new literalism."[16]

---

15. Patrick, *Old Testament Law*, 201.
16. Ibid., 201.

While Patrick's general observation (that the law book now finds a royal function) would here be accepted, his interpretation of that function (that it is legislative) must be questioned. Five features of the Josiah story actually point in another direction than the rise of "incipient statutes...[a] new literalism":

a. According to 2 Kings, when Josiah "heard the words of the book of the law, he tore his garments" (22:11). Josiah's response was immediate, for the book made it clear to him that "great is the wrath of Yahweh which burns against us" (22:13). Nonetheless, Josiah did not regard the penalties stated in the law book as certain. Instead, to find out what God would in fact do in the present case, Josiah sent a delegation to Huldah the prophetess: "Go inquire (דרשו) of Yahweh...concerning the words of this book that has been found" (22:13). Evidently, Josiah understood the statements of the law book as typical (evoking fear), but the book's stipulations do not automatically apply to the present case. The ruling of heaven *for this case* must be oracularly discovered. It is Huldah (not the book) who reveals heaven's ruling: "Thus says Yahweh, behold, I am bringing evil to this place... [But] because your [Josiah's] heart was tender...you will be gathered to your grave in peace" (22:16–20).

It has been frequently questioned why Josiah needed to consult an oracle when he had already read (and obviously understood) the law book. If, as Patrick deduces, the law book is here being equated to divine law, the oracle is superfluous. Some scholars have supposed Josiah wanted to verify the book's authenticity through the oracle.[17] But Josiah's response betrays no question about the book's authenticity. Others suppose Josiah needed a "true interpreter of the book."[18] But Huldah's response is not presented as an interpretation of the book but a direct word from Yahweh. Josiah already understood the meaning of the book: "great is the wrath of Yahweh" (22:13). What the account expects is that the book caused Josiah to know *the disposition of God* toward Judah (i.e. his great wrath). What Josiah did not know from the book was *how God would actually deal* with

17. Anthony F. Campbell and Mark A. O'Brien, *Unfolding the Deuteronomistic History: Origins, Upgrades, Present Text* (Minneapolis: Fortress, 2000), 458; Renita J. Weems, "Huldah, the Prophet: Reading a (Deuteronomistic) Woman's Identity," in *A God So Near: Essays on Old Testament Theology in Honor of Patrick D. Miller* (ed. Brent A. Strawn and Nancy R. Bowen; Winona Lake, Ind.: Eisenbrauns, 2003), 324–25.

18. Hobbs, *2 Kings*, 319.

Judah in the present case.[19] For an actual ruling on this case, he needed an oracle. Josiah's law book gives insight into divine justice, but it does not give statutory rulings.

b.   Josiah learned two things from Huldah: that God is going to judge Judah (22:16–17), and that God does take repentance into account when preparing judgment (22:18–20). Perhaps in view of the latter discovery, Josiah called a national assembly at the temple (23:1–3).[20] At that assembly, Josiah read the law book and the officials and people joined him in an oath "to uphold the words of this covenant, the ones written in this book" (23:3). So far so good, but scholars have often jumped to the conclusion that this covenant ceremony ratified a "law code" or "national constitution" for Judah.[21] There is certainly an important, *ritual* use of the law book in this temple ceremony (as, Exod 24:3–8; Deut 31:9–13).[22] The supposition that a "constitutional convention" is here in view, however, derives more from modern political theory than from the evidence of the text.

Had this national covenant been a legislative enactment, Deuteronomy's commandments would thus be enacted from that point. What actually follows shows something very different. At least twenty times in the subsequent narrative, the king issues commands.[23] These royal decrees (and not the law book) are the actual instruments of reform. It is nowhere said that the people or officers act according to the law book; it is only the royal decree that is shown to be effectual. It is true that the king's commands are said to accord with the law book (23:21, 24–25). The law book is certainly seen as provocative for righteous rule. Nonetheless, it is only the royal command which is shown to be legally effecttive. It is inappropriate to impose modern notions of democratic constitutionalism on the temple covenant ritual of 2 Kgs 23:1–3.

19.   Paul R. House, *1, 2 Kings* (NAC 8; Nashville: Broadman & Holman, 1995), 384. Cf. Niditch, *Oral World*, 102–4.

20.   C. F. Keil, *The Books of the Kings* (trans. James Martin; vol. 3 of C. F. Keil and F. Delitzsch, *Commentary on the Old Testament*; 10 vols.; Grand Rapids: Eerdmans, 1978), 482.

21.   E.g. Weinfeld, *Deuteronomic School*, 164; S. Dean McBride, "Polity of the Covenant People: The Book of Deuteronomy," in Christensen, ed., *Song of Power*, 62–77; Cogan and Tadmor, *II Kings*, 296; Fritz, *1 & 2 Kings*, 402–3; House, *1, 2 Kings*, 387.

22.   Jackson, *Studies*, 141.

23.   2 Kgs 23:4, 5, 6, 7, 8a, 8b, 10, 11a, 11b, 12, 13, 14, 15b, 15c, 16b, 18, 19, 20, 21, 24.

c. In general, Josiah's commands do accord with Deuteronomy.[24] But he also "contradicts" Deuteronomy's statements in significant respects. For instance, Josiah is presented as a king everywhere governing the cultus, both in its reforms (23:4–20, 24) and in its operation (23:21–23). However, as Bernard Levinson remarks, "Deuteronomy's Law of the King (Deut. xvii 14–20) denies the king any role…in the cultus," and conversely, "Deuteronomy's cultic laws envision no role whatsoever for the monarch."[25] It is difficult to reckon this king's dominance over the cultus with the stipulations of Deuteronomy (if, indeed, Josiah read Deuteronomy as prescriptive stipulations). Furthermore, Deuteronomy assigns the teaching of law to *the priesthood*—even the king is to sit under Levitical tutors (Deut 17:18). In Josiah's reform, however, it is the king who teaches the law book to the people—*including the priests* (23:2–3).[26] If Josiah is implementing Deuteronomy as legislation, his own role is curiously out of step with what Deuteronomy prescribes. "Deuteronomy's king," J. G. McConville summarizes, "is nothing like King Josiah."[27]

d. Another discrepancy emerges in Josiah's exclusion of local priests from the altar in Jerusalem. Deuteronomy 18:6–8 provides for the full participation of regional priests in the central cultus: "Now if a Levite comes from one of your towns (anywhere in Israel where he resides, and comes whenever he desires) to the place which Yahweh chooses, then he shall serve in the name of Yahweh his God, like all his brothers the Levites who are there before Yahweh. They shall eat equal portions…" Whether it is a permanent transfer to the central shrine here in view, or a temporary "tour of duty," is not important at the present juncture.[28] In either case, local Levites are assured full participation in both the

24. For a comprehensive list of parallels, see Paton, "Origin of Deuteronomy," 325–26.

25. Bernard M. Levinson, "The Reconceptualization of Kingship in Deuteronomy and the Deuteronomistic History's Transformation of Torah," *VT* 51 (2001): 523–26.

26. Gary N. Knoppers, "Rethinking the Relationship between Deuteronomy and the Deuteronomistic History: The Case of Kings," *CBQ* 63 (2001): 400.

27. McConville, *Deuteronomy*, 33. Cf. J. G. McConville, "Deuteronomy, Book of," in *Dictionary of the Old Testament: Pentateuch* (ed. T. Desmond Alexander and David W. Baker; Downers Grove, Ill.: InterVarsity, 2003), 190; Levinson, "Reconceptualization of Kingship," 534.

28. On a permanent move, see Nelson, *Deuteronomy*, 229. On temporary visit, see J. G. McConville, *Law and Theology in Deuteronomy* (JSOTSup 33; Sheffield: JSOT Press, 1986), 146–47; idem, *Deuteronomy*, 299.

services and food of the temple (and they may come "whenever they desire"). In Josiah's reform, however, outlying priests were excluded from full privileges: "Then he brought all the priests from the cities of Judah, and he defiled the high places where the priests sacrificed... However, the priests of the high places did not go up to the altar of Yahweh in Jerusalem, but they ate unleavened bread in the midst of their brothers" (2 Kgs 23:8–9).

Josiah's centralizing program forcibly transferred the regional priests to Jerusalem.[29] There, they received food from the cultus; however, they were prohibited from service at the altar. "Josiah... found it necessary," John Gray deduces, "to modify the prescription concerning the rural priests."[30] Richard Nelson's expression is sharper (and suggests a justification): "The king even violates Deuteronomy 18:6–8 to attain complete decontamination."[31] Other scholars likewise recognize the problem, and W. Boyd Barrick highlights the attitude towards the law book thereby indicated: "This alone invalidates the assertion that 'Josiah followed the religious philosophy of the book of Deuteronomy to the letter'."[32] Whether or not this singular discrepancy is as decisive as Barrick supposes, it does contribute to the overall sense that Deuteronomy is not here regarded as a statutory law code. Second Kings commends Josiah as a king ruling "according to the law book," while unashamedly showing him in contradiction to various Deuteronomic provisions.

e. Heretical acts of previous kings are cited five times in this account, with Josiah systematically reversing them: "He deposed the pagan priests whom the kings of Judah had appointed" (23:5); "He did away with the horses which the kings of Judah had appointed for the sun" (23:11); "The altars...which the kings of Judah...[and] Manasseh had made...the king pulled down" (23:12); "The king defiled the high places...which Solomon the

29. That they were *Yahwistic* priests is confirmed by their ascription as "brethren" in v. 9.

30. Gray, *I & II Kings*, 735.

31. Nelson, *1–2 Kings*, 258.

32. W. Boyd Barrick, *The King and the Cemeteries: Toward a New Understanding of Josiah's Reform* (VTSup 88; Leiden: Brill, 2002), 9 n. 28 (responding to Sara Japhet, "From the King's Sanctuary to the Chosen City," in *Jerusalem: Its Sanctity and Centrality to Judaism, Christianity, and Islam* [ed. Lee Levine; New York: Continuum, 1999], 9). Barrick also offers an alternate reading of 2 Kgs 23:8–9 which "lessens somewhat but does not eliminate the conflict with Deut. 18:6–8" (pp. 187–96). Cf. von Rad, *Deuteronomy*, 28.

king of Israel had built" (23:13); "The altar…which Jeroboam… built…he pulled down" (23:15). Josiah is portrayed as a righteous king in contrast to earlier kings.[33] *But he is still an absolute monarch like they were.* He is not shown to implement a law code as a replacement (or limit) to royal prerogative. He enjoys the same power as did his predecessors; he simply exercises his dictatorial power in consistency with the Mosaic religion. "Before him there was no king like him, who turned to Yahweh with all his heart…according to the law of Moses" (23:25). There is no diminishing of royal authority under a new "constitutional monarchy" in this narrative. Nor is the law book presented as a statutory document. It is simply the model by which Josiah's rule is vindicated as righteous in contrast to the acts of his ancestors.

There is indeed an exalted status—a "new attitude" per Patrick—ascribed to the law book in DtrH. The uses of law writings seen in the previous chapter included *popular* education; so lofty a status as instruction for kings was either not known, or at least not emphasized, in the pre-Deuteronomic literature. This "new" status of the law book as instructive even for kings does not appear, however, to have turned the law book into statutory legislation. There is actually another explanation for the law book's exalted role in the Josiah story.

In his ground-breaking study of ancient "book-find" legends, Wolfgang Speyer explained the traditional importance of written texts for cult reforms.[34] Various ancient Near Eastern and Mediterranean societies based cultic reformation on the discovery of lost temple documents. Nabonidus, for instance, desired to restore the *Šamaš* shrine in Sippar in the sixth century. According to Nabonidus' inscription, a former king (Nebuchadnezzar) had attempted the same restoration but his efforts proved inadequate. In order to ensure a more successful reformation, Nabonidus reports:

> I made investigations and gathered the ancients of the town… I told them: "Look for the ancient foundation-stone [i.e. containing the Temple documents[35]]…" The erudite persons looked for the ancient stone of

33. Nelson (*1–2 Kings*, 252) titles the pericope "Josiah, the Best King Ever."
34. Wolfgang Speyer, *Bücherfunde in der Glaubenswerbung der Antike: Mit einem Ausblick auf Mittelalter und Neuzeit* (Hypomnemata 24; Göttingen: Vandenhoeck & Ruprecht, 1970).
35. "The foundation-stone contains the document of the 'original temple' and enables Nabonidus to undertake his restoration works" (Thomas C. Römer, "Transformations in Deuteronomistic and Biblical Historiography: On 'Bookfinding' and Other Literary Strategies," *ZAW* 109 [1997]: 8; cf. Joan G. Westenholz, "Writing for

foundation, imploring Shamash, my Lord, and praying to the great Gods, they inspected the apartment and the rooms and they saw it. They came to me and told me... My heart jubilated and my face was radiant.[36]

With this find, the *Šamaš* temple could be properly rebuilt, surpassing Nebuchadnezzar's impotent attempt. For DtrH, Josiah also is a reformer king surpassing earlier reformers (e.g. Hezekiah and Joash). In order to show this, the ancient Near Eastern "book-find" story was a natural choice and, indeed, this "cultic reform" polemic appears to be the book's fundamental role in the Josiah account.

It is noteworthy that, in several other ancient Near Eastern discovery legends, the initial "find" leads to an oracle request by the king. Lowell Handy has shown Esarhaddon's hesitation to restore Esaglia without a further oracle, and also Nabonidus' insistence on an oracle before making restorations to the Nannar cultus. Bringing this evidence to bear on the Josiah story, Handy asks:

> Why was it at all necessary for the king to inquire of Yahweh since Josiah is presented as having clearly understood that the scroll found in the temple was from God and the information contained within it was perfectly, if ominously, clear and reliable?... Like Esarhaddon and Nabonidus, Josiah...is not content with the [written] word of the deity which has come to him even though he believes it to be valid. Instead, Josiah sends for a double-check on the divine will.[37]

Handy's expression, "double-check on the divine will," may be misleading. As Handy affirms, Josiah was already persuaded of the text's veracity when he found it (cf. 2 Kgs 22:11, 13).[38] The discovery, though

Posterity: Naram-Sin and Enmerkar," in *Kinattūtu ša dārâti: Raphael Kutscher Memorial Volume* [ed. A. F. Rainey; Tel Aviv: Tel Aviv University, 1993], 213–14). Steinkeller discusses several cuneiform texts which refer to foundation stones (or tablet boxes) in temples said to contain ritual copies of such texts as the Gilgamesh Epic and the Cuthean Legend of Naram-Sin (Piotr Steinkeller, "Studies in Third Millennium Paleography, 2. Signs ŠEN and ALAL," *OrAnt* 20 [1981]: 243–49; cf. Donald J. Wiseman, "A Gilgamesh Epic Fragment from Nimrud," *Iraq* 37 [1975]: 157–63). Eduard Naville ("Egyptian Writings in Foundation Walls, and the Age of the Book of Deuteronomy," *Proceedings of the Society of Biblical Archaeology* 29 [1907]: 232–42) compiled evidence of ritual texts (including cultic law books) placed into the masonry of ancient Egyptian temples and discovered by later renovators.

36. Translation from Römer, "On 'Bookfinding,'" 8.

37. L. K. Handy, "The Role of Huldah in Josiah's Cult Reform," *ZAW* 106 (1994): 40, 48.

38. Cf. Nabonidus' full persuasion of the implications of his discovery prior to his inquiry: "[Sin's] certain command I awfully heeded...[but] I worried..." (translation from Handy, "Huldah," 44).

of obvious moment, did not itself prescribe action. Something more authoritative was needed to authorize action: a divine oracle. The need for an oracle alongside the "book-find" is typical for ancient cultic reforms. Additionally, Handy finds the promise of peace for the reforming king a further indicator of a typical genre: "That the king is going to have peace because he was moved by the word of the god is also a standard motif."[39] Esarhaddon and Nabonidus (like Josiah) are granted words of peace from the deities. Such similarities—book-finding, oracles, and promises of peace—lead to the suspicion that the Josiah story draws upon typical ancient Near Eastern reform ideals.[40] Josiah's "book-find" was not included because of any supposed statutory import now accorded to texts; rather, a "lost and found" text enabled Josiah to overthrow current tradition by identifying his reform with the long-forgotten "ancient way."

Book discoveries were featured, according to Speyer, "in order to lend to reform work the light of a golden age of great holiness."[41] In some cases, forgeries were planted to facilitate a desired reform.[42] Whether authentic or manufactured, "the idea of the holy book, which is discovered in a grave or a temple, was very common in antiquity."[43] For Josiah to overturn traditions as deeply entrenched as those founded by Solomon (23:13), just such a warrant was required: hence the importance for connecting his reformation to an ancient "law book" found in the temple, and for portraying a "law book" as used by this king in his reforming efforts.

This is probably why Josiah's reforms are exclusively *cultic* in the account. He is seen tearing down altars, defrocking priests, burning idols, and restoring the Passover. He is nowhere said, however, to remove corrupt officers, to care for the poor, or to otherwise institute reforms in matters of justice. Social wrongs are elsewhere berated in the prophetic and DtrH literature as causes of divine disfavor (e.g. Isa 10:2; 1 Kgs 21). One can suspect that Josiah's piety would also lead to improvements in matters of social justice. However, such is not the concern of this narrative. The Josianic reforms which the law book is used to justify are cultic reforms. This fact strengthens the conclusion that the law book receives exalted status in this account because the king required an instrument

39. Handy, "Huldah," 51.

40. For discussion of the integrated forms behind this account, see Long, *2 Kings*, 255–56.

41. Speyer, *Bücherfunde in der Antike*, 125: "[U]m einem gerade angefertigten Werk den Schein höheren Alters und großer Heiligkeit zu verleihen."

42. Ibid., 20–21, 126–28.

43. Ibid., 19: "[W]ar im Altertum die Vorstellung vom heiligen Buch, das in einem Grab oder Tempel entdeckt wird, weit verbreitet."

that overreached current, cultic traditions and brought to his reform "the light of a golden age of great holiness."[44]

Patrick is correct to note as significant the centrality of the law book in Josiah's reforms. It is saying too much, however, to regard this as indicating "incipient statutes." There is no "constitutional convention" portrayed here. What is here portrayed is a king whose status as a righteous reformer is made possible by his discovery of ancient cultic descriptions—and he uses them as descriptions, not as prescriptive stipulations.

2. *Verbal Strictures in Deuteronomy*

Patrick also points to certain rhetorical features of Deuteronomy as indicating prescriptivism. He writes, first of all:

> The evidence for this new understanding appears in a few admonitions in the lawbook of Deuteronomy, for example: "Everything that I command you, you shall be careful to do; you shall not add to it or take from it." (Deut. 12:32) This warning against adding to or subtracting from the text betokens an identification of the text with the law."[45]

Patrick also highlights a second, related kind of statement in Deuteronomy: "statements in the sermonic conclusion of the book, for example: 'If you obey the voice of Yahweh your God, to keep his commandments and mandates *which are written in this lawbook....*' (30:10, author's translation) The italicized clause evidences a significant shift in the relation of rules of law and the law; the will of God is now fixed in [written] rules."[46]

These two "verbal stricture" statements—(a) text-preservation injunctions and (b) written law/"the law" equation—need to be examined more closely.

In regard to the first of these: Deuteronomy twice exhorts not "to add to" nor "to take away from" the words of this law collection (Deut 4:2; 13:1 [EV 12:32]). Patrick perceives in these injunctions an indication of legal comprehensiveness—that is, the law collection is being billed as a comprehensive code with every law inscribed in it. But is this concern for *textual* integrity actually an indication that Deuteronomy is viewed as a comprehensive law code?

---

44. Cf. n. 41, above.
45. Patrick, *Old Testament Law*, 200. Cf. Dale Patrick, "God's Commandment," in *God in the Fray: A Tribute to Walter Brueggemann* (ed. Tod Linafelt and Timothy K. Beale; Minneapolis: Fortress, 1998), 109; McConville, *Deuteronomy*, 103; Bernard M. Levinson, *Deuteronomy and the Hermeneutics of Legal Innovation* (Oxford: Oxford University Press, 1998), 14–15, 48.
46. Patrick, *Old Testament Law*, 200–201 (emphasis original).

The "do not add/take away" formula is a well-known scribal convention for protecting texts from alteration. The closing lines of the Neo-Babylonian *Erra Epic*, for instance, employ a similar formula: "(The deity) revealed it to him during the night, and in the morning, when he recited (it), he did not skip a single (line) nor a single line (of his own) did he add to it... May this song (= the poem) last forever!..." (5.[19].40–59)[47]

A fourteenth-century treaty between Suppiluliumas (of Hatti) and Kurtiwaza (of Mitanni) includes the same kind of formula in its prologue: "Whoever will remove this tablet from before Tessub, the lord of the *kurinnu* of Kahat, and put it in a hidden place, if he breaks it or causes anyone else to change the wording of the tablet—at the conclusion of this treaty we have called the gods to be assembled...as witnesses...."[48]

In addition to such *literary* and *treaty* materials, warnings to guard the verbal integrity of other kinds of material are also known, including official letters,[49] prophecy (Jer 26:2), wisdom literature (Prov 30:5–6), and law collections. In the case of law collections, LL and LH notably conclude with instructions not to change their words. Hammurabi states:

> May any king who will appear in the land in the future, at any time, observe the pronouncements of justice that I inscribed upon my stela. May he not alter the judgments that I rendered and the verdicts that I gave... (But) should that man not heed my pronouncements, which I have inscribed upon my stela, and should he...change my pronouncements... may the great god Anu...curse his destiny... (LH 48.59–94; 49.18–52; cf. LL 21.36–22.52)

The common oriental concern for ensuring the integrity of texts is evident. The presence of this concern in LH, reinforced by a long list of blessings and curses, is particularly significant. As it is the comparison of LH with contemporary practice documents which forced recognition that such collections functioned descriptively (not prescriptively), it can hardly be argued that a similar concern for textual integrity in Deuteronomy is indicative of emerging prescriptivism. Patrick's argument that the "do

---

47. Luigi Cagni, *The Poem of Erra* (Sources and Monographs: Sources from the Ancient Near East 1/3; Malibu, Calif.: Undena, 1977), 60. According to Cagni, the large number and broadly dispersed copies of the *Erra Epic* which have been found do, in fact, evince an absence of textual alterations (p. 5).

48. *ANET*, 205. Cf. Muršilis' concern that a present plague is due to someone changing of a treaty without his knowledge, see Hans Gustav Güterbock, "Mursili's Accounts of Suppiluliuma's Dealings with Egypt," *RHA* 18.66 (1960), 59–60, 61.

49. Robert F. Harper, *Assyrian and Babylonian Letters Belonging to the Kouyunjik Collections of the British Museum* (8 vols.; Decennial Publications, University of Chicago 2/4; Chicago: University of Chicago Press, 1892–1914), 1250.

not add/take away" formula indicates prescriptivism is not persuasive: such formulae secure a text *qua* text against corruption.[50] They do not indicate anything about the function of that text. Nor do they mean the text is comprehensive law. All that is indicated by these formulae is that that *this literary witness* to Mosaic justice must not be manipulated.

Patrick's second kind of Deuteronomic expression is weightier. He points to a statement in Deut 30 where the law book is apparently identified with oracular law. Beginning with the relevant line from Deuteronomy, Patrick writes: "'If you obey the voice of Yahweh your God, to keep his commandments and mandates *which are written in this law-book....*' (30:10, author's translation) The italicized clause evidences a significant shift in the relation of rules of law and the law; the will of God is now fixed in [written] rules."[51] As set out in the first chapter of this project, the defining characteristic of a legislative text is when the text *is itself* "the law" (versus a description of law). On the face of it, Deut 30:10 does appear to equate oracular law ("the voice of Yahweh your God") and law writings ("in this law book"). At face value, this could be an indication of a prescriptive understanding of Deuteronomy. But how does this equation come to appear in the Deuteronomic law book which Patrick himself admits is more descriptive than legislative? The evidence is more complicated than it looks at first blush.

Deuteronomy itself is composed with a descriptivistic attitude toward older law writings. The Deuteronomic law collection repeatedly identifies itself as a restatement of the older, Sinai law. It does not claim to be giving new law; it purports to restate the old: "This is the law that Moses placed before the sons of Israel...when they came out of Egypt" (Deut 4:44–45; cf. 1:5; 4:1–14; 5:2, 22; 6:1, 22–24; 10:1–5; etc.) There is one exception to this. After re-presenting the Horeb covenant (4:44–28:68), Deut 28:69 (EV 29:1) introduces a new Moab covenant (28:69–30:20 [EV 29:1–30:20]).[52] This new covenant is explicitly identified as new:

50. Michael Fishbane, "*Varia Deuteronomica*," *ZAW* 84 (1972): 350. Cf. E. Leichty, "The Colophon," in *Studies Presented to A. Leo Oppenheim: June 7, 1964* (ed. Robert D. Biggs et al.; Chicago: University of Chicago Press, 1964), 150–51; A. Leo Oppenheim, *Ancient Mesopotamia: Portrait of a Dead Civilization* (Chicago: University of Chicago Press, 1977), 150–51, 240–41; Eleonore Reuter, "Nimm nichts davon weg und füge nichts hinzu! Dtn 13,1 seine alttestamentlichen Parallelen und seine altorientalischen Vorbilder," *BN* 47 (1989): 107–14; Jean-Pierre Sonnet, *The Book within the Book: Writing in Deuteronomy* (BibInt 14; Leiden: Brill, 1997), 46.

51. Patrick, *Old Testament Law*, 200–201.

52. Alexander Rofé, "The Covenant in the Land of Moab (Deuteronomy 28:69–30:20): Historico-Literary, Comparative, and Form-Critical Considerations," in Christensen, ed., *Song of Power*, 269–80; Nelson, *Deuteronomy*, 3, 11, 338–39.

"These are the words of the covenant that Yahweh commanded...in the land of Moab, besides the covenant that he made with them at Horeb." Deuteronomy (at least as framed by chs. 4–11 and 27–30) is presented with a discerning awareness of what is "new" and what is the "old" restated. The core of Deuteronomy is regarded as a faithful restatement of the Sinai law.

This concern for restatement is further evident in Deuteronomy's broad dependence (especially Deut 12–26) on BC. In at least 22 places, Deuteronomy reuses laws from BC. However—and here is where Deuteronomy's own *descriptivistic* attitude toward law writings emerges—Deuteronomy does not simply restate BC; nor does Deuteronomy merely amplify BC. There are significant changes introduced in Deuteronomy's appropriation of BC. Deuteronomy professes to retell the old law faithfully, yet it introduces significant changes to BC's stipulations (as well as the Exodus Decalogue).[53] A few examples will suffice here:

Topic	BC's Stipulation (Exod 20:23–23:19)	Deuteronomy's Stipulation
Altars	Multiple altars authorized (20:24)	Single altar centralized (12:1–28)
Slavery	Male slaves released after six years; female slaves not released; rite for voluntary chattel slavery conducted at the shrine (21:1–11)	Male and female slaves released after six years; masters provide generous "severance package" on release; rite for voluntary chattel slavery conducted at the house (15:12–18)
Marriage/ Adultery	A man who seduces a virgin either marries her or pays a fine equal to the bride-price (22:16–17)	A man who seduces a virgin either marries her (and can never divorce her) or pays a fixed fine of 50 shekels of silver (23:28–29); numerous additional provisions on virginity, adultery, divorce, and marriage also given (e.g. 22:13–30; 24:1–4)

53. Gary Alan Chamberlain, "Exodus 21–23 and Deuteronomy 12–26: A Form-Critical Study" (Ph.D. diss., Boston University Graduate School, 1977), especially 108–40, 165; Patrick, *Old Testament Law*, 97; Nelson, *Deuteronomy*, 5; Crüsemann, *The Torah*, 201–4 (Crüsemann believes Deuteronomy is even structured after the pattern of BC [p. 202]). The nature of the relationship between Deuteronomy and BC is debated, largely because of the kinds of features here noted. Van Seters (*Diaspora*) reverses the relationship, so that BC follows Deuteronomy. Such a proposal reverses the relationship, but does not explain its nature. Most scholars still recognize Deuteronomy as dependant on BC.

Carcass disposal	Animals dying naturally to be thrown to dogs (22:31)	Animals dying naturally may be sold to foreigners (14:21)
Septennial release	Land left fallow (23:10–11)	Debts released (15:1–11)
Gleaning	Poor (and beasts) may eat from crops left fallow in the seventh year (23:10–11)	Poor may glean after the reapers each harvest (24:19–21)
Festivals	Three feasts are Unleavened Bread, Harvest, and Ingathering (Passover conducted at home); these three are celebrated by the males (23:14–17; cf. 12:1–50; 34:18–25)	Three feasts are Passover/Unleavened Bread (now combined), Weeks, and Booths; these are celebrated at the central shrine with men, women, and children (16:1–17)
National institutions	(Not addressed in BC)	Institutions such as monarchy, courts, priests, prophecy, and the army described (16:18–20:20)

The nature of these changes are fairly consistent. Deuteronomy adapts the older stipulations for the new conditions of a landed people with a central shrine and a more developed government. But how these adaptations are "passed off" as a restatement of the Sinai laws is puzzling—that is, it is puzzling if the Sinai statements (*qua* statements) are presumed to be the divine law. If, on the other hand, the Sinaitic law statements were regarded as a record of how law was applied at the time when the Sinai covenant was made (but were not themselves the fixed definition of that law), Deuteronomy's representation is coherent. The voice of Moses in Deuteronomy offers a re-application of the same law as it would now apply in the new situation of Israel.

This, in fact, is what Deuteronomy claims: the same law as that learned at Sinai is being faithfully re-proclaimed *as it applies now*. Deuteronomy repeatedly addresses its law stipulations to "today's" Israel: "Yahweh our God made a covenant with us in Horeb...with us, who are all of us alive here today" (5:2–3). This updated proclamation, as seen in the preceding table, involved updated practices too. What is interesting is that these modifications are sometimes explicitly made. For instance, the Deuteronomic altar law (which banned the local altars allowed in BC) is introduced: "You shall not [when you settle the land] do according to all that we are doing here today..." (12:8). That is, the former practice (local altars) is openly acknowledged. The use of local altars is accepted as the proper way to practice the law of sacrifice prior to settlement. However, *the same law* requires a new application (a central altar) once the land is settled. Deuteronomy therefore has no qualms about explicitly stating the old stipulation and the new side-by-side, while calling them the same law. For the Deuteronomic tradents, the old law book was not itself the law but an idyllic witness to the law. Deuteronomy makes use of the received law writings (e.g. BC) as descriptive treatises on divine law.[54]

All this is to say that Deuteronomy itself, as a law collection, looks very much like a descriptivistic compilation. This recognition sets a problematic backdrop for Patrick's reading of Deut 30:10 (cited on p. 68, above). Patrick perceives in that passage an equation of written law with actual law; but this is an attitude which Deuteronomy's compilers do not seem to have possessed. Patrick recognizes this problem when he writes:

> The text of the Deuteronomic Law [itself] does not exhibit this new conception. Moses' address displays a striking freedom in its adaptation and restatement of the materials the author inherited from the Book of the Covenant. The author shows no compulsion to adhere to the letter of the divine law. Moreover, the style and tone of the Deuteronomic presentation of law is so imprecise and homiletical that the very idea of strict adherence is virtually meaningless. It is ironic that Deuteronomy should become the text which gave rise to the understanding of law as a body of written rules.[55]

Patrick therefore avers:

> The verses in the book of Deuteronomy exhibiting this new understanding of law are either isolated elements within the lawbook or a part of the Deuteronomistic framework. I would ascribe all of them[56] to the school which sprang up in Judah following the discovery of the book in the temple and its adoption as the basis of Josiah's reform.[57]

54. Contra Levinson, *Legal Innovation*. Levinson supposes that the authors of Deuteronomy claimed fidelity to the old law (and employed BC language) as a ruse—"to purchase the legitimacy and authority that their reform agenda otherwise lacked" (p. 21). Levinson's thesis, however, is fundamentally self-contradictory. It requires that Deuteronomy's audience both knew BC well (in order to perceive Deuteronomy's subtle reuses of BC's phrases) yet simultaneously did not know BC (in order not to recognize Deuteronomy's drastic changes). Levinson's work highlights the tension, but does not resolve it. (Joe Sprinkle offers a similar criticism in his review of Levinson, *Legal Innovation, JETS* 42, no. 4 [1999]: 720–21.)

55. Patrick, *Old Testament Law*, 201 (cf. pp. 97–141). Cf. Dale Patrick, "Deuteronomy," in *Chalice Introduction to the Old Testament* (ed. Marti J. Steussy; St. Louis, Miss.: Chalice, 2003), 64–65.

56. Though Patrick refers to "all of them," as though there are many such expressions, he only actually identifies two: 13:1 (EV 12:28) (discussed above, pp. 66–68), and 30:10 (presently under discussion).

57. Patrick, *Old Testament Law*, 201. Sonnet is skeptical of ascribing Deuteronomy's "writing texts" to later redaction, since the concern with texts is central to Deuteronomy's structure (Sonnet, *Book within the Book*, 5–6).

Patrick ascribes the Deut 30:10 equation of law writings and divine law to a Josianic-era editor. It has already been shown, however, that Josiah's reform does not offer a plausible period for a prescriptive editing of Deuteronomy. Therefore, two alternatives remain: either Deut 30:10 is an addition from some *other* period yet to be identified, when the law writings did come to be perceived as legislation; or, the phrase here is a *figurative* equation (i.e. the law book is being rhetorically, but not actually, equated to divine law). The latter possibility could be supported from the immediate context, which reads as follows:

> Yahweh your God will cause you to abound in all the deeds of your hand…if you will give heed to the voice and Yahweh your God to keep his commandments and his statutes (that which is written in this book of the law)… For this commandment which I command you today—it is not too perplexing for you, neither is it far away. It is not in heaven, that you should say, "Who will ascend for us into the heavens and bring it to us, that we may hear it and do it?" Neither is it over the sea, that you should say, "Who will cross over the sea for us and bring it to us, that we may hear it and do it?" For the word is very near to you—in your mouth and in your heart—in order to do it. (30:9–14)

The lesson here advanced is that this law book makes it simple for every Israelite to learn God's will. The imagery is that of the ancient hero epics, where heroes such as Gilgamesh must traverse the heavens and seas to find teaching on eternal life.[58] No Israelite will ever have to embark on such a difficult odyssey to find the divine secrets of life: the law book brings this instruction on "life and good" (v. 15) within reach for all Israel (cf. 4:5–8).[59] Thus the law book is a popular lesson book on divine righteousness rather than a legislative code of government. It is equated with the oracular command of Yahweh as a rhetorical device to underscore the insight into God's will made possible by this text (without necessarily supposing that all of God's will is now contained in this book).

The expression in v. 14 seems to confirm that it is the book's didactic value (not any regulatory function) that is in view: the book is studied (it is "in your mouth") and its lessons are learned (they are put "in your heart"). Just living is not the result of acting upon a text, but acting from the instructed heart. There is no regulatory enforcement of this book in view; the law book is, in Deut 30, a text for the people's instruction. This

---

58. McConville, *Deuteronomy*, 429; Peter C. Craigie, *The Book of Deuteronomy* (NICOT; London: Hodder & Stoughton, 1976; repr., Grand Rapids: Eerdmans, 1994), 365; Nelson, *Deuteronomy*, 349–50.

59. Cf. Agur's use of the "no need to ascend to heaven" *and* "do not add/take away" formulae (Prov 30:3–6).

looks more like Bernard Jackson's popular didacticism than a community "rule of law."[60]

In light of the immediate context, and the nature of Deuteronomy as a whole, it is probably best to read Deut 30:10 as a rhetorical device rather than a philosophical statement about the nature of law. It fortuitously matches the defining characteristic of statute law, but its own immediate context undermines any effort to read this text as introducing so radical a concept here.

Even if one were to insist that Deut 30:10 does equate the law with written law, it can hardly be an attitude native to Deuteronomy. It would have to be seen (as Patrick affirms) as a later editorial gloss. The source of that gloss would need to be established, and the seventh-century reforms of Josiah do not provide the convenient solution Patrick assumed.

II. *Westbrook on Deuteronomic Law Writings*

Westbrook also connects the rise of prescriptivism with the Deuteronomic school. His argument is more sophisticated, however. First of all, Westbrook does not posit so radical a shift as Patrick. For Westbrook, the Deuteronomic evidence points to an "intermediate stage" between descriptivism and prescriptivism.[61] Second, Westbrook finds his evidence

60. See p. 38, above.

61. Westbrook identifies "stages" of legal development, which can be summarized as follow: (1) The "first stage" of Hebrew law writing produced *descriptive* treatises. Israel's earliest law writings (e.g. BC) were treatises on law, but not themselves "the law." (2) Westbrook then identifies an "intermediate stage" of development with a beginning point and an ending point. (2a) The intermediate stage began with Deuteronomy, which (for Westbrook) evinces a new idea of law writings as *statutory*. With Deuteronomy, Hebrew law writings came to be viewed as *being* "the law." However, this Deuteronomic innovation did not achieve widespread acceptance until the time of Ezra. (2b) Ezra marks the end point of the intermediate stage, as it is in Ezra's Jerusalem (under Persian influence) that a *prescriptive* use of law writings came to be the community norm. These law writings, however, were still formulated in terms of concrete examples. They could never be true, comprehensive law codes as long as they contained a limited circle of precedents. (3) For Westbrook, the "final stage" of legal development emerged when Greek philosophy provided the means whereby laws could be organized into abstract categories and definitions. By this time, however, the Torah had become a fixed canon and could not simply be rewritten. Nonetheless, the *methods* of Greek philosophy made it possible for Hebrew "jurists" to use the fixed law writings as a comprehensive legal source. The Mishnah (and rabbinical exegesis) show(s) this effort to find comprehensiveness in the Hebrew law writings by discerning categories and definitions. See several of Westbrook's studies: "Origins of Legislation," 222; "Biblical Law," 3–4, 7–8; "Codification," 43–44; "Ancient Near Eastern Law," 20–21; *Studies*, 7.

in the Deuteronomic debt-release cycle (Deut 15:1–15). Rather than focusing on law-book rhetoric, Westbrook notes something significant in the character of an actual Deuteronomic law.

It is Westbrook's handling of this Deuteronomic debt-release law which is important. His arguments can be summarized, as follows, for subsequent discussion.[62] First, ancient Near Eastern kings typically published a debt-release edict (a *mīšarum* edict) if economic oppression was widespread. Such edicts only cancelled *present* debts, however. Debt release was typically, therefore: a royal prerogative, accomplished by edict, and retrospective. Second, in Deut 15, however, debt release is recast in a *prospective* law writing—a law text which, without mention of the king, calls for debt release every seven years. Thus, "legislation became detached from the legislator" and "the ultimate prerogative of the king, to decree a cancellation of debts, is made automatic and cyclical."[63] This cyclical debt release, for Westbrook, marks the beginning of Israel's conception of law writings as statutory. Westbrook supports this reading of Deut 15 with: (1) a historical witness to this debt release law's expected import (Jer 34); and (2) a contemporary parallel (Solonic Athens).

Each of these points will be taken up below. Aspects of Westbrook's argument can be accepted; however, certain conclusions he draws will be challenged, resulting in a different interpretation of the "intermediate stage" of legal development reflected by the Deuteronomic writings.

1. *The Typical Nature of Debt Release*
It was a pre-eminent duty of kings in the ancient Near East to defend the poor and helpless against the oppression of the powerful. This included the rescue of the poor from creditors who abused their power over them. Ideally, the poor and weak could seek deliverance from such oppression by appealing to the king's court. Sometimes, however, such economic oppression was widespread. The king might come to recognize not only isolated instances, but widespread oppression. In such instances, the king could announce a *general* debt release (a *mīšarum* edict)[64] for the whole kingdom or specific cities.[65]

---

62. Westbrook's various statements on this subject can be found in: "Origins of Legislation," 219–22; *Property and the Family in Biblical Law* (JSOTSup 113; Sheffield: JSOT Press, 1991), 16, 36–57; "Covenant Code," 28; "Social Justice in the Ancient Near East," in *Social Justice in the Ancient World* (ed. Morris Silver and K. D. Irani; Westport, Conn.: Greenwood, 1995), 160–61; "Codification," 42–43.

63. Westbrook, "Codification," 42.

64. The typical expressions are *mīšarum šakānum* ("to establish justice") and *andurānum šakānum* ("to establish liberation"). For a discussion, see Moshe

Such an edict might be likened to a modern "class action" lawsuit, where a vast number of individual cases are handled by one verdict. Note, for example, the presentation of Tudhaliya IV's edict, where a case is brought to him (as judge) by "class action" (all the oppressed of the land): "... the men of Hatti all began to bow down to me, and they spoke as follows: O great king... Are you not able to judge in matters of justice? Behold, evil people...have utterly destroyed...the feudal holdings and the *šarikuwa* tenants..."[66]

The rest of the fragmentary document reports the specific releases Tudhaliya handed down—his verdicts "to enforce justice" (*mīšarum šakānum*)—in response to this plea. The nature of these edicts as "judicial verdicts" helps to explain their prescriptive nature in contrast with the non-binding law collections.[67] Westbrook explains, "There is no doubt as to the legislative character of the edicts: they are reforms expressly dated to a specific point in time at which their provisions come into effect and there is ample evidence, direct and indirect, of their effect upon legal relations."[68]

Whereas the law collections described legal ideals *generically* (without obliging court activity), a written edict was aimed at a *specific* situation with specific remedies and was obliging.[69] The edict was not a statement of ideals, but a judicial act addressing a specific—that is, *present*—crisis. Only obligations existing *at the time of the edict* were cancelled, therefore. Such release proclamations were not only practiced in Mesopotamian lands, but in Israel as well. The example of Zedekiah (Jer 34) is

Weinfeld, *Social Justice in Ancient Israel and in the Ancient Near East* (Jerusalem: Magnes, 1995), 75.

65. A *mīšarum* edict was also typically announced on a new king's ascension to his throne, thereby consolidating power and showing himself a defender of the poor (Weinfeld, *Social Justice*, 10).

66. Raymond Westbrook and Roger D. Woodard, "The Edict of Tudhaliya IV," *JAOS* 110, no. 4 (1990): 641. Cf. Westbrook, "Origins of Legislation," 215.

67. Westbrook calls them "administrative acts" (Westbrook, "Origins of Legislation," 216–17; *Property*, 50).

68. Westbrook, "Tudhaliya IV," 642. Cf. Finkelstein, "Ammi-Ṣaduqa's Edict," 100–104; J. J. Finkelstein, "Some New *Misharum* Material and its Implications," in Güterbock and Jacobsen, eds., *Studies in Honor of Benno Landsberger*, 233–46. Actually, scholars differ as to whether the written edict was *itself* legislative, or if the *oral act* of release was alone prescriptive and the written edict was an aid to its implementation or simply a literary record of that binding oral act. On this discussion, see Gregory C. Chirichigno, *Debt-Slavery in Israel and the Ancient Near East* (JSOTSup 141; Sheffield: JSOT Press, 1993), 86–87; cf. Westbrook, "Origins of Legislation," 215–16 n. 60.

69. Finkelstein, "Ammi-Ṣaduqa's Edict," 91–92.

particularly notable, and will be discussed later (cf. also 1 Kgs 12:3–17; Isa 61:1; Ezek 46:17).[70]

2. *The Nature of the Deuteronomy 15's Debt Release*

Deuteronomy does something unusual with the traditional debt release: "At the end of seven years you shall make release, and this is the manner of the release: every creditor, the loan of his hand which he lent to his fellow, he shall not require of his fellow—his brother—for Yahweh's release has been proclaimed" (Deut 15:1–2). Concerning this provision, Westbrook writes: "The content of the law is a debt-release decree, such as we have seen were common throughout the Ancient Near East. But in this version there is a significant difference; the effect of the law is pro-spective, not retrospective. The release has been changed into a cyclical event…"[71]

Westbrook notes two facts: (1) the topic of Deut 15 is a topic com-monly treated in royal edicts; and (2) Deut 15 is prospective (indeed, cyclical) in how it envisions debt release. Both of these facts are correct. It is Westbrook's conclusion from these facts which needs to be ques-tioned: namely, that this law writing has therefore been ascribed with the force of a prospective edict (i.e. statute law).[72] Westbrook's conclusion is plausible, but it is a speculative hypothesis which needs to be critiqued.

Westbrook's first observation is that the topic of Deut 15 (debt release) is a topic commonly treated in royal edicts. This in itself is not remark-able. Topics found in edicts and court verdicts often overlap with topics in the law collections. After all, the same issues ought to be expected in the legal literature as are found in actual legal instruments.[73] Simply because a topic characteristic of the edict has been included in a law collection does not mean the *force* of the edict is also brought into the collection. It is the instrument (edict or law collection) which typically determines the force of the provision, not *vice versa*.

This point is fully understood by Westbrook. He himself has demon-strated this point in connection with the Mesopotamian materials, noting how Ammiṣaduqa's *mīšarum* edict practically quotes from his great-great-grandfather's law collection (LH):

70. Weinfield, *Social Justice*, 75–96; Donald J. Wiseman, "The Laws of Hammurabi Again," *JSS* 7 (1962): 167–68.
71. Westbrook, "Origins of Legislation," 220.
72. "It is this combination of the two ancient sources of law [i.e. the *edict* incor-porated into a *law collection*] that turns the law code into a statute whose text may be cited as authoritative in a court of law" (Westbrook, "Origins of Legislation," 222).
73. Westbrook, "Origins of Legislation," 204; Finkelstein, "Ammi-Ṣaduqa's Edict," 103.

"If a debt seizes a man and he gives his wife, son and daughter in sale or *ana kiššātim* [debt-slavery], they shall serve in the house of their purchaser or holder for three years; in the fourth year their freedom shall be established." (LH §117)

"If a citizen of Numhia, Emut-balum, Idamaraz, Uruk, Isin, Kisurra (or) Malgium has been bound by a debt and has given [hims]elf, his wife or [his *child*] in sale, *ana kiššātim*, or in pledge, because the king has established equity for the land, he is released, his freedom is established." (Ammiṣaduqa's Edict §20)[74]

The very presence of Ammiṣaduqa's edict to enforce an ideal already published in LH shows the ineffectual nature of LH. If the debt-slave release in LH was itself binding, no edict would have been necessary. It required an instrument with prescriptive force—an edict—to enforce the release idealized in LH. Westbrook's point in drawing this comparison is that various legal ideals (including debt release) can be *discussed* in a law collection. Those "discussions" can even serve as the model for real edicts. However, a royal edict is necessary *to enact* an enforceable measure. It is not the topic which carries prescriptive force, but rather the instrument. This distinction can be displayed in the following table:[75]

Instrument	Direction of Intent	Nature of Intent
Law Collection	Prospective	Idyllic (Descriptive)
Edict/Court Verdict	Retrospective	Actual (Prescriptive)

Normally, then, a debt-release discussion *in a law collection* should be regarded as idyllic (not prescriptive). That is the normal conclusion to be drawn—unless other factors indicate differently. It is in this connection that Westbrook points to his second fact: that Deut 15 is *prospective* in how it envisions debt release.

Of course, law writings are generally prospective in a limited way: they envision typical instances in which certain judgments would be expected. They are "precedents," of a sort, and thus prospective examples.[76] Thus, for instance, LH and BC both take up the topic of debt-slavery by describing the number of years an individual slave should serve (Exod 21:2; LH §117). In a limited, precedential manner, the law writings are typically prospective. Deuteronomy 15, however, envisions a *general* debt release. Furthermore, that debt release is tied to *a regular*, *automatic cycle* of seven years. This is unique. Nowhere else does a

---

74. Translation from Westbrook, "Social Justice," 154, 157.
75. Cf. Westbrook, "Origins of Legislation," 215–19.
76. Ibid., 218.

known ancient Near Eastern law writing take up the idea of a general debt release on a regular cycle. This is no mere precedent, but an automatic system. It is in this second fact that Westbrook finds the grounds for his conclusion that the idea of statute law arose in the Deuteronomic school.

Westbrook's position is well argued and plausible. It is not, however, certain. There is another plausible explanation for this unique instance of cyclical debt release which Westbrook does not appear to have considered. This alternate explanation will need to be outlined next. Initially, it is only intended to offer this explanation as a possible alternative to that of Westbrook. Only after setting both side-by-side can they then be tested (by reference to relevant practice materials) and a conclusion drawn between them.

Westbrook places significant weight on the uniqueness of the Deuteronomic debt-release cycle. He is probably correct to suspect that something peculiar about the Deuteronomic attitude toward law writings, in contrast with other ancient Near Eastern peoples, has produced this unique vision of cyclical debt release. Rather than assuming that legislative thinking must be present for this peculiar law provision to have emerged, there is another well-known distinctive of Hebrew law writing which also can explain the same phenomenon. That distinctive trait of Hebrew law writing (and particularly Deuteronomy) is the tendency to integrate cultic laws with judicial laws. Unlike other ancient Near Eastern peoples, the Hebrews incorporated cultic law writing into the typically judicial law-collection genre. In other ancient Near Eastern societies, cultic practices were recorded in priestly texts (and often kept secret). The publicized law collections of other ancient Near Eastern peoples were "a strictly secular institution."[77] It may be this distinctive tendency of Hebrew law writings that explains the uniqueness of this *cyclical* debt-release law.

Scholars already recognize that Deut 14:22–16:17 collates a series of prospective cycles related to the Hebrew cultus:[78]

---

77. S. Paul, *Studies*, 8, 9 n. 1. Cf. Crüsemann, *The Torah*, 10.

78. E.g. Jeffrey H. Tigay, *Deuteronomy* (JPS Torah Commentary; Jerusalem: The Jewish Publication Society, 1996), 141; A. D. H. Mayes, *Deuteronomy* (NCB; London: Marshall, Morgan & Scott, 1981), 243; Nelson, *Deuteronomy*, 191; Eugene H. Merrill, *Deuteronomy* (NAC 4; Nashville: Broadman & Holman, 1994), 239; cf. McConville, "Deuteronomy," 184. Scholars have occasionally identified Deut 14:22–16:17 with the sabbath commandment; see Georg Braulik, "The Sequence of the Laws in Deuteronomy 12–26 and the Decalogue," in Christensen, ed., *Song of Power*, 321; Jeffries M. Hamilton, *Social Justice and Deuteronomy: The Case of Deuteronomy 15* (SBLDS 136; Atlanta: Scholars Press, 1992), 99–135.

14:22–27	Annual tithe cycle
14:28–29	Triannual tithe cycle
15:1–11	Septennial debt-release cycle
(15:12–18)	(Slave-release law[79])
15:19–23	Annual first-born animal-sacrifice cycle
16:1–17	Annual festivals cycle (Passover, vv. 1–8; Weeks, vv. 9–12; Booths, vv. 13–17)

By definition, cultic calendars are prospective and cyclical. Israel was, of course, not alone in its fascination with cycles, including cycles of seven (e.g. the weekly sabbath and seven-year cycles) as well as annual, equinoctial, and monthly cycles. What was unique about Israel was its tendency to incorporate such *cultic* cycles into its law collections. Notwithstanding this unique way of recording such cycles, similar cycles—with connected rites—were observed throughout the ancient world. And sometimes these cycles incorporated acts of economic or political significance.

Ugarit, for instance, included a septennial fallow year in its calendar (as did Israel; Exod 23:10–11). C. H. Gordon explains the Ugaritic conviction that

> if one seven-year period ends in real or simulated famine, it will be followed by seven years of plenty... In the sabbatical year the land is to lie fallow...not because of any principles of soil chemistry, but because the ending of one cycle without a harvest was believed to bring on a seven-year cycle of plenty.[80]

Therefore, a forced famine had to be implemented every seventh year. In an agrarian society of subsistence living, such a practice would have had profound—even devastating—results if literally implemented (cf. 1 Macc 6:49–54). Gordon suspects that the Ugarit cult accomplished its septennial famine ritually (as part of the harvest festival), without

79. The slave release law interrupts the series of cyclical laws, though verbally it is closely tied to vv. 1–11 (Nelson, *Deuteronomy*, 192). It is probably appended as a limitation on the debt release law. Although *debts* are projected for general release every seven years (vv. 1–11), debt-*slaves* (vv. 12–18) are still expected to complete a full, six-year term of service before being released. This is a significant limitation on the practicality of the debt release, since it was as a result of debt that such slavery occurred; yet Deut 15 makes clear debt-*slaves* are not released until their term of service is through.

80. Cyrus H. Gordon, *Ugaritic Literature: A Comprehensive Translation of the Poetic and Prose Texts* (Rome: Pontifical Biblical Institute, 1949), 5, 57–62. Cf. idem, "Sabbatical Cycle or Seasonal Pattern? Reflections on a New Book," *Or* 22 (1953): 79–81; Edward Neufeld, "Socio-Economic Background of Yōbēl and Šemiṭṭā," *RSO* 33 (1958): 53–124; Westbrook, *Property*, 42–43.

necessitating a literal famine. Scholars are likewise divided on the literalness and nature of Israel's fallow-year cycle.[81] Leaving aside questions of implementation, the fallow-year law illustrates how cyclical, cultic calendars could include prospective acts of considerable economic import.

Facets of the Mesopotamian *akītu* (or, so called "New Year" or "Enthronement") festival might likewise be noted. The purpose of this festival was, as Mark Cohen explains, "the reenactment of the triumphal moment when the god first entered and claimed his city."[82] This cyclical "re-enthronement" of the deity was paralleled by the ritual "re-enthronement" of the human king. Scholars are divided as to whether the king's right to rule was literally decided in the ritual, or if it was a symbolic re-investiture.[83] The cultic literature nonetheless *envisioned* the practice in realistic terms, as though the king's reign was actually determined in that festival.

The *akītu* festival is also known to have concluded with "ritual activities which symbolized [the god's] setting in order the [city's] administration."[84] Henri Frankfort explains, "In Mesopotamia the concord [between nature and society] was…felt to be unstable; and the community united on numerous occasions, and notably at each New Year, in an effort to strengthen or restore it."[85] To what extent this ritual social ordering might have included economic re-alignments can only be guessed.[86] The *akītu*

81. For discussion, see Chirichigno, *Debt-Slavery*, 302–11; Cornelis Houtman, *Exodus: Volume 3 (Chapters 20–40)* (trans. S. Woudstra; Historical Commentary on the Old Testament; Leuven: Peeters, 1999), 251–55.

82. Mark E. Cohen, *The Cultic Calendars of the Ancient Near East* (Bethesda, Md.: CDL Press, 1993), 440.

83. For discussion of the arguments, see M. Cohen, *Cultic Calendars*, 450. Perhaps both functions of the royal review actually took place. In some instances, priests may have employed the power of the festival to "divinely dethrone" a weak and undesired king. In other instances, the king's appointed "review" before the god may have been "merely" symbolic (recalling that symbolism itself is powerful).

84. M. Cohen, *Cultic Calendars*, 453.

85. Henri Frankfort, *Kingship and the Gods: A Study of Ancient Near Eastern Religion as the Integration of Society and Nature* (Chicago: University of Chicago Press, 1978), 277.

86. There are at least two Nuzi documents which indicate actual release edicts pronounced in connection with the New Year festival, on which see Manfred Müller, "Sozial- und wirtschaftspolitische Rechtserlässe im Lande Arrapḫa," in *Beitrage zur sozialen Struktur des alten Vordersien* (ed. Horst Klengel; Schriften zur Geschichte und Kultur des alten Orients 1; Berlin: Akademie-Verlag, 1971), 56–57; Weinfeld, *Social Justice*, 93–94. It is also known that individual slave releases often took place in connection with temple rites (Driver and Miles, *Babylonian Laws*, 1:225–26).

festival included two high consultations to "determine destiny" for the city that year. The combination of such "determinations of destiny" with the "setting in order" of the administration certainly suggests that any changes made were tailored to the particulars of the year's oracles.[87] There do not appear to have been *fixed* administrative acts connected with this festival.[88] There is no precise parallel here to the specific debt-release cycle envisioned in Deut 15. Nonetheless, there is in these features of the *akītu* festival further illustration of ancient cults readily *expecting socio-political "re-alignments" according to a cyclical, cultic calendar*. Whether such projected re-alignments were accomplished literally or ritually (or by some combination of both) is not, for the present, significant. It is sufficient to have indicated this much: cultic cycles, by their very nature, were ascribed with regularity, and they could include prospective economic and political "corrections" within their scope.

That Deut 15 expects Israel's God to proclaim a debt release septennially remains unique in the ancient Near Eastern literature. Westbrook is correct to see an unparalleled provision here. But does this unique provision necessarily mean a "new intellectual climate" and "the transformation to true prospective legislation" was at work in the community that formed it?[89] It may simply be Deuteronomy's way of upholding one of its cultic ideals (divine kingship) by projecting a royal release proclamation into the cultic cycle.

Supporting this view is the fact that the septennial release is not "new prospective legislation" but actually goes back in principle to BC, where a cyclical "release" (שמטה) was declared *for the land*: "Six years you shall sow your land and gather its produce, but the seventh year you shall leave it fallow (ותשמטנה), that the poor of your people may eat…" (Exod 23:10–11). The stated purpose of that BC release was a concern for the poor. The Deuteronomic provision calls itself by the same title (שמטה) and incorporates the same concern for the poor (vv. 4–11). In other words, Deut 15 is not creating a new statutory cycle; it is merely updating an

---

87. M. Cohen, *Cultic Calendars*, 439.

88. Among the fixed prayers of the Babylonian *akītu* festival are petitions for Marduk to "Establish freedom for the citizens of Babylon!" and to "Grant release to your city, Babylon!" These prayers do not use technical terms of royal release edicts and must therefore be regarded as more generic in their intent. Nonetheless, they do indicate the expectation that the "determination of destiny" and ensuing "administrative re-ordering" at the culmination of the festival would in some manner secure real liberty to Babylon's citizens. See M. Cohen, *Cultic Calendars*, 442–43.

89. Westbrook, "Origins of Legislation," 219.

existing release-law cycle.[90] The Deuteronomic version of the release is *recast in terms of a royal debt release.* Deuteronomy states its reason for a septennial release thus: "At the end of seven years you shall make release...*for Yahweh's release has been proclaimed*" (vv. 1–2). Moshe Weinfeld has pointed out that, "In its content and stylistic structure, the commandment in Deuteronomy 15:2–3 is reminiscent of the Mesopotamian proclamations of *mīšarum*."[91] Through an extensive comparison with Ammiṣaduqa's *mīšarum* edict, Weinfeld shows the royal edict form of the Deut 15 release. This is generally recognized, and Deut 15 explicitly places this royal declaration on Yahweh's lips. Jeffrey Tigay appropriately writes, "Here it is God—Israel's divine king—who establishes remission."[92] This declaration is not a new piece of prospective regulation; it is an old BC cycle now re-shaped to include the Deuteronomic doctrine of Yahweh's kingship.

These observations establish the possibility (as an alternative to that of Westbrook) that Deut 15 was drafted as a cyclical debt release for theological reasons (not legislative reasons). Just as the BC fallow year was a religious cycle (rather than economic),[93] so its new formulation continues to be theological (rather than becoming a fixed, economic release edict). It may be part of the Deuteronomic concern to "reapply" BC within its own polemic. This possibility stands in contrast to the alternative proposed by Westbrook: that dissatisfaction with the king who failed to declare timely release edicts led, not only to the drafting of a statutory release cycle, *but to the invention of the idea of statute law.* If Westbrook's thesis is correct, Deut 15 marks an important intellectual revolution in Hebrew law. If the alternative just presented is correct, however, Deut 15 is not quite so innovative as Westbrook supposes. Its uniqueness from other ancient Near Eastern debt-release writings is not due to a new "intellectual revolution"; it is rather one of the many results of Israel incorporating its cultic rites into its law collections.

Fortunately, there is a release narrative in Jer 34 which references Deut 15. An examination of this law-practice narrative will help to determine

90. Chirichigno, *Debt-Slavery*, 263; Nelson, *Deuteronomy*, 194; McConville, *Deuteronomy*, 258–59; Craigie, *Deuteronomy*, 236; Christopher J. H. Wright, "What Happened Every Seven Years in Israel? Old Testament Sabbatical Institutions for Land, Debt and Slaves," *EvQ* 56 (1984): 132–38.

91. Weinfeld, *Social Justice*, 163–68.

92. Tigay, *Deuteronomy*, 146. Cf. Wright, "Every Seven Years," 132. Merrill sees a royal God theology behind each of the cyclical rites in Deut 14:22–16:17 (Merrill, *Deuteronomy*, 239–56).

93. Alt, *Essays*, 128–29.

between Westbrook's statutory view of Deut 15 and the alternative just constructed. It is in this law-practice evidence that one can discern how the Deuteronomic redactor of Jer 34 expected this law writing (Deut 15) to be used.

3. *Debt Release in Jeremiah 34*

It is a remarkable stroke of good fortune that a narrative text citing Deut 15 is available. Though layers of editing are suspected in the present form of the account, Jer 34 provides an important witness to how the provision in Deut 15 was understood by the Deuteronomic redactors. Jeremiah 34 is the account of Zedekiah's "proclamation of liberty" during the Babylonian siege:

> ...King Zedekiah made a covenant with all the people which were in Jerusalem to proclaim freedom (לקראדרור) to them, that each man should set his slave...free, so as not to enslave a Jew—a man his brother. And all the officials and all the people who entered into the covenant obeyed, each man setting his slave and each man his maidservant free, so as not to enslave them again. So they obeyed and set them free. But they turned around after that, and they took back the slaves...which they had set free... Then the word of Yahweh came to Jeremiah from Yahweh, saying, "Thus says Yahweh the God of Israel, I made a covenant with your fathers...saying, *'At the end of seven years, each man shall set free his Hebrew brother who was sold to you and served you six years, and you shall set him free from you [citing Deut 15].'* But your fathers did not listen to me and did not incline their ears. You recently turned and did what was right in my eyes, by proclaiming freedom (לקראדרור) each man to his fellow... Then you turned and defiled my name when you took back, each man his slave...which you had set free... (Jer 34:8–16)

Most scholars (including Westbrook) regard the Deuteronomy citation (vv. 13b–14) as a Deuteronomic gloss.[94] The original narrative reports the eighth-century prophet's rebuke of Judah's kings for their failure to aid the poor. Westbrook states: "By and large, the Israelite kings failed to institute such decrees. For this they are bitterly criticized by some of the

---

94. Nicholson, *Tradition*, 64; Winfried Theil, *Die deuteronomistische Redaktion von Jeremia 26–45: Mit einer Gesamtbeurteilung der deuteronomistischen Redaktion des Buches Jeremia* (WMANT 52; Neukirchen–Vluyn: Neukirchener Verlag, 1981), 38–43; Niels Peter Lemche, "The Manumission of Slaves—The Fallow Year—The Sabbatical Year—The Jobel Year," *VT* 26 (1976): 51–53; Westbrook, *Property*, 16 n. 4. Contra Helga Weippert, *Die prosareden des Jeremiabuches* (BZAW 132; Berlin: de Gruyter, 1973), 86–106; Jack R. Lundbom, *Jeremiah 21–36: A New Translation with Introduction and Commentary* (AB 21B; New York: Doubleday, 2004), 561.

prophets, such as Jeremiah."[95] The Jeremiah narrative was later adapted (under the Deuteronomic pen) to include reference to the Deut 15 release law as the expected norm for such proclamations.

All this can be accepted, and shows the practical implications (even for the king) which the Deuteronomic school expected the law writings to have. The mere presence of the Deuteronomy citation as a standard for measuring the king's conduct is an indication of the "new attitude" toward law writings within the Deuteronomic school already seen in Patrick's evidence. However, Westbrook goes beyond such a recognition of Deuteronomy's importance as a descriptive paradigm; Westbrook sees in this text his postulated "coup" that removed the power of debt release from the king. Even as edited under the Deuteronomic pen, however, Jer 34 does not support this supposition. An examination of this account reveals the following problems with positing the idea of "legislation" to the use of Deut 15 here:

a.   The Deuteronomic editor freely changes the provision in the way he cites it. He actually "mixes" two laws into one: the *timing* of the Deut 15:1–11 *debt* release, and the *subjects* of the Deut 15:12–18 *slave* release.[96] It is only *debt* release which the Deuteronomic cycle envisions "at the end of *seven* years" (15:1). The provision actually goes on to indicate that, despite a cyclical debt release, debt-*slaves* are still expected to fulfill an entire *six* year's service (15:12–18). In Jer 34, the cyclical expectation of the debt-release law is quoted, but made to refer to the manumission law: "At the end of seven years [Deut 15:1] each man shall set free his Hebrew brother who was sold to you... [Deut 15:12]" (Jer 34:14). Some scholars perceive even further sources here integrated: Helga Weippert suspects the use of דרור in the context derives from the Leviticus version of the release laws (Lev 25:10) since Deuteronomy only uses the expression שמטה;[97] and Gerald Keown points to Exod 21:2 for the exclusively male reference in the citation (אחיו העברי, Jer 34:14), since it varies

95.   Raymond Westbrook, review of Moshe Weinfeld, *Justice and Righteousness in Israel and the Nations: Equality and Freedom in Ancient Israel in the Light of Social Justice in the Ancient Near East*, *RB* 93 (1986): 605.

96.   Lundbom, *Jeremiah 21–36*, 560–61; Robert P. Carroll, *Jeremiah: A Commentary* (OTL; London: SCM Press, 1986), 648–49; Westbrook, *Property*, 16–17 n. 4.

97.   Weippert, *Jeremiabuches*, 91. Cf. William L. Holladay, *Jeremiah 2: A Commentary on the Book of the Prophet Jeremiah Chapters 26–52* (Hermenia; Minneapolis: Fortress, 1989), 238; Lemche, "Sabbatical Year," 52.

from Deuteronomy's inclusion of women (העבריה, Deut 15:12).[98] These other choices may be regarded as stylistic.[99] However, the confusing of Deut 15:1 and 12 substantially changes the release law. Jeremiah 34 presents the release law as a cyclical release of slaves—*something Deut 15 as written actually explicitly avoids.*[100] The Deuteronomic glossator, though desiring to measure Zedekiah in terms of Deut 15, does not seem to have felt compelled to make this measurement according to the terms of his law text as written.[101] He is only concerned with the ideal that slaves are to be duly released in Yahweh's kingdom.

b.   There is a further problem which arises from the way Deut 15 has been adapted. The resulting amalgam of debt/slave release laws creates a confusion about timing. As cited in Jer 34, the release law reads: "At the *end of seven years* each man shall set free his Hebrew brother who…served you *six years*" (Jer 34:14). Are debt-slaves to be released at the end of seven years, or at the end of six years? The former timing derives from the Deuteronomic debt-release cycle; the latter from the slave-release law. As incorporated together here, a contradiction results.[102] Either the redactor has been careless, or else he is not really concerned about the accurate timings of the release laws cited. He does not expect the law writing to define precisely when release proclamations are made. It is the principle *that* slaves (specifically, "your brother Hebrews"[103]) be released at appropriate intervals that is in view.

c.   Not only is the law citation internally inconsistent (at least verbally), it also does not actually say anything about the "crime" of Zedekiah. As Niels Peter Lemche has noted, "the quotation from the law referred to in v.14, does not correspond to the contents of the royal edict."[104] The manumission declared by Zedekiah

98.   Keown et al., eds, *Jeremiah 26–52*, 188–89.

99.   E.g. the דרר word-play in v. 17, and the inclusion of women already in vv. 9–11.

100.   See n. 79, above.

101.   Charles L. Feinberg, *Jeremiah: A Commentary* (Grand Rapids: Zondervan, 1982), 240–41.

102.   While the MT reading retains the contradictory "seven" and "six," the LXX version of Jer 41:14 gives "six" in both instances. The LXX reading is certainly an early effort to correct the contradiction which was original.

103.   Note the repeated emphasis on the *brotherhood* principle in Deut 15:2, 12; Jer 34:9, 14; Neh 5:7–8.

104.   Lemche, "Sabbatical Year," 51–52.

in the narrative was a universal release proclaimed *during a social emergency* (the Babylonian seige). The cited law (at least as it is cited) concerns the release of slaves *at certain calendar years*.[105] The Deuteronomic law is a "statutory mismatch" for the actual circumstances it was cited to critique. Either the Deuteronomic glossator failed to notice this incongruity, or (more likely) the citation is being used to illustrate a principle of righteous government. It is not appealed to as a prescription for when and how releases ought to occur.

d.   Finally (and perhaps most importantly for evaluating Westbrook's hypothesis), nowhere in the Jeremiah narrative is the king's authority to pronounce release edicts replaced or constrained. No other institution is expected to enforce the release law. Nor is the king himself called to pronounce releases according to a certain, codified schedule. Rather, the king is still upheld as the one who holds authority to pronounce release proclamations (vv. 8–10). He is, in fact, commended by Yahweh for having independently determined the circumstances warranting a release (v. 15). The only thing for which Zedekiah is rebuked is his going back on his דרור proclamation (v. 16). If the Deuteronomic editor intended "to replace the untrustworthy royal prerogative" with a written statute,[106] he has not revealed that expectation here. There is nothing actually in the text to demonstrate this intent: Westbrook supposes a "political coup" that is not expressed.

In light of these observations, Westbrook's explanation for the Deut 15 debt-release cycle must be regarded as doubtful. There is no evidence to support his supposition that the Deuteronomic writers desired to replace the royal prerogative with a statutory debt release. On the contrary, the evidence points more strongly toward the alternative: that Deut 15 is part of a cultic presentation of Yahweh's royalty. This conclusion, it has already been seen, is supported by the release law's placement within a series of cultic cycles. Furthermore, it has now been seen that

---

105.   Nahum M. Sarna ("Zedekiah's Emancipation of Slaves and the Sabbatical Year," in *Orient and Occident: Essays Presented to Cyrus H. Gordon on the Occasion of his Sixty-Fifth Birthday* [ed. Harry Hoffner; AOAT 22; Neukirchen–Vluyn: Neukirchener Verlag, 1973], 143–49) has suggested that Zedekiah's edict was during a sabbath year, but others have shown the improbability (if not impossibility) of this (W. Holladay, *Jeremiah*, 2:239; Westbrook, *Property*, 16–17 n. 4). Moreover, even if Zedekiah's release was during a sabbath year, it remains a problem that the Deuteronomic *debt* release was septennial but not the *slave* release.

106.   Westbrook, *Property*, 16.

the Zedekiah practice narrative employs Deut 15 as a religious/ethical exemplar, but not a legislative norm.[107] This practice narrative shows that the Deuteronomy text's influence on debt release is theological not statutory, and that the authority to proclaim actual release edicts *remains* in the hands of the king (Jer 34:8, 15).[108]

These points do not undermine the accuracy of the facts Westbrook has brought to light (especially the uniqueness of the prospective debt release in Deuteronomy). They do, however, call for a less ambitious conclusion. It ought not be supposed that Deuteronomic scribes invented the idea of written legislation as a replacement for kings. The "intermediate stage" represented by the Deuteronomic law looks like an enhanced juridical treatise (even kings are taught by it), but law writings are not yet perceived as *being* "the law." This conclusion is not completely at variance with Westbrook (or Patrick), but it is significantly less ambitious.

4. *Debt Release in Solonic Athens*
One final aspect of Westbrook's argument for legislative thinking in the Deuteronomic literature is his proposed source for such innovative uses of law writings: namely, Solonic Athens.[109] Operating on the assumption that the Deuteronomic school does originate with the Josianic reforms (seventh century), Westbrook cites legal developments taking place "at the same time in Athens."[110] Prescriptive ideas of written law are known to have emerged in Greece. "If Aristotle is to be believed," writes Westbrook, "a similar process took place a little later in the case of Solon,[111] whose most famous measure was his *seisachtheia*, a retrospective cancellation of debts and debt-slavery on the universal Near Eastern pattern, but who in addition, '...made the people free both at the time and *for the future* by prohibiting loans secured on the person'..."[112]

---

107. The law book is employed here in a manner similar to that already seen in connection with Josiah's reign. Josiah *made and kept* a Deuteronomy-based covenant with all the people and was thereby shown to be a righteous king. Zedekiah is, on the contrary, shown to make a Deuteronomy-based covenant with all the people *and break it*—thereby showing himself to be an unrighteous king.

108. Cf. Tigay, *Deuteronomy*, 145.

109. See pp. 18–23, above.

110. Westbrook, "Origins of Legislation," 220.

111. Bernard Jackson ("Modelling Biblical Law: The Covenant Code," *Chicago-Kent Law Review* 70 [1995]: 1757) notes the timing problem of Westbrook's argument: Josiah is seventh century; Solon is sixth century. Would it be more reasonable to suppose that Solon borrowed from Josiah?

112. Westbrook, "Origins of Legislation," 220 n. 73, quoting Aristotle, *Ath. pol.* 6.1 (emphasis Westbrook's).

Collections, Codes, and Torah

In one of his early articulations of this point, Westbrook seems to suggest a common legal evolution was occurring in Judah and Greece, so that this concrete Greek evidence might explain developments in Judah without actual contact between them.[113] More recently, however, he has suggested actual contact (diffusion) behind Greco-Judean legal developments.[114] Thus far, however, no evidence of such contact has been produced.[115]

III. *Deuteronomic Attitudes toward Law Writings*

In the foregoing dialog with Patrick and Westbrook, significant evidence for a "new attitude" towards law writing has been identified. Within the Deuteronomic literature, there is what might be regarded as a "new" or at least "heightened" concern for the law writings *as a paradigm of righteousness even for kings.* This does seem to be a development beyond the *popular* education uses previously ascribed to the law writings. In this sense, these other scholars are correct to note new law-writing attitudes in connection with the Deuteronomic school. In fact, this development can be defined even more precisely. A trio of texts from Deuteronomy and Joshua will next be examined in order to further elucidate the nature of Deuteronomic attitudes toward law writings. In these texts, it will be seen that this "official" interest in law writings within the Deuteronomic heritage is not flat; there is development even between Deuteronomy and DtrH in the nature of this royal law book esteem.

1. *Deuteronomy 17:18–20*
It was seen in the previous chapter that Deuteronomy participates in the expectation of *oracular* source law. Immediately following a Deuteronomic description of an oracular high court (17:8–13), Deuteronomy offers its ideal for kingship (vv. 14–20). Israel is granted permission, upon possessing the land, to set up a king "like all the nations that are around" (v. 14). There are, however, five ways in which the Hebrew king

113. "This is not the forum in which to discuss the vexed question of cultural connections between the Ancient Near East and pre-classical Greece. Suffice it to say that from the Near Eastern perspective, early legal sources like Drakon's law...are immediately recognizable as the culmination of a two thousand year-old tradition..." (Westbrook, "Origins of Legislation," 220 n. 74).
114. Westbrook, "Covenant Code," 28: "The later biblical codes—the Deuteronomic and Priestly codes—share something of the intellectual ferment of contemporary Greek sources and thus some taste of their new legal conceptions."
115. Van Seters, *Diaspora*, 43–44.

must *not* be like the kings of surrounding nations: he must be a native Israelite (v. 15); he must not multiply horses for himself (v. 16); he must not accumulate numerous wives (v. 17a); he must not amass "excessive silver and gold" (v. 17b); and finally, he must "write for himself a copy of this law in a book, from before the Levitical priests. So it shall be with him, and he shall read from it all the days of his life" (vv. 18–19). The stated purpose for this final provision is "that he will learn to fear Yahweh his God by keeping all the words of this law and these statutes and doing them, so as not to lift up his heart above his brothers nor turn from the commandments, right or left…" (Deut 17:19–20).

As the only (explicit) passage in Deuteronomy about Israel's king, this text has attracted extensive interest. Most commentators recognize that its emphasis is on making the king *like* his brothers rather than exalted above them—"the model Israelite."[116] Some commentators have seen the absence of normal regal functions as a Deuteronomic attempt to neutralize the king completely.[117] Such a conclusion is reading too much out of silence, however; it presupposes a legalistic reading of the text (i.e. that those duties not mentioned are presumed not to exist). Actually, the text *does* state that Israel's king would be "like [the kings of] all the nations that are around" (v. 14). The Deuteronomic king is explicitly a typical ancient Near Eastern king, with only five exceptions. (Indeed, that the king is instructed not to multiply horses, wives, and money would imply that this king is still Israel's military commander, dynastic/diplomatic head, and tax administrator.)

It is the last of the five exceptions on the Deuteronomic king—that he is to copy and daily read the law book—which is of particular interest here. "Writing is often associated with royal figures in the ancient Near East," Jean-Pierre Sonnet observes, before going on to state that "The recourse to writing by royal rulers reportedly extended to the publication or recording of legal stipulations, as in Hammurapi's Code; 'I wrote my precious words on my stela,' the king five times boasts in the epilogue to the code…"[118] It is not remarkable to find the Deuteronomic king writing (copying) laws. What is unusual is that this king is writing laws *for*

---

116. E.g. Sonnet, *Book Within the Book*, 71, 78; McConville, *Deuteronomy*, 295–96; Nelson, *Deuteronomy*, 222–25; Norbert Lohfink, "Distribution of the Functions of Power: The Laws Concerning Public Offices in Deuteronomy 16:18–18:22," in Christensen, ed., *Song of Power*, 349; Gerald E. Gerbrandt, *Kingship According to the Deuteronomistic History* (SBLDS 87; Atlanta: Scholars Press, 1986), 112.

117. E.g. Levinson, "Kingship," 522; idem, *Legal Innovation*, 138–43; Knoppers, "Rethinking the Relationship," 393–415.

118. Sonnet, *Book within the Book*, 72–73.

himself. He himself is the recipient of the law book he writes out: "the Torah 'book''s arch-reader," per Sonnet.[119]

There are instances in the wider ancient Near East of wisdom texts intended for the instruction of princes.[120] Also, Hammurabi expected subsequent rulers to read his law compilation: "May any king who will appear in the land in the future, at any time, observe the pronouncements of justice that I inscribed upon my stela..." (LH 48.59–49.17). Nowhere in the ancient Near Eastern materials, however, is there an instance of a king enjoined to write out a law book for himself (and one which contains limiting instructions on his own reign).[121] He who in other nations is chief law *teacher*, has for Israel become the first law *student*. Like the preceding four stipulations, the book-reading stipulation is intended to make Israel's king "like his brothers" (vv. 19–20; cf. 6:6–9; 11:18–21).

In other words, study of the law book is (for Deuteronomy) a *non-kingly* activity. This is so much the case that calling the king to daily law-book study is expected to keep him on a peer level with the general public in the land.

2. *Joshua 1:8*

The book of Joshua opens with another instruction to study "the book of the law"—an instruction undoubtedly modeled from the Deut 17 passage just discussed.[122] Its use in this instance is remarkably different, however. In Deut 17, law-book study was presented as a means for keeping the king equal with his brothers; Josh 1:8, however, emphasizes the law book's potential to exalt Joshua as leader of the Israelites above his brethren.

It has been popular to regard the opening chapter of Joshua as an "Installation Formula," establishing Joshua as Israel's leader in matters of peace and war.[123] Moshe Weinfeld, and more recently Lori Rowlett,

119. Ibid., 78.

120. E.g. Ashurbanipal's *Advice to a Prince* (translation from W. G. Lambert, *Babylonian Wisdom Literature* [Oxford: Clarendon, 1960], 113–15).

121. Sonnet, *Book within the Book*, 78.

122. John Gray, *Joshua, Judges, Ruth* (NCBC; Grand Rapids: Eerdmans, 1986), 60; Lori L. Rowlett, *Joshua and the Rhetoric of Violence: A New Historicist Analysis* (JSOTSup 226; Sheffield: Sheffield Academic Press, 1996), 137–41.

123. Norbert Lohfink, "Die deuteronomistische Darstellung des Übergangs der Fëhrung Israels von Moses auf Josue: Ein Beitrag zur alttestamentliche Theologie des Amtes," *Schol* 37 (1962): 32–44; J. Roy Porter, "The Succession of Joshua," in *Proclamation and Presence: Old Testament Essays in Honour of Gwynne Henton Davies* (ed. John I. Durham and J. Roy Porter; London: SCM Press, 1970), 102–32; Dennis J. McCarthy, "An Installation Genre?," *JBL* 90 (1971): 31–41.

have defined the passage as more precisely a "War Oracle" (focusing only on Joshua's call to lead Israel in war).[124] In any case,[125] there is a clear focus on Moses' leadership in the passage, and on Joshua as his rightful successor.[126] It is an account justifying his installation to rule.

In this account, Joshua is introduced as "the servant of Moses" (Josh 1:1), Moses himself having been Yahweh's "servant" (v. 2). It is because Joshua was Moses' servant that he is now the one to "arise" and lead the people after Moses' death (v. 2). God will give Joshua the land "just as I promised to Moses" (v. 3). As Yahweh "was with Moses, so I will be with you" (v. 5). Later in the passage, Joshua's first command as the new leader of the people is introduced as an explicit continuation of Moses' program: "Remember the word that Moses the servant of Yahweh commanded you..." (v. 13). Joshua recounts the Mosaic "plan of entry" which Joshua now purposes to continue (cf. vv. 13–15/Deut 3:18–22). It is "the land that Moses the servant of Yahweh gave you" (v. 15) that Joshua promises to confirm to the trans-Jordan tribes. Finally, the people respond by accepting Joshua as the legitimate heir to Moses: "Just as we obeyed Moses in all things, so we will obey you. Only may Yahweh your God be with you, as he was with Moses!" (v. 17). There is an extensive effort in this chapter to introduce Joshua as Moses' rightful successor and the one to see through the settlement envisioned by him.

It is within this identification of Joshua with Moses that the law book is assigned to Joshua's attention:

> Only be strong and very courageous, being careful to do *according to all the law that Moses my servant commanded you*. Do not turn from it to the right or the left, that you may have good success wherever you go. *This book of the law* shall not depart from your mouth, but you shall meditate in it day and night, that you may be careful to do according to all that is written in it. For then you will make your way prosperous, and then you will have good success. (Josh 1:7–8)

Most commentators regard these verses as a late insertion.[127] This presentation of the law book may reflect the ideals of a later stage in the Deuteronomic school. There is, in any case, a difference in this instruction's

124. Weinfeld, *Deuteronomic School*, 45 n. 5; Rowlett, *Rhetoric of Violence*, 122–37.

125. Butler denies the presence of any form in Josh 1 (Trent C. Butler, *Joshua* [WBC 7; Waco, Tex.: Word, 1983], 6).

126. Ibid., 13.

127. Robert G. Boling (*Joshua: A New Translation and Commentary* [AB 6; Garden City, N.Y.: Doubleday, 1988], 124) regards vv. 7–8 as original. For a critique of Boling and a discussion of the majority arguments for its later insertion, see Rowlett, *Rhetoric of Violence*, 137–41.

function here from its function in Deut 17. Rather than making a ruler equal to his fellow Israelites, daily law-book reading is now presented as that which sets Joshua apart as Moses-like and kingly. This being the case, an examination of the text shows that the nature of this further development still falls short of making the law book a prescriptive "constitution."

a. First of all, the repeated, second person singular verbs and pronouns affirm that the law book is being assigned for Joshua's personal edification:

> ...be strong and very courageous (חזק ואמץ)...
> ...all the law that Moses my servant commanded you (צוך).
> ...do not turn (אל־תסור) from it...
> ...that you may have good success (תשכיל) wherever you go (תלך).
> ...this book of the law shall not depart from your mouth (מפיך)...
> ...and you shall meditate (והגית) in it day and night...
> ...that you may be careful to do (תשמר לעשות) according to all that is written in it.
> ...then you will make your way prosperous (תצליח את־דרכך)...
> ...then you will have good success (תשכיל). (vv. 7–8)

The assignment of the law book is to Joshua individually, not to "the government" (e.g. elders and priests) as a whole.[128] It is for ensuring the effectiveness of his own way, not the way and arrangement of the nation, that Joshua studies this law book. Even though the *connotation* of law book study is different here from Deut 17, the *nature* of the practice (*personal* edification) is consistent.

b. Second, confirming and expanding on the above, the stated purpose of Joshua's book study is for his "effectiveness" (תצליח) and "insight" or "success" (תשכיל)—statements of a markedly sapiential character.[129] These expressions do not suggest the use of this book as prescriptions for governance, but rather instructions for wise leadership. The similarity between Josh 1:8 and Ps 1:3 (another Deut 17:18 parallel) is well-known and suggestive.[130] Psalm 1:3 promotes "meditation on the law of Yahweh" as bringing effectiveness to *any* Israelite (i.e. the אשרי־האיש of Ps 1:1). In the Joshua parallel, *the commander of Israel* is expected to find his powers of insight and effectiveness enhanced by regular contemplation in this text. That Joshua's effectiveness

128. Cf. the discussion of Josh 23:6, below.
129. Boling, *Joshua*, 125.
130. J. H. Eaton, *Psalms of the Way and the Kingdom: A Conference with the Commentators* (JSOTSup 199; Sheffield: Sheffield Academic Press, 1995), 19, 22, 26, 129.

in his vocation (דרכך תשכיל, v. 8) has ramifications for all Israel
is the obvious reason why his law-book study is particularly
important. Nevertheless, there is nothing in the text that distin-
guishes Joshua's use of the law book as a code of governance. It
seems rather to be a source of wisdom for Joshua.[131]

c.   Finally, it remains the words of Joshua (not the words of the
      book) to which the nation is subjected, and by which the dis-
      obedient are judged: "Then they answered Joshua, 'All that you
      have commanded us we will do, and wherever you send us we
      will go. Just as we obeyed Moses in all things, so we will obey
      you... Any man who rebels against your commandment and dis-
      obeys your words, whatever you command him, shall be put to
      death'..." (vv. 16–18).

There does seem to be a distinction between the use of the law book
in Josh 1 from its use in Deut 17. In the present text, the law book is
envisioned as a document which lends authority to the leader. In the
formerly examined text, the law book contributed to the "commonness"
of the leader. Nonetheless, it would be overstating the evidence to
identify this development with a prescriptive use of the law book.

3. *Joshua 23:6*
A third text which needs attention appears at the close of Joshua and is
closely related to the previous text.[132] In Josh 23:6, it is Joshua (rather
than Yahweh) who extols the law book. He assembles "all Israel, its
elders and heads, its judges and officers," and exhorts them "to do all that
is written in the book of the law of Moses, turning aside from it neither
to the right nor the left" (vv. 2, 6).[133] The nature of this exhortation,
however, again lacks connection with court regulation or government
administration:

a.   This law book fidelity is summarized as "clinging to" (דבק) Yah-
      weh and "loving" (אהב) him (vv. 8, 11)—"two verbs which are
      not at all legalistic."[134] This may admittedly be due to the sermonic

131.   Some scholars emphasize the martial nature of this passage to the exclusion of civil responsibilities being in view; see, e.g., Rowlett, *Rhetoric of Violence*,
125–26.

132.   On the connections between 1:6–9 and 23:6, see Boling, *Joshua*, 523–24.

133.   Here is one text overlooked by Jackson (pp. 37–38, above) where judges
are charged to observe the law book. This exception does not undermine Jackson's
basic conclusions, however: the nature of this official attention to the law book in
Josh 23 (as here shown) is not prescribing jurisprudence.

134.   E. John Hamlin, *Inheriting the Land: A Commentary on the Book of Joshua*
(ITC; Grand Rapids: Eerdmans, 1983), 187.

nature of the charge. However, it may just as readily (as the following points would seem to confirm) reflect the sermonic use presupposed for the law book itself.

b.   The prohibitions which are specified in connection with the law book (in vv. 7–13) are those of strict separation from the communities of the land rather than regulations for the community of Israel: "that you may not mix with these nations remaining among you (v. 7)."[135] Trent Butler observes: "The major concern of the Deuteronomic law is now [beginning in v. 7] summarized. Israel's identity hangs on her uniqueness… She must avoid all contact with the nations in order to avoid all temptation from their gods… Israel must do everything in her power to avoid losing her unique identity…"[136] It is not internal regulation, but international non-relation, which is the purpose attached to the law book.[137] The appearance given is that of a textbook on holy war rather than a constitution of state.

c.   Most significantly, it is upon Joshua's abdication of government (not his organizing of it) that he commends this book to Israel's tribal leaders. It is not in his execution of government that Joshua so uses the law book, but in his stepping down from leadership. The Deuteronomic transfer of the law book to Joshua at the beginning of his leadership (1:8), and its transfer at the end of Joshua's rule to the tribal leaders (and that in the absence of a single successor) confirms what was earlier noted. The law book ascribed in Deut 17 to make the king "more like" his brothers has in DtrH become a symbol distinguishing leadership.

This last point is not only discernible within the book of Joshua; subsequent succession narratives in DtrH likewise involve a frequent exhortation to observe the Mosaic law book.[138] Concurrent with this rising

135.   Hamlin (*Inheriting the Land*, 183–85) identifies "four temptations" of mixing with the Canaanites which "show a progression in terms of the degree of subjection" to their gods.

136.   Butler, *Joshua*, 255–56.

137.   Hamlin maintains that the prominence of international concerns in this chapter as tied to the seven-fold use of גוים: "The word 'nations' (Heb. *goyim*) appears seven times in Joshua 23, and nowhere else in the entire book… The sevenfold occurrence of this word corresponds to the two lists of seven 'nations' at the beginning (3:10) and end (24:11) of the Joshua story" (Hamlin, *Inheriting the Land*, 180).

138.   1 Kgs 2:3; 2 Kgs 11:12; 14:6; 22:8, 11–13, 16; 23:3, 21, 24. Cf. 1 Chr 16:40; 2 Chr 17:9; 23:11, 18; 25:4; 31:3; 34:14–15, 21, 24, 30–31; 35:26.

"official" importance of the law book, the evidence of legal *practice* texts in DtrH confirms the absence of prescriptive operation for those law writings.[139]

IV. *Conclusions*

In this chapter, the Deuteronomic attitude toward law writings has been considered. This has been pursued in particular dialog with the evidence produced by Patrick and Westbrook, and has been supplemented with a further review of law book texts in Deuteronomy and DtrH. It has been seen that Patrick and Westbrook are correct in their perception of a "new attitude" between earlier uses of law writings and that evinced in the Deuteronomic literature. However, it is anticipating the eventual result of prescriptivism—reading it into the evidence too early—to ascribe these Deuteronomic developments as "incipient statutes" or "true prospective legislation." Rather, the Deuteronomic materials show that the practice of law writing, once employed for *popular* education, is now also employed for guiding (and measuring) national officials in their loyalty to the ancient religion.[140]

In fact, one of the most important developments of the Deuteronomic school was the production of a particular law book (Deuteronomy) as an ideal compilation of Mosaic paradigms. As LH was to become the pre-eminent compendium on justice (revered and studied for over a millennium) in the Mesopotamian sphere, the book of Deuteronomy was to gain prominence as Israel's ideal treatise on religious fidelity and social justice.

The Deuteronomic tradition evinces important developments in the Hebrew view of law writings, and in the identification of one particular law book (Deuteronomy restating BC for a new day) as ideal. Nonetheless, the uses of written law in DtrH are still essentially descriptive (sapiential and symbolic), rather than prescriptive (where the text *is* "the law").

139. Cf. pp. 59–63, above.
140. This development might be compared to Westbrook's "juridical treatise" idea (see pp. 12–15, 32–34, above), although here the law book is being used as a *cultic*, rather than juridical, treatise.

Chapter 4

WRITTEN LAW IN PERSIAN-ERA YEHUD

It is not surprising to find scholars connecting prescriptivism with the reforms of Ezra and Nehemiah. Whereas the Deuteronomic literature esteems the law book in general terms, the Ezra–Nehemiah account cites the law book in reference to a whole series of specific measures.[1]

Raymond Westbrook perceives the "full bloom" of statutory law in Ezra–Nehemiah. As seen in the previous chapter, Westbrook places the genesis of legislative thinking in the Deuteronomic school. It is Ezra, however, whom Westbrook sees as making this new way of using law writings the community norm:

> Described as a priest and a "scribe skilled in the torah of Moses," he may be credited with laying the jurisprudential foundations of Jewish Law as we understand it today. For he and his fellow priests read "from the book, from the torah of God, with interpretation" before the assembled people (Neh. 8:1–8). Thus the legal system became based upon the idea of a written code of law interpreted and applied by religious authorities.[2]

In Westbrook's view: Deuteronomic scribes first devised the potential for employing law writings as statutes, and this innovation achieved general currency under Ezra's "legal experts." But does the fact that Ezra wanted the people to understand the law book mean that he expected it to provide statutory rulings? To state the alternative: Could this not be a further instance of Israel's law book being employed after, what Westbrook calls, "the Mesopotamian concept of a law code as a pedagogical tool"?[3] Ezra's citations clearly show that the law book has been accepted

1. Most scholars regard Ezra–Nehemiah as a single corpus (although distinct sources can be discerned). For helpful discussion of this scholarship, see Michael W. Duggan, *The Covenant Renewal in Ezra–Nehemiah (Neh 7:72b–10:40): An Exegetical, Literary, and Theological Study* (SBLDS 164; Atlanta: Society of Biblical Literature, 2001), 30–37.

2. Westbrook, "Biblical Law," 3–4.

3. Ibid., 7. Cf. Hammurabi's desire for the lay person to understand his stele: LH 48.3–19.

as a *practical* text. It would need to be determined whether the law book is cited as statutory (i.e. stipulations to be enforced) or as an academic ideal (i.e. legal/cultic wisdom).[4] Westbrook and others have persuasively shown that the *absence* of law-text citations in practice-records shows a lack of practical use, and thus the absence of prescriptivism (being one kind of practical use). The *presence* of citation therefore indicates practical use of the law text. It would need still to be determined whether that practical use is prescriptive (i.e. implementation of written stipulations) or descriptive (e.g. didactic). Westbrook has not offered such an examination of the Ezra–Nehemiah use of the law book.

Bernard Jackson also sees prescriptivism emerging in Ezra–Nehemiah. He points to the integration of didactic and ritual uses of the law book in the public assembly recounted in Neh 8:7–8. In that passage, Ezra combines "the traditional ritual reading" of the law book "with a didactic function." The text is not only read, but explained. This public reading is followed by a gathering of "specialists" for further study (8:13). "It is in this context," Jackson writes, "that we should locate the transformation of the biblical legal collections into 'statutory' texts, binding upon the courts and subject to verbal interpretation."[5] Jackson supports this deduction through several further points. He appeals, on the one hand, to Peter Frei's theory of "imperial authorization." According to Frei (whose theory will be discussed, shortly), Persia ratified the Torah as a legislative code for Yehud. Jackson cites Frei's theory affirmatively. Jackson also suggests that the ascription of Israel's law collections to the eternal God (rather than a temporal king, which was lacking in the post-exilic period) could explain "the emergence of the idea of enduring law in ancient Israel."[6] For Jackson, therefore, it is the connection of the Pentateuch law writings with Yahweh that made them an *enduring* ideal, while Frei's "imperial authorization" led to their *legislative* use. The Neh. 8 narrative shows the result: Ezra's legalistic attention to the Torah.

But does Neh 8—or the other law-book applications in Ezra–Nehemiah —actually reveal "the transformation of the biblical legal collections into 'statutory' texts, binding upon the courts and subject to verbal interpretation"? Something is happening in Ezra–Nehemiah's exalted view of the law book, but Jackson stops short of testing his hypothesis about the nature of the law book in Ezra–Nehemiah.

4.   Westbrook ("Law Codes," 253–58; "Origins of Legislation," 202; *Studies*, 2–5) has emphasized the practical import of law writings when employed as reference works, without thereby making them legislation.
5.   Jackson, *Studies*, 141–42; cf. his "'Law' and 'Justice,' " 222; "Modelling Law," 1763.
6.   Jackson, *Studies*, 162.

Frei's theory of "imperial authorization" has often been cited in relation to the present question.[7] In his study, Frei compiled evidence for
Achaemenid involvement in the law compositions of subject peoples as
wide-ranging as Egypt and Asia Minor. From this evidence, he posited a
standard Persian practice of imperially endorsing local norms: "The legal
norms of a local body...were elevated to the status of imperial legislation."[8] For Frei, Ezra 7:26 indicates imperial authorization of Ezra's
Torah, where Torah is (in Frei's reading) called at once both "the law of
your God" and "the law of the king."[9] Frei's argument is simply to suggest a way in which the Pentateuch was formed (and gained hegemony)
as the Jewish law book. However, other scholars (such as Jackson, noted
above) have picked up on Frei's thesis as a possible explanation for how
Israel's law writing ("the [custom] law of your God") might have
actually become a legislative code ("the [statute] law of the [Persian]
king"). Frank Crüsemann cites Frei for this conclusion: "There was a
policy of the Persian empire...which sanctioned local law through the
empire, recognizing it as binding... Thus the traditional law of the God
of Israel, simultaneously became the [statutory] law of the Persian
empire for the Jews."[10]

Whether Persia had such a policy, and whether the integration of
various traditions into one Torah was instigated by Persian initiative, is
not of concern here.[11] Even if such a policy did exist, it remains doubtful
that this mechanism would make Torah legislative. Persia itself did not
have a prescriptive law code. In his Behistun inscription, Darius I boasts
of his faithfulness to uphold *dāta* (i.e. law). However, his *dāta* is the just
order of society—a justice which is clearly identified with his own *ad
hoc* rulings—not a written code.[12] In other words, Persia does not seem

7. Peter Frei and Klaus Koch, *Reichsidee und Reichsorganisation im Perserreich*
(OBO 55; Freiburg: Universitätsverlag, 1984); Frei, "Die persische Reichsautorisa-
tion."
8. Frei, "Persian Authorization," 38.
9. Ibid., 11–12; on Nehemiah's authorization, see pp. 13–15.
10. Crüsemann, *The Torah*, 336–37. Cf. Jackson, *Studies*, 142; David M. Carr,
Reading the Fractures of Genesis: Historical and Literary Approaches (Louisville,
Ky.: Westminster John Knox, 1996), 327–33; Rainer Albertz, *A History of Israelite
Religion in the Old Testament Period* (trans. John Bowden; 2 vols.; OTL; Louisville,
Ky.: Westminster John Knox, 1994), 2:446–49; Jon L. Berquist, *Judaism in Persia's
Shadow: A Social and Historical Approach* (Minneapolis: Fortress, 1995), 137–39.
11. Frei's thesis (though initially influential) has come under criticism, as recently
in Watts, *Persia and Torah*.
12. L. W. King and R. C. Thompson, *The Sculptures and Inscription of Darius
the Great on the Rock of Behistûn in Persia: A New Collation of the Persian, Susian,*

to have had an imperial statute book. In fact, in the well-documented polemics of ancient Greece and Persia, Persia's lack of prescriptive law was one of the prominent reasons Greece regarded Persia as "barbarian."[13] As participants in the ancient Near Eastern "rule of kings" (and not "rule of written law"), it would be remarkable to find Persia introducing statutory law on its subject territories.

Excursus: The Law of the Medes and Persians

Scholars sometimes point to the "law of the Medes and Persians which cannot be revoked" (Dan 6:8; cf. Esth 1:19; 8:8) to illustrate a supposed Persian penchant for writing statutory law (Jackson, *Studies*, 142–43; Westbrook, "Codification," 43; Crüsemann, *The Torah*, 349–50; Carr, *Reading the Fractures*, 329; Frei, "Persian Authorization," 30–31). However, these "injunctions" are more like royal edicts or court verdicts (addressing specific, present cases); they are not legislation. Three instances are relevant.

(1) *Esther 1:10–22.* In Esth 1, it is the banishment of Queen Vashti (for disobeying King Ahasuerus) that is written up "among the laws of the Medes and Persians." Notably, Ahasuerus issued this decree in response to a law (he was not drafting a law). It was after consulting with wise men to determine what extant custom law *already had to say* (v. 15) about Vashti's disobedience that Ahasuerus gave his verdict to enforce that law. Furthermore, the verdict itself was pronounced *orally*. The purpose for its further *inscription* was not to make it binding upon Vashti—the oral verdict was sufficient for that. The verdict was written in order to publish it *for its propagandistic value*—that other women in the kingdom might learn to revere their husbands (vv. 17–19, 22). The "law of the Medes and the Persians" looks more like a publicly inscribed collection of court verdicts than a source of law.

(2) *Esther 3:1–15.* The written edict of Ahasuerus appointing the destruction of the Jews (Esth 3:1–15) is also presented as a judicial verdict. It is not statutory law. In this pericope, the Jews (epitomized by Mordecai; v. 5) are summarily charged with rebellion: "they do not keep the king's laws" (v. 8). Ahasuerus is therefore led to render a judgment against the whole race. Once again, Ahasuerus is enforcing already extant laws by his judgment; he is not creating law. This verdict is written down to facilitate its widespread enforcement (as is known to have been done with ancient Near Eastern edicts). In the further unfolding of the account, Esther appealed Ahasuerus' judgment against her race and succeeded in turning his heart. Notwithstanding his change in heart, the inscribed verdict "cannot be revoked" (8:8). Another

and Babylonian Texts, with English Translations, Etc. (London: British Museum, 1907). Cf. Lester L. Grabbe, *Ezra–Nehemiah* (London: Routledge), 148–49; Joseph Blenkinsopp, *The Pentateuch: An Introduction to the First Five Books of the Bible* (New York: Doubleday, 1992), 239; Fitzpatrick-McKinley, *Transformation*, 148; Josef Wiesehöfer, *Ancient Persia: From 550 BC to 650 AD* (trans. Azizeh Azodi; New York: I. B. Tauris, 2001), 31, 33.

13. Discussed further in Chapter 6, below.

edict is issued empowering the Jews to defend themselves (8:9–14). There is no concept of "creating statute law" in this account, only a very typical, ancient Near Eastern ideal of irrevocable court verdicts (see further, below) and written edicts.

(3) *Daniel 6:1–29 (EV 5:31–6:28)*. A third example of Persian law writing appears in Dan 6. In this account, Daniel's enemies are looking for a way to bring a charge against (עלה) him, but his virtue is spotless. The only way they can make a charge stick is by creating a loyalty test, with a verdict predetermined against those who fail it. It is the inclusion of a test to expose a certain kind of person to be punished (rather than specifically naming a person) which gives this verdict a limited legislative resemblance. It is clear, nonetheless, that Darius' decree is a test to expose *real and present* disloyalty: it is put in place with a specific time limit. For 30 days (v. 8 [EV v. 7]) no one is to pray to any god but Darius. This is not, therefore, a statute creating a new law binding on future violators; it is *a test* designed to expose *a real and present threat* to the king's cultic authority. The fundamental thinking here is still retrospective. The perpetrator of the purported threat (Daniel) merely needs to be exposed by a test before the verdict can be applied. When Daniel is exposed as the one whom the king has condemned, Darius "labored till the sun set to rescue him." However, the verdict could not be changed (vv. 15–16 [EV vv. 14–15]). That a royal verdict is irrevocable is not surprising (see further, below). Although the inclusion of a test is unusual, the "law of the Medes and Persians" again looks like a collection of written court verdicts, not a statute book.

The historicity of these three narratives is widely questioned. Their portrayal of Persian court verdicts as irreversible is, nonetheless, reliable. Diodoros also reports an instance when the Persian king issued a verdict in his wrath. "Once the king's passion had cooled," Diodoros reports, the king regretted his ruling, "but all his royal power was not able to undo what was done." The condemned prisoner was executed (Diodoros, *Hist.* 17.30.1–7). LH also denies the right of any judge to change a verdict once written down: "If a judge…deposits a sealed opinion, after which he reverses his judgment…he shall give twelvefold the claim of that judgment; moreover, they shall unseat him from his judgeship…" (LH §5). It was a characteristic feature of ancient Near Eastern justice that *a judicial verdict*, once written down, could not be changed. This permanence of verdicts may have to do with the idea of the king's inspiration in judgment (and perhaps, in some societies, that of all judges; cf. LH §5). The king's wrath against injustice is divine; even the king's own later reflections must not change that divinely inspired verdict. (Cf. Prov 16:10; 21:10; cf. also Esth 7:7, 10.)

In fact, a closer look at what "the law of the Medes and Persians" actually refers to is telling. Daniel 6:16 (EV v.15) offers this explanation: "Recognize, O king, that it is a law of the Medes and Persians that no injunction or statute which the king makes may be changed." In other words, the "law of the Medes and Persians" does not necessarily refer to the book and its contents; the term refers to the unwritten custom that royal injunctions, once written down, cannot be reversed. The book is called by that name, not because it *contains* the law of the Medes and Persians, but because it contains a written record of royal injunctions on cases which, according to the law of the Medes and Persians, cannot be revoked. This statement in Daniel further suggests that the written book is not itself a source of law, but a record of orally pronounced verdicts.

The Persian verdicts/edicts of Daniel and Esther do not show a Persian penchant for legislation as often assumed by scholars. In further confirmation of the above findings, direct evidence of actual Persian law descriptions (like the Behistun inscription), as well as the witness of Greek/Persian legal polemics (see Chapter 6, below), confirm that Persia lacked written legislation.

Persia may or may not have endorsed Torah as Yehud's "official law book"; but if it did, it would require something more to show how this "authorization" could have made Torah statutory. James Watts has suggested that

> A better analogy for understanding such Persian interventions in local cults and laws may be the modern practice of designating various symbols, commodities, and events as "the official X" of a city, state, or nation... The Persians may have designated the Pentateuch as the "official" law of the Jerusalem community simply as a token favor, with little or no attention to that law's form or content.[14]

Watts' alternative simply illustrates the point: even if Persia gave some sort of imperial countenance to Israel's law book, this in itself does not mean it became legislative. In order to resolve that latter question, something more needs to be established. In particular, an examination of relevant practice-evidence from Yehud would be required—a study of Ezra–Nehemiah's actual uses of the law book.

Anne Fitzpatrick-McKinley also doubts Frei's thesis as a viable mechanism for the rise of prescriptivism in Israel.[15] She nonetheless shares the common expectation that Ezra's law book use was statutory. Fitzpatrick-McKinley explains Israel's transformation from descriptivism to prescriptivism through reference to Jack Goody's theories on the "fixation" and "decontextualization" of texts.[16] Fitzpatrick-McKinley

---

14. Watts, *Persia and Torah*, 3.
15. Fitzpatrick-McKinley, *Transformation*, 147–48.
16. Jack Goody, *The Logic of Writing and the Organization of Society* (Cambridge: Cambridge University Press, 1986); idem, *The Oriental, the Ancient, and the Primitive: Systems of Marriage and the Family in the Pre-Industrial Societies of Eurasia* (Cambridge: Cambridge University Press, 1990), 409–15. Fitzpatrick-McKinley also draws upon Watson's legal-transplant theory (to explain the *contents* of Israel's law writings—that they are borrowed rather than indigenous) and Lingat's study of Indian *dharma*'s reconceputalization as legislation (as a comparative model for a change in the *use* of Israel's law writings). (Alan Watson, *Legal Transplants: An Approach to Comparative Law* [Edinburgh: Scottish Academic Press, 1974]; idem, *Society and Legal Change* [Edinburgh: Scottish Academic Press, 1977]; idem, *The Evolution of Law* [Oxford: Blackwell, 1985]; Robert Lingat, *The Classical Law*

concludes that, without a king as the source of law for Yehud, the scribal texts of ancient legal wisdom became an independent (i.e. "decontextualized") institution. Exegesis of these "decontextualized" texts became the source for new rulings (i.e. legislation). "The roots of such a process go back to Ezra"; "[it is] Ezra whose 'textual task' is to seek from torah new divine teachings or to explain older teachings making them meaningful in the present."[17] Although Fitzpatrick-McKinley's work has met with criticism (perhaps too severely at points), her basic intuition is not unreasonable. Even if deemed a reasonable hypothesis, however, whether it fits the actual practice evidence in Ezra–Nehemiah remains untested. Was the "decontextualized" law book of Ezra–Nehemiah employed as a *source* of legal rulings?

Each of the above proposals stops short of testing the law-practice narratives of Ezra–Nehemiah. That the law book was regarded as a *practical reference* for Ezra is patent. But was the law book a source of rulings (prescriptivism), or a treatise of ancient examples (descriptivism)?[18] It is such an examination of the practice evidence that is needed in order to determine the nature of Yehud's attitude toward law writings. There are intractable historical problems surrounding the Ezra–Nehemiah accounts, and these will be discussed below. Nonetheless, it can be stated for now that the Ezra–Nehemiah measures "according to the law book" offer important law-practice materials for assessing the way in which law writings were used in Persian-era Yehud.

The scholar who has come closest to providing such an examination is Michael Fishbane. In his study of *Biblical Interpretation in Ancient Israel*, Fishbane discusses certain instances of the law book's use in Ezra–Nehemiah. It is not the purpose of Fishbane's treatment, however, to assess the nature of law writings in Ezra–Nehemiah. Rather, he *presupposes* their legislative nature: "Despite the fact that the biblical legal corpora are formulated as prototypical expressions of legal wisdom, *the internal traditions of the Hebrew Bible present and regard the covenantal laws as legislative texts.*"[19] It is the validity of this presupposition which needs to be determined. Do "the internal traditions of the Hebrew Bible" represent the law writings as legislative? The problems with the reasons offered by Fishbane for this presupposition have already been noted (pp. 48–50, above). Fishbane consequently begins his treatments

of India [Berkeley: University of California Press, 1973]; cf. Jackson, "Dharma to Law.")

17. Fitzpatrick-McKinley, *Transformation*, 172 n. 68, 175.
18. Niditch (*Oral World*, 95) poses a similar question.
19. Fishbane, *Biblical Interpretation*, 96 (emphasis original).

of Ezra–Nehemiah with a legislative function for Israel's law book presupposed. He seeks to explain how Ezra derived his rulings from the law book's wording ("innerbiblical exegesis") without first asking *whether* Ezra was verbally constrained in the first place. In other words, Fishbane shows how Ezra must have used the law writings *if* he regarded those writings as prescriptive; he does not, however, demonstrate *that* this was the case. This makes Fishbane an important discussion partner in the present chapter; nonetheless, conclusions about Persian-era attitudes toward law writings cannot be drawn prior to an assessment of the relevant law-practice materials.

It is such an examination which has generally been missing from scholarly attributions of prescriptivism to Ezra; and it is such an examination which will next be offered.

I. *Law Book Citations in Ezra–Nehemiah*

The reliability of Ezra–Nehemiah as a historical source is controversial. Many scholars accept the so-called "Nehemiah Memoir" (in Neh 1–7; 12:27–43; 13:4–31), various Aramaic documents (e.g. Ezra 4:11–16, 17–22; 5:7–17; 6:3–5, 6–12; 7:12–26), possibly the Hebrew document in Ezra 1:2–4, and other such imbedded sources as authentic.[20] But the problematic chronology of the work (Who came first, Ezra or Nehemiah?), its remarkable claims (Did Ezra really bring 25 metric tons of gold and silver to Jerusalem, and that without military escort?), and other issues lead many scholars to question its overall historicity. While dating of the composition varies widely, most cite the late fifth century as the likely date of its primary compilation (with later redaction in subsequent periods).[21]

The present study is not dependent on resolving the account's historicity. All that is here of concern is the account's legal ideals. In particular: How, in view of Ezra–Nehemiah, should the ideal Jewish leader use the Torah? Whether a historical Ezra and Nehemiah provided this ideal, or whether these leaders are literary constructs, is not here important. It is only the fact that an ideal practitioner of the law book has been portrayed in this work that is of present concern. As a work rooted in the late Persian era, Ezra–Nehemiah offers a useful source of legal attitudes in

20. For discussion, see Lester L. Grabbe, *Judaism From Cyrus to Hadrian*. Vol. 1, *The Persian and Greek Periods* (Minneapolis: Fortress, 1992), 30–42.

21. Samuel Pagán, "Ezra, Nehemiah, and Chronicles," in Stuessy, ed., *Chalice*, 125; Crüsemann, *The Torah*, 336; H. G. M. Williamson, *Ezra, Nehemiah* (WBC 16; Waco, Tex.: Word, 1985), xxxv–vi; Grabbe, *Ezra–Nehemiah*, 102–22.

Yehud, even if not a reliable source of history.[22] Ezra–Nehemiah is therefore useful for the present study, despite its historical problems.

The law book is clearly a major theme in Ezra–Nehemiah,[23] but there are anomalies between the content of the Torah and the way it is applied. These anomalies are well known, but there are a number of ways to explain them. The explanations advanced by scholars can be summarized as follows:

a.   Some scholars deduce that Ezra's law book was an early (and somewhat different) text from what became the Pentateuch. Either Ezra had a complete Pentateuch slightly different from its present form, or Ezra had certain law collections (Deuteronomy, the Priestly "Code," and/or the Holiness "Code") which were further modified when adapted into the Pentateuch. Anomalies between the Pentateuch and Ezra's uses of it are, therefore, evidence of an earlier stage of the Pentateuch.

b.   Some scholars attribute anomalies to Ezra's exegetical methods. Ezra is said to have had legal texts essentially the same as those in the present Pentateuch, and verbal links demonstrating such correspondences are emphasized. Discrepancies are then explained as arising through inner-biblical comparison, etymological expansion, and other proto-midrashic methods. Ezra drew "new" applications from old law writings by exegetical technique.

c.   Some scholars have concluded that none of the above alternatives are satisfactory. While Ezra's law book was probably an indirect "cousin" of the Pentateuch, his law book is too fundamentally different to have been in the same lineage. It has been proposed that Ezra's law book was analogous to the Qumran community's *Temple Scroll*—a law book indirectly related to, but substantially different from, the Pentateuch.[24]

22. Even early Hellenistic-era documents, in order to appear authentic, can be written in keeping with Persian-era institutions (Frei, "Persian Authorization," 8, 11; Crüsemann, *The Torah*, 336).

23. The Mosaic law is mentioned throughout (e.g. Ezra 3:2–4; 7:6, 10–11; 10:3; Neh 1:5–9; 8:1–18; 9:3–34; 10:29–36; 12:44; 13:1–5). Additionally, a "commandment of the prophets" (for which no single source can be identified) is quoted in Ezra 9:10–12, 14; a "commandment of the (Davidic) king" regarding worship appears in Neh 11:23; 12:24, 45.

24. The *Temple Scroll* analogy is that of Cornelis Houtman, "Ezra and the Law: Observations on the Supposed Relation Between Ezra and the Pentateuch," in *Remembering all the Way...: A Collection of Old Testament Studies Published on the Occasion of the Fortieth Anniversary of the Oudtestamentisch Werkgezelschap in Nederland* (ed. Bertril Albrektson *et al.*; OTS 21; Leiden: Brill, 1981), 110. See the response offered by Williamson, *Ezra, Nehemiah*, xxxviii.

d.   Finally, a fourth possibility which the present study opens up is that the disparities between Pentateuch law writings and Ezra's applications may indicate his lack of constraint by Pentateuchal stipulations. It is possible that Ezra did not view written law as binding (i.e. prescriptive). He used (and cited) the Torah as a pre-eminent description of Yahwistic ideals as practiced by Moses, yet he freely applied Torah's ideals without obligation to Torah's stipulations. In other words, Ezra used the Pentateuch as a descriptive law collection, not prescriptions to be enforced.[25]

In what follows, seven texts where the law book's use is problematic will be examined.[26] Proponents for the various explanations just noted will be enlisted in the examination.

1. Discrepancy 1: Ezra 6:18—Classification of Priests and Levites
After the completion of Ezra's temple-building program, a dedication ceremony was held:

> Then the sons of Israel, the priests, and the Levites, and the rest of the sons of the exile conducted the dedication of this house of God with joy. They offered sacrifices to dedicate this house to God—100 bulls, 200 rams, 400 lambs, and 12 he-goats for a sin-offering for all Israel (according to the number of the tribes of Israel). And they set the priests in their divisions, and the Levites in their bands, for the service of God at Jerusalem as written in the book of Moses (ככתב ספר משה). (Ezra 6:16–18)

Cornelis Houtman sums up the problem succinctly: "In *Ezra vi 18* the classification of priests and Levites happened with an appeal to 'the prescription of the book of Moses.' The Pentateuch does not know such a classification. It comes from David; see I Chron. xxiiiff. (cf. Exod xxix; Lev. viii; Num. iii–iv; viii 5–26)."[27] Houtman believes that the Davidic courses must have been redacted into Ezra's law book. None of the extant

25.   An additional explanation is that Ezra simply misrepresented the Torah. This explanation generally appears in polemical scholarship of Muslim and Samaritan traditions (Camilla Adang, *Muslim Writers on Judaism and the Hebrew Bible: From Ibn Rabban to Ibn Hazm* [Leiden: Brill, 1996], 246–48; Moses Gaster, *Samaritan Eschatology: The Belief of the Samaritans in Immortality, Resurrection, Future Punishment and Reward, the Taheb and the Second Kingdom* [The Samaritan Oral Law and Ancient Traditions 1; London: Search Publishing, 1932], 258).
26.   The anomalies here presented are not an exhaustive list, but are sufficient to indicate the pervasiveness and nature of the problem and its possible solutions. For further examples, see Houtman, "Ezra and the Law," 103–6; Grabbe, *Ezra–Nehemiah*, 146; Joseph Blenkinsopp, *Ezra–Nehemiah: A Commentary* (London: SCM Press, 1988), 155.
27.   Houtman, "Ezra and the Law," 104.

versions of the Torah include the Davidic courses of Levites, however. Therefore, Houtman deduces that Ezra's law book was a different Torah from the preserved versions. Ezra's version of the Torah had the Levitical divisions appointed by David (1 Chr 23–26) retrojected to Moses.

H. G. M. Williamson notes Houtman's argument, but presents an alternative. Williamson identifies this ascription as a partisan gloss. A pro-priestly editor added the Mosaic citation in "a concern for the safeguarding of priestly privileges."[28] There are, however, several problems with Williamson's alternative. First of all, this Mosaic citation appears in the Masoretic Text (MT), in the Septuagint (LXX), and in 1 Esd 7:9. If this citation is a partisan gloss, it occurred early enough to influence all these traditions. More importantly, in Neh 12:24, the Levitical courses *are* assigned to David: "according to the commandment of David the man of God, division by division." One might expect more consistency if a pro-priestly editor sought to tie the Levitical courses to Moses instead of David. Recourse to a partisan glossator seems inappropriate here.

Joseph Blenkinsopp proposed a literary purpose for assigning the Levitical orders to Moses. The pericope which immediately follows concerns the holding of the Passover (6:19–22). Since the Passover "had to be carried out in conformity with Mosaic law," the writer may have felt compelled to tie the priestly orders (established in the preceding dedication ceremony) to Moses.[29] That Ezra 6:18 concludes an Aramaic pericope, with the Passover pericope beginning a Hebrew section, renders Blenkinsopp's explanation tenuous. It seems unlikely that the Aramaic-language dedication ceremony was worded with the Hebrew-language Passover narrative in view.

Lester Grabbe explains that it was only *the work done* by the priestly orders (not the orders themselves) which are being called "according to the writings." "The priests and Levites," he explains, "organized according to their divisions, performed the work as written in the law of Moses."[30] This would be reasonable if the text read, "And they set the priests in their divisions, and the Levites in their bands, *for the service of God as written in the book of Moses*" (v. 18). However, the full expression is actually, "...for the service of God *at Jerusalem* as written in the book of Moses." It is difficult to make the Torah citation refer only to the "service of God" when that service is framed on both sides by Davidic ordinances: the Levitical courses *and* Jerusalem. It seems the whole arrangement is being connected with Moses.

---

28. Williamson, *Ezra, Nehemiah*, 84.
29. Blenkinsopp, *Ezra–Nehemiah*, 131.
30. Grabbe, *Ezra–Nehemiah*, 25.

One further alternative which might be noted is that offered by D. J. A. Clines. Clines notes that the *main* division indicated in Ezra 6:18—that of the priests and the Levites—is Mosaic. The citation could simply be intended to show that the main divisions were Mosaic.[31] This is actually similar to Grabbe's approach, as it focuses on what is clearly Mosaic in the passage and overlooks what is Davidic. It seems, however, that the final line—"according to the writing of Moses"—is intended to explain everything just described: the sacrifices, the priestly and Levitical courses, the work, and the place (Jerusalem).

None of these explanations seem satisfactory. Even Houtman's view (that David's courses were re-ascribed to Moses in Ezra's law book) can be countered by the fact that the Levitical courses *are* ascribed to David in Neh 12:24 (cf. Ezra 3:10; Neh 12:34, 45–46). The Davidic courses had not been retrojected to Moses, but were still known to have derived from David. It would seem, therefore, that the only explanation for this Torah citation is that the writer simply did not perceive any substantial difference between the Mosaic and Davidic priestly orders.

The law book of Moses is not being cited as a source book of stipulations. There is no need for each detail of the ceremony to find a stipulation in the Mosaic book in order for the whole to qualify as "according to the writings of Moses." The law book is being cited as the ideal of Yahwism which the indicated measures (whatever their various sources) altogether realize. That is all that is being said. Drawing on the more extensive, temple system of priestly courses appointed by David was simply an effective way to fulfill *Mosaic* Yahwism in the post-exilic context. It remains the Mosaic vision, even if not Moses' original stipulations, that stands behind the arrangements instituted at the Second Temple dedication.

Support for this view might be found by comparing the various ascriptions of the Levitical orders to Moses (Ezra 6:16–18) or David (Neh 12:24). In Ezra 6:16–18, the main focus of the narrative is on sacrifices. The sacrificial cultus was originally patterned by Moses. The re-establishment of the sacrificing cultus (even though according to Davidic stipulations) was therefore said to be in keeping with the Mosaic law book. In Neh 12:24, however, where music is prominent (and sacrifices are present but secondary; vv. 30, 43, 45), the *Davidic* command is at the forefront (cf. vv. 35, 45–46). The concern therefore is not to connect practices to texts,[32] but to connect ideals to the right personage (restored

---

31. D. J. A. Clines, *Ezra, Nehemiah, Esther* (NCB; Grand Rapids: Eerdmans, 1984), 96.

32. Much less *written* texts: it might be noted that nowhere are David's commands said to be written in a book. The only *written* ideal in view is that of Moses.

sacrifices to Moses; restored psalmody to David). The Levitical orders can be ascribed to either David or Moses depending on the context.[33] All this bespeaks a concern for the law book as a pattern by which to authenticate the renewed cultus, but not a source book for its stipulations.

2. *Discrepancy 2: Nehemiah 8:13–18—Feast of Booths*

In Neh 8:13–18, Ezra gathers the heads of the community together to study the Mosaic law book. Based on what they find written there, the Feast of Booths is reinstituted. The Feast of Booths is discussed in the Pentateuch in several places (Lev 23:33–43; Num 29:12–39; Deut 16:13–17; 31:10–13). The Neh 8 narrative fits most closely with the instructions of Lev 23. It is the two so-called "Priestly" accounts (Lev 23; Num 29) that identify the date as the seventh month (Lev 23:34; Num 29:12/Neh 8:14) and the length of the feast as eight days with a solemn assembly on the eighth day (Lev 23:36, 39; Num 29:35/Neh 8:18). Of these two texts, however, it is only Lev 23 that calls the people to gather tree boughs (Lev 23:40/Neh 8:15) and to live in booths (Lev 23:42/Neh 8:14) for the festival. Of the various Pentateuchal regulations for the Feast of Booths, Lev 23 provides the best all-round match for Neh 8.[34] Even taking the best match, however, there are significant problems. The principal problems can be displayed in three parts, as follows:[35]

Problem a. Instruction on *what* to gather—

Lev 23:40 calls for *fruit and branches* to be gathered: "You shall take…the fruit of choice trees, branches…and boughs…"	*Neh 8:15* calls *only for branches* to be gathered: "Go out to the hills and bring branches…as it is written."

Problem b. Instruction on what *kinds* of flora to gather—

Lev 23:40 specifies: "You shall take…the fruit of choice trees (פרי עץ הדר), branches of palm trees (כפת תמרים) and boughs of leafy trees (וענף עץ עבת) and willows of the brook (וערבי־נחל)…"	*Neh 8:15* specifies: "Go out to the hills and bring olive branches (עלי־זית) and wild olive branches (ועלי־עץ שמן), myrtle branches (ועלי הדס), palm branches (ועלי תמרים) and branches of leafy trees (ועלי עץ עבת)…as it is written."

---

33. Or they can be distinguished, as in 2 Chr 23:18.

34. Williamson, *Ezra, Nehemiah*, 294; Duggan, *Covenant Renewal*, 95–98.

35. Other problems observed by commentators include: Ezra's reading law *throughout* the feast; the absence of mention of the Day of Atonement; the emphasis on *proclamation* in this text as a legal requirement; and the summons *to Jerusalem*. These further details will not be taken up here, though some of them further indicate the extent of the inconsistencies between stipulations and practice.

Problem c. Instruction on *how to use* the flora gathered—

Lev 23:40 expects the branches, fruits, and foliage to be used *in a festal procession:* "You shall take the fruit of choice trees, branches... and boughs...and you shall rejoice before Yahweh your God for seven days."	*Neh 8:15* expects the branches to be used *in booth construction:* "Go out to the hills and bring branches...to make booths, as it is written."

Notwithstanding these discrepancies, the Neh 8 narrative claims that Yehud's leaders reinstituted the festival based on what "they found written in the law that Yahweh commanded by the hand of Moses" (v. 14), "as it is written" (v. 15), and "according to the ordinance" (v. 18). How is this problem to be explained?

Williamson shows a way to alleviate some of the tension. He argues that the narrative is only concerned to highlight the zeal *of the laity* in response to the public reading of the law book (vv. 1–12). Aspects of the autumn festival conducted by the Levites are therefore not mentioned—such as the Day of Atonement (Lev 23:26–32) and the festival sacrifices (Num 29). Those aspects of the autumn festival which are mentioned in Neh 8 are those which show the initiative of the laity.[36] Williamson's observation could explain Problem a, that "fruit" is overlooked: "The present proclamation is dealing with materials for the making of booths, and thus need not be expected to correspond with the separate stipulations concerning produce for the festival."[37] The foliage for the *corporate* procession would have included fruit and branches, but the narrative's concern with *individual* booth construction only mentions the branches. Williamson's explanation is helpful, but does not resolve the whole problem.

Fredrick Holmgren points to a statement in v. 17 as a possible explanation for the differences. In that verse, it is said that "the sons of Israel had not done thus since the days of Joshua the son of Nun." The differences could derive from traditions which had not been observed since Joshua.[38] Holmgren offers another source for the variations, but does not account for the triple insistence that this festival was carried out according to the pattern written by Moses. Houtman believes the apparent

36. Williamson, *Ezra, Nehemiah*, 293–97.
37. Ibid., 295.
38. Fredrick Carlson Holmgren, *Israel Alive Again: A Commentary on the Books of Ezra and Nehemiah* (ITC; Grand Rapids: Eerdmans, 1987), 127–28. Cf. Yehezkel Kaufmann, *History of the Religion of Israel*. Vol. 4, *From the Babylonian Captivity to the End of Prophecy* (Dallas: Institute for Jewish Studies, 1977), 380–82.

inconsistencies are irreconcilable, and that Ezra's Torah must have been different from the extant Pentateuch.[39]

Another solution, and perhaps the most successful thus far, is that of Fishbane. Fishbane proposes a way around the most difficult point of problem—namely, Problem c, the use of the branches. Fishbane views Ezra as the progenitor of Judaic midrash and seeks to explain his handling of the law book according to midrashic techniques.[40] In this instance, Fishbane believes Ezra employed *etymology* to re-interpret the Torah instructions:

> Although Neh. 8:14–17 is [not]…a citation and enforcement of the exegetical plain sense of Lev. 23:39–42…the levitical instructors nevertheless engaged in legal exegesis. A close comparison of the citation in v. 14 (to 'dwell…in booths') with the proclamation in v. 15 (to 'build booths' out of local tree species) suggests that the latter is an interpretation of the former based on an etymological exegesis of the noun 'booths'. Faced with a legal prescription to build סכה, but with no indication as to its manner of construction, the levitical instructors apparently started with the fact that the noun סכה is derivable from the verbal stem סכך 'to cover over (with branches)'. On this basis they interpreted the Torah command to dwell in booths as implying that one must dwell in 'branched' shelters…[41]

Fishbane's explanation shows how a prescriptive attitude toward the exact wording of the written law could be honored while drawing out new applications not evident in the static text. Ezra, according to Fishbane, called for the use of the branches for booth construction based on "what was written"—that is, based on detailed, etymological examination of the words used in Lev 23. Others follow Fishbane in this reading. Blenkinsopp, for instance, concurs that, by midrashic etymology, that which was deduced from the very words of the text came to be viewed as part of the law's obligation.[42]

Taken together, the explanations proposed by Williamson and Fishbane could resolve Problems a and c. The only remaining problem not resolved by these scholars is Problem b, the change in the kinds of trees indicated. Williamson supposed that this problem could be dismissed

---

39. Houtman, "Ezra and the Law," 104–5.
40. Fishbane, *Biblical Interpretation*, 107–13. See also his "Midrash and the Meaning of Scripture," in *The Interpretation of the Bible: The International Symposium in Slovenia* (ed. Joze Krašovec; JSOTSup 289; Sheffield: Sheffield Academic Press, 1998), 553.
41. Fishbane, *Biblical Interpretation*, 111.
42. Blenkinsopp, *Ezra–Nehemiah*, 291–92.

due to the fact that Neh 8 is talking about branches used for a *different purpose* than Lev 23. One might expect, he reasons, different kinds of trees to be involved for different activities.[43] This only sidesteps the problem of how Neh 8 can claim to have appointed these species "as it is written." Fishbane does not offer any insight into the midrash that could explain the change in kinds of trees, although this does not mean such a midrash is not possible. In view of Fishbane's lexical insight for the booths, it must be allowed that a similar lexical process (yet to be discerned) could stand behind the foliage choices. A prescriptivistic explanation for the Feast of Booths variations is therefore possible.

Clines, however, offers a simpler solution for the change in foliage: "As for the names of the trees, the present list may reflect Ezra's interpretation of the law (cf. Ezra 9:1) in the light of which types of trees were now available... The Leviticus passage may have been interpreted by Ezra as referring to categories of trees."[44] Clines is suggesting that Ezra read the list of trees in Lev 23 as descriptive rather than prescriptive. Rather than seeing the four kinds of trees as *prescribed*, Ezra understood the named trees as *describing* the kinds of foliage Moses used. To say the same thing another way: Lev 23 reports the kinds of trees which Moses prescribed in the Sinai wilderness; Ezra followed Moses' example by prescribing appropriate foliage for the same festival in the environs of post-exilic Yehud. So long as Ezra was following the model of Moses in shaping his own proclamation, Ezra could say that his tree list was devised "according to what was written." Clines summarizes: "...nor do the trees prescribed there [in Lev 23] coincide with those here [in Neh 8], nor does the Leviticus passage say what is to be done with the boughs. All this may mean that Ezra's copy of Leviticus differed in minor points from our own, but the last item leads us to think that we are dealing here not with variant texts, but with a contemporary reinterpretation of the law."[45]

Fundamental questions of how law writings were viewed has not entered into Clines' examination. His choice of terms (e.g. "reinterpretation") suggests that Clines expects Ezra was compelled to tie his regulations to the wording of Torah.[46] This, however, is not necessary. If Ezra

---

43. Williamson, *Ezra, Nehemiah*, 295.

44. Clines, *Ezra–Esther*, 187.

45. Ibid., 187.

46. Clines (ibid., 187) goes on to say, "Ezra would doubtless have argued that what the law implied it also commanded." It seems Clines is endeavoring to justify what he instinctively sees (a descriptive use of Moses) without violating prescriptive assumptions (i.e. that the written law is the source of stipulations, and all rulings

viewed the law writing as a *typical* ideal, he would not have needed to tie his own instructions to its stipulations. He proclaimed instructions that would fulfill, in contemporary circumstances, the same festival Moses celebrated as described in the law book.

A prescriptive approach (drawing principally on Fishbane's insight) could explain Ezra's use of the Torah in Neh 8, though it requires significant assumptions. It seems more reasonable to suspect Ezra viewed Torah as a historic ideal, not the source of stipulations for the present situation.

(Discrepancies 3–6: Provisions of the Nehemiah 10 Covenant)
Further points of discrepancy occur in the community covenant recorded in Neh 10. Because the covenant is presented in one passage (10:31–40 [EV 10:30–39]),[47] the four relevant difficulties will be introduced together and then examined individually.

Nehemiah 10 records that all the people (leaders and laity) drew up a covenant,[48] whereby they devoted themselves "to walk in the law of God which was given by the hand of Moses the servant of God, and to keep and to do all the commandments of Yahweh our Lord, and his judgments and his statutes" (10:30). The subsequent document lists the specific ways in which the people intend so to observe "the law of God given by Moses." Further statements within the covenant itself—"as it is written" (vv. 35, 37)—also indicate the intention to tie the covenant stipulations to the law book of Moses. However, there are discrepancies between Torah's stipulations and those of the covenant.

These further discrepancies, which appear in the Neh 10 covenant, can be displayed up front as follows:[49]

---

must be shown to be *innately* required by it—explicitly or implicitly). Cf. D. J. A. Clines, "Nehemiah 10 as an Example of Early Jewish Biblical Exegesis," *JSOT* 21 (1981): 111–17.

47. Only Hebrew citations will be given in the subsequent discussion of this passage.

48. It is not clear whether Ezra or Nehemiah was the key figure behind this covenant. For the sake of simplicity, this study will consider Ezra as the leading covenanter without thereby intending to ignore the text's lack of clarity on this matter.

49. For other possible discrepancies in Neh 10, see Houtman, "Ezra and the Law," 103–6. On the overall structure and aims of the covenant, see David A. Glatt-Gilad, "Reflections on the Structure and Significance of the *ʾamānāh* (Neh 10,29–40)," *ZAW* 112, no. 3 (2000): 386–95. For a table displaying each of the covenant provisions and their Pentateuchal parallels, see Duggan, *Covenant Renewal*, 287.

Discrepancy 3. Prohibition against intermarriage:

Deut 7:1–3 lists specific Canaanite peoples with whom Israel is not to intermarry upon settlement: "…the Hittites, the Girgashites, the Amorites, the Canaanites, the Perizzites, the Hivites, and the Jebusites…when Yahweh your God gives them over to you…you must devote them to destruction… You shall not intermarry with them, giving your daughters to their sons or taking their daughters for your sons." (Cf. Exod 34:11–16)

Neh 10:31 reinstitutes this restriction for post-exilic Yehud, and with different people-groups in view: "We will not give our daughters to the peoples of the land, and we will not take their daughters for our sons." (Cf. 13:23–27; Ezra 9:1)

Discrepancy 4. Prohibition against purchases on the sabbath:

(There is no prohibition against making purchases on the Sabbath day in the Torah.)

Neh 10:32: "If the peoples of the land bring their goods and any grain on the sabbath day, to sell—we will not take from them on the sabbath, or on a holy day."

Discrepancy 5. Institution of an annual temple tax:

Exod 30:12–16 reports a one-time census tax (half a shekel) at the inauguration of the tabernacle: "When you take the census…each shall give…half a shekel…for the service of the tent of meeting…"

Neh 10:33–34 obliges the covenanters to an annual temple tax of a third of a shekel: "We also…will give of ourselves a third of a shekel per year for the service of the house of our God…"

Discrepancy 6. Institution of a wood offering —

(There is no wood offering in the Torah.)

Neh 10:35 requires a wood offering "as written in the law": "We…have also cast lots for the wood offering, to bring it…for burning upon the altar…as written in the law."

3. *Discrepancy 3: Nehemiah 10:31—Prohibition Against Intermarriage*

Intermarriage is a thematic concern in Ezra–Nehemiah.[50] An injunction against intermarriage appears at the top of the list of the covenanted responses to Torah. The relevant provisions in the Pentateuch are the following:

50. Kenneth G. Hoglund (*Achaemenid Imperial Administration in Syria-Palestine and the Missions of Ezra and Nehemiah* [SBLDS 125; Atlanta: Scholars Press, 1992], 236–40) calls it "the primary emphasis in the [Ezra–Nehemiah] narratives."

> ...Behold, I will drive out before you the Amorites, the Canaanites, the Hittites, the Perizzites, the Hivites, and the Jebusites... You shall tear down their altars...lest...you take of their daughters for your sons, and their daughters whore after their gods and make your sons whore after their gods. (Exod 34:11–16)

> When Yahweh your God brings you into the land...and clears away many nations before you, the Hittites, the Girgashites, the Amorites, the Canaanites, the Perizzites, the Hivites, and the Jebusites...then you must devote them to destruction... You shall not intermarry with them, giving your daughters to their sons or taking their daughters to your sons, for they would turn away your sons from following me... (Deut 7:1–5)

Elsewhere in the Pentateuchal laws, the possibility of intermarriage with non-Hebrew women is countenanced (e.g. Deut 21:10–14).[51] The focus of the above injunctions was to protect the Israelites from adopting Canaanite worship on settlement, not to prohibit all intermarriage with non-Hebrew peoples. Ezra and Nehemiah evidently considered the conditions of the Jewish re-settlement similar enough to those of the first settlement to re-assert the same prohibition. What is significant, however, is that the terms of the Torah laws are altered to fit contemporary circumstances.

Within the Neh 10 covenant, a generic statement ("the peoples of the land") replaces the specific ethnic groups contained in the Pentateuch laws. The closely related injunctions in Ezra 9.1 and Neh 13.23 make it clear which "peoples of the land" are now intended—contemporary adversaries like the Moabites and Ammonites not included in the Pentateuch laws: "The sons of Israel...have not separated themselves from *the peoples of the land*...from the Canaanites, the Hittites, the Perizzites, the Jebusites, the Ammonites, the Moabites, the Egyptians, and the Amorites. For they have taken some of their daughters to be wives ..." (Ezra 9:1–2; cf. Neh 13:23).

All this shows Ezra's concern to apply old Torah prohibitions to a new situation. It is clearly the "old Torah" that he has before him: the Canaanites, Hittites, Perizzites, and Jebusites died out long before. They are mentioned here to make the Mosaic connection; nonetheless, it is the current "problem peoples" not mentioned in the Pentateuch but incorporated at the end of Ezra's list which are the real aim of his use of the Mosaic doctrine.[52] To make such free adjustments to Torah stipulations,

---

51. Cf. the idealized marriage of David's grandfather Boaz to a *Moabitess* (Ruth)—one of the very people groups prohibited by Ezra–Nehemiah "according to the law book." Dating for the book of Ruth, and thus the relevance of this evidence here, is contested.

52. Clines, "Neh 10," 115–16.

however, probably evinces a descriptivistic view of the Pentateuch law writings. The Mosaic law book, itself, is treated as a situational application of law. Actual law is an unwritable divine ideal; Moses' records show the way he applied justice to his time. When Ezra finds how Moses applied divine justice to circumstances similar to his own, Ezra makes a customized application of the same practice for his own day. His reference to the Mosaic law book is not as a source code of stipulations, but as an exemplar—a role model. By citing the Mosaic exemplar, Ezra can show his own prohibition (and it is unconcealedly *his own* prohibition) to have a noble precedent.

Few would disagree that Ezra–Nehemiah "updates" the Mosaic injunction. However, those who view Ezra's use of the Pentateuch as legislative are compelled to explain his modified stipulations. Fishbane has offered the following explanation.

Fishbane begins his explanation with the intermarriage injunction in Deut 7:1–5. He then produces another Deuteronomic prohibition (Deut 23:4–9), whereby Moabites, Amonites, Edomites, and Egyptians were refused access to the cultic assembly. Fishbane suggests that Ezra might have drawn upon the similar wording of both these prohibitions to create a midrashic combination of them:

Deuteronomy	*Ezra*
7:1–2: "...the <u>Hittites</u>, the Girgashites, the <u>Amorites</u>, the <u>Canaanites</u>, the <u>Perizzites</u>, the <u>Hivites</u>, and the <u>Jebusites</u>...you shall not intermarry with them..."	9:1–2: "...the sons of Israel...have not separated themselves from the peoples of the lands with their abominations, from the <u>Canaanites</u>, the <u>Hittites</u>, the <u>Perizzites</u>, the <u>Jebusites</u>, the *Ammonites*, the *Moabites*, the *Egyptians*, and the *Amorites*..."
23:4–9: "No *Ammonite* or *Moabite* may enter the assembly of Yahweh... An *Edomite*... [and] an *Egyptian*...in the third generation may enter the assembly of Yahweh."	

Fishbane states, "Accordingly, the mechanism for prohibiting intermarriage with the Ammonites, Moabites, etc. was an exegetical extension of the law in Deut. 7:1–3 effected by means of an adaptation and interpolation of features from Deut. 23:4–9."[53]

---

53. Fishbane, *Biblical Interpretation*, 117. Cf. Kaufmann, *Religion of Israel*, 4.384–5; Holmgren, *Alive Again*, 71–72.

It is possible, therefore, to incorporate the "people of the land" posing a present threat to Ezra's Yehud into the old Pentateuchal injunction through exegetical means. Two problems with Fishbane's proposal weaken the likelihood that Ezra was employing such a technique. First, if the list of peoples in Ezra 9:1 does draw from Deut 23:4–9, it is remarkable that the "Edomites" were not also included. Post-exilic Judaism's bitterness toward the Edomites was especially pronounced (e.g. Ps 137; Obadiah). Second, a parallel passage in Neh 13:23 names the "women of *Ashdod*, Ammon, and Moab." To sustain Fishbane's argument, it would be necessary to find a textual source for including the *Ashdodite* women in Ezra–Nehemiah's legal definition for "people of the land." Phillip Sigal points the way for just such an argument: "Based upon Zekh. 9:6, '*mamzer* will inhabit Ashdod' many think *mamzer* originally referred to an ethnic group. In that event Deut. 23:3 which prohibits *mamzer* would refer to Ashdodites."[54]

The definition of ממזר as an ethnic term is dubious. In Deut 23, ממזר seems more closely paralleled to the "crushed or castrated" than the subsequent ethnic exclusions. Also, the reference to Ashdodites as ממזר in Zech 9:6 is most likely a derisive reference to their mixed population after foreign domination (i.e. "mongrels/bastards").[55] In any case, the fact remains that the Ashdodites are not mentioned in Deut 23. What Sigal's insight offers is a *midrashic* means for incorporating Ashdodites into the Deuteronomy prohibitions (through the medium of Zechariah's prophecy). If Fishbane is correct when he ties Ezra's list of prohibited peoples to a merging of Deut 7 and 23, Zech 9 would need to be further referenced as a source for the Ashdodites.

It is one of the strengths of midrash that such verbal links can be exploited to produce new regulations out of old texts. Such practices are well-documented for late Second Temple Judaism. Whether Ezra and Nehemiah adopted such methods for their intermarriage injunctions seems dubious. There is, in fact, no indication that Ezra felt compelled to justify his changes to the excluded-peoples list. For the present, it can be allowed that an exegetical explanation for the Ezra–Nehemiah intermarriage injunctions is possible, but a descriptivistic reference requires fewer assumptions.

54. Phillip Sigal, *The Emergence of Contemporary Judaism*. Vol. 1, *The Foundations of Judaism from Biblical Origins to the Sixth Century A.D.* Part 1, *From the Origins to the Separation of Christianity* (PTMS 29; Pittsburgh: Pickwick, 1980), 139.

55. Victor P. Hamilton, "מַמְזֵר" (#4927), *NIDOTTE* 2:971.

4. *Discrepancy 4: Nehemiah 10:32—Prohibition Against Purchases on the Sabbath*

None of the Mosaic sabbath laws prohibit the right to make purchases on the sabbath day.[56] Nevertheless, in a covenant purporting to implement "the law of God given by the hand of Moses" (v. 30), the following provision has been adopted: "If the peoples of the land bring their goods and any grain on the sabbath day, to sell—we will not take from them on the sabbath, or on a holy day" (v. 32). How Ezra created a prohibition against buying (even food) on the sabbath, and identified it as part of "the law given by Moses," is a nearly insurmountable problem for the prescriptive theory of Hebrew law. Thus Houtman's claim that Ezra's Torah was different from extant versions.[57] Some scholars have attempted solutions to the problem.

According to Chaim Tschernowitz, v. 32 is actually a round-about prohibition against labor on the sabbath. Because the Jews could not work on the seventh day, Gentiles were hired to tend their crops for them on that day. This hiring of servants to work on the sabbath was a direct violation of the Torah prescriptions (e.g. Exod 20:8). According to Tschernowitz, it was the produce from the day's gathering in Jewish fields which was being brought into the city for sale. Ezra was not, therefore, giving a new requirement; he was (indirectly) addressing the problem of work being done on Jewish property by hired laborers.[58] This explanation seems strained. Besides, the parallel narrative in Neh 13 makes it clear that the items being sold included produce from Jewish farms *and other goods besides*:[59] "In those days, I saw in Judah people treading wine presses on the sabbath, and bringing in heaps of grain… wine, grapes, figs, and all kinds of loads… I warned them when they sold food. Tyrians also, who lived in the city, brought in fish and all kinds of goods and sold them on the sabbath …" (Neh 13:15–16). Tschernowitz's explanation serves to highlight the difficulty.

Fishbane admits there is no stipulation in Moses' law book that prohibits sabbath purchases. He does note a provision by the prophet Jeremiah, however, which Ezra may have drawn upon.[60] In Jer 17.21–22

56. Exod 20:8–11; 23:12; 31:13–17; 34:21; 35:2–3; Lev 23:3; Deut 5:12–15; cf. Exod 16:22–30; Num 15:32–35.
57. Houtman, "Ezra and the Law," 105.
58. Chaim Tschernowitz, *Toledoth ha-Halakah*, 2:114–15, per Kaufmann, *Religion of Israel*, 4:424.
59. The relationship between Neh 10 and 13 is widely discussed. The former lists obligations covenanted, and the latter describes the same obligations neglected. The "historical" order of the two is debated.
60. Fishbane, *Biblical Interpretation*, 129–34.

the Deuteronomy sabbath law (5:12–14) is quoted almost word for word. However, in Jeremiah's quotation new stipulations are interpolated into the command. Fishbane displays the prophet's interpolation thus (new material in *italics*):

Deut 5:12-14	*Jer 17:21-22*
Heed the Sabbath day to sanctify it— as YHWH, your God, commanded you: six days you may labor and do all your work, but the seventh is the Sabbath of YHWH, your God; do not do any work ...	Be heedful *and do not bear a burden on the Sabbath day and bring it into the gates of Jerusalem; and do not take any burden from your homes* on the Sabbath day; do not do any work; you shall sanctify the Sabbath day, as I commanded *your forefathers*.[61]

According to Fishbane, it was Jeremiah who introduced a prohibition of *selling* into the Hebrew sabbath law (cf. Amos 8:5). Ezra "exegetically applied this prohibition" to restrain *buying* as well.[62] Fishbane's argument pushes back the main work of innovation upon Jeremiah, which Jeremiah justified through two techniques: (1) he placed this expansion of the sabbath law on the lips of the Lord: "thus says Yahweh" (17:21); and (2) he claimed that this new provision was *actually part of* the Sinai declaration "commanded [to] your forefathers" (17:22–23). Fishbane marvels at these seemingly chimerical assertions:

> In sum, such a revelation…which presumptively cites regulations hitherto unrecorded as known and ancient is most remarkable. It points, at the very least, to the need in ancient Israel to camouflage and legitimate its exegetical innovations… Indeed, inner-biblical legal exegesis contains many other instances whereby the old revelation is misrepresented to one degree or another; but there is none like Jer. 17:21–2 where exegetical innovations are so brazenly represented as a citation of the old revelation by YHWH himself.[63]

Ezra apparently shared this need "to camouflage and legitimate…exegetical innovations." In a prescriptive-law society (especially with a closed law code which cannot be amended) strict adherence to what is written meant that new regulations, if added, would have to be made to look like part of the old. According to Fishbane, Ezra used Jeremiah's innovation as a basis for further expanding the sabbath prohibitions. Furthermore, he succeeded in passing it off as though it were part of "what God gave to Moses" (Neh 10:30) as Jeremiah had done. Other

61. Ibid., 132 (emphasis original). Cf. Clines, "Neh 10," 114–15.
62. Ibid., 133.
63. Ibid., 134. Cf. Michael Fishbane, *The Garments of Torah* (Indianapolis: Indiana University Press, 1989), 10–11.

scholars—including Joseph Blenkinsopp, H. G. M. Williamson, Mark Throntveit, Jacob Myers, and Yehezkel Kaufmann—share Fishbane's intuition that new legislation is being passed off as though it were old.[64]

Not all scholars agree. Holmgren does not think Ezra was shrouding new law under old garments. Ezra's regulation (indeed, Jeremiah's) was a faithful application of the "spirit" of the Torah sabbath law. Holmgren writes, "Although the teaching here does not reflect the 'words' of Torah concerning Sabbath observance, it does reflect the 'spirit' of Torah."[65] Clines has drawn a similar conclusion:

> The sabbath law, which in each of its formulations specifically enjoins rest from work...nowhere defines buying food as work... The presence of Gentile merchants in Nehemiah's Jerusalem raised the legal question whether simply to *buy* was breaking the law. No "God-fearer"...would have had much doubt about the answer, but a public definition was desirable.[66]

Both Clines and Holmgren recognize that Ezra faced new circumstances not faced by Moses. When, therefore, he sought to apply the sabbath law witnessed to by Moses, he was free to overlook—that is, he did not have to exegetically re-interpret—the Mosaic stipulations. The explanation of Clines and Holmgren seems the most satisfactory at this point, and it is an explanation which essentially ascribes to Ezra a descriptivistic use of Torah. The ancient law book shows how Moses applied Yahwistic righteousness in his day, but does not prescribe to Ezra how the same righteousness should be applied in his day.

5. Discrepancy 5: Nehemiah 10:33–34—Institution of an Annual Temple Tax

Another discrepancy in the Nehemiah covenant relates to the appointment of an annual temple tax of one-third shekel. This provision introduces two unprecedented features: first, the Pentateuch knows of no *one-third* shekel tax (the closest parallel is a one-half shekel tax); and second, that one-half shekel tax was connected with a one-time census—it was not *annual* (Exod 30:12–16; 38:25–26).

Clines has endeavored to overcome the first of these problems (the discrepancy in amount) by introducing a difference between the Median

---

64. Blenkinsopp, *Ezra–Nehemiah*, 315; Williamson, *Ezra, Nehemiah*, 334; Kaufmann, *Religion of Israel*, 4:385; Jacob M. Myers, *Ezra–Nehemiah* (AB 14; Garden City, N.Y.: Doubleday, 1965), 178; Mark A. Throntveit, *Ezra–Nehemiah* (IBC; Louisville, Ky.: John Knox, 1992), 109.

65. Holmgren, *Alive Again*, 139.

66. Clines, *Ezra–Esther*, 205–6.

shekel *coin* and the shekel *weight*. However, the former being 5.6 grams and the latter around 11.4 grams, the 1/2 = 1/3 ratio does not work.[67] Other attempts to explain the discrepancy by changes in monetary weights have similarly proven unhelpful.[68] Blenkinsopp offered a "common sensical" approach to the change in amount: "We may assume that taxation tends inexorably to increase."[69] Blenkinsopp therefore reasons that the half-shekel tax in the Priestly corpus was actually *later* than the one-third shekel tax of Ezra–Nehemiah. Those sharing Blenkinsopp's view note that a half-shekel tax was introduced under the Hasmonean era and continued into New Testament times.[70] This view may reverse the direction of the discrepancy, but it does not resolve it. Menahem Haran (followed by Williamson) concludes that the Neh 10 tax-amount was "based on a midrashic interpretation of the half-shekel [tax]."[71] No details of *how* the change was derived is offered, however. Such an explanation provides a title for the change ("midrash"), but does not really explain it. It is difficult to avoid the conclusion that there is no *textual* basis in the Torah for setting a *one-third* shekel value on the temple tax.

Furthermore, it is difficult to justify (textually) the establishment of an *annual* temple tax. Williamson approaches this second problem by explaining reasons why an annual tax became necessary: Darius' patronage may have lapsed after his death; the new, monetary economy of Persia may have made the need for "cash as well as kind" gifts more pressing; and so forth. He also demonstrates that the Ezra provision does show a close connection with the Mosaic census tax: both are "for the service of the house of our God" and both are "to make atonement for Israel" (Exod 30:15–16/Neh 10:33–34).[72] Thus Williamson's commentary provides helpful insight into the reason why the tax was instituted annually, and helps to confirm the connection of that tax with Exod 30, but he stops short of explaining how the change from a one-off to an annual tax was justified. Contrary to the general admission of scholars,[73] Myers has sought to resolve the problem by reading Exod 30:13 as an *annual* tax. He does not, however, base this move on any evidence in

67. Ibid., 171, 207.

68. For summary of other attempts, see Jacob Liver, "The Half-Shekel Offering in Biblical and Post-Biblical Literature," *HTR* 56 (1963): 182 n. 18.

69. Blenkinsopp, *Ezra–Nehemiah*, 316.

70. Liver, "Half-Shekel Offering"; Josephus, *War* 7.216–18; *Ant.* 18.312; Matt 17:24–27.

71. Menahem Haran, "Behind the Scenes of History: Determining the Date of the Priestly Source," *JBL* 100 (1981): 323. Cf. Williamson, *Ezra, Nehemiah*, 336.

72. Williamson, *Ezra, Nehemiah*, 335.

73. Especially Liver, "Half-Shekel Offering."

Exod 30. He begins with the fact of Ezra's annual tax (and that of Joash; see below). The fact of Ezra's annual tax is used as grounds for supposing Exod 30 to have had the same in view.[74] This simply begs the question.

There may be, as Haran and Williamson proposed, a midrash to explain how one-half becomes one-third, or how a census becomes an annual tax. Without any plausible sketch of what that midrash might have entailed, however, such an appeal feels more like a side-stepping of the problem than a real solution. Yet without some creative, exegetical midrash, there can be no justification for these blatant changes to Torah's stipulations (if read as prescriptive law).

If, on the other hand, the Yehud covenanters understood the Torah as an authoritative model, but not legislation, then such innovation is completely natural. The Mosaic example illustrates the congregation's responsibility to provide for the national shrine in times of need, so that their atonement might not fail. In Moses' day, needed support was raised through a one-off, half-shekel census tax. This exemplar illustrates the kind of burden which might be expected of the people; it does not prescribe the universal method or amount of such taxation. Ezra was able to impose a one-third shekel tax (valued according to the economics of his situation) and to impose it annually (due to the perpetual difficulties of the time). But this was *his own* stipulation, not one drawn from Torah. That is, "according to the law book of Moses" does not mean that Ezra instituted a Mosaic law, but that he drafted a new law harmonious in some way with Moses' example.

Support for this conclusion might be found in the Chronicler's account of Joash's reformation (2 Chr 24:4–14; cf. 2 Kgs 12:4–15). Joash is also said to have funded his temple renewal through taxation. Like Ezra, Joash did so through an annual tax (probably continued until the renovation was completed). Like Ezra, Joash defended his tax by reference to the Exod 30 census. Joash's example (as recounted by the post-exilic Chronicler) seems to confirm the likelihood that Persian-era Judaism used Torah as a descriptive model, and did not feel constrained to enforce its stipulations.[75]

74. Myers, *Ezra–Nehemiah*, 178.
75. Joash used this tax for the *fabric* of the temple. Ezra (like Moses) used it for the *service* of the temple. In this respect, Joash's application of the Exod 30 tax law is even more remarkable than Ezra's, further indicating the flexibility of the Mosaic example on this tax. In both Joash's and Ezra's reforms, the congregation is taking responsibility to perpetuate atonement—the *idea* behind the Exod 30 census (v. 16). Thus, even though the *stipulations* of Exod 30 are not being upheld by Joash, he too is acting with good precedent: "according to the Mosaic pattern."

6. *Discrepancy 6: Nehemiah 10:35—Institution of a Wood Offering*

The institution of a wood-offering rota represents another innovation not contained in the Mosaic writings. Nevertheless, Neh 10 identifies this injunction as one to be carried out "as written in the law" (v. 35). Once again, Houtman sees this as indication Ezra's Torah was different from any extant version. Clearly the perpetual fire on the altar shows a need for wood (Lev 6:2–13), but the Pentateuch contains no "wood offering" requirement.[76]

Blenkinsopp and Williamson point out that wood provision had originally been made by the Gibeonites. They were appointed "hewers of wood and drawers of water…for the altar of Yahweh, even unto this day" (Josh 9:27). There would have been no need for a wood offering in pre-exilic Israel.[77] Post-exile, however, it became necessary to make new arrangements for wood. Ezra looked to the Torah for guidance to do so.

Two possible texts might have provided Ezra with the needed insight. First, the Pentateuch does speak of the congregation's duty to bring oil for the ever-burning lamp (Exod 27:20). Second, it is the priests' responsibility to ensure the fire at the altar does not expire: "The fire on the altar shall be kept burning… The priest shall burn wood on it every morning…it shall not go out" (Lev 6:12–13). These paradigms could have led Ezra to introduce the new, jointly congregational/priestly wood offering as "according to the writing." Such a conclusion could readily be drawn by the precedential value of these Torah examples; or, if Ezra was a tradent of midrashic interpretation, one might envision him melding the two instructions into a new command for "the priests, the Levites, and the people" to provide wood (v. 35). This stipulation of Ezra could, therefore, be conceived as either a midrashic reuse of Torah prescriptions, or a new law after the Mosaic pattern.

7. *Discrepancy 7: Nehemiah 5:1–13—Nehemiah's Lawsuit*

The final passage from Ezra–Nehemiah to be examined in this study is different from those preceding. The foregoing texts are those where the law book is cited. The text now to be considered is a law-court proceeding. Remarkably, however, there is *no* citation of the law book in this setting—even though Mosaic norms are arguably in view. The narrative is part of the so-called "Nehemiah Memoir." In this entry of his memoir, Nehemiah records the economic distress of Jewish peasants and his response to it. The account can be summarized as follows.

---

76. Houtman, "Ezra and the Law," 106.
77. Blenkinsopp, *Ezra–Nehemiah*, 317; Williamson, *Ezra, Nehemiah*, 336.

The typical strains of subsistence living in Yehud had been exacerbated by a famine (v. 3) and by imperial taxes (v. 4). As a result, many Jews were compelled to borrow in order to feed their families (v. 2), to pay the king's tax (v. 4), and possibly to pay for the replanting of their lands (v. 3). This indebtedness was not, in itself, the cause of trouble. Uproar arose as Jewish creditors began to seize mortgaged property from their brother Jews. Loans had been guaranteed against the people's fields and houses (vv. 3–5). Now these properties were being seized (vv. 5, 11). The people's means of income was therefore lost to them, while the debts remained outstanding. Thus, with debts to pay but no means of income, it was inevitable their families would be forced into slavery to work off the debts. It was this hopelessness, already beginning to collapse in upon them, that drove these destitute Jews to Nehemiah's court: "Now behold, we are subjecting our sons and our daughters to slavery, and some of our daughters are subjugated already, and there is no power in our hands—our fields and our vineyards belong to others" (v. 5). Nehemiah responded with characteristic passion ("now it enraged me exceedingly," v. 6) and typical deliberation ("so I took counsel with myself," v. 7). Nehemiah's solution was to call "a great assembly." There he persuaded the moneylenders, under solemn oath, to release all collateral back to the owners and to cease from requiring pledges (vv. 10–13).

Several details of the account need to be established in order to clarify the problem Nehemiah sought to resolve. First of all, there is a textual question in Nehemiah's plea to the creditors in v. 11: "Restore to them please, this day, their fields, their vineyards, their olive orchards, and their houses, and _____ (MT: ומאת/or, emend as: ומשאת) the silver, the grain, the new wine, and the oil which you have been loaning to them."

Most scholars interpret the MT reading as a percentage—either a specific percentage ("a hundredth," being one per cent per month),[78] or as a term simply meaning "interest."[79] In either case, the implication of the MT reading is that, in addition to requiring pledges, *interest* was being charged. There is, however, no clear reference to interest elsewhere in the narrative. Apart from this instance, the whole account is aimed at the

78. E.g. Edward Neufeld, "The Rate of Interest and the Text of Nehemiah 5.11," *JQR* 44 (1953–54): 194–202; F. Charles Fensham, *The Books of Ezra and Nehemiah* (NICOT; Grand Rapids: Eerdmans, 1982), 195; L. H. Brockington, ed., *Ezra, Nehemiah and Esther* (The Century Bible; London: Thomas Nelson, 1969), 124–25. Most scholars recognize 12% per year as low, with 20% being the Persian-era norm.

79. E.g. Williamson, *Ezra, Nehemiah*, 240–41; Mervin Breneman, *Ezra, Nehemiah, Esther* (NAC 10; Nashville: Broadman & Holman, 1993), 205; Blenkinsopp, *Ezra–Nehemiah*, 255.

problem of property distraint. For this reason (and due to the awkward-
ness of the MT reading) a number of scholars have suggested the emended
reading, ומשאת ("and the pledged property").[80] Rather than a two-fold
instruction—to return seized property (v. 11a) *and* waive interest charges
(v. 11b)—the verse would then read simply as a requirement to release
all seized property: "Restore to them please, this day, their fields, their
vineyards, their olive orchards, and their houses—the property pledged
for the silver, the grain, the new wine, and the oil which you have been
loaning to them." Although the MT reading cannot be absolutely ruled
out, this reading seems more plausible. If correct, it would mean that
interest was not an issue in Nehemiah's case.

A second detail requiring resolution is the extent of Nehemiah's
release. Did Nehemiah require creditors to forgive all debts, or did he
merely require the return of property held in pledge? The former is often
assumed, although the latter seems more likely. As already noted, the
cause of the people's uproar was not the provision of loans, but the loss
of their means of livelihood as mortgaged property was seized: "We are
subjecting our sons and daughters to slavery…and there is no power in
our hands—our fields and our vineyards belong to others" (v. 5).

Nehemiah's measure is intended to reverse *this* misfortune and does
not say anything about annulling debts—only restoring property (v. 11).
The question arises, however, whether a full release of debts might be an
automatic result of restoring pledges. Some commentators see this as the
implication inherent in the creditors' response to Nehemiah: "'Restore to
them…the property pledged for the [goods]…you have been loaning to
them.' Then they said, 'We will restore, and we will not seek (לו נבקש)
from them. Thus we will do as you have said'" (vv. 11–12). Does the
promise, "we will not seek," indicate the creditors' foregoing all repayment? It is often assumed that they are promising two things: to restore
distrained property, and to expect no reimbursement for the original
loan.[81] This is doubtful, however, as Nehemiah never asked the creditors
to release outstanding debts—only to return property. It would be a
remarkable transformation in attitude for the tight-fisted creditors suddenly to offer to "require nothing more" in the way of debt repayment as
well. More likely, the agreement is simply to restore distrained property
now, with a promise not to turn around and retake it later (cf. Jer 34:11).

80. E.g. *BHS*; Clines, *Ezra–Esther*, 169; Robin Wakely, "נשא" (#5957),
NIDOTTE 3:178.

81. E.g. Holmgren, *Alive Again*, 112; Myers, *Ezra–Nehemiah*, 131; Blenkinsopp,
Ezra–Nehemiah, 260; Williamson, *Ezra, Nehemiah*, 241; Robert North, *Sociology of
the Biblical Jubilee* (AnBib 4; Rome: Pontifical Biblical Institute, 1954), 205.

The absence of any direct object for the verb בקש indicates that the pledges released are also the object no longer to be sought. By so doing, the creditors "do as you said"—they fulfill the demands Nehemiah placed upon them (but nothing more).

Nehemiah's injunction is best understood as focused on the restoration of seized collateral. The debts remain outstanding. Nehemiah himself had been granting loans on collateral to the poor (v. 10)—though he (it seems) was not seizing pledged lands. In general, granting loans to those in distress was regarded as a deed of kindness (e.g. Deut 15:7–8). It is doubtful that Nehemiah intended to restrain the wealthy from "seeking all further payment" from their brethren, thereby effectively halting loans. He simply put an end to property seizure, whereby the people were inevitably doomed to slavery when they failed to produce income. This is probably why there is no mention of restoring debt-slaves in Nehemiah's demands. Debt-slavery was only an impending (though inevitable) fear, few having been put into such bondage at this point (v. 5). Even after Nehemiah's action, family members might still be required to work off a debt if it could not be repaid.[82] However, with a moratorium on all pledged-land foreclosures, the people retained the means to redeem themselves and their kin. This is what Nehemiah protected. It was the problem of distraint—not usury, debt-slavery (directly), or loans—that Nehemiah confronted.[83] This clarification helps focus attention, now, on the particular legal issues relevant to the case.

The juridical nature of the account is apparent. It begins with the helpless and oppressed, both men and women, "crying out" (צעקת גדולה) to the royal governor for protection (v. 1). Verses 1–5 record the specific appeals raised. It was typical of ancient jurisprudence that "the court was brought into being by the appeal."[84] Nehemiah responds with appropriate zeal, showing himself to be the judge of the helpless: "Now it enraged me exceedingly when I heard their outcry and these words" (v. 6). He therefore pressed charges (ואריבה) against the creditors, which are recorded: "By loans under pledge (משא), you are pledging a man to his brother!" (v. 7). In this charge, Nehemiah is exposing the heart of the problem: by lending under a pledge of *property*, it is actually the *persons* of brother Jews that are being put in jeopardy. There follows then "a great assembly" (קהלה גדולה) where Nehemiah reasons with the defendants before witnesses (the gathered community; cf. Ruth 4:4, 11). This

---

82. Grabbe points out the need of the creditors (including Nehemiah; Neh 5:10) to be protected from ruin, as well (Grabbe, *Ezra–Nehemiah*, 47).

83. Clines, *Ezra–Esther*, 166, 169; Wakely, *NIDOTTE* 3:178.

84. Boecker, *Law and Justice*, 33. Cf. Fensham, *Ezra and Nehemiah*, 191 n. 2.

reasoning continues until a resolution acceptable to all is concluded— "Then [the creditors] said, '...We will do as you have said'... And all the assembly said, 'Amen'" (vv. 12–13)—which resolution is then sealed with a sacral oath (v. 13).

It is immediately striking that the whole case unfolds in the typical ancient Near Eastern fashion, with the judge as a wise man enraged at injustice and able to satisfy all sides of the debate by his wise negotiation. He negotiates a solution with obvious sensitivity to social customs (i.e. loan, pledge, debt, and debt-slavery practices, etc.) There is, however, no appeal to an authoritative law text. The judge is one who, by his own great wisdom and sense of justice ("so I took counsel with myself," v. 7), through brilliant reasoning no one can dispute ("they were silent and could not find a word to answer," v. 8), brings a solution accepted as just by both the charged ("we will do as you have said," v. 12) and the victims ("all the assembly said, 'Amen,'" v. 13). Ludwig Köhler's typification of ancient "justice in the gates" is apropos at this point:

> The legal assembly...is the organization for reconciliation. It grows up out of a practical need. It does not go beyond this in its actions nor in its outlooks. It intervenes when it must, but does not intervene any further than it must. It has no desire to provide systematic law. Nor does it act in systematic legal ways, but its sole endeavor is to settle quarrels and to guard the well-being of the community. To judge means here to settle.[85]

Nehemiah is such a judge. He is not an executor of the law book. He is rather a mediator between the contradictory rights of two parties, offering a way of reconciliation that protects everyone and the overall community. This is significant for the present study. If Persian-era Yehud was the setting where "the legal system became based upon the idea of a written code of law,"[86] and "the transformation of the biblical legal collection into 'statutory' texts, binding upon the courts" occurred,[87] it is remarkable that the law book was never brought to bear in Nehemiah's court. In a set of narratives where the Mosaic law book is constantly invoked to justify cultic reforms, it is significant that this detailed court record completely overlooks any reference to that law book as a source of jurisprudence.

Most commentators sense some influence from the Torah in Nehemiah's thinking. Various ideals from the Lev 25 Jubilee are particularly

---

85. Ludwig Köhler, *Hebrew Man: Lectures Delivered at the Invitation of the University of Tübingen December 1–16, 1952, with an Appendix on "Justice in the Gate"* (trans. P. R. Ackroyd; London: SCM Press, 1956), 156.

86. Westbrook, "Biblical Law," 4.

87. Jackson, *Studies*, 142.

notable in the Nehemiah courtroom story.[88] Both passages emphasize the fear of the Lord as a reason to forego economic claims (Lev 25:17, 36, 43/Neh 5:9). Both passages seek to preserve ancestral property (Lev 25:27–28, 41/Neh 5:3–5, 10–11). Both passages are concerned to guard against the enslaving of fellow Israelites (Lev 25:39, 46/Neh 5:5, 7–8). Both passages emphasize brotherhood as a grounds for charitable loans (Lev 25:14, 25, 35–36, 39, 46–48/Neh 5:1, 5, 7–8). And if usury is part of the Nehemiah case, a further parallel emerges (Lev 25:36/Neh 5:11). It is difficult to miss these significant parallels.

The following Exodus provision is even more directly relevant to Nehemiah's argument:

> If you loan money to my people—the poor who are with you—do not play the pledge-snatcher (לא־תהיה לו כנשה) over them, nor shall you exact interest of them. If you claim a pledge, (say) your fellow's garment, you shall return it to him before sundown, for it is his only covering, it is his garment for his body. What will he sleep in? For it will be, when he cries out to me, that I will hear, for I am gracious. (Exod 22:24–26 [EV vv. 25–27]; cf. Deut 24:10–13)[89]

While Torah consistently discountenances *interest* on loans between Israelites (Exod 22:24; Lev 25:36–37; Deut 23:20–21 [EV vv. 19–20]), a loan secured with property (נשא; משא) was deemed appropriate (Exod 22:27–28 [EV vv. 26–27]; Deut 15:2; 24:10–13). The above passage from BC includes both a frank opposition to usury and an exhortation to handle collateral with grace (as God is gracious). Nehemiah, likewise, acknowledges the general propriety of secured loans. Without any indication of guilt,[90] Nehemiah readily identifies himself with the practice: "Even I, my brothers, and my servants, are lending (משים) them silver and grain under pledge" (Neh 5:10). Nehemiah nowhere disparages loans under pledge; he condemns distraint which leaves the debtor with no means to avoid subsequent bondage: "By loan under pledge, you are pledging a man to his brother!" (v. 7). Nehemiah's defense of the individual with no means of income after property distraint is in direct harmony with the defense of the debtor in Exod 22, whose seized garment is his only covering: "What will he sleep in?"

---

88. E.g. Blenkinsopp, *Ezra–Nehemiah*, 259; Leslie C. Allen and Timothy S. Laniak, *Ezra, Nehemiah, Esther* (NIBC 9; Carlisle: Paternoster, 2003), 111; Williamson, *Ezra, Nehemiah*, 238–39; Lemche, "Sabbatical Year," 53–54; North, *Sociology of the Jubilee*, 205–6.

89. See Blenkinsopp, *Ezra–Nehemiah*, 258–59; Williamson, *Ezra, Nehemiah*, 238; Clines, *Ezra–Esther*, 168.

90. Contra Holmgren, *Alive Again*, 111–12; Fensham, *Ezra and Nehemiah*, 194–95. Cf. Blenkinsopp, *Ezra–Nehemiah*, 259–60.

Did Nehemiah actually reflect on these (or other[91]) texts when he "took counsel with himself"? Many commentators cannot avoid this suspicion: "He was facing a conflict between social classes, which he solved on the basis of principles taught in the Pentateuch."[92] *If* Nehemiah did reference Torah, he referenced it as a juridical treatise; he never drew upon its authority to bind the creditors to a "legally prescribed" course of action. Instead of citing texts as binding, he obliged the creditors by invoking: their fear of Yahweh and a divine curse (vv. 9, 12–13); their obligation as brother Jews (vv. 7–8); their national pride (v. 9); their own moral sensibilities (v. 9); and the pressure of public sensibilities (vv. 7, 13).[93] Furthermore, the creditors never appeal to any text to defend their legal rights ("they could find not a word to answer," v. 8).[94] And at the end of the trial, the verdict implemented was "these words" which Nehemiah had spoken (vv. 12–13): the only prescriptive order emerging from the narrative *is the verdict stipulated by Nehemiah.*[95]

This scenario is startling if post-exilic Yehud was reorganized under Torah as a statutory constitution. As seen, there is plenty of Pentateuchal material Nehemiah could have drawn upon to justify his verdict. That he turned, however, to traditional forms of persuasion—and not to the law book—is telling. That this lack of judicial citation from the law book is paralleled by frequent cultic law book citations in Ezra–Nehemiah is even more telling. The resulting appearance is very similar to that of Josiah's reforms. Citation of the law book is an important basis for restoring a defunct cultus. It is not used prescriptively for that reform, however. Nor is the book cited at all for social reform.[96] There is actually no evidence in Ezra–Nehemiah of any effort to enforce Torah judicially.

---

91. Other Torah parallels sometimes mentioned by commentators include Exod 21:1–11; Deut 15:1–2, 7–11; 24:10–13.

92. Breneman, *Ezra–Esther*, 202. Cf. Williamson, *Ezra, Nehemiah*, 239; Allen and Laniak, *Ezra–Esther*, 111; Holmgren, *Alive Again*, 114.

93. Myers, *Ezra–Nehemiah*, 131; Clines, *Ezra–Esther*, 166, 168–69; Fensham, *Ezra and Nehemiah*, 196; Blenkinsopp, *Ezra–Nehemiah*, 259–60; Williamson, *Ezra, Nehemiah*, 238–39.

94. Cf. Köhler, *Hebrew Man*, 158–60.

95. Cf. Neh 13:6–31.

96. Cf. Fried's insight that Ezra's rescript was *"to appoint judges,"* not to institute a law code. It was for purposes of public and judicial education that Ezra's law book was introduced in connection with that rescript. Ezra's judges were being equipped to adjudicate in keeping with *custom* law (i.e. the "law of your God" and the "law of the king"). See Lisbeth S. Fried, "'You Shall Appoint Judges': Ezra's Mission and the Rescript of Artaxerxes," in Watts, eds., *Persia and Torah*, 63–89; cf. Ezra 7:25–26.

*   *   *

A summary of the texts examined above is in order at this point. Seven problem texts for ascribing prescriptivism to Persian Yehud have here been presented: (1) the *Davidic* temple courses were said to have been established in keeping with the *Mosaic* law book; (2) specific stipulations for observing the Feast of Booths "according to the law" were seen to be different from what the Torah actually states; (3) prohibitions against intermarriage were seen to go beyond the terms of Moses' proscription; (4) making purchases on the sabbath was seen to be nowhere prohibited in the Torah, yet such was prohibited "according to Torah" in Persian Yehud; (5) an annual temple tax (of one-third shekel) was seen somehow to have been identified with a one-time census tax (of one-half shekel) in the Pentateuch; (6) a wood offering rota was seen to have been appointed "as written in the law," although no such wood offering appears in Torah; (7) Nehemiah was seen to have been handed down a court ruling in evident harmony with Torah's teachings, yet he sourced his verdict in all manner of moral, cultic, and social sources of authority—but never the Torah book.

While more or less plausible possibilities have been advanced by numerous scholars to resolve various of these problems, the overall effect is persuasive. Ezra–Nehemiah does not display concern for the enforcement of Torah's stipulations. What the records show is a concern to demonstrate that the post-exilic *cultus* was reformed in harmony with the Mosaic religion. The expression, "according to the book of Moses," does not mean the Mosaic *stipulations* are being applied; it means *Ezra's new stipulations* are crafted in keeping with Mosaic Yahwism.

It was noted, nonetheless, that several of Ezra's anomalous practices actually can be reckoned with the written stipulations of Torah through midrashic exegesis. Fishbane has shown how Ezra could have employed "etymological midrash" to derive the booths-from-branches prescription out of Lev 23 (#2, above), "midrashic extension" to meld two distinct Deuteronomy texts and produce the updated intermarriage proscription (#3, above), and "midrashic innovation" to take a *Jeremiah* sabbath command and "camouflage" a deduction from it as Mosaic (#4, above). By demonstrating these three possible exegeses, Fishbane has opened the way to speculate on others too.

The fact remains, however, that nowhere in Ezra–Nehemiah is such exegetical activity actually indicated. The law-interpretation scene in Neh 8 is the setting where one might suppose such lexical studies would have occurred if they occurred, but the Neh 8 law-reading "with interpretation" is more likely a matter of translating from Hebrew to Aramaic rather than exegesis. (These features of the Neh 8 exposition will be discussed further, below; pp. 134–36.) Two problems with Fishbane's thesis therefore emerge. First, the writers of Ezra–Nehemiah show no concern to record any lexical grounds for Ezra's anomalous Torah responses. In other words, if Ezra felt constrained to show how his stipulations were the very stipulations of the Torah, the compilers of the account (and presumably the audience it was written for) did not share this need. Nothing in the narrative shows midrash taking place: the anomalies are not felt to need exegetical support.[97] Second, the whole theory that Ezra engaged in the kind of midrashic exegesis Fishbane posits for him is anachronistic. Vocable-constrained exegesis is a known practice of late Second Temple rabbinics. Fishbane draws this late practice all the way back to Ezra, and ascribes to him a remarkably advanced set of midrashic tools for his period.[98]

David Weiss Halivni finds that the earliest halakhic midrash can be demonstrated is the second century BCE.[99] The evidence from that period reflects midrashic praxis that was relatively straightforward (i.e. interest in the text's plain meaning). It was not yet characterized by the complex forms of etymology, word-linkages, and the like which would later develop. Halivni explains, "The word 'simple' is crucial to this discussion of Midrash, for only the simple Midrash—the one that springs forth easily from the text, as against the 'complex,' heavy one that requires the assistance of hermeneutical principles—is old, before the time of Hillel."[100]

In the first century BCE, Hillel (ca. 30–39 BCE) first articulated a systematic set of rules for complex midrash. Hillel claimed to have learned these rules from his teachers, so they could date somewhat earlier. Nonetheless, Hillel's exegetical methods do not seem to have been widely

97. Hindy Najman, "Torah of Moses: Pseudonymous Attribution in Second Temple Writings," in *The Interpretation of Scripture in Early Judaism and Christianity: Studies in Language and Tradition* (ed. Craig A. Evans; JSPSup 33; Studies in Scripture in Early Judaism and Christianity 7; Sheffield: Sheffield Academic Press, 2000), 211–12.

98. Childs and Sanders raise similar questions; see Brevard S. Childs, review of Fishbane, *Biblical Interpretation*, JBL 106, no. 3 (1987): 512–13; J. A. Sanders, review of Fishbane, *Biblical Interpretation*, CBQ 49 (1987): 303.

99. David Weiss Halivni, *Midrash, Mishnah, and Gemara: The Jewish Predilection for Justified Law* (Cambridge, Mass.: Harvard University Press, 1986), 18–37. Cf. David Daube, "Rabbinic Methods of Interpretation and Hellenistic Rhetoric," *HUCA* 22 (1949): 239–64; R. C. Musaph-Andriesse, *From Torah to Kabbalah: A Basic Introduction to the Writings of Judaism* (trans. John Bowden; London: SCM Press, 1981), 59.

100. Halivni, *Midrash*, 34.

understood in his day. As the Palestinian Talmud famously reports: "Even though he [Hillel] would exposit Midrash abundantly [to prove his point], they did not accept his conclusions" (*y. Pesaḥ* 6:1 [33a]).[101]

In other words, complex midrash can only be presupposed in the first and second centuries BCE (and it would appear to be a relatively recent development for that time). If Ezra–Nehemiah witnesses to a community employing the Torah prescriptively, however, Fishbane has shown the extent to which verbal adaptation would have had to be present much earlier. If Ezra was drawing his stipulations from the Torah's text, he was not employing Halivni's "simple midrash" (i.e. the plain meaning), but anticipating Hillel's "complex midrash." This seems a lot to presume, especially since the fact remains: Ezra–Nehemiah never includes any midrashic explanations. It seems that showing consistency with the general vision of Torah was all Ezra–Nehemiah needed to do.[102] The practice evidence indicates that Torah was a practical—but *historic-descriptive*—law collection in Persian Yehud.

II. *Law Book Study in Ezra–Nehemiah*

The evidence treated above leads to the conclusion that post-exilic Judaism continued to employ the Hebrew law writings descriptively. This conclusion has been drawn from examination of the law-practice evidence in Ezra–Nehemiah. It is this kind of study which has hitherto been lacking.

There is, however, another front which needs to be addressed. Most scholars who posit prescriptivism with Ezra–Nehemiah also point to a new emphasis on *understanding* the law book in Ezra–Nehemiah.[103] While the practice evidence warns against overstating this new emphasis on studying texts, its presence is significant. This new emphasis is particularly pronounced in Neh 8. In the first part of that passage, a public reading of the law book *was accompanied by Levitical explanation* (vv. 1–12). In the second part of the passage, a private gathering of community leaders *was accompanied by Ezra's explanation* (vv. 13–18). (It was in that latter gathering that the Feast of Booths arrangements, discussed earlier, were formulated; pp. 108–112, above.)

101. Translation from ibid., 19.
102. Najman, "Torah of Moses," 212–13.
103. Jackson, *Studies*, 141–42; Westbrook, "Biblical Law," 3–4; Fitzpatrick-McKinley, *Transformation*, 174–75; Michael Fishbane, "From Scribalism to Rabbinism: Perspectives on the Emergence of Classical Judaism," in *The Sage in Israel and the Ancient Near East* (ed. John G. Gammie and Leo G. Perdue; Winona Lake, Ind.: Eisenbrauns, 1990), 440–41.

There is nothing novel in the use of a law book for the education of "a wise and understanding people."[104] Some sort of public reading with explanation might be presupposed for earlier periods than Ezra–Nehemiah, since law writings were previously used for public instruction and ritual. Nehemiah 8, in other words, may not be recording a strictly new practice.[105] Notwithstanding that possibility, Neh 8 does introduce a remarkable new emphasis. Nowhere else is *public understanding* of the law book deemed a matter of such concern. For instance, the account of Josiah's public law-reading lacks any talk of the people understanding what was read to them (2 Kgs 23:1–3). It might be argued that the people's repentance, and their giving way to the destruction of their idols, presupposes some sort of explanation and understanding in the Josiah law-book reading. But the emphasis in the Josiah narrative focuses only on the *king's* response to the writings; Ezra–Nehemiah is novel in its new concern to highlight the *public* understanding of the law book.

This emphasis on popular understanding is coupled with a record of Ezra leading the leaders in further study. There is evidence for law book study by Israel's leaders in pre-exilic times (e.g. Deut 17:19; 31:9; Josh 1:8; 23:6); nonetheless, the Nehemiah passage is unique in its concern to describe such a study. This description of Yehud's leaders engaged in Torah study might be a way of showing their qualification to serve as the community's rulers in the absence of a king (whose traditional task it was "to read Torah day and night"). One might suspect propagandistic value behind a narrative about the leaders' Torah study. That this leadership study is told in concert with the story of *public* exposition, however, shows that there is more behind this portrayal. There is, in Ezra–Nehemiah, a new emphasis on study of the law book *by all levels of Jewish society.*

Fishbane is among those who note this development. He fittingly calls it an "axial shift" in biblical history—one of "the axial transformations that mark the onset of classical Judaism."[106] Fishbane correctly notes that law-book study has now become, in the post-exilic period, a central feature of the Hebrew faith, thus deserving ascription as an "axial" development. It seems necessary, however, once again to caution against reading too much of later Judaism into this Persian-era development. More specifically, Fishbane sees in these developments an early expression of

104.   Exod 12:26–27; 18:20; Deut 4:1–10; 6:6–9, 20–25; 31:10–13; cf. pp. 38, 46–48, above.

105.   So James W. Watts, review of Jackson, *Studies, RBL* 02/2003. Online: http://bookreviews.org/pdf/1404_3083.pdf.

106.   Fishbane, "From Scribalism to Rabbinism," 440.

that Judaic doctrine (well known after 70 CE) whereby law-book study replaces aspects of the temple services.[107]

Fishbane's basic thesis on this point derives from three Ezra–Nehemiah texts:

> The first is the almost offhand archival notice concerning the loss of the *ʾûrîm* and *tûmmîm*, the ancient priestly devices for mantic practice (Neh 7:65). The second is the rather explicit account of a national convocation in the year 458 BCE, at which time Ezra led the people in a public event of Torah instruction (Neh 8:1–8)... [Third, and] of central importance is the depiction of Ezra himself... We are told that "Ezra set his heart to investigate (*lidrôš*) the Torah of YHWH, and to do and teach (both) law and ordinance in Israel" (v. 10).[108]

In Fishbane's view, this series of texts indicate the cessation of normal methods for divine inquiry, and their replacement with exegetical study. In other words, study of Torah has become the means whereby the divine will is received—Torah has become the *source* of rulings for *present* questions, not just a *record* of *past* rulings. It has already been shown that Ezra's actual rulings cannot be readily explained by reference to the stipulations of Torah. The practice evidence does not support the idea that texts were Ezra's source for rulings. But what about the aforementioned texts Fishbane highlights?

A new post-exilic emphasis on community-wide Torah study is certainly emerging in Ezra–Nehemiah. Fishbane's three texts depicting this "axial shift" will next be examined, each in turn.

1. *Nehemiah 7:65: Demise of the* אורים ותומים

Fishbane rightly highlights a significant problem in early Second Temple manticism: the loss (or demise) of the אורים ותומים. This problem is reported by Nehemiah in this manner:

> Then my God put it into my heart to assemble the nobles and the officials and the people to be enrolled by genealogy... The following [among the Levites] were those who...could not prove their father's houses or their descent... The governor told them that they were not to partake of the most holy food until a priest with אורים ותומים should arise. (Neh 7:5–65; cf. Ezra 2:62–63)

Divine revelation had not ceased completely for Ezra's Yehud. The prophets Haggai and Zechariah in particular had important, oracular

---

107. Cf. Michael Fishbane, *The Exegetical Imagination: On Jewish Thought and Theology* (Cambridge, Mass.: Harvard University Press, 1998), 129–32.

108. Fishbane, "From Scribalism to Rabbinism," 440–41.

input in the temple rebuilding program (Ezra 6:14). Nonetheless, a significant decline in the mantic capacity of the Second Temple appears to have marked its inferiority to the First Temple.[109] The Ezra–Nehemiah incident mentioning the אורים ותומים reflects on this decline. Whether this decline should be understood as a complete loss of mantic oracles is debatable. The Talmudic tradition holds that the אורים ותומים, and other mantic features, "were present, but they were not as helpful (as before)" (*b. Yoma* 21b). This seems to be the implication of Ezra–Nehemiah: "Ezra 2:63 (Neh 7:65) does not say that the people in question had to wait 'until UT [אורים ותומים] should appear for the priest,' as if UT were lost. Instead it says: 'until a priest for *(lĕ)* Urim and Thummim should appear…'."[110] There was not necessarily so absolute a loss of inquiry as Fishbane supposes.

It is not necessary, however, to resolve whether mantic appeals were completely lost or weakened in Persian Yehud. In either case the citation from Neh 7 indicates that a certain "difficult case" (cf. Deut 17:8) could not be resolved because of this incapacity. What is important to note is the lack of any alternative deemed to be available. A ruling for a "difficult case" is required; however, the inability to resort to the אורים ותומים leaves the officials unable to source any answer. The expectation here portrayed is that *no* ruling for such a "difficult case" can be offered "until a priest with (or for) *ʾûrîm* and *tûmmîm* should arise." Rather than supporting Fishbane's idea that "exegetical praxis has functionally coopted older mantic techniques of divine inquiry,"[111] the opposite would appear to be the case. Where no mantic inquiry is possible, no solution to the "difficult cases" (once answered by oracle) can be obtained.[112]

2. *Nehemiah 8: Public Torah Reading*
Second, Fishbane points to the Neh 8 assembly where the law book was read and explained. Fishbane is correct to observe a "new emphasis" on law-book instruction in this narrative. However, that this development

---

109.   Ezek 10; *m. Soṭ.* 9:12; *b. Yoma* 21b; *b. B. Bat.* 12a.

110.   Cornelis van Dam, *The Urim and Thummim: A Means of Revelation in Ancient Israel* (Winona Lake, Ind.: Eisenbrauns, 1997), 220.

111.   Fishbane, "From Scribalism to Rabbinism," 441.

112.   In Williamson's view (*Ezra, Nehemiah*, 37), the governor expected appeal to the אורים ותומים to be possible once the cultus was fully operational. Van Dam further points out that the sons of Haqqoz (among those "not to partake…until a priest with אורים ותומים arise") *do* appear elsewhere in the narrative in full exercise of priestly offices (Ezra 8:33; Neh 3:4, 21). Does this mean further genealogical proof was found, or that the אורים ותומים were operational again? See Van Dam, *Urim and Thummim*, 219.

shows a replacement of oracles with new exegetical techniques (i.e. midrash)—or that this scene should be read as describing legal exegesis at all (as many scholars do)[113]—is, in fact, doubtful. It is unlikely the explanation which accompanied Ezra's reading went much beyond translation from Hebrew to Aramaic.

James Kugel explains:

> The language of Babylon, where the elite of Judea had been borne off captives, was Aramaic... [The] returnees might therefore presumably be in need of help in understanding Hebrew Scripture... Moreover, even those who stayed behind in Judea during the exile, though they continued to speak their native idiom, were not exempt from linguistic difficulties. For their spoken idiom was...corrupted by neighboring dialects (see Neh. 13.24). For this reason, both the Judean exiles and those who stayed behind might be in need of that most basic act of interpretation, translation into an idiom more familiar to them.[114]

The exiles in Jerusalem evidently had some rudimentary knowledge of Mosaic law even before Ezra arrived (Ezra 3:2, 4). Ezra, however, was "a scribe quick (מהיר) in the law of Moses" (Ezra 7:6). Persian scribes were trained to translate between languages efficiently; this was evidently one of Ezra's skills. The Neh 8 scenes (public reading/leadership study) involve at least this basic idea of Hebrew to Aramaic translation. Many scholars believe this to be the sense intended by the remark in v. 8: "so they read in the book...translating (מפרש)..."[115] In addition to translation, one can expect that some sort of Targum-like explanation took place. This is generally recognized in the further elaboration of v. 8: "and they gave its sense (ושום שכל) so [the people] understood the reading (ויבינו במקרא)." It is here that legal exegesis would need to be introduced. But does this translation-with-explanation introduce an exploration of lexical etymologies—midrash sufficient to derive, for instance, instructions about booth-making from the verbal root for סבכות?[116] This is a lot to accept.

It seems a big step to take what is manifestly a basic translation exercise *among a community which hardly knows Biblical Hebrew*, and to suggest that Ezra led those same people *in detailed studies of Hebrew*

113. See n. 103, above.
114. James L. Kugel, "The Need for Interpretation," in James L. Kugel and Rowan A. Greer, *Early Biblical Interpretation* (ed. Wayne A. Meeks; Philadelphia: Westminster, 1986), 28.
115. Cf. the Aramaic use of the same root in Ezra 4:18; see Fishbane, *Biblical Interpretation*, 108–9; Blenkinsopp, *Ezra–Nehemiah*, 288; Myers, *Ezra–Nehemiah*, 154; Najman, "Torah of Moses," 206–7).
116. See p. 110, above.

etymologies in order to source answers to difficult questions unsolvable by oracles. Nehemiah 8 does show an important effort in public education from the written Torah, but it does not show legal exegesis. Nor, in fact, is there any indication that oracles are being substituted by this exercise.[117] The emphatic explanation connected to the Ezra reading in Neh 8 is significant; there are no grounds, however, for seeing such nuanced exegesis here—much less exegesis as a replacement for oracles.

3. Ezra 7:10: Ezra's "Inquiry"

Perhaps Fishbane's most significant evidence for such a "replacement" is his third text: "Ezra set his heart to inquire (לדרש) in the law of Yahweh and to do and teach statutes and judgments in Israel" (Ezra 7:10). Fishbane writes:

> This is no mere depiction of a routine priestly function of ritual instruction, in the manner of some older pentateuchal accounts (cf. Lev 10:11). It is, rather, an extension and virtual transformation of this role. Special significance thus lies in the fact that the very idiom used to describe Ezra's activity ("*lidrôs* the Torah of YHWH") is a precise reworking of an ancient formula used to indicate oracular activity (cf. "to consult *[lidrôs]* YHWH," 1 Kgs 22:8). Since Ezra's textual task is to seek from the Torah new divine teachings (or explication of older ones) for the present, there is a sense in which exegetical praxis has functionally coopted older mantic techniques of divine inquiry.[118]

This use of an oracular term (דרש) in connection with Ezra's Torah study certainly invites the possibility of such a "replacement" as Fishbane has posited. However, the term דרש has broader usage than cultic inquiry. Its meaning, when a deity is its object (e.g. Exod 18:15) or when used in connection with the shrine (e.g. Deut 17:9, 12), is normally mantic inquiry. When some other setting or object (like a book) is in view, however, the term indicates "to seek" or "to study."[119] Thus a man seeks his lost sheep (Deut 22:2) and enemies seek the Psalmist's life (Ps 38:13 [EV v. 12]). More directly parallel to the present text: the memory of God's works are *studied* by all who delight in them (Ps 111:2); the singer of Ps 119 three times devotes himself to "study your precepts"

117. Fishbane (*Biblical Interpretation*, 108–9) notes that מפרש often occurs in connection with oracular legal decisions, but he also recognizes that the same term can mean "translation" between languages as in Ezra 4:18, and that the latter meaning is more likely here.

118. Fishbane, "From Scribalism to Rabbinism," 441. Cf. his "Midrash and Meaning," 553.

119. David Denninger, "דרש" (#2011), *NIDOTTE* 1:996–98.

(Ps 119:45, 94, 155); and a written study on another text is called a מדרש (2 Chr 24:27; here, a commentary on the book of Kings). These latter parallels show that when דרש appears with a text or body of tradition as its object, its normal indication would be pious *study* without necessarily supposing oracular results. It would seem probable that Ezra's study of Torah falls in line with this lexical norm, since no reference to the cultus is tied to his book-דרש.

A survey of other uses of the term in Ezra–Nehemiah helps to confirm its use in both cultic and non-cultic senses within this corpus. In two places, the term is used in reference to "seeking Yahweh" with cultic overtones:

> Now...the enemies of Judah...said to them, "Let us build with you, for we inquire (נדרוש) of your God as you do..." (Ezra 4:1–2)

> [The Passover] was eaten by the sons of Israel who had returned from exile, and also by everyone who had joined them and separated himself from the uncleanness of the peoples of the land to seek (לדרש) Yahweh, the God of Israel. (Ezra 6:21)

Elsewhere, however, the term is used in reference to study that is non-oracular. For instance, after exposing the prevalence of mixed marriages, Ezra appointed commissions in each city "to investigate (לדריוש) the matter" (Ezra 10:16). In reference to the enemies of the Jews, Ezra cites the ultimatum "never to seek (לא־תדרשו) their peace and prosperity" (Ezra 9:12).

In other words, the Ezra narrative evinces both cultic and "mundane" uses of the term דרש. Whether Ezra's דרש-study *in the Torah* indicates a new method of mantic inquiry (rather than its *natural* meaning where a *text* is in view—i.e. study) is not obvious. To provide further evidence, Fishbane points out, "This somewhat mantic or inspired dimension of study is underscored by the fact that, in this very context, Ezra is twice described as one who has the 'hand of YHWH...upon him' (vv 6, 9)."[120] However, this double expression is quite notably not connected with Ezra's study of the law book:

> This Ezra went up from Babylon. (Now he was a scribe skilled in the law of Moses which Yahweh the God of Israel gave.) And the king gave him *(as the hand of Yahweh his God was with him)* all his requests... On the first day of the first month, he began the ascent from Babylon; and on the first day of the fifth month he entered into Jerusalem *(for the good hand of his God was upon him)*, for Ezra set his heart to study in the law of Yahweh and to do and teach statutes and judgments in Israel. (Ezra 7:6–10)

120. Fishbane, "From Scribalism to Rabbinism," 441.

It is the fact that Ezra received from the king "all his requests" (v. 6) and then managed to complete his trek to Jerusalem in safety and speed (v. 9) that lead to the double ascription of "the good hand of his God upon him." These ascriptions of "the hand of God" on Ezra do not refer to inspired book study; they refer to God's getting him to Jerusalem with speed and safety.[121] Indeed, the whole reason God carried Ezra to Jerusalem was because Ezra "set his heart" to teach Torah "in Israel" (v. 10); but it is the *travel* of Ezra that is the concern of this passage, and it is the remarkable efficiency of his trip which is the mark of God's hand prospering him. This understanding is confirmed by the parallel account of Ezra's trip to Jerusalem in Ezra 8, where Ezra attests, "the hand of our God is on all those seeking him for good" (v. 22). Notably, the hand of God is thus on *all* the traveling exiles (not just upon Ezra). This expression is not being used to denote mantic activity connected to law-book study, but rather divine care in travel.[122]

*   *   *

Fishbane is correct to locate an "axial shift" in the post-exilic attitude toward the law writings. The text (by this point comprising the Pentateuch) is being emphatically promoted as a book for study by all levels of society: "everyone who has understanding" (Neh 8:2, 3).[123] Fishbane is also correct to note the presence of a close relationship between ancient texts and the ruling applied "according to" them. One might expect that verbal similarities might occur when a practitioner (like Ezra) is acting with a juridical treatise (like the Torah) at hand.[124] However, to adduce that this new emphasis on study and practical reference to the Torah means *the text* (as signs or as stipulations) has become *the source* for *present* rulings is unnecessary and anachronistic. Fishbane ascribes

---

121. Clines, *Ezra–Esther*, 100–101.

122. Fishbane ("From Scribalism to Rabbinism," 444–45) also cites examples in Dan 9–10 (especially 9:3; 10:21) to support his claim that books were being use for injury in the Persian era. In neither of these further examples, however, is Daniel actually said to derive answers from a book. Rather, after reading the book of Jeremiah, Daniel is perplexed and, *turning away from the book*, "turned [his] face to the Lord God, seeking (לבקש) him by prayer and pleas for mercy with fasting and sackcloth and ashes" (9:3; cf. 10:2–3). In other words, the book did *not* provide answers but prompted questions. Daniel employed *prayer and fasting* to seek oracular answers to the dilemma raised by the book. Daniel subsequently received divine answers through visions (not exegesis).

123. It is probably in this period that the Deuteronomic instruction for *kings* to study Torah day and night (Deut 17:18–20; Josh 1:8) received reformulation for the average Israelite in Ps 1.

124. Cf. Ammiṣaduqa's use of LH, on pp. 76–77, above.

too much of later practices to Ezra when he asserts: "Historically consdiered [*sic*], Ezra is the first master of the midrashic *parole*—for he 'inquires' *(doresh)* of the 'Torah of the Lord' (in Ezra 7:10) as former generations 'inquired' of God for a living oracle (2 Kgs 22:5, 8). His act...thus conjures new meanings from God's *langue*."[125]

The "axial shift" in Ezra's Judaism is less dramatic than that. The law book has become a focus of understanding for the whole community. This development can still be regarded as the origin of classical Judaism as a religion centered on book study. However, it anticipates too much to ascribe in Ezra's time: exegetical practices only demonstrable much later; the doctrine of book study as a replacement for the temple (e.g. oracles) which is only actually demonstrable much later; or the introduction of "'statutory' texts, binding upon the courts."[126]

III. *Conclusions*

To the extent that Ezra–Nehemiah is a reliable witness to Persian-era institutions, it can be concluded from this study that the Torah continued to be used descriptively—even if it was "used more."[127] Even for scholars who regard Ezra–Nehemiah as more properly belonging to early Hellenistic-era Jerusalem (and thus reflecting that period's ideals), the results of this study still stand. The finding that the literary construct

125. Fishbane, "Midrash and Meaning," 553. Cf. his *Garments of Torah*, 16–18.
126. Citing Jackson, *Studies*, 142.
127. The focus of this study has been limited to Ezra–Nehemiah. Following Fishbane, Schniedewind has proposed a similar replacement of oracle with the law book in Chronicles (William M. Schniedewind, *The Word of God in Transition: From Prophet to Exegete in the Second Temple Period* [JSOTSup 197; Sheffield: Sheffield Academic Press, 1995]). Of particular relevance here, Schniedewind shows that the Chronicler employed the expression "word of Yahweh" for the preserved (i.e. written) oracles of past prophets. Whether this means that *"Torah* replaced prophecy and the prophetic office became unnecessary" (p. 137) seems overstated in light of the actual continuation of prophecy post-exile (e.g. Haggai, Zechariah, Malachi). More to the point, Shaver has shown the same characteristic anomalies in the law-practice materials of Chronicles as here noted in Ezra–Nehemiah (Judson R. Shaver, *Torah and the Chronicler's History Work: An Inquiry into the Chronicler's References to Laws, Festivals, and Cultic Institutions in Relationship to Pentateuchal Legislation* [BJS 196; Atlanta: Scholars, 1989]). Schniedewind, Fishbane, and others correctly observe a "new centrality" ascribed to the biblical texts post-exile. But the continuing appeal to (and inability to replace) oracles post-exile, the indication of practice-evidence that the writings were used idyllically (not prescriptively), and an absence of law writings in courtroom adjudication, cautions against introducing legislative concepts prematurely into the Persian era.

"Ezra" used the Torah descriptively would simply be moved to that period. It would thus appear that the descriptivism of pre-exilic Israel continued into early Hellenistic Jerusalem through the medium of Persian-era practices. (More will be said in the next two chapters about Hellenistic-era legal ideals.)

The conclusion in the present chapter (in regard to Persian-era ideals) has been established through an examination of the practice materials of Ezra–Nehemiah, and in connection with "book study" texts noted by other scholars as indicative of "axial" period developments. Scholars have generally noted the latter (a new emphasis on book study) without testing subsequent conclusions against the former (law-practice evidence). Taking both kinds of evidence into account in this chapter, a qualified result as emerged: the law book continues to be viewed descriptively in Persian Yehud—but it is now viewed much more widely. Torah understanding has become a duty of the whole community. This is a significant development.[128]

Another significant development ought to be mentioned. Ezra's law-book citations include references to Deuteronomy and the so-called "Priestly Laws" and "Holiness Laws." Furthermore, the confession in Neh 9–10 draws upon a broad sweep of Pentateuchal history, including Abraham, the exodus, the wilderness wanderings, as well as the conquest (i.e. Joshua). The Ezra–Nehemiah law book therefore appears "similar to, if not yet fully identical with, our Pentateuch."[129] This is a significant expansion from the focus on Deuteronomy generally assumed in DtrH. It is not a change in *how* the law book was used, but it is an important expansion in the *contents* of Israel's law collection.

This latter development—the compilation of the Pentateuch in Ezra's Yehud—is widely accepted. A particular problem integral to this development has to do with the numerous, internal incongruities within the Pentateuch. Particularly when viewed as a legal corpus, the presence of contradictory stipulations and different traditions in one collection seems remarkable. It is to explain this problem that theories such as Frei's "imperial authorization" have been produced: such theses attempt to explain how (apparently) contradictory legal norms came to be integrated into a single collection. It is generally believed that it must have been a compromise measure between competing parties, all of which

128.   Duggan's insight (*Covenant Renewal*, 108) is indicative: law book readings are described as many times within Ezra–Nehemiah (four times: Neh 8:1–12, 13–18; 9:3; 13:1) as in the rest of the Hebrew Bible combined (four times: Exod 24:7; Josh 8:34; Jer 36:10, 13, 21; 2 Kgs 23:2/2 Chr 34:30).

129.   Williamson, *Ezra, Nehemiah*, xxxix. So also Blenkinsopp, *Ezra–Nehemiah*, 152–7; Grabbe, *Ezra–Nehemiah*, 56, 146–47.

were simply happy to have their own norms included in the final "consti-tution" despite the unwieldy result.[130]

How such a compromise measure (if it was one) could be accepted can be more readily appreciated in light of the present study. The Pentateuch was used (and arguably compiled) in this period as a collection of historic descriptions, not as a prescriptive code.[131] How Moses enforced a law at Sinai and how the same Moses differently enforced that law in another setting (e.g. in Moab) are, for the Pentateuch's community, sim-ply historic events, not contradictory prescriptions. It is outside the scope of the present study to resolve matters of the Pentateuch's redaction; nonetheless, Torah's use in Persian Yehud—the point of interest here—has been examined. It seems most reasonable to conclude that the law writings were employed as a practical treatise but not as statute law.

*   *   *

The results of this project thus far should be summarized. Scholars have generally dated the prescriptivization of Israel's law writings (or the beginning of that phenomenon) to the seventh or fifth centuries. The preceding chapters (Chapters 3 and 4) have disputed those conclusions. It has not been denied that new levels of importance were ascribed to the Mosaic law writings in the periods mentioned. There does appear to have been a rising esteem attached to the law writings, particularly in con-nection with the Josian and Ezran reforms. But does the rising eminence of a particular, ancient law collection necessarily mean that that text is "becoming *the* law"? There is a subtle, but critical, problem here.

As set out at the beginning of this project, the distinction between a law code (prescriptive) and a law collection (descriptive) is one of *essence*, not just *importance*. By *essence* is meant what a book is and how it is used; by *importance* is meant how highly a book is respected or how much it is used. A certain collection of ancient love songs, for instance, came to be attached to the Solomonic court: the Song of Solomon. Though ascribed to the king, the songs did not change from *poems about love* into *precepts on lovemaking*.[132] Perhaps a more relevant example is

---

130. Morton Smith, *Palestinian Parties and Politics that Shaped the Old Testa-ment* (New York: Columbia University Press, 1971), 173; Blenkinsopp, *The Penta-teuch*, 240–41; Crüsemann, *The Torah*, 339–45; James W. Watts, *Reading Law: The Rhetorical Shaping of the Pentateuch* (The Biblical Seminar 59; Sheffield: Sheffield Academic Press), 137; Levinson, *Legal Innovation*, 153.

131. Cf. p. 47 n. 66, above.

132. Michael V. Fox, *The Song of Songs and the Ancient Egyptian Love Songs* (Madison: University of Wisconsin Press, 1985), 247–50; Duane A. Garrett, "Song

the book of Proverbs. The proverbs are frequently called "laws" and "commandments" (Prov 1:8; 2:1; 3:1; 4:2, 4; 6:20, 23; 7:1, 2; etc.), and they have been ascribed to the royal court (1:1). Many even "prescribe" proper court procedure (e.g. 8:16; 18:17–19; 24:23–26; 29:1–14; 31:1–9). Nevertheless, this affiliation with royal authority (and even direct address to judges) does not change their essential nature. By ascribing these wisdom "laws" to King Solomon, they became Israel's *pre-eminent* wisdom sayings. They remain, however, maxims *about* wisdom; they did not *become* wisdom (as though wisdom could ever actually be embodied in words!)[133]

In a similar manner, the official endorsement of a particular collection of writings about law—the Mosaic law collection—would certainly heighten their importance. This, however, would not necessarily change their essential use. They remain legal ideals. There is no real basis, in the periods examined thus far, for supposing Israel had come to the idea that law itself (any more than love or wisdom) could be embodied by words. To the modern Western mind (as the heirs of Greco-Roman culture), it is hard to think about law *without* thinking of a text.[134] It might be suspected that the reverse would have been the case for the ancient Near Eastern judge: a text might describe, but never could it *be*, "the law."

Scholars interested in the re-characterization of Israel's law writings as legislation have naturally been drawn to these two periods heretofore discussed because they are periods of reformation. In cultic restoration, written records from the ancient cultus offered propagandistic grounds to justify radical acts. By citing ancient writings, practices entrenched in living memory could be overthrown without being sacrilegious. It is because these are cult reforms that the law book features prominently. The fact that Josiah actually conducts his reforms in ways contrary to Deuteronomy's stipulations underscores the need to avoid overstating the implications of his law-book appeals.[135] The same is true of Ezra and Nehemiah, with the additional evidence of Nehemiah's court case (Neh 5:1–13).[136] In a narrative text so keen to show the law book's use in

of Songs," in Duane A. Garrett and Paul R. House, *Song of Songs/Lamentations* (WBC 23B; Nashville: Thomas Nelson, 2004), 90–91.

133.   Roland Murphy, *Proverbs* (WBC 22; Nashville: Thomas Nelson, 1998), xxv–vi; Richard J. Clifford, *Proverbs: A Commentary* (OTL; Louisville, Ky.: Westminster John Knox, 1999), 5.

134.   "A classical Greek could think of a law as a physical object" (MacDowell, *Law in Athens*, 42).

135.   See especially points c and d on pp. 61–62, above.

136.   See pp. 105–28, above.

connection with Jerusalem's restoration, the fact that Nehemiah's civil suit was conducted by traditional custom law and sealed with cultic oaths confirms this finding. The concern for the law book is, in these texts, to justify radical changes to extant cultic tradition. The evidence should not be over-read as the rise of legislative thought in Israel.

Instead of identifying periods of incipient legislation in Israel, what scholars have identified in these two periods are turning points in the *content* and *esteem* of Torah. The Josiah reform serves to introduce the importance of *Deuteronomy* as the pre-eminent description of fidelity to Yahweh. The Ezra reform serves to introduce the whole *Pentateuch* as the pre-eminent description of Yahwistic order. There is, consequently, significant development in Israel's Torah itself attributable to these periods. In terms of esteem, the traditional use of law writings for *popular* instruction seems to have given way in DtrH to a particular connection with royal symbolism. By Ezra's time, Torah was emphasized for the edification of leaders *and* commoners—"as many as had understanding" (Neh 8:2). Scholars are correct to note the development of Torah's *content* and *esteem* in these reforms; but it is assuming too much to posit in these periods an innovation in the *nature* of law writing.

An important implication of the findings thus far is to challenge the current consensus on the timing of Torah's prescriptivization. These findings push the period for Israel's recasting of the Torah as legislation *into the Hellenistic era*. In many ways, this is actually a "common sensical" conclusion. Prescriptive legislation is known to have been innovated in classical Greece.[137] It would not be surprising to find Israel's own development along these lines emerging under Greek domination. Scholars have frequently sensed Greece as an "obvious" source for Israel's own reconceptualization of law writings; however, the reigning consensus positing legislative activity in Persian-era Yehud has hindered scholars from adequately exploring this possibility. Even those who do recognize the stamp of Hellenism on Torah's prescriptivization have felt compelled to explain the Greek dynamic in ways that fit the Persian-era timing.

Westbrook, for instance, perceives that some form of Greek contact stands behind Israel's legislative adaptation of Torah. However, his view that Josiah and Deuteronomy inaugurate Torah's prescriptivization has forced him to look for that Greek influence as early as the seventh century. Because Solon was instituting legislative reforms in Athens in roughly that period, Westbrook has posited a connection between the

---

137. See pp. 18–23, above.

two, though evidence for it is lacking.[138] Westbrook's basic intuition—that Hebrew thinking about written law was influenced by Greece—may yet be proven correct. But his speculation that such influence took place in the seventh century has now been shown to be unnecessary.

Fitzpatrick-McKinley has also sensed the involvement of Greek influence. Fitzpatrick-McKinley uses the reconceptualization of Brahmin *dharma*, in British controlled India, as a comparative model for her study of Torah's transformation. Brahmin *dharma* was ancient scribal wisdom later established as Indian legislation. Remarkably, Fitzpatrick-McKinley recognizes that British domination was a key factor in *dharma*'s transformation: "A modern legal model [British law] is imposed on an ancient compilation [Brahmin *dharma*] leading to a gross misrepresentation of the original functions and intentions of the ancient collection."[139] She immediately recognizes the suggestive implications of this model for her study of Israel's law writings: Greek *nomism* could have had just such an effect on the Hebrew view of Torah. However, because she had already accepted Fishbane's arguments for prescriptivism in Ezra–Nehemiah, Fitzpatrick-McKinley felt constrained to find the basic mechanism of Torah's reconceptualization in the Persian period. She recognizes Persia had no concept of prescriptive law writings, and therefore dismisses the "foreign influence" catalyst of her own comparative model (which was one of three points deduced from it).[140] Following Fishbane and others, Fitzpatrick-McKinley regards Ezra's supposed midrashic activity as the innovation which triggered the prescriptivization of Torah beginning in the Persian era.[141] Later Greek influences, she allows, further shaped the methods of Judaic legal reasoning,[142] but the identification of Torah as legislation had already occurred with Ezran midrash.

In other words, scholars already feel compelled to explain the "Greekness" of Torah's prescriptivization. The supposed evidence of prescriptivism in Persian Yehud has, however, hindered scholars from exploring the straightforward explanation of this likeness: that Torah's prescriptivization occurred in the Hellenistic period. An important aspect of the present project has been accomplished in the preceding chapters by critiquing those conclusions which have tied scholars to pre-Hellenistic theories for Torah's reconceptualization. Having dismissed the grounds

---

138. See pp. 87–88, above.

139. Fitzpatrick-McKinley, *Transformation*, 147.

140. Ibid., 148.

141. With Ezra "we come to the final influence which brought about the identification of torah with legislation, that is the practice of exegesis" (ibid., 172).

142. Ibid., 21, 148.

for positing Torah's re-characterization in these earlier periods, it will now be possible to do what scholars have sensed but not yet systematically documented: to explore the fundamental mechanics behind Judaism's reconceptualization of Torah under the influence of Hellenic domination.

What follows in the next two chapters will offer one plausible set of hypotheses for how this change in Israel's attitude toward the Torah came about. In doing so, this project enters what is really a separate argument from what has gone before. To the extent that the preceding chapters have proven persuasive, the general conclusion can now be accepted that Torah's reconceptualization took place not prior to the Hellenistic era. The question which remains, however, is: How did this occur? What were the mechanics of so significant a transformation? In the following two chapters, two possible mechanisms for this change will be indicated, along with evidence that Torah indeed did come to be used legislatively in the Hellenistic era.

Chapter 5

WRITTEN LAW IN HELLENISTIC-ERA JUDEA I:
PTOLEMAIC COURT REFORMS

Having dealt in the preceding chapters with unlikely periods for Torah's reconceptualization, an alternative explanation should now be offered. In this and the following chapter, it will be suggested that this shift in Jewish legal thinking occurred in the Hellenistic era through two basic mechanisms. The present chapter will explore the first of these: namely, the *administrative structure* of the Ptolemaic court system which, it will be argued, facilitated Torah's re-casting as legislation in fact. The subsequent chapter will then explore a second mechanism: namely, the *social philosophy of law* brought by the Greeks which, it will there be argued, made Judaism's characterization of Torah as legislation popularly attractive—indeed, virtually irresistible.

Admittedly, the conclusions which will be offered in this and the following chapter must remain hypothetical. There are, unfortunately, gaps in the extant material for the early centuries of Greek rule in Judea: "large and exasperating gaps" to use Lester Grabbe's expression.[1] Especially when documenting an interest as narrow as the use of written law, relevant material from Ptolemaic-era Judea (the late fourth to third centuries) simply is not available. Coming into the Seleucid era (the second to early first centuries), more material is available: the Apocryphal writings and certain of the Qumran scrolls begin to emerge in that period. Some of these Seleucid-era writings will be useful later in this and subsequent chapters. It is, however, the absence of evidence for the early centuries of Greek rule in Judea (the Ptolemaic era) that has left a material gap in present scholarship on the subject. No amount of scholarly magic can fill that hole, and any effort to postulate answers in that hole will remain hypothetical. What follows will offer a plausible account for certain legal developments in Ptolemaic Judea; but it should be recognized up front that it cannot attempt to be anything more than a hypothesis.

1. Grabbe, *Judaism*, 1:204.

A further distinction needs to be made up front. It is one thing to identify a period when, and to hypothesize the processes whereby, Torah came to be *regarded* as prescriptive; it is another matter to document the ways in which different strands of Judaism *practiced* Torah as prescriptive. The first is a matter of Torah's re-characterization as being a law code; the second is a matter of describing the ways in which different Jewish sects believed Torah's "prescriptions" should be interpreted and applied. The former is the conceptual shift in how Torah is to be used; the latter is the practical ramifications of that new function actually being worked out. Chapters 5 and 6 will endeavor to demonstrate the former as having occurred in the Hellenistic period: Torah came to be widely regarded in Judaism as *being* "the law" during the Hellenistic period. Two mechanisms contributing to that reconceptualization will be posited. Chapter 7 will show, however, that the practical implications of this "new use for Torah" were not necessarily neat and tidy. In that chapter, it will be seen that the *practice* of "prescriptive Torah" continued to evolve in diverse and complex ways long after the initial re-characterization of Torah—indeed, into the Roman era. But first, it is necessary to establish that Torah came to be regarded as a law code in the Hellenistic era, and to indicate the mechanisms which likely contributed to this new function for Torah.

The first of the two mechanisms for Torah's reconceptualization—the administrative structure of the Ptolemaic court system—is the focus of the present chapter. More specifically, Ptolemy II (Philadelphus) instituted a set of court reforms around 275 BCE, which, though only recoverable in its basic framework, offers a persuasive explanation for the legal transformation here postulated. Some background matters—(1) the legal activities of Alexander the Great and (2) the legal activities of Ptolemy I (Soter)—will prepare the ground for a closer examination of these reforms under Ptolemy II.

I. *Alexander's Legal Activities*

The fourth-century conquests of Asia Minor and the East by Alexander III ("the Great") had not been his own contrivance. It was his father Philip II who consulted the Delphic oracles about subjugating Persia.[2] Furthermore, the "Greek cities" (πόλεις) which Alexander planted in conquered lands were not formed strictly of his own genius. Aristotle

2. N. G. L. Hammond, *Philip of Macedon* (London: Duckworth, 1994), 165–70; A. H. M. Jones, *The Greek City from Alexander to Justinian* (Oxford: Clarendon, 1979), 1–2.

(legendarily Alexander's "tutor") was writing about the *isonomic polis* ideal at the time of Alexander's reign.[3] Alexander was no lone ideologue—but he was the one who carried out the conquest prepared by his father, and who built "rule of law" πόλεις throughout his new empire as epitomized by the classical philosophers.

What does seem to have been uniquely Alexander's idea, however, was his aggressive interest in establishing these cities, not only for Greek colonists, but as a force for the "civilization" of the "barbarians" as well.[4] Due to Alexander's death shortly after completing the conquest of Persia, it is not clear exactly how he would have governed the lands he subjugated had he lived to rule them in peace. At least two things, however, can be stated about his short rule. First, as just noted, Alexander intended to introduce civilized institutions in the barbarian East.[5] Second, though one-sided in theory, in reality this institutional give-and-take between conqueror and conquered was more complex. Alexander was clearly enamored with certain aspects of eastern culture. Far from merely bringing Greek ideals to the orient, he also imposed aspects of Eastern culture on his fellow Greeks and Macedonians.[6] Contrary to the term, the process commonly regarded as "Hellenization" was a complex of cultural conflicts and amalgamations, rather than a one-way imposition of Greek ideals. Within this give-and-take, however, the influence of one uniquely Greek ideal can be noted: the introduction of "the rule of (written) law."[7]

It is this limited aspect of Hellenization that is of interest in this (and the following) chapter. Through focus on this particular Hellenistic ideal, however, it must not be supposed that the whole nature of Hellenistic influences were "one way."

3. E.g. Aristotle, *Pol.* 3.6.3: "It is preferable for the law to rule rather than any one of the citizens, and according to this same principle, even if it be better for certain men to govern, they must be appointed as guardians of the laws and in subordination to them..."

4. For stylistic reasons, the terms "civilized" and "barbarian" will appear hereafter without quotation marks. These terms are nonetheless used throughout this thesis to indicate the Hellenistic representation that certain peoples or institutions were "barbarian" or "civilized," without thereby concurring with those designations.

5. A. Jones, *Greek City*, 4.

6. E.g. Arrian, *Anab.* 7.4.4–8. Cf. François Hartog, *Memories of Odysseus: Frontier Tales from Ancient Greece* (trans. Janet Lloyd; Edinburgh: Edinburgh University Press, 2001), 102.

7. In the opinion of Morton Smith ("Hellenization," in *Emerging Judaism: Studies on the Fourth and Third Centuries B.C.E.* [ed. Michael E. Stone and David Satran; Minneapolis: Fortress, 1989], 125–26), the introduction of prescriptive law was the one, truly Greek innovation within the complex give-and-take of "Hellenization."

Alexander's own efforts to establish Greek πόλεις—with Greek law codes—can be seen in extant documents from his reign. Upon his liberation of the Greek island-city Chios from Persian control, for example, Alexander issued the following prescript:

> ...from King Alexander to [the] *demos* of the Chians. All the exiles from Chios are to return; the form of government in Chios is to be demos. Law-drafters are to be chosen, who shall draft and revise the laws, in order that nothing may be contrary to the democracy or the return of the exiles; the results of the revision and drafting are to be referred to Alexander...[8]

In addition to restoring constitutional democracy to restored Greek cities like Chios, Alexander also established new constitutional cities in conquered lands and settled them with his soldiers.[9] Most celebrated among these Alexandrian settlements is Alexandria in Egypt. Alexander founded his Egyptian capital in 332 with, as A. H. M. Jones reports,

> ...its own code of laws, modelled substantially on those of Athens, and an elaborate system of law courts, again modelled on the Athenian jury system... It had its magistrates, and, though this is not directly attested, there can be no doubt that it had its council and popular assembly.[10]

That Alexander introduced Greek legal ideals into the Mediterranean world is hardly questionable. What impact this introduction had on native peoples' thinking about law writings—specifically in "back-country" Judea—is what is of concern here. It is not likely that these early efforts of Alexander had much effect on countryside regions (ἡ χώρα) like Judea. Local adjudication undoubtedly continued according to local norms—at least until such times as military conquest was translated into local administration.

The replacement of the Persian-era administration over Judea with Greek rulers began immediately after Alexander's conquest.[11] A Greek

---

8. Translation from Roger S. Bagnall and Peter Derow, *Greek Historical Documents: The Hellenistic Period* (SBLSBS 16; Chico, Calif.: Scholars, 1981), #2. (= Marcus N. Tod, *A Selection of Greek Historical Inscriptions*. Vol. 2, *From 403 to 323 BC* [Oxford: Clarendon, 1948], #192.)

9. The exact number of Alexandrias actually founded by Alexander himself is not clear; lists of 9 to 18 are not uncommon (P. M. Fraser, *Cities of Alexander the Great* [Oxford: Clarendon, 1996]).

10. A. Jones, *Greek City*, 3. On the Alexandrian claim to have adopted Athens' law code, see *P. Oxy.* #2177. For an extant collection of Alexandrian laws: *P. Hal. I* (portions in: Bagnall and Derow, eds., *Greek Historical Documents*, #104).

11. Victor A. Tcherikover, *Hellenistic Civilization and the Jews* (trans. S. Applebaum; Philadelphia: The Jewish Publication Society of America, 1961), 58–59;

στρατηγός was placed over the region, and the old Persian office פחה ("governor"), known from coinage to have been operating in Judea into the fourth century, disappeared.[12] Hecataeus of Abdera, writing early in the Greek period, only knows of the high priest as ruler in Jerusalem.[13] Such evidence indicates that the installation of Greek bureaucracy over Judea began directly after their military subjugation. However, it also indicates that, at least for the time being, Greek administration was largely regional. Local government was still in the hands of native leaders—the high priest in the case of Judea. It is unlikely that the Jewish leaders would have had reason (or perhaps even awareness) to change the way legal affairs were handled. In fact, Hecataeus' description of the high priest suggests that law was still being sourced through oracles during the time he wrote:

> ...they call this man the high priest, and believe that he acts as a messenger to them of god's commandments. It is he...who in their assemblies... announces what is ordained, and the Jews are so docile in such matters that straightway they fall to the ground and do reverence to the high priest when he expounds the commandments to them...[14]

Hecataeus' description certainly looks like law oracles being cultically sourced (rather than sourcing law from the legal exegesis of texts). Josephus' account of Alexander's visit to Jerusalem also seems to suggest a continuation of "the old way of doing law" in Judea into the early years of Greek domination:

> After saying these things to Parmenion [Alexander's general], he [Alexander] gave his hand to the high priest and...entered the city. Then he went up to the temple, where he sacrificed to God... When the high priest asked that they might observe their country's laws and in the seventh year be exempt from tribute, he granted all this...[15]

It is doubtful Alexander actually visited Jerusalem in person. It may have been his general Parmenion, commissioned to subjugate Syria while Alexander marched south along the coast to Egypt, who received Jerusalem's surrender. Nevertheless, while the personal involvement of Alexander may have been invented for apologetic effect, the basic point of Josephus' account is that Jerusalem retained its native customs under

Martin Hengel, *Judaism and Hellenism: Studies in their Encounter in Palestine During the Early Hellenistic Period* (trans. John Bowden; 2 vols.; London: SCM Press), 1:24–25.

12. Uriel Rappaport, "The First Judean Coinage," *JJS* 32 (1981): 1–17.
13. Diodoros, *Hist.* 40.3.5. Cf. Tcherikover, *Hellenistic Civilization*, 58.
14. Diodorus, *Hist.* 40.3.1–7.
15. Josephus, *Ant.* 11.8.5.336–38.

Alexander's dominion. This is likely accurate. There is no reason to suspect that the Jews were immediately drawn into (or would even have noticed) Greek "ways of doing law." Jerusalem's institutions probably remained largely unchanged during Alexander's reign.[16] Without clearer evidence, of course, conclusions cannot be established. Nevertheless, there are no compelling grounds to suppose that written law was viewed any differently in Alexander-era Judea than in earlier periods, and, in fact, Hecataeus' account seems to confirm otherwise. Source law remained an unwritten ideal into the early years of Greek dominion.

II. *Ptolemy I's Legal Activities*

After Alexander's death in 323, the empire was divided among his generals. Ptolemy I, whose Ptolemaic Empire controlled North Africa, was the first to lay claim upon Palestine. Antigonus "the One-Eyed," however, whose Seleucid Empire ruled Macedonia, Greece, and Asia Minor, seized control of Palestine in 315. In the 22 years between Alexander's death and the final defeat of Antigonus (in 301), Palestine was traversed by armies seven or eight times.[17] Palestine became the site of constant military occupation and, for centuries to follow, would continue to be a conflict zone between the Ptolemaic kingdom in Egypt and the Seleucid kingdom in Syria. The impact of these years of military activity on local institutions is not clear. Once Antigonus was defeated, however, the Ptolemaic dynasty consolidated its rule over Palestine and would hold it for a century. Palestine (as part of the region "Syria–Phoenicia") was incorporated into the vast Ptolemaic economy.

Ptolemy I organized his domains, including Judea, into administrative units. He adopted the native division of Egypt into *nomes*, and he applied a similar pattern for dividing outlying provinces into *hyparchies*.[18] Two principal officers in each of these *nomes/hyparchies* were the στρατηγός (the military head of security for the district) and an οἰκονόμος (the chief economic officer for the district). With an elaborate bureaucracy and other various offices functioning around this structure, Ptolemy administered his kingdom with rigorous detail.[19] It is not insignificant that the

16. Cf. Peter Schäfer, *The History of the Jews in the Greco-Roman World* (London: Routledge, 2003), 5–6.

17. Hengel, *Judaism and Hellenism*, 1:14.

18. In addition to Syria–Phoenicia (which included Judea), the Ptolemaic provinces included Cyrenaica, Cyprus, and numerous smaller holdings in Asia Minor, around the Aegean, and in Ionia.

19. Roger S. Bagnall, "Ptolemaic Administration" (Appendix I), in Bagnall and Derow, eds., *Greek Historical Documents*, 253–55.

titles of the various Ptolemaic offices were adapted from those of traditional Greek property managers for a wealthy man's private estate.
Indeed, Ptolemy regarded his kingdom as his "house" (his οἶκος),[20] and
his administration seems to have been principally concerned with economic development.

The Ptolemies squeezed immense profit from the lands they ruled.[21]
Among the means introduced to increase productivity, the Ptolemies
were aggressive in applying new technologies and new methods to local
agriculture and industry.[22] In addition to these technical improvements,
Michael Rostovtzeff highlights the contribution of Greek legal theory to
the Ptolemies' success:

> The relations between the working classes and their overlords in pre-
> Ptolemaic times were probably based, not on specific laws and regula-
> tions, but on custom and tradition. In this respect the Ptolemaic régime,
> which in general was a continuation of the past, represents almost a com-
> plete break with it. The Ptolemies, in planning their national economy,
> were not satisfied with custom and tradition. They required more preci-
> sion, more regularity, more logic, and sought therefore to transform the
> old-fashioned traditional relations into relations based on laws, regula-
> tions, orders, instructions, &c...[23]

For instance, written regulations are known to have closely prescribed
agricultural production along the Nile.[24] Each year, as soon as the inundation of the Nile could be measured, local officials compiled detailed
schedules for the next planting season, schedules which were reviewed at
each level of the bureaucracy up to Alexandria. Royal seed stores were
then "let out" to the peasant planters according to the schedules. All of
this was governed by written procedures and written directives from
Alexandria, insuring a maximum return from the Nile plantings. Other
such "revenue laws" were carefully drafted to prescribe every aspect of
the economy, from wine production to banking.[25] Written regulations,

20. Hengel, *Judaism and Hellenism*, 1:19; Michael I. Rostovtzeff, *The Social
and Economic History of the Hellenistic World* (3 vols.; Oxford: Clarendon, 1941),
1:269; Hans Julius Wolff, *Das Recht des griechischen Papyri agyptens in der Zeit
der Ptolemaeer und des Prinzipats*. Vol. 1, *Bedingungen und Triebkräfte der
Rechtsentwicklung* (Munich: Beck, 2002), 31.
    21. See the figures in Hengel, *Judaism and Hellenism*, 1:28–29.
    22. Rostovtzeff, *Social and Economic History*, 1:351–85.
    23. Ibid., 2:1101. Cf. A. Jones, *Greek City*, 2; Smith, "Hellenization," 121–22.
    24. Pierre Vidal-Naquet, *Le Bordereau d'ensemencement dans l'Egypte ptolé-
maique* (Papyrologica Bruxellensia 5; Brussels: Foundation égyptologique Reine
Elisabeth, 1981). Cf. Bagnall and Derow, eds., *Greek Historical Documents*, #87
    25. Bagnall and Derow, eds., *Greek Historical Documents*, #95.

implemented under a heavy handed bureaucracy, made it possible for the Ptolemies to maximize the economic production of their domains.

As best as can be discerned from extant evidence, Ptolemy I's regulations dealt almost exclusively with economic development. In the words of one scholar, Ptolemy I's regulations "had hardly been more than a machinery designed for economic exploitation."[26] The practices of social justice among subject peoples do not appear to have been touched by him. Whether Ptolemy I's practice of regulating economic production through written law would have had much effect on Judea's conception of its own social-justice writings (the Torah) is doubtful. It is not until the reign of his heir—Ptolemy II (Philadelphus)—that a challenge to traditional methods of adjudication can be posited.[27]

Fortunately, documentation of Ptolemy II's court reform has been preserved in the papyrological sources. It is possible to recover both the basic contours of the system established by Ptolemy,[28] and something of its effects on native legal traditions. Unfortunately for present purposes, however, the extant sources illumine its effects in *Egypt*—not Judea directly. Nonetheless, interaction with Ptolemy's reforms in Egypt will provide a useful framework for analyzing the sparse Judean evidence and postulating whether Ptolemy's policies brought similar effects there.

This study of the Ptolemaic court reforms will therefore proceed in the following four sections: (1) identification of Ptolemaic juridical policies *in Egypt*, followed by (2) examination of *Judean* evidence to determine the extent to which the same policies can be said to have operated there. Having in these initial sections identified the *structure* of the Ptolemaic reform, the subsequent sections will consider its *effects* on subject peoples and their perceptions of their ancient law writings. Specifically, this study will (3) consider the impact of that Ptolemaic juridical system on native uses of law writings *in Egypt*, followed by (4) an examination of *Judean* evidence to determine what can be said about the impact of the Ptolemaic court system on Judean uses of Torah. In essence, the present

---

26. Hans Julius Wolff, "Plurality of Laws in Ptolemaic Egypt," *RIDA* 7 (3d ser.) (1960): 210.

27. Ibid., 196–98; idem, *Das Recht der Ptolemaeer*, 1:26. The oldest extant papyrus from Ptolemaic Egypt is a marriage contract dating from early in the time of Ptolemy I (311 BCE). In that contract, arbitration arrangements are spelled out *as part of the contract*. A codified system of arbitration would come into force under Ptolemy II, so that later contracts could simply refer to "the διάγραμμα(τα)," where standard arbitration procedures had been codified (*P. Eleph. 1*; = Bagnall and Derow, eds., *Greek Historical Documents*, #122).

28. Hereafter, whenever Ptolemy (the king) is used without a number, it is Ptolemy *II* that is being referred to.

chapter explores the impact of Ptolemaic justice where the evidence is strong (in Egypt) in order then to consider the feasibility of postulating a similar impact in Judea (where the evidence is weak).

III. *The Juridical System of Ptolemy II—in Egypt*

As already noted, the initial efforts of Ptolemy I to consolidate his empire were primarily economic. It was not until Ptolemy II that a program was instituted to unify the judicial system of disparate subject peoples. Particular reference will here be made to the works of the late Hans Julius Wolff, a recognized authority on the Ptolemaic legal system.[29]

Wolff points out the intractable complexity of governing a society as diverse as the Ptolemaic Empire, with large numbers of Macedonian, Greek, Thracian, Illyrian, Syrian, Jewish, and other immigrant peoples, as well as native Egyptians. Initially, the king and his army were essentially military occupiers and not really a national government, properly speaking. Native and transplant communities operated according to their own varied customs, with the Greek conquerors resorting to their military officers for governance.[30] Initially, the concern of the conqueror was to establish control over the production of wealth, while in matters of justice:

> They were not interested, nor in the position, to force Hellenistic legal ideas upon the native inhabitants, since they [the Egyptians] held firmly to their deeply rooted religion and ancient customs. And naturally, it would also have been politically and psychologically inconceivable to subject the conquerors under the jurisdiction, and thus the linguistically and materially incomprehensible law, of the despised natives.[31]

29. Especially Wolff, "Plurality of Laws"; idem, *Das Justizwesen der Ptolemäer* (MBPF 44; Munich: Beck, 1962); *Das Recht des griechischen Papyri agyptens in der Zeit der Ptolemaeer und des Prinzipats*. Vol. 2, *Organization und Kontrolle des privaten Rechtverkehrs* (Munich: Beck, 1978); idem, *Das Recht des griechischen Papyri agyptens in der Zeit der Ptolemaeer und des Prinzipats*. Vol. 1, *Bedingungen und Triebkräfte der Rechtsentwicklung* (Munich: Beck, 2002).

30. An exception would have been the three Greek πόλεις—Alexandria, Ptolemais, and Naucratis—which had constitutional political systems and law codes (Wolff, *Das Recht der Ptolemaeer*, 1:43–46).

31. Ibid., 1:26: "Waren sie weder interessiert noch in der Lage, den in ihrer Religion tief verwurzelten und an uralten Sitten festhaltenden Landeseinwohnern hellenische Rechtsvorstellungen aufzudrängen. Und noch unvorstellbarer wäre natürlich politisch wie geistig die Unterwerfung der Eroberer unter die Gerichtsbarkeit und damit das sprachlich und inhaltlich unverständliche Recht der verachteten Eingeborenen gewesen."

Egyptian justice, therefore, continued unchanged according to longstanding, native traditions. Though justice had been the prerogative of the divine Pharaoh and his officers (*śrw*) in the hoary past, from the Twentieth Dynasty (c. eleventh century) onward the priests increasingly became Egypt's dispensers of justice.[32] By the time of the Greek conquests, Egyptian justice was firmly the provenance of priests who "pronounce[d] sentence at the 'portal-where-justice-is-given' (*rwt-di-Mꜣꜥt*)" in the temples.[33] These native practices continued during the early Ptolemaic years while Ptolemy I was consolidating the economic productivity of the domain.

The first effort to strengthen the royal government by consolidating justice was that of Ptolemy II. Even this reform was cautious in its design, however: Ptolemy more or less authorized the existing plurality of legal traditions without materially changing them; he "merely" brought them under a single royal bureaucracy. It was around 275 BCE that Ptolemy enacted the διάγραμμα instituting this reform. Its essential framework is identifiable in a court record (dated 226) which summarizes the resulting legal system as follows:

> ...the code of regulations (τὸ διάγραμμα)...directs us to give judgment... on all points that any person knows or shows us to have been dealt with in the regulations of king Ptolemy (ἐν τοῖς βασιλέως Πτολεμαίου δια-γράμμασιν), in accordance with the regulations (κατὰ τὰ διαγράμματα)[;] and on all points not dealt with in the regulations, but in the civic laws (οἱ πολιτικοὶ νόμοι), in accordance with the laws[;] and on all other points to follow the most equitable view (γνώμη δικαιοτάτη)...[34]

As part of his reform, Ptolemy codified standard regulations (τὰ δια-γράμματα) for many spheres of society. The exact extent of that legislative code is not known, but it must have been broad. Wolff notes evidence for royal regulations on assault and battery, and on debt default, to illustrate something of its scope.[35] This body of royal legislation, however, was not comprehensive. The above διάγραμμα indicates how Ptolemy integrated subject customs into a hierarchical system topped by his own regulations. In all matters of justice where the king's regulations (τὰ διαγράμματα) provided direction, the courts were obligated to

32. See Jean-Marie Kruchten, "Law," in *The Oxford Encyclopedia of Ancient Egypt* (ed. Donald B. Redford; 3 vols.; New York: Oxford University Press, 2001), 2:280.

33. Kruchten, "Law," 2:282. Cf. S. Allam, "Egyptian Law Courts in Pharaonic and Hellenistic Times," *JEA* 77 (1991): 115–19.

34. *CPJ*, #1.19.

35. Wolff, "Plurality of Laws," 208–9. Cf. *Das Recht der Ptolemaeer*, 1:51–52.

implement those.[36] Authority was secondarily granted to a category of law called πολιτικοὶ νόμοι, which included the "civil laws" of a πόλις or other people group (this term will be discussed further, shortly). Finally, in cases where neither royal regulation (τὰ διαγράμματα) nor the appropriate civil laws (οἱ πολιτικοὶ νόμοι) provided direction, judges were to rule according to general equity (γνώμη δικαιοτάτη).[37]

In theory, the Ptolemaic hierarchy of laws is simple enough; implementation by courts, however, would have been complex. Alongside this hierarchical system of laws, Ptolemy also authorized a pluralistic system of courts: principally the δικαστήρια and the λαοκριταί.[38]

The δικαστήρια were courts which heard the cases of Hellenes.[39] (By "Hellene," of course, it must not be assumed that *ethnic* Greeks alone are in view. "Hellene" referred to all those peoples which had transplanted from a foreign land as part of the new, Hellenic order. Hence, not only Greek colonists, but Thracians, Syrians, and Jews as well, belonged to the designation "Hellene" in Egypt.[40]) The λαοκριταί were the pre-exist-

36. *CPJ*, #1.19. Note that τὰ διαγράμματα means specifically, τοῖς βασιλέως Πτολεμαίου διαγράμμασιν (especially lines 42–43). Cf. Charles Bradford Welles, "New Texts from the Chancery of Philip V of Macedonia and the Problem of the 'Diagramma,'" *AJA* 42 (1938): 245–60.

37. The expression τῇ δικαιοτάτη γνώμη ("general equity") is a standard provision of Greek law. Aristotle admitted that one problem with the "rule of law" is the impossibility of pre-defining every potential dispute. To accommodate this problem, Aristotle quoted the δικαιοτάτη γνώμη formula from the Athenian judicial oath: "But the law first specially educates the magistrates for the purpose and then commissions them to decide and administer matters that it leaves over 'according to the best of their judgment (τῇ δικαιοτάτη γνώμη),' and furthermore it allows them to introduce for themselves any amendment that experience leads them to think better than the established code" (Aristotle, *Pol.* 3.11.4). Where written law appeared, it was prescriptive; where written law was lacking, magistrates decided by "general equity" and proposed laws to fill the gap thus exposed for the future. That a specific provision for δικαιοτάτη γνώμη appears in Ptolemy's διάγραμμα further shows that Ptolemaic courts did not leave judges free to decide cases according to "judicial equity" *except* where no prescription already existed.

38. In addition to these two main systems of courts, two less extensive courts can also be identified: the πόλεις courts operating according to the relevant *polis* constitution; and the κοινόδικον, concerning which little can be determined beyond its name (Wolff, "Plurality of Laws," 201–2; idem, *Das Justizwesen der Ptolemäer*, 53–56; idem, *Das Recht der Ptolemaeer*, 1:84–85).

39. Wolff, "Plurality of Laws," 199–200; *Das Justizwesen der Ptolemäer*, 37–48.

40. Sylvie Honigman, "The Birth of a Diaspora: The Emergence of a Jewish Self-Definition in Ptolemaic Egypt in the Light of Onomastics," in *Diasporas in Antiquity* (ed. Shayne J. D. Cohen and Ernest S. Frerichs; Atlanta: Scholars Press, 1993), 94.

ing Egyptian priest-magistrates adopted into the imperial judicial system.[41] The λαοκριταί specialized in dispensing justice for the native peoples (hence the title) in accordance with native law.

Presiding over both court systems, and representing the unifying agent in the system as a whole, was the εἰσαγωγεύς. The εἰσαγωγεύς was a royal officer appointed by the king. The exact scope of his duties are unclear, but they included the authority to seat judges, introduce lawsuits, pronounce the judgment decided by the court, and see to the execution of the court's judgment.[42] Writes Wolff,

> [The εἰσαγωγεύς] was understood to represent the king, thus forming a link between the government and the judges who, though not appointed by the sovereign, did, none the less, derive their jurisdiction from a royal *diagramma* prescribing the circumstances and forms of their activities.[43]

With this basic structure now indicated, one clarification should be added. The earlier cited court record (p. 155, above), in which the hierarchy of law sources is described, occurs in the records of a δικαστήριον (not a court of the λαοκριταί). It is the Hellene courts (δικαστήρια) which appealed to the πολιτικοὶ νόμοι in matters not regulated by royal legislation. Wolff identifies the πολιτικοὶ νόμοι of these Hellene courts as

> the laws of Hellenic *poleis* or other non-Egyptian groups[,] citizens or members of which lived in Egypt. In other words, the decree...instructed the judges [of the δικαστήρια] to decide issues not covered by any *diagramma* in agreement with those statutes [to which] parties claim[ed] a common citizenship or ethnical affiliation...[44]

41. Wolff, "Plurality of Laws," 200–201; idem, *Das Justizwesen der Ptolemäer*, 48–53. Wolff was uncertain whether the λαοκριταί was a continuation of native Egyptian courts, or a creation of the Ptolemaic διάγραμμα for handling native law. Allam has shown, however, that the λαοκριταί was a native institution (Allam, "Egyptian Law Courts").

42. Wolff, "Plurality of Laws," 199 n. 21, 204–5; *Das Justizwesen der Ptolemäer*, 39–41. On the presence of the εἰσαγωγεύς in the native Egyptian courts, see Herbert Thompson, *A Family Archive from Siut: From Papyri in the British Museum, Including an Account of a Trial Before the Laocritae in the Year B.C. 170* (Oxford: Oxford University Press, 1934), xix, 12; J. D. Ray, *The Archive of Hor* (Texts from Excavations, Memoirs 2; Excavations at North Seqqâra, Documentary Series 4; London: Egypt Exploration Society, 1976), #19.15–19.

43. Wolff, "Plurality of Laws," 199–200; idem, *Das Justizwesen der Ptolemäer*, 44–45, 50–51; Allam, "Egyptian Law Courts," 124–25.

44. Wolff, "Plurality of Laws," 214. Cf. idem, "Faktoren der Rechtsbildung im Hellenistisch-Römischen Aegypten," *Zeitschrift der Savigny-Stifung für Rechtsgeschichte romanistiche Abteilung* 70 (1953): 38–44; idem, *Das Recht der Ptolemaeer*, 1:55–58. Modrzejewski modifies Wolff's position, arguing that Ptolemy

Hence the term πολιτικοὶ νόμοι, or "civic laws," of the parties before the court. There would have been, Wolff suspects, a limited circle of royally recognized πολιτικοὶ νόμοι ("The laws issued with royal approval for those groups to observe, to which a certain autonomy has been granted...").[45] Papyrological evidence does show that distinctive law writings of subject peoples were identified by this term in adjudication.[46]

The terminology is different, however, in connection with the λαοκριταί. In the native courts of Egypt, the secondary body of law is called τῆς χώρας νόμοι ("the law of the country"), not πολιτικοὶ νόμοι. From all appearances, however, the terms are generally analogous.[47] The native courts were authorized to administer their ancient customs (τῆς χώρας νόμοι), just as Hellenes were authorized to live according to their πολιτικοὶ νόμοι. What was of principal importance for the Ptolemaic agenda was that, under this new arrangement, "both the Greek *dikasteria* and the Egyptian *laokritai*...[were] operating by virtue of his *authorization*."[48] All law now derived from the sovereignty of the king (see the diagram, below). According to Wolff,

> The king's objective in launching his project of judicial reform was...to solidify into permanent and normal government under the supreme authority of the king what up to then had hardly been more than a machinery designed for mere economic exploitation and backed by nothing but the power of the armed forces... An *integrated legal system*, depending on and sanctioned by the royal will, was one of the conditions prerequisite to the attainment of the political goal.[49]

intended πολιτικοὶ νόμοι to mean the various law codes of different peoples, but that few transplant communities actually brought law texts with them. Thus in practice, per Modrzejewski, πολιτικοὶ νόμοι came to mean the "legal κοινή" of the Hellenes (Joseph Mélèze-Modrzejewski, "The Septuagint as *Nomos:* How the Torah Became a 'Civil Law' for the Jews of Egypt," in *Critical Studies in Ancient Law, Comparative Law and Legal History* [ed. John W. Cairns and Olivia F. Robinson; Oxford: Hart, 2001], 192). Wolff rebuts Modrzejewski's arguments in his *Das Recht der Ptolemaer*, 1:55–58. For the purposes of the present study, it is one instance on which Modrzejewski and Wolff agree that will prove of interest: namely, the Jewish importation of Torah into Egypt (pp. 169–73, below).

45. Wolff, *Das Recht der Ptolemaer*, 1:55: "die mit königlicher Billigung erlassenen Gesetze derjenigen Körperschaften zu verstehen sein, denen eine gewisse Autonomie zugestanden war."

46. See pp. 169–73, below.

47. Wolff, "Plurality of Laws," 214–17; idem, *Das Justizwesen der Ptolemäer*, 51–52. Cf. Joseph Mélèze-Modrzejewski, *The Jews of Egypt: From Ramses II to Emperor Hadrian* (trans. R. Cornman; Edinburgh: T. & T. Clark, 1995), 109–10.

48. Wolff, "Plurality of Laws," 204.

49. Ibid., 209–10.

Simplified Diagram of the Ptolemaic Juridical Reform

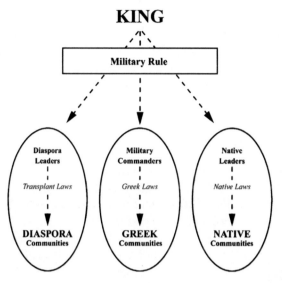

Pre-Reform: The king ruled as an occupying power, with subject people groups operating as distinct communities under their own leaders.

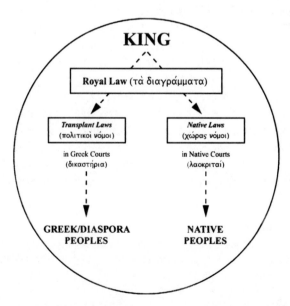

Post-Reform: The king establishes a government system to unify his subjects into one community, with himself as the source of justice (leader) for all.

As time went on, the initial design of Ptolemy underwent further modi-
fication so that the above outline is certainly not representative of the
system throughout the whole Ptolemaic period.[50] Nevertheless, what has
been reviewed above indicates the basic shape of Ptolemy's consolida-
tion of justice within his kingdom—at least in Egypt. It remains to be
considered whether this hierarchical system of courts and law traditions
was also implemented in the province of Syria–Phoenicia (and, specifically, in Judea).

IV. *The Juridical System of Ptolemy II—in Judea*

Unfortunately, there is little legal material from the Ptolemaic period for
Judea. This circumstance makes it difficult to ascertain whether the
Ptolemaic judicial order discussed above extended into that province.
There are, nonetheless, some suggestive clues.

Two documents in the Zenon papyri indicate the presence of royal
judges (δικασταί) in Syria–Phoenicia: a 259 BCE deed of sale for a slave
girl in Birta (in Ammon) lists a δικαστῆς among six witnesses to the
transaction;[51] and a record of a sale of pickled fish which took place in
Palestine (perhaps near Gaza) around the same time identifies Nossos the
δικαστῆς as one of the recipients.[52] Whether these royal judges were in
the province operating in δικαστήρια along the lines defined in the
Ptolemaic διάγραμμα, or whether they were royal judges attached to
military garrisons in the territory, has been debated. Both of these Zenon
records also include military personnel, thus leading some to the latter
hypothesis. Normally, however, disputes within military units were
settled by garrison officers,[53] and "no judge is mentioned in the military
κατοικίαι of Ptolemaic Egypt."[54] If these δικασταί were, indeed, attached
to military garrisons, it is an unusual occurrence. Roger Bagnall has suggested that these judges could have been attached to military garrisons
specifically for handling matters related to crown finance.[55] It is also
possible, however, that these records of δικασταί in Syria–Phoenicia

50. Ibid., "Plurality of Laws," 202–3.
51. C. C. Edgar, *Catalogue Général des Antiquités Egyptiennes du Musée du Caire: Zenon Papyri* (5 vols.; Cairo: Imprimerie de l'Institut Français d'Archéologie Orientale, 1925–28), #1.59003.
52. Edgar, *Zenon Papyri*, #1.59006.
53. *CPJ*, #1.1.
54. *CPJ*, #1.1.
55. Roger S. Bagnall, *The Administration of the Ptolemaic Possessions Outside Egypt* (Columbia Studies in the Classical Tradition 4; Leiden: Brill, 1976), 22.

indicate the operation of δικαστήρια for the Hellenes in Syria–Phoenicia, and that the Ptolemaic διάγραμμα published roughly 15 years earlier was operating in this province as well as Egypt. Such is a plausible way to account for the Zenon records, but it cannot be verified without more solid evidence. Some additional facts may add to its plausibility.

Further insight into Ptolemy's juridical administration of Syria–Phoenicia can be discerned through extant ordinances (προστάγματα) regulating the registration of livestock and slaves in that province.[56] Dated to the year 260, these ordinances addressed several specific problems. In them, the royal administration mandated the registration of all cattle by a certain date (with tax benefits and penalties, accordingly). The problem of natives being enslaved by Greeks for defaulting on debts was also therein rectified. Since the royal economy depended on maintaining a "free" peasant class to pay rents and taxes and to work the lands, the Ptolemies generally limited slavery. Apparently debt-slavery was getting out of hand and needed to be addressed. What is of special interest here is that, in the course of these ordinances on slavery, specific reference is made to a codified body of royal law (τὸ διάγραμμα), which is referred to as the source for needed regulatory details on these matters:

> And for the future no one shall be allowed to buy or accept as security native free persons on any pretext, except for those handed over by the superintendent of revenues in Syria and Phoenicia for execution, for whom the execution is properly on the person, as it is written in the law (τὸ διάγραμμα) governing farming contracts.[57]

This decree does not give any indication of a law-code hierarchy operating in Syria–Phoenicia; but it does provide a clear witness to the force of royal legislation (τὸ διάγραμμα)—not just irregular decrees (προστάγματα) or military rule—in Syria–Phoenicia.

This decree on slavery would have violated Jewish customs (assuming Jewish custom continued in general harmony with the Mosaic pattern).[58] Unlike Ptolemy's decree, the Mosaic pattern does countenance debt-slavery (e.g. Deut 15:11–12), including the specific expectation that foreigners might enslave Hebrew debtors (e.g. Lev 25:47–52). On this point, the Ptolemaic rule might have been more attractive than the Mosaic example. Nonetheless, Mosaic tradition also expected that, after six years

56. Herbert J. Liebesney, "Ein Erlass des Königs Ptolemaios II Philadelphos über die Deklaration von Vieh und Sklaven in Syrien und Phönikien (PER Inv. Nr. 24.552 gr.)," *Aeg* 16 (1936): 257–91 (= Bagnall and Derow, eds., *Greek Historical Documents*, #95).

57. Bagnall and Derow, eds., *Greek Historical Documents*, #53.

58. So Diodoros, *Hist.* 40.3; Josephus, *Ant.* 11.25.338–39; 12.1.8.

of service, debt-slaves would be released (e.g. Exod 21:2; Deut 15:12–14). Furthermore, foreign holders of Hebrew debtors should release them upon redemption by the family (e.g. Lev 25:47). These allowances were denied, however, by the Ptolemaic decree just cited: Ptolemy enforced all royal enslavements as permanent. Certainly this was not the only matter in which Ptolemaic regulation would have contradicted Jewish tradition. If the hierarchical law system employed by Ptolemy in Egypt was not in operation in Syria–Phoenicia, some other way would have been required for handling discrepancies between Ptolemaic policy and the "deeply rooted religion and ancient customs" of the Jews.[59] That both the operation of royal legislation (τὸ διάγραμμα), and the presence of δικασταί, can be documented in Syria–Phoenicia is suggestive that the legal system appointed around 275 included Syria–Phoenicia as well as Egypt.[60]

This would not be remarkable. Although there is little documentation of Ptolemaic justice in Syria–Phoenicia, it seems Ptolemaic administration, generally, operated consistently in Egypt as in the neighboring provinces—what Bagnall calls "the central core of the empire" (i.e. Cyprus, Cyrenaica, Syria–Phoenicia, and Egypt).[61] In his examination of administrative material from the Ptolemaic provinces, Bagnall has concluded,

> …Is it possible to see and formulate any overall system of administration for the empire as a whole…? The answer…is, I suggest, a qualified yes… What we have here [i.e. in the administrative patterns of the "central core" provinces] is the closest thing one can find in the Ptolemaic kingdom to a standard form of administration, a "Ptolemaic norm"… The outer provinces [i.e. those not belonging to the "central core"] all in common lack certain characteristics of the first group…[62]

The preponderance of bureaucratic officers which can be documented in Syria–Phoenicia, extending the king's interest down to the local level, and the consistency of those offices and activities with the administration in Egypt and other "central core" provinces suggests a general pattern of consistency in Ptolemaic administration.[63] All this adds to the plausibility

59. Cf. n. 31, above.

60. Whereas the Jews belonged to the general class "Hellene" in the Egyptian context, in the Palestinian context the term "Hellene" would refer to all non-Jews. In Palestine, Jews would be the λαός; Jewish law (Torah?) would be the χώρας νόμος; and Jewish courts (sanhedrins?) the λαοκριταί.

61. Bagnall, *Ptolemaic Possessions*, 240.

62. Ibid., 240–41.

63. Bagnall, *Ptolemaic Possessions*, 24: "If allowances are made for differences in the ecology and economy of Egypt and Syria, it is fair to conclude that there was a

that the Ptolemaic law system, specifically, may have been consistently applied throughout the "central core" of the empire. It can be regarded as plausible—even likely due to evidence for royal διαγράμματα and δικασταί in Syria–Phoenicia—that Ptolemy's consistent administration of the "central core" empire did not make an exception in the matter of justice. The Jews of Judea may very well have had their native law courts (i.e. sanhedrins?) and traditions authorized by Ptolemy in a manner analogous to the λαοκριταί of Egypt. The lack of evidence must leave this conclusion hypothetical—but it is plausible.

This conclusion will be accepted as a working hypothesis for the present project. It remains now to determine what *effect* this Ptolemaic court system had on the Egyptians and Jews in their use of their respective law writings. Once again, documentable conclusions are possible in connection with the effects of this policy in Egypt. Drawing demonstrable conclusions from the Egyptian material (in the next section) will open the way to make sense of sparse evidence from Judea.

V. *The Impact on Native Law—in Egypt*

Like many other ancient peoples, the ancient Egyptians are known to have maintained law writings. In contrast with the Mesopotamians, who inscribed their law writings in stone and clay, the Egyptians made extensive use of papyri. Very little has therefore survived of Egypt's ancient law writings. One law collection which has survived is the so-called "Legal Manual of Hermopolis" (*P. Mattha*).[64] It contains provisions on real estate, marriage, inheritance, and family law. In addition to this actual law writing, extensive indirect evidence attests to the Egyptian practice of writing down "laws" (demotic: *hp*). In one survey of the evidence, Egyptologist Donald Redford concludes,

> The evidence, though more extensive than one might have expected, is yet inadequate to help us decide whether *hpw* ever refers to codified law. For one thing, one looks in vain for any word or phrase in the Egyptian language that conveys the idea of *codification*. For another, as we have seen, statements of legal principles within the realm of jurisprudence

close resemblance between the two areas of administration. This is especially true in the relationship of king, city, and *chora*. Had we more evidence the similarities might be more or less striking, but it is unlikely that our basic perception of likeness will be altered." Cf. Grabbe, *Judaism*, 1:190–91, 215–18.

64. K. Donker van Heel, ed., *The Legal Manual of Hermopolis (P. Mattha): Text and Translation* (Uitgaven vanwege de Stichting Het Leids Papyrologische Instituut 11; Leiden: Papyrologisch Instituut, 1990).

belong within the categories of *sḥrw* and *shȝyt*, not code. Examples of *hpw* that have been vouchsafed to us fall within the category of circumstantial applications of the law, not of statements of principle.[65]

Redford's cautiousness is reflective of the field. Though once Egyptologists might have assumed Egypt had legislation,[66] it is now recognized that this assumption is both anachronistic and unsupported. The evidence points toward idyllic law collections, maybe even juridical models of precedential value,[67] but not prescribed penalties.[68] This understanding is drawn in part from the aforementioned lack of evidence for prescriptive law writings (i.e. the lack of actual law codes, as well as lack of citations in extant court materials and a lack of appeals to law writings in extant juridical narratives) and the lack of legal vocabulary (i.e. "in their legal deeds the Egyptians used everyday language").[69] It is also drawn from positive evidence: principally that it was *maᶜat* (not *hp*) which was held as the source of justice;[70] and it was the living voice of the divine pharaoh, gradually replaced by the oracular consultations of the priests (not law writings), which provided the prescriptive voice of *maᶜat* in matters of adjudication.[71] Egyptians did put *hpw* in writing (as Mesopotamians wrote *kittûm*, Hebrews wrote תורה, and Persians wrote *dāta*); nonetheless, custom and *maᶜat* are the only sources of justice certain to have held force in courts.

The matter which is of interest in the present project is, what effect the integration of the Egyptian λαοκριταί into the Ptolemaic bureaucracy had on how the old law writings came to be used. Wolff (and others) have shown that, under the oversight of the royal εἰσαγωγεύς in the λαοκριταί

65. Donald B. Redford, "The So-Called 'Codification' of Egyptian Law under Darius I," in Watts, ed., *Persia and Torah*, 145.

66. This was the assumption once supported by reference to a tomb painting of Rekh-mi-rēꜥ, pictured in his judgment seat with forty scroll-like objects (called *sšmw*) laid before him. It has since been demonstrated, however, that *sšmw* are "rods" for flogging criminals, not law scrolls. See Norman de Garis Davies, *The Tomb of Rekh-mi-rēꜥ at Thebes* (The Metropolitan Museum of Art Egyptian Expedition 11; New York: Plantum, 1943), 31–32.

67. So Aristides Théodoridès, "The Concept of Law in Ancient Egypt," in *The Legacy of Egypt* (ed. J. R. Harris; Oxford: Clarendon, 1971), 308–9.

68. Kruchten, "Law," 2:277–82. For a review of the question, see Russ VerSteeg, *Law in Ancient Egypt* (Durham: Carolina Academic Press, 2002), 3–14.

69. Théodoridès, "Concept of Law," 291.

70. Kruchten, "Law," 2:277–78; Redford, "So-Called 'Codification'," 138–40; VerSteeg, *Law in Egypt*, 20–23.

71. Kruchten, "Law," 2:281–82; Nicolas C. Grimal, *A History of Ancient Egypt* (trans. Ian Shaw; Oxford: Blackwell, 1992) 57–58.

(and in δικαστήριον cases where Egyptian law bore relevance), the Egyptian law writings came to be used as legislation binding on the courts. Although Egypt's native law writings do not appear to have been drafted as legislation, the Greek conquerors apparently expected that any *written* law could be equated with legislation: "The Greeks took *hp* to be the exact equivalent of νόμος."[72] This led to such misunderstandings as that of Diodoros of Sicily. Diodoros (*Hist.* 1.94.1–95.4) famously compiled a list of Egyptian "lawgivers," in which law writing pharaohs were described as great legislators. Redford writes,

> Far too much has been made of Diodoros's list of Egyptian lawgivers. The very notion of "lawgiver" is wholly alien to Egyptian tradition. The "ancestors" en bloc or individually were often singled out as having bequeathed written precepts worthy of continued use as standards of living, but these fell within the category of worldly wisdom. None encompassed "lawgiving."[73]

Diodoros was not alone in the supposition that Egyptian *hp*-writings could be equated to nomistic legislation. The Ptolemaic διάγραμμα earlier discussed appointed Egyptian *hp*-writings to operate *as law codes* in Greek-administered courts.[74] The impact this had, even on how native Egyptians came to regard their inherited law writings, is indicated in court papyri from the period. Wolff documents various instances of native Egyptian litigants prosecuting their cases using demotic laws.[75] For purposes of illustration, the so-called "Trial of Hermias and the Χοαχυταί" (117 BCE) can here be noted.[76]

The case involves a Greek military officer, Hermias, who claimed family ownership of a property in the Theban Nome. The property was, however, being inhabited by a native Egyptian named Horos whose family conducted their business as χοαχυταί (conductors of funerary services) from that place. Hermias sued before a Greek court (δικαστήριον) for possession of the said property.

In the closing arguments, the record reports extensive appeals to various kinds of legal documents by both parties: royal ordinances (προστάγματα, 4.30); administrative acts (χρηματισμοί, 4.23); letters (ἐπιστολαί,

72. Redford, "So-Called 'Codification,'" 139. Cf. Kruchten, "Law," 2:277–82; Charles F. Nims, "The Term *Hp*, 'Law, Right,' in Demotic," *JNES* 7 (1948): 243–60.
73. Redford, "So-Called 'Codification,'" 135–36.
74. Wolff, "Plurality of Laws," 216.
75. Ibid., 211–12.
76. Ulrich Wilcken, *Urkunden der Ptolemäerzeit: Älter Funde* (2 vols.; Papyri aus Oberägypten 2; Berlin: de Gruyter, 1957), #2.162. (= Bagnall and Derow, eds., *Greek Historical Documents*, #110.)

4.25); an amnesty declaration (τὸ φιλάνθρωπα πρόσταγμα/ ἀπολελευ-
κότων, 5.22; 7.13); specific provisions of law (e.g. νόμος βεβαιωσέως,
4.20–21) belonging to the πολιτικὸς νόμος (e.g. 7.9); and, even though
the case was being heard before a Greek court (δικαστήριον), certain
Egyptian laws (χώρας νόμοι) concerning the validity of contracts are
cited:

> And he [Hermias' lawyer, Philokles] (read) sections from the native law
> (καὶ ἐκ τοῦ τῆς χώρας νόμου μέρη) about disregarding it if anyone
> produces to the court a contract that has not been guaranteed by oaths,
> and if anybody produces a false contract it is to be torn up... (4.17–20)

With this appeal to Egyptian law, Hermias' lawyer was attempting to
invalidate Horos' claim to the property by questioning the validity of his
contract.

In the final verdict, the arguments by Hermias' lawyer failed. Horos'
lawyer (Deinon) ably satisfied the court on each of Philokles' charges,
including his challenge to Horos' contractual claim to the land. As part
of his rebuttal, Deinon produced "Egyptian contracts, translated into
Greek...in which the father of the accused...purchased [the property in
dispute]" (5.4–10). Furthermore, Deinon turns Philokles' appeal to Egyptian law on its head as he argues,

> that if they were judged before the λαοκριταί by the laws which he
> [Philokles, for Hermias] cited, he [Hermias] had to prove first that he was
> the son of Ptolemaios and the mother whom he named and that his
> ancestors whom they claimed were of the kinsman, before his claim could
> be heard at all about any matter, and that after these proofs he could ask
> [Horos] for proofs about the house... (7.2–8)

Hermias' basis for claiming the property was that it was an inheritance
belonging to his family over many generations (though neither he nor his
father had personally lived there). Deinon was showing that, under the
χώρας νόμος of the λαοκριταί, the burden of proof was upon Hermias to
prove his claim to the property first; only after proving his own claim
could he even request a valid contract from Horos. That, at least, is the
way the case would proceed "if they were judged before the λαοκριταί
by the [χώρας] νόμοι."

There are several points of interest to note before proceeding. First of
all, the fact that Horos possessed an *Egyptian* contract to the land should
have put this case within the provenance of the λαοκριταί. The year
before the Trial of Hermias, the king had issued an ordinance clarifying
the proper jurisdiction for contracts:

...Egyptians who have made an agreement with Greeks in Greek contracts shall give and receive satisfaction before the χρηματισταί [successors of the δικαστήρια]; but all Greeks who make agreements (with Egyptians) in Egyptian contracts shall give satisfaction before the native judges in accordance with the national laws; and suits of Egyptians against Egyptians...[shall] be decided before the native judges in accordance with the national laws.[77]

Of course, there was no contract between Hermias and Horos directly; nonetheless, Horos' Egyptian contract required handling under Egyptian law. This is undoubtedly why Hermias' lawyer cited a χώρας νόμος when he challenged Horos' contract. Furthermore, this would explain why Horos' lawyer cited a further provision of the χώρας νόμοι in defense, and even charged the Greek court to handle this point of the case "the way the λαοκριταί would handle it." These arguments show how the Egyptian law writings were being cited as binding upon judicial decisions. In fact, not only the λαοκριταί themselves were obliged to enforce the χώρας νόμοι, but the Greek judges were obliged to honor the stipulations of the χώρας νόμοι in cases belonging within its jurisdiction.

A second point of interest in this case is that Deinon (a Greek lawyer) is reported to have read out a section of the χώρας νόμοι for the Greek court. Wolff deduced that "a Greek version of the τῆς χώρας νόμοι does seem to have existed in the latter part of the second cent[ury]."[78] Wolff's suspicion was established some years later, when a Greek translation of the Hermopolis Manual from the Ptolemaic era was found (*P. Oxy.* #3285). Concerning this find, Joseph Mélèze Modrzejewski wrote,

In 1978, the British scholar John Rea published a papyrus from Oxyrhynchos (XLVI 3285), which established the fact that, probably under the reign of Ptolemy II Philadelphus, the demotic Case Book [i.e. the "Law Manual of Hermopolis"] had been translated into Greek... It seems to have been the "official version" of the compendium, accepted, if not commissioned, by the Ptolemaic monarchy.[79]

Modrzejewski is speculating when he credits Ptolemy II for commissioning the translation of this Egyptian law collection. His basic point is

77. Bagnall and Derow, eds., *Greek Historical Documents*, #45 (= *P. Tebt.* #1.5).
78. Wolff, "Plurality of Laws," 212 n. 56.
79. Modrzejewski, *Jews of Egypt*, 106. Cf. idem, "Law and Justice in Ptolemaic Egypt," in *Legal Documents of the Hellenistic World: Papers from a Seminar arranged by the Institute of Classical Studies, the Institute of Jewish Studies and the Warburg Institute, University of London, February to May 1986* (ed. Markham J. Geller and Herwig Maehler; London: The Warburg Institute, 1995), 8.

nonetheless sound and supported by the Hermias case. It would be necessary, under the Ptolemaic court system and its law code hierarchy, for Egyptian law writings to be accessible to Greek-speaking courts. Translations were used in just this manner, as Deinon's citation demonstrates. The overall indication is that the Egyptian law writings had become a recognized source of law—even, in certain instances, for Greek courts. The basis of Horos' victory in this particular case, however, depended on more than the Egyptian law code.

Horos' lawyer also cited a royal amnesty decree (τὸ φιλανθρώπα πρόσταγμα) to defend his client. In that royal decree, the record explains, "the very great sovereigns released everyone under their rule from all offenses up to Thouth 19 of the 53rd year," according to which Deinon argued, "the contracts deposited by [Horos] are unassailable and...the possession and ownership of the house are guaranteed for Horos and his associates from the same amnesty..." (7.13–17). It will be recalled that, under the Ptolemaic legal system, whatever the lower law codes (χώρας νομοί or πολιτικοὶ νόμοι) may require, royal legislation overruled wherever there was overlap. After showing that the χώρας νομοί actually favored Horos' position (rather than Hermias'), Horos' lawyer went on to invoke a royal amnesty issued the previous year, thereby trumping the whole debate. The king had begun an economic reform after a period of recent unrest. As part of that reform, he had issued a general amnesty.[80] Horos' lawyer appealed to this act as part of his defense.

In the final verdict, the scribe reports that the court identified three grounds for its decision in Horos' favor:

> [1] Since...Hermias had introduced no title deed..., And [2] since Horos and his associates had deposed that their ancestors had bought the said house...in accordance with an Egyptian contract...and [3] since they deposed a section of a royal decree issued in the 26th year about amnesty... It was ordered [to Hermias], "Do not make a claim." (9.4–25)

In the end, the case was decided by Hermias' lack of evidence to support his claim to the property (as the λαοκριταί would have required), and by the deposition by Horos of two bases for his own claim to it: an Egyptian contract governed by the χώρας νομοί, and a certain royal decree.

This case illustrates, in one well-preserved record, the intertwining uses of royal regulation and various subordinate laws, including πολιτικοὶ νόμοι and χώρας νομοί, in the years following Ptolemy's reform. Even complicated cases between Greek and Egyptian litigants

---

80. This amnesty is also extant: *P. Tebt.* #1.5 (= Bagnall and Derow, eds., *Greek Historical Documents*, #45).

could be handled with the various legal sources operating hierarchically —including the native Egyptian law writings. Perhaps the most intriguing feature of this case, however, is what it reveals about Horos and his family.

Horos (an Egyptian), leaning upon the eloquence and learning of a Greek lawyer (Deinon), *discovered how to use his own native law writings along with Greek law codes in a "rule of law" court.* In fact, by doing so, he—an Egyptian commoner—was able to defeat the advances of a powerful Greek military officer against him in a Greek court. If this case is at all typical, native Egyptians had learned to use their native law writings prescriptively (and effectively so) in connection with the Ptolemaic court system.

The case just cited occurred several generations after Ptolemy's initial reforms. The scarcity of λαοκριταί court material makes it difficult to assess how Egyptians *initially* responded to prescriptivistic ways of using their native law writings, or to what extent they were conscious of the change taking place. Nevertheless, it can now be posited that such a reconceptualization did take place in connection with the pluralistic court system of Ptolemy II. It is Wolff who initially reconstructed Ptolemy's court bureaucracy along the lines described above. However, Wolff does not seem to have recognized the "descriptive-to-prescriptive" shift thereby brought about. For Wolff, the change was primarily one of legitimacy: laws which had originally been legitimized through Egyptian authorities had come to operate under the authorization of a foreign occupier and enforced by Greek bureaucracy.[81] In light of more recent trends in the understanding of ancient law writings in Egypt, it can now be suggested that something more subtle—but potentially more profound —was taking place through the re-authorization of native law by Ptolemy. Egyptian law which had once operated according to custom was now expected to operate by written codes.

It is not, however, the presence of this transition in Egyptian native law that is here of concern, but the matter of transition in how Hebrew law writings were used. Though the Egyptian law example just cited is only of heuristic interest, there is actually evidence for the prescriptivization of *Torah* in Ptolemaic Egypt as well. Prior to the examination of *Judean* law practice under the Ptolemies, this evidence for Jewish use of the Torah in Egypt under the Ptolemies deserves note.

There was, after all, a large Jewish population in Ptolemaic Egypt. One might appropriately wonder whether the Jewish law writings would have gained status as a valid πολιτικὸς νόμος within the Ptolemaic court

81. Wolff, "Plurality of Laws," 216–17.

structure. Wolff, followed by Modrzejewski, has produced evidence confirming this very point.[82]

The 226 BCE court record cited earlier in this chapter—in which the basic framework of Ptolemy's διάγραμμα is preserved—is actually from a case between Jewish litigants in Krokodilopolis. A Hellene Jew named Dositheos had accused Herakleia, a Jewess, of publicly accosting him, spitting on him, and tearing his coat (causing 200 drachmas worth of damage). Among the various justificatory documents which Herakleia submitted to the court was the Ptolemaic διάγραμμα previously cited. The relevant section of the Herakleia case, quoted more fully, reads,

> ...the code of regulations (τὸ διάγραμμα) which was handed in by Herakleia among the justificatory documents directs us to give judgment...on all points that any person knows or shows us to have been dealt with in the regulations (τὰ διαγράμματα) of king Ptolemy, in accordance with the regulations (τὰ διαγράμματα)[;] and on all points not dealt with in the regulations (τὰ διαγράμματα), but in the civic laws (οἱ πολιτικοὶ νόμοι), in accordance with these laws[;] and on all other points to follow the most equitable view (ἡ γνώμη δικαιοτάτη)[;] but when both parties have been summoned before the court and one of them is unwilling to put in a written statement or plead his case or acknowledge defeat[?]...he shall be judged guilty of injustice.[83]

Evidently, Herakleia had a defense prepared which would have invoked πολιτικοὶ νόμοι under the authority of Ptolemy's διάγραμμα. Unfortunately for modern scholars (though certainly a relief to Herakleia), Diosdoros failed to pursue his charges. After filing his complaint and getting a court date set, Diosdoros failed to appear for the actual trial. Consequently, it was the last line of the διάγραμμα which was invoked by the court: the case was dismissed without argument because Diosdoros was "unwilling to put in a written statement or plead his case."

Because the case did not go forward, there is no record of how Herakleia actually intended to defend herself. Nonetheless, by her submitting the διάγραμμα among the legal documents to be cited in her defense, one of two things can be supposed: either Herakleia intended to invoke a πολιτικὸς νόμος to defend herself (she cited the διάγραμμα to establish her right to do so), or else Herakleia expected Diosdoros to invoke a πολιτικὸς νόμος in his case, and she desired to establish the legal

---

82. Ibid., 215; idem, *Das Recht der Ptolemaeer*, 1:55; Modrzejewski, "Law in Ptolemaic Egypt"; *Jews of Egypt*, 99–119; idem, "Jewish Law and Hellenistic Legal Practice in the Light of Greek Papyri from Egypt," in Hecht et al., eds., *Jewish Law*, 75–99; idem, "LXX as *Nomos*."
83. *CPJ*, #1.19.

grounds for appealing to a royal διάγραμμα.[84] Modrzejewski believes that the former was the case. He believes that Herakleia intended to cite "the provisions on violence inflicted upon others in the book of Exodus (Ex. 21.18–27)."[85] Presumably Herakleia's interest in that text, according to Modrzejewski, was to limit Diosdoros' claims to the torn coat. Since Exodus discountenances charges for bodily assault where recovery has taken place, Diosdoros would only be able to require reimbursement for the coat and nothing more. In any case, because the trial did not proceed, it is impossible to know for certain what Herakleia had in mind. This document suggests, but does not prove, that the Mosaic law writings could be submitted to an Egyptian court as the Jewish πολιτικοὶ νόμοι.

Another document, however, provides further help. In a much-discussed court record from the Fayyum, a 218 BCE appeal against certain divorce settlements specifically invokes "the πολιτικὸς νομός of the Jews." What is extant of the document pleads, as follows:

> To King Ptolemy greeting from Helladote, daughter of Philonides. I am being wronged by Jonathas, the Jew[…] He has agreed in accordance with the law of the Jews (ἐχ […κατὰ τὸν νόμον π]ολιτικὸν τῶν [□ἰου]δαίων)[86] to hold me as wife […] Now he wants to withhold […] hundred drachmas, and also the house […] does not give me my due, and shuts me out of my house […] and absolutely wrongs me in every respect. I beg you therefore, my king, to order Diophanes the strategos to write to […] the epistates of Samareia not to let […] to send Jonathas to Diophanes in order.[…] Farewell.
> Year 4, Dios 3, Phamenoth 27.
> Helladote daughter of Philonides concerning dowry and […][87]

Helladote is either a Jewess with a Greek name, or perhaps an ethnic Greek. Modrzejewski believes the latter to be the case. He believes that Helladote (a Greek woman) married Jonathas (a Jew) under a Jewish marriage contract, not realizing that Jewish law did not secure her the

---

84. Alternately, one might suppose Herakleia knew Diosdoros was not going to appear and invoked the διάγραμμα in anticipation of his abandoning his claim. This, however, is unlikely: the record indicates Herakleia had submitted "justificatory documents" (plural: τὰ δικαιώματα βουλομένης). In other words, she had a fuller defense prepared than was needed when Diosdoros failed to appear. Indeed, the report states that Herakleia was "willing [or, prepared] to defend her case" (*CPJ*, #1.19). Herakleia's submission of the διάγραμμα was indeed, therefore, because of the relevance of a πολιτικὸς νόμος for her case.

85. Modrzejewski, "LXX as *Nomos*," 192.

86. "The reading πολιτικὸν τῶν ἰουδαίων is certain; [κατὰ τὸν νόμον], restored by Wolff, is highly likely" (Modrzejewski, "LXX as *Nomos*," 194; cf. *CPJ*, #1.128).

87. *CPJ*, #1.128.

same dowry rights as Greek marriage contracts.[88] Under a typical Greek marriage contract, divorce provided for the full restoration of the dowry to the wife and further ensured that a husband would not drive his wife out of the home (Helladote's two specified complaints).[89] Under the provisions of Torah, however (at least as written), divorce is completely one-sided: Deut 24:1 simply requires that a man, finding "something displeasing" in his wife (MT: ערות דבר; LXX: ἄσχημον πρᾶγμα), give her a writing of divorcement and "send her out of his house" (MT: ושלחה מביתו; LXX: καὶ ἐξαποστελεῖ αὐτὴν ἐκ τῆς οἰκίας αὐτοῦ). This seems to be exactly what Jonathas has done. It may be that Helladote, as a Greek wife to a Jewish husband, has been rudely awakened to the lack of protection she has under a *Jewish* contracted marriage.[90] That she is appealing to the king to give orders to the local court to defend her suggests that the local courts have already rejected her case. It may be that, because Jonathas is acting in complete accord with the πολιτικὸς νόμος of the Jews, the courts cannot intervene.

Victor Tcherikover offers a slightly different explanation. Tcherikover believes that Helladote and Jonathas are both Jewish. He notes that, in the above reconstruction, there is a space of about ten characters unexplained: "It may be that Ἰουδαία stood after the name of the plaintiff [Helladote], or ἀνδρός μου [attached to Jonathas] at the end of the lacuna." Nevertheless, Tcherikover agrees on the basic point, that this is the case of a marriage "performed in a Jewish office," and that Helladote is appealing for the standard rights of a Hellenistic marriage contract. Many details of this case must be acknowledged as unclear. Nevertheless, as even the more cautious Tcherikover concludes: "...we have here the only instance in the Greek papyri of Jewish national law being applied to the legal life of members of the Jewish community [in Egypt]."[91] It is certainly hard not to discern here a place for Torah as an allowable—and used—πολιτικὸς νόμος of the Jews in Ptolemaic courts.

88. Modrzejewski, "LXX as *Nomos*," 193–97.
89. Commenting on *CPJ*, #1.128, the editor of *CPJ*, Victor Tcherikover, states: "The obligation of the husband not to drive his wife out of the house (ἐκβαλεῖν) is a usual clause in every marriage contract of the Ptolemaic period" (p. 238).
90. All that is here being suggested is that marriage *problems* could be appealed to a Greek law court which enforced written law. This does not mean that *the marriage itself* was contracted according to law book stipulations. In other words, it might be expected that marriages continued to be contracted according to unwritten customs (especially since the Jewish law book does not provide marriage prescriptions). It is only when a problem emerges *that brings the marriage into the courtroom* that a code (e.g. Torah) of adjudication is imposed.
91. *CPJ*, #1.128.

Although, as Tcherikover notes, this is the only extant papyrus explicitly identifying Jewish law as πολιτικὸς νόμος, other papyri demonstrate legal enforcement of certain Jewish norms, such as interest-free loans and rest on the sabbath, albeit without specifying the Torah as a law source.[92] None of these other documents provide the kind of evidence that would be necessary to establish that the Jewish Torah operated regularly as a courtroom code. They are, however, the kinds of evidence one would expect to find if such were the case. At minimum, the Helladote document shows that Torah was a Ptolemaically authorized πολιτικὸς νόμος for the Jews in Egypt. By Jonathas' apparent success against Helladote's claims in the local courts, it further appears that at least some of the Jews in Egypt learned to use their native written law as a courtroom law code. In other words, not only is there evidence that *Egyptian* law writings received a legislative interpretation in Ptolemaic Egypt, Jews in Egypt likewise came to view *the Hebrew Torah* as courtroom law.[93]

The matters discussed in this chapter thus far provide the basis for asserting this thesis: the Ptolemaic court reform (of 275 BCE) offers a likely mechanism for the reconceptualization of descriptive law collections as prescriptive law codes in fact. This appears to have taken place at least in Ptolemaic Egypt. It remains now to see whether such a shift can be discerned in Ptolemaic *Judea*.

VI. *The Impact on Native Law—in Judea*

It is, once again, the paucity of materials from Ptolemaic Judea that makes the demonstration of legal institutions in that society practically impossible. It is also this "black hole" which has left vital questions unanswered in present scholarship, thus necessitating creative efforts to get at answers. Framed by what has been seen in the preceding sections about Ptolemaic government and its effects on the legal thinking of subject peoples in Egypt, what follows will draw on two documents that contain evidence (even if sketchy) for similar effects in Ptolemaic Judea.

Though relevant documents from within the Ptolemaic era itself are lacking, a set of early *Seleucid* decrees offer a useful window back into the Ptolemaic administration of Jerusalem. The two decrees are preserved

92. Modrzejewski, *Jews of Egypt*, 112–19.

93. Modrzejewski further supposes that the earlier discussed translation of *demotic* law writings into Greek (pp. 167–68, above) can be compared to the Aristeas legend, according to which Ptolemy commissioned the translation of Torah into Greek (the LXX). He believes a reasonable case can be made that the Jewish πολιτικὸς νόμος was not just the Torah, but the LXX Torah specifically (especially Modrzejewski, "LXX as *Nomos*").

by Josephus: Antiochus III's "Letter to Ptolemy" (the Seleucid governor of Syria–Phoenicia) concerning certain rights accorded the Jews in Jerusalem (*Ant*. 12.3.138–44), and a simultaneously published "Public Statute" concerning certain details of Jewish law (*Ant*. 12.4.145–46).[94] These documents have received attention in the past both with regard to their authenticity and for their reflection on Seleucid imperial policy.[95] It does not seem, however, that anyone has yet considered the usefulness of these documents as indication of Jewish political expectations *coming out of the Ptolemaic period*, and thus their potential help for ascertaining circumstances in Judea during the (late, at least) Ptolemaic era.

Due to the fact that it is Josephus (a historian of inconsistent reliability) who preserves these documents, a long history of debate has surrounded them. Nevertheless, extensive studies by Elias Bickerman—"La Charte séleucide de Jérusalem" (1935) and "Une proclamation séleucide relative au temple de Jérusalem" (1948)[96]—have gained general acceptance among scholars as consolidating the facts in those debates and concluding their authenticity. Though Josephus exaggerates the implications of the texts in the way he uses them, "It is his apologetic use of the text which is false, and not the document itself."[97] The history of these arguments need not be rehearsed here. It will be sufficient to note that other proclamations of Antiochus, as well as actual stele inscriptions, have established the kinds of indulgences granted and the language in these documents as typical.[98] A consensus has therefore emerged with respect to their authenticity.

94. Josephus also preserves a letter purportedly from Antiochus III to Zeuxis the satrap of Lydia (*Ant*. 12.4.148–53), but its authenticity is doubtful. Cf. Jörg-Dieter Gauger, *Beitrage zur jüdischen Apologetik: Untersuchungen zur Authentizität von Urkunden bei Flavius Josephus und im 1. Makkabäerbuch* (BBB 49; Cologne: Hannstein, 1977, as well as his "Formalien und Authentizitätsfrage: noch einmal zum Schreiben Antiochus III. an Zeuxis. (Jos. Ant. Jud. 12: 148–53) und zu den Antiochos-Urkunden bei Josephus," *Hermes* 121 (1993): 63–69.

95. For a survey of the discussion, see Ralph Marcus, "Antiochus III and the Jews (Ant. XII. 129–153)" (Appendix D), in *Josephus* (trans. H. St. J. Thackeray et al.; 13 vols.; LCL; London: Heinemann, 1958–65), 7:743–66; Grabbe, *Judaism*, 1:246–47.

96. Elias Bickerman, "La Charte séleucide de Jérusalem," in *Studies in Jewish and Christian History* (3 vols.; AGJU 9; Leiden: Brill, 1980), 2:44–85; repr. from *Revue des Etudes Juives* 100 (1935); idem, "Une proclamation séleucide relative au temple de Jérusalem," in *Studies*, 2:86–104; repr. from *Syria* 25 (1946–48).

97. Bickerman, *Studies*, 2:65: "C'est son usage apologétique du texte qui est faux et non le document lui-même."

98. Charles Bradford Welles, *Royal Correspondence in the Hellenistic Period: A Study in Greek Epigraphy* (Chicago: Ares, 1934), #38–43; Bickerman, *Studies*,

Scholars have been interested in these materials for what they reveal concerning the policies of Antiochus III and concerning early Seleucid-era Judaism in Judea. What is of interest here, however, is what these Antiochan documents may preserve about Ptolemaic Judea and its legal institutions. The viability of this approach must therefore be explained, and will be done by way of introducing the texts.

For nearly a century, the Ptolemies had maintained possession of Syria–Phoenicia (despite several attempts by the Seleucids to take the region). This Ptolemaic dominance fell, however, after Ptolemy V came to the throne in Egypt. Egypt was already weakened by previous conflicts, and Antiochus III exploited this weakness to seize control over the province in 201. The Jews in Jerusalem evidently saw the writing on the wall for their Ptolemaic overlords and threw their support behind the Seleucid invaders.[99] After the Ptolemaic forces were driven from Jerusalem, Antiochus published the two documents preserved by Josephus: a decree to reward the Jews for their loyalty, and a related (by all appearances, contemporaneous) public statute. They are cited here in full:[100]

Letter to Ptolemy (Ant. 12.3.138–44)
(138) King Antiochus to Ptolemy, greeting. Inasmuch as the Jews, from the very moment when we entered their country, showed their eagerness to serve us and, when we came to their city, gave us a splendid reception and met us with their senate and furnished an abundance of provisions to our soldiers and elephants, and also helped us to expel the Egyptian garrison in the citadel, (139) we have seen fit on our part to requite them for these acts and to restore their city which has been destroyed by the hazards of war, and to repeople it by bringing back to it those who have been dispersed abroad.

(140) In the first place we have decided, on account of their piety, to furnish them for their sacrifices an allowance of sacrificial animals, wine, oil and frankincense to the value of twenty thousand pieces of silver, and sacred *artabae* of fine flour in accordance with their native law, and one thousand four hundred and sixty *medimni* of wheat and three hundred and

2:44–104; Y. H. Landau, "A Greek Inscription Found Near Hefzibah," *IEJ* 16 (1966): 54–70; John Ma, *Antiochus III and the Cities of Western Asia Minor* (Oxford: Oxford University Press, 1999), 111–12.

99. Welles notes that Amyzon also recognized the Seleucids were on the rise. According to Welles, a successful campaign by Antiochus in the East "gave him enormous prestige in the minds of his contemporaries." Amyzon, like Jerusalem, switched loyalty from their Ptolemaic overlords in favor of Antiochus and was rewarded for it; see Welles, *Royal Correspondence*, #38.

100. Translation from Ralph Marcus in Thackeray, et al., *Josephus*, 7:71–77. For a full discussion of these documents, see Bickerman, *Studies*, 2:44–104; Tcherikover, *Hellenistic Civilization*, 82–89.

seventy-five *medimni* of salt. (141) And it is my will that these things be made over to them as I have ordered, and that the work on the temple be completed, including the porticoes and any other part that it may be necessary to build. The timber, moreover, shall be brought from Judaea itself and from other nations and Lebanon without the imposition of a toll-charge. The like shall be done with the other materials needed for making the restoration of the temple more splendid.

(142) And all the members of the nation shall have a form of government in accordance with the laws of their country, and the senate, the priests, the scribes of the temple and the temple-singers shall be relieved from the poll-tax and the crown-tax and the salt-tax which they pay.

(143) And, in order that the city may the more quickly be inhabited, I grant both to the present inhabitants and to those who may return before the month of Hyperberetaios exemption from taxes for three years. (144) We shall also relieve them in future from the third part of their tribute, so that their losses may be made good. And as for those who were carried off from the city and are slaves, we herewith set them free, both them and the children born to them, and order their property to be restored to them.

Public Statute (Ant. 12.4.145–46)
(145) It is unlawful for any foreigner to enter the enclosure of the temple which is forbidden to the Jews, except to those of them who are accustomed to enter after purifying themselves in accordance with the law of the country. (146) Nor shall anyone bring into the city the flesh of horses or of mules or of wild or tame asses, or of leopards, foxes or hares or, in general, of any animals forbidden to the Jews. Nor is it lawful to bring in their skins or even to breed any of these animals in the city. But only the sacrificial animals known to their ancestors and necessary for the propitiation of God shall they be permitted to use.[101] And the person who violates any of these statutes shall pay to the priests a fine of three thousand drachmas of silver.

There are three concerns which Antiochus addresses in the first of these documents (his "Letter to Ptolemy"). Each of these concerns relate to his single, overall interest in *restoration*.[102] It is Antiochus' stated desire to reward the Jews for their loyalty by "restor[ing] their city" (ἀμείψασθαι καὶ τὴν πόλιν αὐτῶν, §139). This reward is clarified by three commitments: to restore the temple; to restore Jewish government; and "to repeople [Jerusalem] by bringing back those who have been dispersed abroad" (§139). Each of these three purposes are stated at the front of the

101.   Bickerman, *Studies*, 2:97: "Il n'est permis de se servir que des bêtes de boucherie traditionnelles, parmi lesquelles il est aussi prescrit de choisir les victimes pour Dieu." / "Of the animals traditionally butchered, it is only permitted to use those which are also prescribed for selection as sacrifices for God."
102.   Tcherikover, *Hellenistic Civilization*, 88.

letter; the body documents respective measures for their accomplishment.[103]

That the respective measures are each presented as specifically *restorative* is not insignificant. In the case of the first two (the πόλις institutions), it is specifically stated that their present disorder is because they were "destroyed by the hazards of the war" (§138). The Jews' reasons for siding with the Seleucids over the Ptolemies in the recent war are not completely clear. As was often the case in such wars, the Jews probably had to predict who was most likely to win and throw their support to the right side in order to avoid retaliatory action afterward. According to Antiochus' letter, the Jews had aligned with him from the outbreak of the war ("from the very moment when we entered the country," §138). Such disloyalty to the Ptolemaic forces then holding the city would have led to serious conflict. Antiochus' letter explicates this fact, stating that the Jews "also helped us to expel the Egyptian garrison in the citadel" (§138). It might be inferred that the destruction suffered by the temple (located beside the citadel) was from this conflict.[104] The Jewish authorities in Jerusalem would also, undoubtedly, have been suspended by the Ptolemaic forces trying to maintain control.[105] This might explain a need to "restore" the government, as well. That the senate (γερουσία) of Jerusalem came to greet Antiochus on his arrival to the city (§138) would indicate that this main organ of the restored government already existed. The ruling body Antiochus authorized for Jerusalem was not a new civic order, but is identified as an existing body reauthorized (albeit under the Seleucid rather than the Ptolemaic throne).[106] Even the repopulation measures were restorative, since some of the people had been "carried off from the city" during the war (§144).[107] Antiochus, in this decree, is rewarding the Jews for making the "right" choice in the war by restoring the πόλις to its pre-war—that is, its Ptolemaic—condition.[108]

It is this theme of "πόλις restoration" that renders these measures useful for the present purposes. Actual Ptolemaic-era records would be preferable; in their absence, these Antiochan decrees offer an alternative

103. Measures for "restoring the Temple" (12.3.140–41); "restoring the government" (12.3.142); "repeopling the city" (12.3.143–44); see Bickerman, *Studies*, 2:47.

104. Bickerman, *Studies*, 2:51–52, 56.

105. Ibid., 2:69.

106. Ibid., 2:48–49; Hengel, *Judaism and Hellenism*, 1:25–26.

107. Bickerman, *Studies*, 2:64.

108. Note a similar decree to Amyzon, in which Antiochus restores the privileges Amyzon enjoyed "even under Ptolemy" (Welles, *Royal Correspondence*, #38 [v. 5]; cf. n. 99, above).

means of insight into the institutional order to which the Jews had grown accustomed under the Ptolemies. Whether or not Antiochus, in fact, restored Jerusalem to its pre-war order, these decrees were intended to look like such a restoration. This material can therefore be expected to present, even if only in vague contours, a convincing portrayal of Jerusalem's institutional order in the Ptolemaic era.

The first point which will be observed in the Antiochan decrees is their indication of Jerusalem's legal plurality. That is, the basic shape of the Ptolemaic doctrine of pluralism might be discerned in the Antiochan restoration. In his "Letter to Ptolemy," Antiochus addressed the restoration of Jewish government in this manner: "And all the members of the nation (πάντες οἱ ἐκ τοῦ ἔθνους) shall have a form of government in accordance with the laws of their country…" (§142). The Jewish law here in view was not authoritative for the whole city, only for those of the Jewish ἔθνος. Antiochus is acting "to restore their city" (§138), so that it is not the Jews throughout the whole empire who are receiving this privilege; nonetheless, it is only the Jewish ἔθνος within the city (and by implication the Judean environs) that is being placed under Jewish law.[109]

One might wonder what government existed for non-Jews in Jerusalem. If Josephus knew, he was not interested in preserving that information. One might also wonder whether this plurality of laws might have been a feature of *Seleucid* policy, rather than reflecting the Ptolemaic order of Jerusalem restored. Antiochus was known to grant special privileges to cities, and to allow certain cities their own laws. However, it is not clear whether such privileges were normally defined by ἔθνος, as here. Under Seleucus II (247–226 BCE), the Smyrnans praised the king for "preserving the autonomy and democracy for the demos." Under Antiochus III, the Iasians honored him for "preserving the democracy and autonomy" of the city. Other cities under Antiochus' rule were likewise granted various kinds of "semi-autonomous" statuses.[110] A grant of political institutions to a specific ἔθνος within a city, however, does not appear to be elsewhere attested.[111] Unfortunately, extant evidence of Seleucid administrative policy is too sparse to know whether the authorization of πόλις institutions for a particular ἔθνος within a city is indeed unique; nonetheless, the present arrangement is at least unusual in this regard. This feature of the Antiochus decree may indicate that Antiochus

109. Bickerman, *Studies*, 69–70.
110. Ma, *Antiochus and the Cities*, 150–74.
111. One possible exception to this is the dubious "Letter to Zeuxis," wherein Antiochus purportedly grants "their own laws" to a group of Jews in Lydia and Phrygia (Josephus, *Ant.* 12.4.148–53; see n. 94, above).

was restoring Jerusalem to the *status quo* plurality attained under the Ptolemaic court system. That is, the Antiochan "Letter to Ptolemy" hints at the reality of some form of Ptolemaic legal plurality having been operative in Jerusalem.

Antiochus' "Public Statute" offers potential confirmation to this suspicion. This statute (πρόγραμμα), inscribed and posted at the city gate,[112] would have been superfluous if the Jewish law and government were appointed for the whole city. The animals indicated were already "forbidden to the Jews" (§146) by their own law; this royal act was added to restrain *non-Jews* from offending the Jewish sense of sanctity in Jerusalem. Bickerman explains, "This warning was not futile. In the Greek (or Hellenized) world, though participation in sacrifice was often refused to a foreigner, this did not prevent him from entering the temple."[113] It took a royal decree to restrain *everyone* from bringing into the city those animals already "forbidden to the Jews." The proclamation also restricted non-Jews (ἐξεῖναι, "foreigners"[114]) from entering the temple precincts, except after "purifying themselves in accordance with the law of the country" (§145). That such a proclamation was necessary further indicates that the authority restored to the Jewish government involved application of Jewish law to Jews only.[115]

What begins to emerge is the realization that Antiochus' "reward" to the Jews for their loyalty is actually quite restricted. He is not restoring Jerusalem to them in a manner that looks all the way back into the Persian era when the Jewish government controlled the city (cf. Nehemiah's authority to enforce Jewish law on Gentiles in Jerusalem; Neh 13:7–8, 16, 19–21). Antiochus is restoring to the Jews a more limited government to which they had evidently grown accustomed during the Ptolemaic era. As a consequence, the indication is given that some form of pluralistic law system—like that enacted by Ptolemy II in Egypt— must also have been implemented in Judea.

Of particular interest, moreover, is Antiochus' promise to restore to the Jews their native law: "And all the members of the nation shall have a form of government in accordance with the laws of their country (πάτριος νόμος)..." (§142). In Bickerman's view, because the νόμος

112. Bickerman, *Studies*, 2:87–88, 102.
113. Ibid., 2:88: "Cet advertissement n'était pas inutile. Dans le monde grec (ou hellénisé), si la *participatio in sacris* était souvent refusée à l'étranger, on ne l'empêchait pas n'entrer au temple."
114. Ibid., 2:91: "In the context of the Jerusalem Temple, this term indicates all the non-Jews" ("Mis en rapport avec le sanctuaire de Jérusalem, ce terme indiquait tous les non-Juifs").
115. Ibid., 2.93; Tcherikover, *Hellenistic Civilization*, 85.

here authorized is being appointed as a πόλις constitution along the lines of other Greek πόλεις codes (πολιτευέσθωσαν), "The phrase, 'the ancestral laws' indicated…the code of Moses. What is 'the book of the laws of the Jews' (Pseudo Aristeas, v. 30) if not the Pentateuch?"[116] Scholars generally expect that it is the written Torah which was authorized by these terms.[117] In view of the grant's likeness both to the Ptolemaic system it essentially continued, and to other Antiochan constitution grants, this is likely correct. Antiochus III's charter for Jerusalem, in all probability, appoints Torah as the governing law code of Jerusalem Jewry. If this is so, the implications are profound. Not only temple practice—but *the political order* of the Jews—is being "restored" according to the Torah. It has been noted in previous chapters that Israel historically used its law writings as a paradigmatic authority for *cultic* reforms. *Never before has there been indication of Israel's national justice, let alone its political institutions, being constituted "according to Torah."*

Prior to the Antiochus III restoration, law-book-based restorations in Jerusalem had two characteristics. First, such reforms have cited the law book because of a long break in cultic orthopraxy. Citing an ancient holy book was a means of demonstrating that the long gap in proper worship was being bridged. In the Antiochan restoration, however, the temple had only been out of operation for at most four years. The war lasted from 201–200, and Bickerman has identified an outside limit of 197 BCE for the decree's publication.[118] Second, book-guided restorations have traditionally emphasized the use of written law for *cultic* reform. Although written norms were likely deemed useful to instruct social justice as well,[119] none of the previous reforms expected the written law to *prescribe* the operation of government.[120] With the appointment of Torah as

116. Bickerman, *Studies*, 2:71: "La locution 'les lois des ancêtres' indiquait…le code de Moïse. Qu'était 'le livre des lois juives' (*Ps. Arist.* 30) sinon le Pentateuque?"

117. Ibid., 2:71–72, 84–5; Shayne J. D. Cohen, "Religion, Ethnicity, and 'Hellenism' in the Emergence of Jewish Identity in Maccabean Palestine," in *Religion and Religious Practice in the Seleucid Kingdom* (ed. Per Bilde et al.; Studies in Hellenistic Civilization 1; Arhaus: Arhaus University Press, 1990), 218; Tcherikover, *Hellenistic Civilization*, 83–84. This is certainly Josephus' understanding, judging by *Ant.* 12.3.3.142.

118. Bickerman, *Studies*, 2:84.

119. E.g. Westbrook's posited use of law writings as a "juridical treatise" (pp. 12–15, 32–33, above), or Jackson's "wisdom-laws" (pp. 37–38).

120. There is actually little in Torah that can be considered as *prescribing* national institutions. Organs of government are *mentioned* in Torah, but in such a manner as to presuppose their existence rather than to institute them. This is probably why Josephus, in his effort to explain the kind of government which Torah

the Jerusalem πόλις-constitution by Antiochus' decree, there here emerges *the first indication of Israel expecting to prescribe its legal institutions from Torah.*

This discovery must be tempered with the recognition that a Hellenistic king was behind this declaration. Antiochus III was known to have established a number of autonomous and semi-autonomous cities by granting them (written) πόλις-constitutions.[121] It is not surprising that Antiochus would grant Jerusalem a semi-autonomous status by restoring *what he perceived* as their native constitution. Antiochus can be expected to perceive the Jewish law collection as a prescriptive code—he is a Greek king. We therefore cannot take the Antiochan decree as proof that the Jews themselves looked upon the Torah as a prescriptive code. Notwithstanding, Josephus (and presumably his sources) indicates that the Antiochan charter was welcomed by the Jews as a proper arrangement.[122] This document may, therefore, be a reflection that Judean Jews had indeed come to identify Torah as their "native law code" and that they came to this reconceptualization of Torah in connection with the pluralistic law system established there by the Ptolemies.

VII. *Conclusions*

The evidence is too sketchy for certain conclusions. The present chapter has, nonetheless, assembled the extant evidence for a plausible hypothesis. Ptolemy II sought to turn his military occupation of North Africa and Palestine into a more coherent kingdom. An important measure for accomplishing this goal was the unification of law. It would have been impossible to force a new legal order on the vastly different religious peoples under his rule. Consequently, he devised a way to reauthorize the native laws of subject peoples so that their justice would continue

---

allegedly prescribes, could not settle on a clear answer. He at first found Torah prescribing *aristocracy* (*Ant.* 4.17.223–24), then *hierocracy* (*Ant.* 14.2.41). Later he devised the concept of *theocracy* to explain Torah's government (*Ag. Ap.* 2.16.165). Nonetheless, despite his own framing of Torah's governmental "prescriptions" in these ways, Josephus recognized the historical record that Israel had in fact operated under *tribal* and *monarchical* governments. Josephus struggled to reckon the history of Israel's monarchy with the lack of prescription for kings in Torah—not to mention reckoning this monarchical history with his own, civilized distaste for barbarian tyranny (e.g. *Ant.* 6.3.35–37, 4.83–85). Josephus' troubles illustrate the point: the Pentateuchal law writings do not prescribe ancient Israel's political structures.

121. Ma, *Antiochus and the Cities*, 150–74.

122. Josephus, *Ant.* 12.3.134, 153. Cf. Schäfer, *Jews in the Greco-Roman World*, 31–32.

according to their own traditions, but would now be recognized as justice flowing from and enforced by the Ptolemaic crown. Practically, this meant integrating all courts of justice into a unified system with royal officials (εἰσαγωγεῖς) supervising each, with countenanced (even translated) copies of the various approved law codes available, and with judges and lawyers skilled in them. The general contours of this system are relatively well preserved in the Egyptian papyri. Evidence that native peoples in Egypt (including Jewish communities) used their native law writings as courtroom law within this system has also been produced. Little material is available, specifically, to describe the legal activities of Ptolemaic Judea; nonetheless, evidence from two early Antiochan decrees allow the thesis that what demonstrably occurred in Ptolemaic Egypt also occurred in Ptolemaic Judea.

It is reasonable to expect that Judean Jews, in connection with the legal administration of Ptolemy II, learned to use their law writings—the Torah—as a legislative order prescribing native justice and government.

Chapter 6

WRITTEN LAW IN HELLENISTIC-ERA JUDEA II: THE CIVILIZED/BARBARIAN POLEMIC REFORMS

When considering the forces that shaped the Jews' perception of written law in the Hellenistic era, administrative changes imposed from above should be examined (as conducted in the previous chapter). Furthermore, ideological changes embraced from within must also be considered. Alexander had designed his conquest to institute both regime change *and* ideological change in the East.

In the previous chapter, certain administrative systems instituted by the Ptolemaic regime were examined. It was shown that the juridical system installed by the Ptolemies offers a plausible mechanism for the recasting of demotic and Hebrew law writings as courtroom law codes in fact. That, however, is only half the picture. Concurrent with those administrative systems which could have brought Torah into legislative uses, it also can be shown that ideological forces were at work, almost compelling Judaism to insist on a legislative use for Torah. After all, many ideals imposed by Hellenic rulers were resisted by the Jews; that the legislative use of Torah was embraced needs to be explained.

This chapter will assess the evidence for ideological forces making it desirable within Judaism to view Torah as a law code. In particular, it will be seen that various Judaic sects adopted the Hellenistic presupposition that prescriptive law is a necessary mark of civilization. In addition to the military/governmental design of Alexander's conquest, the establishment of model cities (the πόλεις) served to lionize the "superiority" of Greek civilization and to expose the "inferiority" of barbarian ways. Because the "rule of law" was one of the championed marks of civilization, subjugated peoples (like the Jews) had either to accept the attribution "barbarian" or defend their native law writings *as inherently* prescriptivistic.

The present chapter will document the emergence of the latter effort in defense of Israel's native, civilized dignity. What follows will: introduce the development of the civilized/barbarian polemic in Greece and its confrontation with Eastern ideology through Alexander's conquest; survey Jewish Torah apologies reflecting this polemic; and finally, give close examination to one particular set of specimens on Judean defense of Torah—namely, 1 and 2 Maccabees.

I. *The Civilized/Barbarian Polemic*

Cultural contacts between Greeks and Persians—even Greeks and Jews —took place long before Alexander's conquest. Greek wares, artisans, and mercenaries were known in the East[1]—even in Palestine[2]—centuries before the so-called "Hellenistic" era. The fourth-century wars of Alexander do not mark a sudden "discovery" of Eastern and Western cultures, one of the other. Nevertheless, the sharp Greek/rest-of-the-world contrast —and its particular formulation as "civilized vs. barbarian"—was a social construct which emerged initially in Greece, with the sovereignty of written law as one of the marks of the civilized.

The Athenians had developed the political system they called "democracy" over several stages during the seventh to fifth centuries.[3] By the fifth century, the Greeks had learned to pride themselves in their democratic principles, including the rule of written law over them (rather than a sovereign king). Not only philosophers and politicians, but the general public, perceived that Greek democracy—and specifically the "rule of law"—set them apart as a civilized race in contrast to barbarian peoples ruled by "lawless" despots. This comparison (and sense of superiority) was particularly fueled by the successful Greek resistance against Darius and Xerxes in the Persian Wars (490–479 BCE). The Persian Empire had extended its dominion over vast stretches of Mesopotamia and Asia Minor, including Greek colonies in Asia Minor. However, the Persians were unable to subjugate Greece itself. The Persians had huge armies, immense wealth, and a vast empire. By conventional wisdom, the Greeks were no match for the brute force and resources of the Achaemenids. Nevertheless, the Greeks withstood the Persian hordes famously at the Battle of Marathon. It was this otherwise inexplicable success which led the Greeks to magnify their pride in their institutional superiority— especially their superiority for having prescriptive law codes.[4]

1. Margaret C. Miller, *Athens and Persia in the Fifth Century B.C.: A Study in Cultural Receptivity* (Cambridge: Cambridge University Press, 1997).
2. Arnaldo D. Momigliano, "The Hellenistic Discovery of Judaism," in Stone and Satran, eds., *Emerging Judaism*, 130–31.
3. See pp. 18–23, above.
4. Thomas Harrison, ed., *Greeks and Barbarians* (Edinburgh: Edinburgh University Press, 2002), 4.

Herodotus (*Hist.* 7.101–3) reveals this attitude in an interview he describes between Xerxes and Demartus (a Greek at Xerxes' court). Just prior to launching his campaign against the Greek nation, Xerxes reportedly held an interview with Demartus to seek further intelligence concerning his foe. In the interview, Xerxes expresses his incredulity at how a mere alliance of armies from different Greek cities could ever ward off his massive, unified army ruled by a single king: "Nay, let us look at it by plain reason's light: how should a thousand, or ten thousand, or even fifty thousand, if they be all alike free and not under the rule of one man, withstand so great a host as mine?" (7.103).

For Xerxes, it was the fear which he instilled in his soldiers that spurred them to gallantry on the field of battle: "Were they [the Greeks] under the rule of one according to our custom, they might from fear of him show a valour greater than natural, and under compulsion of the lash might encounter odds in the field..." (7.103). Demartus' response, however, illustrates the Greek basis of their perceived superiority: "Free they are [the Greeks], yet not wholly free; for law is their master, whom they fear much more than your men fear you. This is my proof—what their law bids them, that they do; and its bidding is ever the same, that they must never flee from the battle before whatsoever odds, but abide at their post and there conquer or die" (7.104).[5]

For Herodotus, the "rule of law" leads a society "from strength to strength...not in one respect only but in all."[6] Not only was Greek society superior in peacetime because of their written-law democracy, but even their military superiority was attributable to their "rule of law" ideals.[7] Harrison points to the importance of the Persian Wars for popularizing this worldview among the Greeks:

> The Persian Wars were not the single cause of the pejorative portrayal of the Persians and the rise of the [denomination] 'barbarian'. Many of the ingredients of that portrayal...long predate the Persian Wars. Other

5. For discussion of a military law code, see Welles, "Texts from the Chancery," especially 245–46.

6. Herodotus, *Hist.* 5.78 (translation from Hartog, *Memories of Odysseus*, 85).

7. That this was a popular perception in the wake of the Persian Wars can be seen in Aeschylus' tragedy, *Persians*, first performed in 472 BCE. In that play, the superiority of democracy over tyranny, and its contribution to success in war, is a general theme. Cf. Simon Goldhill, "Battle Narrative and Politics in Aeschylus' *Persae*," in Harrison, ed., *Greeks and Barbarians*, 50–61; Thomas Harrison, *The Emptiness of Asia: Aeschylus' Persians and the History of the Fifth Century* (London: Duckworth, 2000), 76–91; Edith Hall, *Inventing the Barbarian: Greek Self-Definition through Tragedy* (Oxford: Clarendon, 1989), 57.

aspects of the later Greek–barbarian antithesis, however—in particular,
the contrast between Greek democracy and oriental despotism—were
very much less marked before the Persian Wars...[8]

It was after the Persian Wars that the concepts of "civilized vs. barbarian" became especially pronounced in Greek thinking, with the "rule of
law" as a keystone for qualifying a civilized society.

It might further be underscored that this new way of classifying
societies was not strictly ethnic (at least in concept), but distinctly
institutional. This is evident, for example, in Herodotus' account of a
panhellenic conference where the Spartans were making known their
intention to abandon democracy and return to monarchy (Herodotus,
Hist. 5.92–93). Socles from Corinth reportedly rose to rebut the Spartan
plan: "...you, Lacedaemonians! are destroying the rule of equals and
making ready to bring back despotism into the cities—despotism, a thing
as unrighteous and bloodthirsty as aught on this earth" (Herodotus, *Hist.*
5.92). To dissuade them from this intent, Socles offered an extended
history of the Corinthian experience with kings, culminating in the gross
brutality of the infamous Periander who murdered his own wife and then
raped her corpse. With such warnings about the gross cruelties of "lawless tyrants," the other Greeks dissuaded the Spartans from returning to
"lawless" monarchy. What is significant in this account from Herodotus
is its indication that the civilized/barbarian construct was not racial but
political. Even the Corinthians were barbarian while they lacked democracy. François Hartog states:

> The frontier between Greeks and the rest was from now on above all
> political, or so the Histories suggest. But the frontier does not simply
> separate Asia and Europe; it runs right through Greece itself, where it
> marks out and renders intelligible the period of tyrannies and the rise of
> isonomic cities...[9]

The "rule of law" became a particularly important measure of a civilized people in Hellenistic thinking. As seen thus far, it was legislation
which particularly distinguished the civilized society, and cultural superiority was now to be regarded as political (rather than racial—or even
by implication religious). One further aspect of this new "ethnography"
should be noted: namely, that the Greek philosophers clearly understood

---

8. T. Harrison, *Greeks and Barbarians*, 3. Cf. J. M. Cook, *The Persian Empire*
(London: Dent, 1983), 98–99; Hall, *Inventing the Barbarian*, 101.

9.   Hartog, *Memories of Odysseus*, 87. Actually, two of three "violator[s] of
rules par excellence" (p. 86) in Herodotus are Greek despots—namely, Periander
and Cleomenes. (Herodotus' non-Greek example is Cambyses the Persian.)

the difference between typical non-binding law writings of the Near East and their own, novel approach to law.

In his *Politics*, Aristotle described various approaches to government, including those "kingships existing among some of the barbarians" (Aristotle, *Pol.* 3.9.3). What is significant in Aristotle's description of barbarian kingship is that he recognizes their practice of law writing. Aristotle and others[10] were well aware that barbarian kings also wrote laws. However, written laws in barbarian societies, according to Aristotle, "enunciate only general principles but do not give directions for dealing with circumstances as they arise" (Aristotle, *Pol.* 3.10.4).[11] That is, in present terminology, barbarian law collections are descriptive of law but are not themselves "the law."

Aristotle explains the philosophical basis for this barbarian approach to law writing through an analogy: barbarians view justice as a skilled trade (ἡ τέχνη) like medicine. In medicine, a doctor diagnoses each case based on his wisdom; it would be unthinkable to bind a doctor mechanically to match symptoms with a pre-composed treatment list. Instead, a doctor (per Aristotle) examines each case according to its own circumstances and by his own wisdom. For barbarians, "[in law as] in an art (τέχνη) of any kind [like medicine,] it is foolish to govern procedure by written rules" (Aristotle, *Pol.* 3.10.4). Aristotle does not agree with this view of law as an "art." In subsequent paragraphs of his work, he proceeds to dismantle the barbarian perspective and shows, in its place, the supremacy of prescriptive law. What is significant to note here is the clarity of the philosopher's understanding of barbarian uses of law writings vs. those denominated as "civilized." The distinction is not merely the possession or non-possession of written compilations. Prescriptivism ("directions for dealing with circumstances as they arise") is the civilized ideal, whereas descriptivism ("laws enunciate only general principles") are the law writings of barbarian despotism.

All this was still a matter of Greek self-perception. The Persian-dominated East does not appear to have had any awareness of this new way of viewing law emerging in Greece. This is not to say that Eastern peoples lacked their own grounds for national hubris. Such peoples as the Egyptians (Herodotus, *Hist.* 2.158), the Hebrews (Deut 32:8–9), and the Persians also perceived themselves in a superior role in the world. However, the defining marks of superiority in the Near Eastern view

10. E.g. also, Plato, *Laws* 3.5.695; Aeschylus, *Persians* §§858–60 (see Hall, *Inventing the Barbarian*, 94); Diodoros, *Hist.* 1.75.6; 1.94.1–95.6.

11. Cf. p. 13, above.

were differently measured. The Near Eastern sense of superiority was measured by religious, rather than political, standards.

This is seen, for instance, in the reciprocal disdain of the Achaemenid kings for the Greeks and other kingdoms. In the Behistun inscription of Darius I, Darius grouped Greek Ionia with twenty-three other peoples held in inferiority, and he cites his own righteousness—not his political constitution—as the source of Persian superiority:

> I am Darius, the great king, the king of kings, the king of Persia, the king of the provinces... By the grace of Auramazda am I king; Auramazda hath granted me the kingdom. (Thus) saith Darius, the king: These are the provinces which are subject unto me, and by the grace of Auramazda became I king of them:– Persia, Susiana, Babylonia...Ionia...twenty-three lands in all...
>
> On this account Auramazda brought me help, and the other gods, (all) that there are, because I was not wicked, nor was I a liar, nor was I a tyrant, neither I nor any of my line. I have ruled according to righteousness... Whosoever helped my house, him I favoured; he who was hostile(?), him I destroyed. (1.1–6; 4.63)[12]

The source of Achaemenid superiority was divinely approved righteousness, not political institutions. Persian kings were immensely wealthy and powerful. Nonetheless, Darius would roundly reject the notion that he was a "lawless tyrant." On the contrary, Darius viewed himself as a champion of justice for the poor. Indeed, Greek Ionia and many other lands were made subject to him by the gods because of this righteousness.

In other words, both Greeks and the Persian-dominated East had a sense of self-superiority. However, they had very different standards by which to measure the superiority of one nation over another. For the Greeks, it was their political institutions—principally their "rule of written law"—which made them civilized and the ancient Near Eastern peoples barbarian. For the overlords of the East, it was the righteousness of the king which established national superiority. What would happen when the two worldviews suddenly and finally collided?

In 331, Alexander marched into the heart of Persia and brought Persepolis, the mighty capital of the Achaemenids, to its knees. Suddenly, Greek superiority—*and Greek explanations for their superiority*—could no longer be ignored. The civilized/barbarian paradigm of the Greeks fell prominently upon the East as the way to measure a superior civilization,

---

12. King, *Behistûn Inscription*, 1–4, 71–72. Cf. LH 1.1–49; 2 Sam 7:8–16; Fried, "Ezra's Mission," 81–84; Dale Launderville, *Piety and Politics* (Grand Rapids: Eerdmans, 2003), 189–90.

with the Greek πόλεις established by Alexander and his successors as tangible propaganda for the new political, economic, and cultural ideals. Among the many ideological challenges which began to churn throughout the ancient world, it is the confrontation of the Greek "rule of law" ideal with traditional ancient Near Eastern legal philosophy that is of present concern. It is only to be expected that oriental societies would be forced to respond to the "rule of law" polemic which was not only propagandized, but implemented in plain view through the Greek πόλεις.

At least three oriental responses to Greek legal ideals might be supposed. First, subjected peoples might accept the characterization of their native custom laws as barbarian and thank the Greeks for teaching them civilized legislation. This was evidently the response Alexander would have wanted,[13] though it was not likely to appeal to the pride of cultures with long and rich histories of their own. Alternatively, subjected peoples might deny that sovereign kings (without law codes) were as oppressive as the Greeks claimed. They might simply deny the Greek stereotypes and hope for a return to self-rule under traditional kingship. But it would be difficult to deny the oppressiveness of "lawless tyranny" with the memory of Persian tyranny on the one hand,[14] and with the self-evident prosperity, lower taxation, and enviable rights of πόλεις citizens on the other. This leaves a third possible response to the civilized/barbarian ethnography: peoples previously under Persia's shadow might agree that *Persian* rule was "lawless" and barbarian. It might nonetheless be argued that such a characterization belongs only to "them"; *"our own" native institutions* had actually been civilized prior to Persian repression.

It was this third alternative that became a common feature of ethnic polemics throughout the subjugated Near East. Not only Jews, but other conquered peoples, tended to accept the basic civilized/barbarian framework of their new conquerors while endeavoring to show that their own native institutions actually anticipated the ideals the Greeks called "civilized." In doing so, however, an essentially Greek philosophy of culture was being embraced. Of present concern is the fact that the classical Greek philosophy of prescriptive law came to be embraced in place of traditional, ancient Near Eastern legal theory.

13. Peter A. Brunt, "The Aims of Alexander," in *Alexander the Great: A Reader* (ed. Ian Worthington; London: Routledge, 2003), 45–53.

14. Cf. Josephus, *Ag. Ap.* 1.22.191; Neh 9:36–37; Esth 3:6, 8–11; Dan 3:6, 19–23; 6:7, 16 (EV vv. 8, 17). For a moderating view on Achaemenid hardship, see Christopher Tuplin, *Achaemenid Studies* (Stuttgart: Steiner, 1996), 164–77.

II. *Diaspora Torah Polemics (the Hellenistic Writers)*

Lionizing a society's virtue through reference to socio-political institutions would have been new to the Near East. Many subjugated peoples learned, however, "to beat their own drum"—even if they did so "to the rhythm of the Greeks." They learned to show how various ideals which Greece considered distinctives of civilization actually originated with themselves.

The Phoenicians, for example, boasted numerous ancient innovators, "above all Cadmus…'from whom Greece learnt writing'."[15] The Egyptians drew attention to an ancient reforming pharaoh, Sesostris, and claimed that his civilizing measures spread throughout the world— including Greece among his beneficiaries.[16] The Egyptians also famously drafted their own list of seven, ancient, legislator-sages to answer the Greek boast of seven, law-giving sages. (Notably, the Egyptian law-givers predate those of Greece.[17]) Sometimes a reverse tactic was taken: oriental peoples could admit the origin of civilized ideals in Greece but claim to come from Greek stock themselves. Agenor the ancient king of Sidon, for instance, was said to descend from Phoronis king of (Greek) Argos.[18] In one way or another, the Greek standards of civilization were being embraced as the right standards to measure by, while seeking to demonstrate some native claim to them. So pervasive were such efforts that Elias Bickerman (following Heinrich Heine) has famously termed this polemic the "universally recognized entrance ticket into European culture."[19]

The Jews were no exception. Hebrew law (as well as Hebrew wisdom) was promoted as the "real source" for the praised Greek ideals of law and wisdom. What is significant in noting this phenomenon is that, by advancing a defense of Torah *according to these terms*, it is the Greek definitions of law (and wisdom) which are being applied to native writings. Thus Torah would be subjected to the likeness of Athenian law in the very process of asserting Hebrew supremacy over Athens. The following survey of Hellenistic-era Jewish writers will illustrate, in fact, what has heretofore been indicated in concept.

---

15. Hengel, *Judaism and Hellenism*, 72 (citing Diogenes, *Lives* 7.30).
16. Diodoros, *Hist.* 1.53.9; 54.1–58.5.
17. Diodoros, *Hist.* 1.94.1–95.4.
18. Hengel, *Judaism and Hellenism*, 72.
19. "Das galt eben als Eintrittsbillet in die europäische Kultur" (Elias Bickermann, "Makkabäerbücher: Buch I–III," in PW, 14.1.786).

Pseudo-Hecataeus (ca. 300 or 100 BCE)

The dating for Pseudo-Hecataeus (in particular Fragment 4, which is the citation here of interest) is debated, with dates suggested ranging from as early as 300 BCE to as late as 100 BCE.[20] Although some have endeavored to show the fragments as genuine, they have been conclusively accepted as a pseudepigraphic Jewish work.[21] The portion of Pseudo-Hecataeus here of interest is preserved by Josephus as follows:

> In another passage Hecataeus mentions our regard for our laws, and how we deliberately choose and hold it a point of honour to endure anything rather than transgress them. "And so (he says), neither the slander of their neighbours and of foreign visitors, to which as a nation they are exposed, nor the frequent outrages of Persian kings and satraps can shake their determination; for these laws, naked and defenceless, they face tortures and death in its most terrible form, rather than repudiate the faith of their forefathers." (Josephus, *Ag. Ap.* 1.22.190–91)

What is noteworthy in this fragment is the expressed agreement with Greek propaganda that Persian monarchs were barbaric despots, while nonetheless distancing the Jews from classification among the barbarians.[22] In fact, not only the Persians, but Hecataeus reports that "their neighbours" and other "foreign visitors" slandered the Jewish laws. The Jews are seemingly being presented as an island of "civilization under law," surrounded by lawless barbarians. The Greeks are thus correct in regarding the East in general as barbarian; nevertheless, the Jews should be recognized as a lone, law-observant civilization in the East.

Aristobulus (ca. 180–145 BCE)

Dated by the scholarly consensus to the second century,[23] Aristobulus is known to have written a commentary on Israel's Torah which was dedicated to one of the Ptolemies (probably Ptolemy VI Philometor;

---

20. Robert Doran, "Pseudo-Hecataeus," in *OTP* 2:906.

21. Doran (ibid., 2:907, 914–16) has supported its authenticity. Ben Zion Wacholder (*Eupolemus: A Study of Judaeo-Greek Literature* [Monographs of the Hebrew Union College 3; New York: Hebrew Union College/Jewish Institute of Religion, 1974], 266–74) presents the arguments for its Judean origin, including five instances where the author "uses the first person to identify himself with Judea." Cf. John J. Collins, *Between Athens and Jerusalem: Jewish Identity in the Hellenistic Diaspora* (Grand Rapids: Eerdmans, 2000), 53.

22. For an interesting, anecdotal instance (ca. 256 BCE) of a native of Syria–Phoenicia showing disdain for being "treated like a barbarian"; see Bagnall and Derow, eds., *Greek Historical Documents*, #114.

23. Carl R. Holladay, *Fragments from Hellenistic Jewish Authors*. Vol. 3, *Aristobulus* (SBLTT 39; SBLPS 13; Atlanta: Scholars Press, 1995), 49–75.

180–145 BCE[24]). His writings are only extant in five fragments, and are referenced in only a handful of additional places (fourteen *testimonia*).[25] Of the five extant fragments, nevertheless, three contain arguments that Greek philosophers and legists derived their ideas from Torah.[26] Furthermore, among the various other *testimonia* by those who had access to Aristobulus' works, Aristobulus is five more times attributed with this argument.[27] In other words, the defense of Torah as the source of Greek thought must have been a significant theme of Aristobulus' Torah commentary in view of its pre-eminence in what can be recovered.

Aristobulus' arguments appear to have been primarily concerned with tracing various philosophical schools to Mosaic origins. For example, according to Clement, "Aristobulus [wrote]…abundant books to show that the [Aristotelian] Peripatetic philosophy was derived from the law of Moses and from the other prophets."[28] Aristobulus also identified Plato as a meticulous student of Torah: "For it is clear that Plato followed the tradition of the law that we use, and he obviously worked through each of the details expressed in it" (further explaining that an earlier Greek translation than the LXX had been available to Plato).[29] Furthermore, "Pythagoras…transferred many things from our traditions into his own doctrinal system,"[30] as did Socrates,[31] Homer, and Hesiod,[32] perhaps even Solon the Athenian law-giver,[33] and others.[34]

Aristobulus' extant arguments do not ascribe legislative ideals, specifically, to the Hebrew Torah; nevertheless, there is at least one indication that he wrote with the legislative philosophy of the Greeks also in view. In a fragment preserved by Eusebius, Aristobulus asserted: "All philosophers agree that it is necessary to hold devout convictions about God, something which our school prescribes particularly well. And the

24. So Clement (C. Holladay, *Aristobulus*, 159).
25. Counts from C. Holladay, *Aristobulus*.
26. Ibid., F3, F4, F5.
27. So Clement (T2, T4), Eusebius (T9, T10), and Jerome (T9a). Eusebius' own ascription of this polemic to Aristobulus is also evident in his introductory material to two of the fragments previously noted (T14, T14a) in connection with F3; see C. Holladay, *Aristobulus*.
28. Ibid., T4.
29. Ibid., T14a, F3.
30. Ibid., F3a.
31. Ibid., F4a.
32. Ibid., F5.
33. Ibid., F5, F5d.
34. E.g. Orpheus (F4), Aratus (F4), Linus (F5), and Callimachus (F5d); see ibid.

whole structure of our law has been drawn up with concern for piety, justice, self-control, and other qualities that are truly good."[35]

Here, Aristobulus' concern for Torah's supremacy as a source of *social justice*, also becomes manifest. One might presume that he means to speak of Torah as a *legislative* code-of-justice, since he cites as his measurement those criteria on which "all philosophers agree." Unfortunately, extant fragments are too sparse to establish details of Aristobulus' thinking on the "rule of law" aspect of Greek philosophy. It would be helpful to know to what extent Plato's "work[ing] through each of the details" of Torah was perceived to include Plato's "rule of law" doctrine.[36] Furthermore, it would be helpful to have Aristobulus' opinion as to which doctrines Aristotle is believed to have derived from Torah, and what Solon learned from Torah (he is at least said to have gained the sabbath principle from Torah).[37]

Due to the fragmentary nature of Aristobulus' works, further clarity seem unlikely. Nevertheless, the above does make clear his influential defense of Torah as the source of current Greek philosophical ideals— and thus Torah itself is believed to *share* those philosophical ideals.

Artapanus (Third to Second Century BCE)[38]

Artapanus wrote about the Hebrew patriarchs and Moses. His writings remain in only three fragments, containing his discussions of Abraham, Joseph, and Moses respectively. Nonetheless, it is well-attested in what is extant that Artapanus viewed the Hebrews as "founders of culture."[39] Abraham, for example, was the first teacher of astrology.[40] Joseph, in his rule over Egypt, invented standard measures and "was the first to divide the land and distinguish it with boundaries" for orderly administration. (Notably, the Ptolemies retained the historic arrangement of nomes for ordering their government in Egypt, which order is thus attributed to Joseph.) It was also Joseph who introduced methods to make barren Egyptian land arable.[41] Moses is most highly esteemed by Artapanus, being described as the inventor of many important technologies, military implements, and also as the inventor of philosophy.[42] Artapanus further

---

35. Ibid., F4.
36. E.g. Plato, *Laws* 7.788A–793D.
37. C. Holladay, *Aristobulus*, F5d.
38. For discussion of dating, see J. Collins, *Athens and Jerusalem*, 38–39.
39. Ibid., 40.
40. John J. Collins, "Artapanus," in *OTP* 2:889–903, F1.
41. Ibid., F2.
42. Boats, masonry tools, water-drawing implements, arms, ox-plowing, even the annual inundation of the Nile are accredited to Moses (J. Collins, "Artapanus," F3).

identifies Moses as the one "called Mousaeus by the Greeks...the teacher of Orpheus,"[43] and as the historical figure behind the Greek Hermes (i.e. the scribe and messenger of the gods).[44]

Too little remains of Artapanus' work to glean a full appreciation of his ideas. It would seem that his particular focus was specifically on showing Hebrew origins for cultural ideals of Hellenistic *Egypt*.[45] To do so, he does not speak of Greek or Egyptian sages studying *Torah*, but he does speak of the Hebrew fathers (especially Moses) as the source of Greek–Egypt's cultural improvements. He also identifies Moses as the teacher from whom various mythical Greek heroes learned. Greek philosophical norms, in other words, are actually a reflection of Israel's own ancient and native ideals.

Pseudo-Aristeas (ca. 150–100 BCE)
The date for the *Letter of Aristeas* and its account of Torah's translation into Greek (the LXX) is variously placed between 250 BCE and 100 CE, with the majority accepting a late second-century BCE date.[46] Although a similar argument for Torah appears in Aristeas as that used by Aristobulus, the argument is approached from the opposite direction. Aristobulus endeavored to show that the Greek philosophers had, in fact, studied Torah; Aristeas takes the reverse argument.

Aristeas recognizes that the classical Greek philosophers do not actually mention the Jews in their writings. He also accepts that no Greek translation of Torah existed before the LXX. Instead, Aristeas exalts Torah as a sort of "hidden treasure" of philosophical wisdom. He describes how Ptolemy and his philosophers were amazed that Torah could have escaped the notice of their forefathers. Now that Torah is being explained to them, however, Ptolemy's court agrees that "this legislation...is very philosophical and genuine" (v. 31), that its teachings are superior even to those "usually ranked to be the wisest of the Greeks," and of course far surpasses anything arising from barbarian peoples ("there is surely no

---

43. Ibid., F3. Collins notes, "Orpheus...is more commonly said to have been the teacher of Mosaeus. Here the relationship is inverted to glorify Moses" ("Artapanus," 898 n. i).

44. Ibid., F3. Collins notes, "Hermes was the Gk. Equivalent of Thoth. The identification with Moses was facilitated by the frequency of the Egyptian name Thutmosis. Thoth was also a lawgiver" (p. 899 n. l).

45. "That he wrote in Egypt cannot be doubted" (J. Collins, *Athens and Jerusalem*, 39).

46. R. J. H. Shutt, "Letter of Aristeas," in *OTP*, 2.8–9; J. Collins, *Athens and Jerusalem*, 98. All subsequent *Aristeas* quotations are from Shutt's translation.

need to mention the rest of the very foolish people, Egyptians and those like them...," vv. 137–38). Through a series of banquet interviews with the Jewish priests, Aristeas repeatedly emphasizes how the king and all the philosophers attend in amazement to every word of their speeches:

> All the assembled company acclaimed and applauded loudly, and the king said to the philosophers, of whom there were many among them, "I think that these men excel in virtue and have a fuller understanding..."
> The philosopher Menedemus of Eritrea said, "Yes, indeed, O King..."
> ...With a loud voice the king complimented and encouraged them all; the audience raised their voices in approval, and especially the philosophers, for these men far surpassed them in attitudes and eloquence...
> ...[The king] addressed them thus: "The greatest benefits have fallen on me through your visit. I have been assisted a great deal by your giving me essential teaching on kingship."
> ...they were manifestly deserving of admiration to me and to the audience, but especially to the philosophers. (vv. 200–201, 235, 294, 296)

In various other allusions throughout the letter, the sages of Torah are shown to be better philosophers than the Greeks' own.[47]

Pseudo-Aristeas thus offers a similar apology as Aristobulus, albeit from another direction. Both argue that Torah stands above all sources of Greek legal and philosophical wisdom. Both cite Greek philosophers as the ones who perceive this greatness (i.e. it is *according to current Greek norms* that Torah is being idealized). The distinction between Aristobulus and Aristeas is that the former sought to show how numerous "big names" of classical Greece studied Torah; Aristeas admits they did not, but notes how much the poorer they were for not having had that privilege.

"How is it," the question at last emerges, "that after such great works were (originally) completed, none of the [Greek] historians or poets took it upon himself to refer to them?" (v. 312).[48] In a slight twist on what has already been indicated, Aristeas avers that a number of Greek writers actually did try to borrow from the Torah. However, "because the legislation was holy...some of those who made the attempt were smitten by God" (v. 313; cf. vv. 31, 314–17). It therefore remained hidden from the Greeks until now.

One might wonder whether Aristobulus' failure to demonstrate dependence on the Torah by Greek philosophers led to this new approach by

47. E.g. the king's immediate audience for the Jewish priests when other foreign dignitaries wait four days for admittance (vv. 174–75), and his esteeming them "men of culture" always welcome in his presence (v. 321).
48. This question is already implied in v. 31.

Aristeas.[49] In any case, they both argue alike that it is according to Greek philosophical—and legal—standards that Torah is to be understood.

Eupolemus (Before First Century BCE)[50]

Eupolemus was a Jew writing in Judea shortly after the Maccabean wars. He is accepted as being the same Eupolemus as the Jewish ambassador to Rome in 1 Macc 8:17–18.[51] From his work *On the Kings in Judea*, five fragments survive. "The extant fragments of the book," writes Martin McNamara, "treat of Jewish history from Moses to the fall of Jerusalem. Eupolemus was concerned in his writing to show that the Jewish people went back further in their origins than the Greeks."[52] He also argues for Greek dependence on Moses, in writing, philosophy, and in law. Alexander Polyhistor cited Eupolemus thus: "And Eupolemus says that Moses was the first wise man, that he first taught the alphabet to the Jews, and the Phoenicians received it from the Jews, and the Greeks received it from the Phoenicians, and that Moses first wrote laws for the Jews."[53]

According to Ben Zion Wacholder, the triad of "wisdom, writing, and law" are not to be read independently. Rather:

> since traditionally the "wise man" became almost equivalent to the great lawgiver, it makes more sense to treat it as…a unitary thought: Moses was the first "wise man"—hence he was the father of "wisdom," the antecedent of (a) Greek philosophy; (b) the alphabet; and (c) written laws… Thus the invention of written law, according to Eupolemus, was the climax of Moses' other benefits bestowed on mankind.[54]

Eupolemus specifically ascribes "the invention of written law" (i.e. legislation as presently observed by the Greeks) to Moses. The Eupolemus text evinces an implicit acceptance of Torah as a Greek-like law code.

Pseudo-Eupolemus (Before First Century BCE)

Two additional fragments ascribed to Eupolemus (but regarded as pseudonymous by scholars[55]) reflect similar dependence polemics. The ancient Hebrew Enoch is said to be "[the inventor of] astrology and other

49. Philo found a middle way: the Greeks did study Torah but never revealed their source due to Greek pride (see p. 19, below).

50. On dating, see Francis T. Fallon, "Eupolemus," in *OTP* 2:861–62. Cf. Martin McNamara, *Intertestamental Literature* (Wilmington, Del.: Glazier, 1983), 222.

51. J. Collins, *Athens and Jerusalem*, 46.

52. McNamara, *Intertestamental Literature*, 222–23. Cf. Wacholder, *Eupolemus*, 76.

53. Fallon, "Eupolemus," F1.

54. Wacholder, *Eupolemus*, 83. Cf. Fallon, "Eupolemus," F1 (p. 865 n. f).

55. Probably the work of a Samaritan (J. Collins, *Athens and Jerusalem*, 47–49).

sciences... Enoch first discovered astrology, not the Egyptians."[56] Further-more, "[although] the Greeks say that Atlas discovered astrology," Pseudo-Eupolemus observes that, "Atlas is the same as Enoch." After Enoch, his son "Methuselah...learned everything through the angels of God, and so knowledge came to us." That is, from Enoch and Methuselah this knowledge came from heaven to men, and then it was Abraham who in turn brought and taught the same to the other peoples. Abraham not only taught Enoch's astrology to the Egyptians, it was also Abraham who taught the cycles of heavenly bodies to the Phoenicians, and "everything else as well."[57]

Eupolemus and Pseudo-Eupolemus both seem to employ a multi-layered view of the development of the various sciences and philosophi-cal ideals venerated in the period. The Hebrew patriarchs received this knowledge from God, and through the mediation of various of the other nations (e.g. astrology through Egypt and writing through Phoenicia), these insights were passed on to Greece. It may be that Eupolemus and Pseudo-Eupolemus reflect an effort to endorse the claims of many ancient peoples to primacy in certain fields of culture, while nonetheless insisting that Israel's patriarchs were the source of all the cultural achievements further developed by these nations.

Cleodemus Malchus (Before First Century BCE)

Due to the legendary travels (and propagation) of Heracles, oriental links to Greece could often be claimed through him. Heracles was commonly thought to have brought Greek cultural ideals to those lands where he left progeny long before the Hellenistic period.[58] Significantly, Cleodemus Malchus is cited by both Josephus (*Ant.* 1.239–41) and Eusebius (*Prep. Gosp.* 9.20.2–4) as having shown that Abraham was the father-in-law of Heracles, and that Abraham was "spreading culture prior to Heracles."[59] But Cleodemus has not left specific claims of a Hebrew source for civilized legal ideals. "Cleodemus refers briefly to Moses the lawgiver," Collins notes, "[but] it would seem that descent from Abraham is more important to him than fidelity to the law."[60]

---

56. Robert Doran, "Pseudo-Eupolemus," in *OTP* 2:873–82, F1. Ben Sira's list of wise men also begins with Enoch (Sir 44:16).

57. Ibid., F1. Cf. Gen 15:5.

58. Dieter Georgi, *The Opponents of Paul in Second Corinthians* (Edinburgh: T. & T. Clark, 1987), 50: "The Greek hero Heracles...was generally considered the conveyer of divine order and [the] founder of human well-being."

59. Robert Doran, "Cleodemus Malchus," in *OTP* 2:886; Georgi, *Opponents of Paul*, 50–51.

60. J. Collins, *Athens and Jerusalem*, 52.

Philo of Alexandria (ca. 30 BCE–ca. 45 CE)
Philo's writings are more intact than those surveyed thus far. Writing from Alexandria, Philo advanced the same general argument of priority for Israel's law code, not only as a source of philosophical wisdom,[61] but also as the first source of legislative ideals.[62]

Philo recognizes that there was a time when even the Hebrews operated without the "rule of law." In particular, he speaks of Abraham and the patriarchs as those who "obeyed the unwritten principle of legislation before any one of the particular laws were written down at all" (*On Abraham* 1.5). Because of their virtue and insight into the natural creation order, the patriarchs did not need written legislation. Philo's work *On Abraham* concludes with this praise:

> But God, adding to the multitude and magnitude of the praises of the wise man [Abraham] one single thing as a crowning point, says that 'this man fulfilled the divine law, and all the commandments of God,' [Gen 26:5] not having been taught to do so by written books, but in accordance with the unwritten laws of his nature..." (*On Abraham* 46.275–76)

Philo places the origin of Hebrew law writing with Moses, *and with this* the introduction of the prescriptive law ideal. Philo does not deny that unwritten customs continue to be an important complement to the written law; however, it is only the written law which is enforceable (*Spec. Laws* 4.28.149–50). Furthermore "a righteous judge" will always tender "a judgment in strict accordance with the [written] law" (*Spec. Laws* 4.10.64). For Philo, although there once was a period when Israel's patriarchs did not have (or need) legislation, the Mosaic law collection was always a prescriptive code. His was also the law code from which the Greeks and all others learned:

> Almost every other nation...have dedicated themselves to embrace and honour them, for they have received this especial honour above all other codes of laws, which is not given to any other code... For they lead after them and influence all nations, barbarians, and Greeks, and the inhabitants of continents and islands, the eastern nations and the western, Europe and Asia; in short, the whole habitable world from one extremity to the other. (*Moses* 2.4.17–20)

In regard to Greek law, Philo is even more explicit, in one place asserting that "lawgivers among the Greeks...transcribed some of the laws from

61. E.g. Philo, *Heir* 45.214; *Alleg. Interp.* 1.33.108; *Posterity* 39.133; *QG* 3.5; 4.152, 167; *Good Person* 8.53–57.
62. Philo (*Migration* 89–93) devoted most of his energies to the allegorical study of Scripture as a philosophical text, but he also insisted on "pay[ing] heed to the letter of the laws" as a legal text.

the two tables of Moses..." (*Spec. Laws* 4.10.61), and in a spirited moment charging Greeks with, "like a thief taking law and opinions from Moses."[63] That the Mosaic laws are the source from which other nations legislate is an obvious fact in Philo's perception, because all nations observe "the sacred seventh day" (*Moses* 2.4.21–22), all nations hold a "great yearly [fast]" (2.4.23–24), and because even a king as noble as Ptolemy Philadelphus desired a translation of the Hebrew laws he could study (2.5.25–7.44). In Philo's polemic, the Mosaic laws were always prescriptive legislation, and other nations have derived the best of their own law systems from what Moses taught them. Peder Borgen, perhaps a bit stereotypically but not inappropriately, sums up Philo's apologetic thus: "He was such an extreme Jew that he referred all ideas and phenomena of value, also including those outside Judaism, to Moses as their origin and/or authentic formulation. Whatever good there was had its source in Scripture and thus belonged to the Jewish nation as its heritage."[64]

The only reason the Greek debt to Moses is not more widely known is because of the pride of the Greeks:

> ...The glory of the laws which [Moses] left behind him has reached over the whole world, and has penetrated to the very furthest limits of the universe; [but] those who do really and truly understand him are not many, perhaps partly out of envy, or else from the disposition so common to many persons of resisting the commands which are delivered by law-givers in different states, since the historians who have flourished among the Greeks have not chosen to think him worthy of mention. (Philo, *Moses* 1.1.2)

Philo's emphasis is not focused on the Mosaic law writings as the original source of "rule of law" philosophy. Philo does recognize the historical reality of peoples operating with unwritten law; nevertheless, he seems to perceive all written law as prescriptive. He believes that Moses wrote the law code from which all others derived right concepts of justice. In doing so, he further illustrates the standard polemic: Israel's law collection was the perfect fulfillment of that which Greek "rule of

---

63. Philo, *QG* 4.152. Cf. Philo, *Moses* 1.5.20–22: the child Moses, taught by the wisest teachers of Egypt and "some being even procured from Greece," quickly surpassed them all. In fact, what Moses learned from these was more "a recollection [of what he already noted on his own] rather than learning [from them]." The picture is similar to Luke's description of Jesus in the Temple: the all-wise child being the one to teach the teachers (Luke 2:46–47). By this description of Moses, Philo undoubtedly intends to show that Torah fulfills the greatest ideals of the Greeks— but not because Moses learned from the Greeks.

64. Peder Borgen, "Philo of Alexandria," in *ABD* 5:341.

law" philosophy sought. In fact, so perfectly does the Mosaic law code meet the requirements of the Greeks that Torah alone never needs amendment:

> But that he himself is the most admirable of all the lawgivers who have ever lived in any country either among the Greeks or among the barbarians, and that his are the most admirable of all laws, and truly divine, omitting no one particular which they ought to comprehend, there is the clearest proof possible in this fact, the laws of other lawgivers... [undergo] various alterations and innovations... But the enactments of this lawgiver are firm...not liable to alteration... (Philo, *Moses* 2.3.12–16)

Philo regards the Torah, not only as a law code, but a law code never needing amendment. Philo's main concern in his writings is to show the philosophical wisdom of Israel's native writings. Courtroom justice does not seem to be a prominent focus of his works. Nonetheless, in advancing his various arguments, Philo does speak of Israel's Torah as having been the nation's prescriptive law code ever since Moses. It was indeed the source of Greek philosophical *and legal* ideals. The "rule of law" norm of Hellenism is accepted by Philo as inherent in Torah.

Flavius Josephus (37–100 CE)

Josephus knew many of the aforementioned apologists. In fact, it was he who preserved several of the writings previously examined. Josephus recognized a powerful, pro-Jewish polemic in the writings of his predecessors, and he conscientiously continued their efforts to identify Israel's Torah as a Greek-like law code. What is particularly interesting in Josephus' argument is that he plainly states his reason for wanting to show Torah as legislation: Israel's claim to be a civilized (not barbarian) nation depends on their having possessed the "rule of law." In his book *Against Apion* (2.15.151–52), Josephus wrote

> I would begin with the remark that persons who have espoused the cause of order and law—one law for all—and been the first to introduce them, may fairly be admitted to be more civilized and virtuously disposed than those who lead lawless (ἄνομος) and disorderly lives. In fact, each nation endeavours to trace its own institutions back to the remotest date, in order to create the impression that, far from imitating others, it has been the one to set its neighbours an example of orderly life under law.

Writing in the Roman era, Josephus demonstrates that the need to shake the barbarian stigma was still keenly felt. Furthermore, he confesses that his own argument is not new, nor unique, but that "each nation endeavours to trace its own institutions" as being that original source of "rule of law" civility. Josephus recognizes the heritage of apologetics here being pieced together from fragments, not only as a Jewish polemic but one which other barbarian peoples employed as well. It is by demonstrating ones own nation to have been the originator of "orderly life under law" that the claim to being "most civilized" can be affirmed. Josephus believes he can prove that the Jews are the genuine font of civilized law:

> Now, I maintain that our legislator is the most ancient of all legislators in the records of the whole world. Compared with him, your Lycurguses and Solons, and Zaleucus, who gave the Locrians their laws, and all who are held in such high esteem by the Greeks appear to have been born but yesterday. Why, the very word "law" was unknown in ancient Greece. Witness Homer, who nowhere employs it in his day;[65] the masses were governed by maxims not clearly defined and by the orders of royalty, and continued long afterwards the use of unwritten customs, many of which were from time to time altered to suit particular circumstances.
>
> On the other hand, our legislator, who lived in the remotest past (that, I presume, is admitted even by our most unscrupulous detractors), proved himself the people's best guide and counsellor; and after framing a code to embrace the whole conduct of their life, induced them to accept it, and secured, on the firmest footing, its observance for all time. (Josephus, *Ag. Ap.* 2.15.154–56)

In Josephus' apology, the Jews had innovated the prescriptive-law philosophy long before Greeks even knew the word "law." In fact, Josephus goes a step further, arguing that the Greeks themselves learned their legal philosophy from the Jews: "...the wisest of the Greeks learnt to adopt these conceptions of God [leading to 'civilized' society and the 'rule of law'] from principles with which Moses supplied them."[66]

As late as Josephus, the stigma of "lawless barbarianism" was still keenly felt. His *Against Apion* was written, in part, because Apion had charged the Jews with being "the most witless of all barbarians, and...the only people who have contributed no useful invention to civilization." The way to defend the civilized nature of Israel (and Israel's God) was, in Josephus' thinking, to show that Israel not only had contributed *something* to the civilization of culture, but in fact had invented *the cornerstone* of civilization itself: "All this tirade will, I think, be clearly refuted, if it be shown that the precepts of our laws, punctiliously practiced in our lives, are in direct conflict with the above description [of Apion]... We are the most law-abiding of all the nations...[and] the first to introduce [laws]" (*Ag. Ap.* 2.14.148–15.152).

---

65. Thackeray, *Josephus*, 1:355 n. a: "The word νόμος appears first in Hesiod; older terms were θέμιστες (Homer) and θεσμοί, 'ordinances'"; cf. Maine, *Ancient Law*, 3–4.

66. Josephus, *Ag. Ap.* 2.16.168; cf. 2.38.281–86. On Greek dependence on Moses for philosophy, see 1.22.161–82.

As Josephus admits, this was not a new argument devised by himself: he points to similar argumentation put forward by others before him (including some of those earlier noted).[67] His was a standard polemic which he had inherited from his predecessors (and which was shared by other ethnicities). Yaacov Shavit has sensed this point:

> Living in a world where Greek political ideals were seen as the supreme model of political life and values, writers such as Josephus and Philo found it vital to compare the "Jewish constitution" with the Greek one. This was done in order to combat negative Hellenistic descriptions of the Mosaic law, and at the same time to see the Torah as a constitution, as the Hellenistic writers did…[68]

*			*			*

The Jewish polemicists of the above survey illustrate an extended heritage through the Hellenistic era of defending Jewish *norms* (especially the precepts of Torah) within an accepted framework of Greek *conventions* (e.g. Greek philosophy and/or the "rule of law"). Eastern peoples had traditionally asserted pre-eminence based on the superiority of their gods and the righteousness of their kings. With the conquest of the Greeks, however, a new framework for ethnic apologetics was forced upon the Orient. At its core was the Greek "civilized vs. barbarian" worldview with the "rule of law" as a definitive mark of a civilized society. Ethnic self-explanation now needed to be expressed in terms of civic institutions (such as the "rule of law") and cultural developments (such as writing, astronomy, etc.). For many peoples of the East, this was accomplished by finding ideological ties to Greece, whose cultural ideals had become universally recognized as the standard of civilization. Often, such efforts involved the identification of some native cultural innovation similar to one of those championed by Greece. Some ancient Greek hero, etymological link, similar myth, or other bridge could then be located and used to show how Greece had, in fact, received that ideal from the said nation.

In the case of the Jews, the Law of Moses provided prime material for such an apologetic, both as a source of wisdom (cf. Deut 4:6) which could now be defined in the systems provided by Greek philosophers,

67.   Hecataeus (*Ant.* 1.7.2.159; 12.4.38; *Ag. Ap.* 1.22.183–205; 2.4.43), Aristeas (*Ant.* 12.1.11–15.118), Cleodemus Malchus (*Ant.* 1.15.240–41), and possibly Artapanus (*Ant.* 2.10.1.238–53; cf. J. Collins, "Artapanus," 2:894).

68.   Jacob Shavit, *Athens in Jerusalem: Classical Antiquity and Hellenism in the Making of the Modern Secular Jew* (trans. C. Naor and N. Werner; London: Littman Library of Jewish Civilization, 1997), 436.

and as a civilizing law code. Such an apologetic, however, actually subjected Torah to Greek conventions. It became generally desirable, in these conditions, for Hellenistic-era Judaism to conceive of its ancient law writings as a prescriptive law code, and to "demonstrate" that it always had been just that.[69]

III. *Judean Torah Polemics (1 and 2 Maccabees)*

The preceding material illustrates the basic premise behind the present chapter: namely, that Torah apologists of the Hellenistic era accepted the civilized/barbarian ethnology. Rather than contradicting period stereotypes (i.e. by defending Israel as having maintained an honorable society under sovereign kings, not law codes), Jewish apologists acceded that "lawless monarchy" is barbarian. Once this presupposition was admitted, it would have been impossible to suppose that Yahweh gave his people a *barbarian* king and law collection. The Torah must have always been a law code, since Yahweh certainly is a civilizing God. The preceding material indicates the widespread employment of such a polemic in *diaspora* Judaism. It will now be helpful to look at evidence for this polemic in *Judean* Judaism—showing thereby both (1) that Torah was being viewed prescriptively in Judea, and (2) that such a view of Torah can be tied to an acceptance of the civilized/barbarian ethnology. This evidence can be found in the writings of 1 and 2 Maccabees. Some preliminary remarks concerning these works will open the way to their use in this project.

First Maccabees can confidently be dated sometime within (or shortly after) the reign of John Hyrcanus (134–104 BCE). The book's closing reference is to "the rest of the acts of John...written in the annals of his high priesthood" (1 Macc 16:23–24).[70] Second Maccabees is more difficult to date. The work is itself based on an older, five-volume work by Jason of Cyrene (2 Macc 2:23) and has been prefixed with letters by those who further adapted it. Due to the friendly attitude toward the Romans evinced in the book, most scholars expect a pre-63 BCE date for its extant form and thus an earlier dating for its source (the five volumes

---

69. Cf. Louis H. Feldman, "Torah and Secular Culture: Challenge and Response in the Hellenistic Period," in *Studies in Hellenistic Judaism* (ed. Louis H. Feldman Leiden: Brill, 1996), 487–503 (especially 492–94).

70. Jonathan A. Goldstein, *I Maccabees: A New Translation with Introduction and Commentary* (AB 41; New York: Doubleday, 1976), 62–63; Robert Doran, "1 Maccabees," in *1 & 2 Maccabees, Job, Psalms* (ed. Adele Berlin et al.; New Interpreter's Bible 4; Nashville: Abingdon, 1996), 22; David Williams, "Recent Research in 1 Maccabees," *CurBS* 9 (2001): 173–74.

of Jason of Cyrene).[71] Since one of the prefixed letters added to the book has been dated to 124 BCE,[72] the book itself is likely older than that. In terms of dating therefore, both works arise within generally the same period: late second to early first century. In fact, Jonathan Goldstein suggests that Jason of Cyrene may have written his work in direct response to the pro-Hasmonean 1 Maccabees.[73] Most scholars are doubtful that the books are so directly related, one being an answer to the other.[74] Nonetheless, there is a roughly contemporaneous dialog in these works—and it is, notably, a dialog of contrary sects.

For instance, 1 Maccabees shows the Hasmoneans as Judah's divinely anointed saviors and warns that all who try to achieve victory apart from them will lose God's favor.[75] Second Maccabees, however, likely derives from a Hassidim party.[76] It presents Judas Maccabeus and his family as of questionable effectiveness and even, at times, of dubious integrity.[77] In the view of 2 Maccabees, it is the Hassidim martyrs who are the heroes of Jewish independence.[78] Furthermore, in addition to such political differences, there are significant theological differences. First Maccabees focuses on deliverance as that which is achieved in the present life, and on glory as one's enduring name in this world. This view is complemented by a willingness to fight defensively on the sabbath day for the sake of preserving Jewish society here and now.[79] For 2 Maccabees, however, glory is that which is attained in a future resurrection whether

71. Doran, "1 Maccabees," 22; idem, "2 Maccabees," in Berlin et al. eds., *1 & 2 Maccabees*, 183.

72. Elias Bickerman, "Ein jüdischer Festbrief vom Jahr 124 v. Chr. (II Macc. 1.1–9)," *ZNW* 32 (1933): 233–54; Jonathan A. Goldstein, *II Maccabees: A New Translation with Introduction and Commentary* (AB 41A; New York: Doubleday, 1984), 24–25; David Williams, "Recent Research in 2 Maccabees," *CBR* 2, no. 1 (2003): 71–72.

73. Goldstein, *I Maccabees*, 64–89.

74. Joseph Sievers, *The Hasmoneans and their Supporters: From Mattathias to the Death of John Hyrcanus I* (South Florida Studies in the History of Judaism 6; Atlanta: Scholars Press, 1990), 9; Williams, "Recent Research in 2 Maccabees," 75.

75. E.g. 1 Macc 5:61–62; see Goldstein, *I Maccabees*, 4–12.

76. E.g. 2 Macc 14:6; see Goldstein, *I Maccabees*, 64–89; idem, *II Maccabees*, 18. Cf. Christian Habicht, *2. Makkabäerbuch* (JSHRZ 1/3; Gütersloher: Gerd Mohn, 1979), 189; Sievers, *Hasmoneans and Supporters*, 7–8.

77. E.g. 2 Macc 10:19–22; 12:40; 14:17, 22–25; see Goldstein, *I Maccabees*, 33, 79–80.

78. E.g. 2 Macc 7:38; 8:5; see Goldstein, *I Maccabees*, 30, 33; Jan Willem van Henten, *The Maccabean Martyrs as Saviours of the Jewish People: A Study of 2 and 4 Maccabees* (JSJSup 57; Leiden: Brill, 1997).

79. E.g. 1 Macc 2:40–41, 51, 62–64; see Goldstein, *I Maccabees*, 12, 79.

or not success is achieved in this world. This view is complemented by an eagerness to die the martyr's death, particularly for refusing to fight on the sabbath.[80] These and other distinctions make it evident that 1 and 2 Maccabees, though treating the same history, represent competing interpretations of that history.[81]

In regard to place of origin, 1 Maccabees was originally written in Hebrew and later translated into Greek; it is generally accepted as having emerged in Judea.[82] The provenance of 2 Maccabees is more complex. It is Greek in style and is frankly identified as deriving from the work of a diaspora Jew: the five volumes of Jason of Cyrene. Many scholars believe 2 Maccabees was likewise composed in the Diaspora. This conclusion is not firm, however. Noting 2 Maccabees' strong focus on the temple, Robert Doran believes "there is no reason why someone living in Jerusalem who was fluent in Greek could not have written it."[83] Jason wrote his five-volume work in the Diaspora; but the epitomization of that work into 2 Maccabees could have taken place in the Diaspora or in Judea. What is clear, in any case, is that 2 Maccabees was accepted by a prominent Jerusalem sect as representative of their views. Both letters appended to the front are addressed from Jerusalem to the Egyptian Jews (2 Macc 1:1, 10). The first of these letters, at least, is genuine (dated 124 BCE, so 2 Macc 1:10);[84] the authenticity of the second is controversial.[85] It is the fact that this text was endorsed by a Jerusalem sect in the late second/early first century that makes it useful for a study of *Judean* views on law. It is indeed fortunate that, amid other themes (e.g. the sanctuary and the fatherland), both works present a prominent concern for law.

In 1 Maccabees, the story opens with certain "transgressors of the law" (1 Macc 1:11) setting up Greek institutions in Jerusalem and the dogged efforts of Antiochus IV to cause the Jews "[to] forget the law" (1:49). Throughout 1 Maccabees, the subsequent wars are repeatedly

---

80. E.g. 2 Macc 6:11; 8:26–27; 12:43–45; see Goldstein, *1 Maccabees*, 12, 30–31, 79.

81. On further differences, see ibid., 33–34, 45–54, 78–84; Doran, "*1 Maccabees*," 7–12; idem, "Independence or Co-Existence: The Response of 1 and 2 Maccabees to Seleucid Hegemony," *SBLSP* 38 (1999): 94–103.

82. Ibid., 20.

83. Ibid., 183. Cf. Robert Doran, *Temple Propaganda: The Purpose and Character of 2 Maccabees* (CBQMS 12; Washington, D.C.: Catholic Biblical Association of America, 1981), 112–13; J. C. Dancy, *A Commentary on 1 Maccabees* (Oxford: Blackwell, 1954), 15; Hengel, *Judaism and Hellenism*, 1:95–96.

84. See n. 72, above.

85. For discussion: Williams, "Recent Research in 2 Maccabees," 72–73.

epitomized as being "war for the law" (2:21–28, 42, 50, 64, 67–68; 3:20–21, 48; 6:59; 10:37; 13:3; 14:29). For 2 Maccabees, Jerusalem was "inhabited in perfect peace" so long as "the laws were well maintained" (2 Macc 3:1). As long as the Jews revered the law (3.15), the Lord guaranteed their security (3:24–40; cf. 11:36; 12:40). More specifically, under the high priest Onias ("a zealot for the laws," 4:2), Jerusalem as a whole had observed Torah. But when the wicked Jason usurped the high priesthood, he "overthrew the lawful order" (4:11) so that even the priests began to be drawn away after "unlawful proceedings" (4:14). With this opening scenario, 2 Maccabees explains the tragic years that followed: "For this reason hardship surrounded [the Jews]...for impiety toward the divine laws is no light matter—as the following history will make clear" (4:16–17; cf. 2:20–22). Although for 2 Maccabees it is the pious laity (rather than Hasmonean zeal) that is the secret to renewal, the Maccabean struggle is alike described as a "struggle for the law" (4:17; 6:1–6, 28; 7:2, 9, 11, 23, 24, 30, 37; 8:21, 23, 36; 11:24, 31; 13:10, 14).

In sum, therefore, 1 and 2 Maccabees preserve two, competing interpretations of the early Seleucid history as held by two Judaic sects in Jerusalem. Within those competing interpretations there is imbedded evidence of Jewish attitudes toward law. The good fortune of possessing two such works enhances their importance for the present study. It means that, where ideological agreement is found between these documents, one can suspect that a truly widespread Judaic ideal has been noted (not just the view of one sect). It will be seen that there are very significant differences between these two works in how they view law; but it will also be seen that important similarities can also be adduced.

The following pages will examine the legal ideals undergirding 1 and 2 Maccabees. Of course, assessment of so pervasive a theme as "law" in these books is a massive project in itself. Ralph Marcus, in 1927, produced a monograph on "law" in the Apocryphal writings.[86] Bernard Renaud, in 1961, produced an important article on "law" in 1 and 2 Maccabees.[87] Unfortunately however, neither of these important works were conducted with sensitivity to the legal categories here at issue: descriptivism (a.k.a. "barbarian lawlessness") and prescriptivism (a.k.a. "civilized law"). A thorough analysis of law in the Maccabean histories, with sensitivity to these categories, is needed. What follows cannot pretend to be the whole of what is needed. Nonetheless, the following discussion

---

86. Ralph Marcus, *Law in the Apocrypha* (New York: Columbia University Press, 1927).

87. B. Renaud, "La loi et les lois dans les livres des Maccabées," *RB* 68 (1961): 39–67.

will identify key evidence from three major strands of legal thought in 1 and 2 Maccabees: (1) the *lexical choices* of each work in relation to Jewish laws and Seleucid laws; (2) the binding force each work ascribes to *Seleucid* laws; and (3) the binding force each work ascribes to *Jewish* laws. Once these three lines of evidence are fleshed out, conclusions will be drawn relevant to the present project.

1. *Lexical Choices in Relation to Law*

Both 1 and 2 Maccabees use a wide range of terms for various legal instruments. First Maccabees uses the word "law" (νόμος) 26 times.[88] Other terms employed in reference to legal imperatives include: "words" (λόγοι),[89] "decrees" (προστάγματα),[90] "customs" (νόμιμοι),[91] "commands" (ἐντολαί),[92] "writings" (βιβλία),[93] "ordinances" (δικαιώματα),[94] "covenants" (διαθῆκαι),[95] "letters" (ἐπιστολαί),[96] "agreement" (στάσις),[97] "judgment" (σύγκριμα),[98] and "oath" (ὅρκος).[99] What is striking is that, amid all these designations, the word νόμος is always reserved for Jewish law. Never is any Seleucid regulation dignified with the important designation, νόμος.

The same pattern is also maintained in the negative. Not only are the rules made by the Seleucids denied the title νόμοι, but also the rules broken by the Seleucids are never called νόμοι either. Seleucid law violators are called "sinners" (ἁμαρτωλοί),[100] doers of "evil" (πονηρός),[101] an "adversary" (διάβολος),[102] "(sons of) arrogance" (οἱ υἱοὶ τῆς

88. 1 Macc 1:49, 52, 56, 57; 2:21, 26, 27, 42, 48, 50, 58, 64, 67, 68; 3:48, 56; 4:42, 47, 53; 10:14, 37; 13:3, 48; 14:14, 29; 15:21.

89. 1 Macc 1:30, 42 (EV v. 43), 50, 51; 2:22, 33, 34, 62; 3:14, 39, 42; 7:10, 11, 15, 27; 9:55, 10:3, 24, 46, 47.

90. Seleucid: 1 Macc 1:60; 2:18, 23; 6:23 / Jewish: 2:68; 10:14.

91. Seleucid: 1 Macc 1:14, 42, 44 / Jewish: 3:21, 29; 6:59 (×2).

92. Seleucid: 1 Macc 2:19, 31; 11:2 / Jewish: 2:53.

93. Seleucid: 1 Macc 1:44 / Jewish: 1:56, 57; 3:48; 12:9 (cf. 16:24) / Spartan: 14:23.

94. Seleucid: 1 Macc 1:13 / Jewish: 1:49; 2:21, 40.

95. Seleucid: 1 Macc 1:11; 11:9 / Jewish: 1:15, 57, 63; 2:20, 27, 50, 54; 4:10.

96. Seleucid: 1 Macc 9:60; 10:3, 7, 17; 11:29, 31; 13:35; 15:1; 16:19 / Jewish: 12:2, 5, 17 / Roman: 8:22; 12:4; 15:15 / Spartan: 12:7, 8, 19; 14:20.

97. Seleucid: 1 Macc 7:18.

98. Seleucid: 1 Macc 1:57 (cf. κρίνω in 1 Macc 11:33).

99. Seleucid: 1 Macc 7:18. On nn. 88–89, cf. Renaud, "La loi et les Maccabées," 39–41.

100. 1 Macc 1:10; 2:44, 48, 62.

101. 1 Macc 1:36; 11:8; 14:14 (cf. 1:15; 7:25).

102. 1 Macc 1:36.

ὑπηρφανίας),[103] or "workers of injustice" (οἱ ἐργαζόμενοι τὴν ἀδικίαν).[104] But only Jewish rule breakers are ever called "lawless" (ἄνομοι,[105] or παράνομοι[106]). The implication is that only the Jewish nation even *has* a law (νόμοι) to be betrayed. The Seleucids are everywhere denied any connection with νόμοι—either as law keepers or law breakers.

The importance of this pattern is heightened when it is seen that the epitomist of 2 Maccabees exercises the same selectiveness. Second Maccabees employs the word νόμος 27 times,[107] also in exclusive reference to Jewish law. Seleucid instruments are described by other terms: "words" (λόγοι),[108] "decrees" (προστάγματα),[109] an "act" (ψήφισμα),[110] "customs" (ἐθισμός,[111] or ἀγωγή),[112] "commands" (ἐντολαί),[113] "letters" (ἐπιστολαί),[114] "policies" (προαίρεσις),[115] "pledges" (δεξιός),[116] "covenants" (συνθῆκαι),[117] a "pact" (διάσταλοις),[118] and "oaths" (ὅρκοι).[119] In the negative also, 2 Maccabees avoids speaking of Seleucids as νόμος-breakers. Like its counterpart, 2 Maccabees employs terms of νόμος-violation (i.e. παράνομοι) almost exclusively in reference to Jewish apostates.[120]

There is one place where Judas does call the Seleucids "law breakers," though not in a manner that undermines the point here being deduced. The author of 2 Maccabees reports:

103. 1 Macc 1:21, 24; 2:47, 49.
104. 1 Macc 9:23. On this term referring to pagans, see Renaud, "La loi et les Maccabées," 46.
105. 1 Macc 2:44; 3:5, 6; 7:5; 9:23, 58, 69; 11:25; 14:14.
106. 1 Macc 1:11, 34; 10:61; 11:21. On nn. 100–106, cf. Renaud, "La loi et les Maccabées," 45–49.
107. 2 Macc 1:4; 2:2, 3, 18, 22; 3:1; 4:2, 17; 5:8, 15; 6:1, 5, 28; 7:2, 9, 11, 23, 30, 37; 8:21, 36; 10:26; 11:31; 12:40; 13:10, 14; 15:9. (Also νομοθετέομαι: 3:15; νομοθεσία: 6:23.)
108. Seleucid: 2 Macc 7:24; 9:5.
109. Seleucid: 2 Macc 7:30 / Jewish: 1:4; 2:2; 7:30; 10:8.
110. Seleucid: 2 Macc 6:8; 12:4 (Joppans) / Jewish: 10:8; 15:36.
111. Seleucid: 2 Macc 4:11 / Jewish: 12:38.
112. Seleucid: 2 Macc 4:16; 6:8; 11:24 (cf. νόμιμος: 4:11; 11:24).
113. Seleucid: 2 Macc 3:7, 13; 4:25; 14:13.
114. Seleucid: 2 Macc 9:18; 11:16, 22, 27 / Jewish: 2:13 / Roman: 11:34.
115. Seleucid: 2 Macc 9:27; 11:26.
116. Seleucid: 2 Macc 4:34; 11:26, 30; 13:22; 14:19 / Jewish: 12:11, 12.
117. Seleucid: 2 Macc 12:1; 13:25; 14:20, 26, 27 (cf. διαστελλόμενον: 14:28).
118. Seleucid: 2 Macc 13:25.
119. Seleucid: 2 Macc 4:34; 7:24; 15:10. (On nn. 107–19, cf. Renaud, "La loi dans les Maccabées," 55–57.)
120. 2 Macc 4:11, 14; 6:21; 13:7 (cf. 5:15).

Then Judas...and those who continued in Judaism [with him]...implored the Lord to take notice of the people, oppressed on all sides, and also to have pity on the temple...and to remember also the lawless (παράνομος) slaughter of innocent children... Then Maccabeus assembled his men... and exhorted them not to be awed by the enemy nor to fear the Gentile (ἐθνῶν) horde which was unjustly coming against them, but to fight bravely, holding before their eyes the outrage lawlessly (ἀνόμως) perpetrated upon the holy place...and moreover the overthrow of the ancestral order (τῆς προγονικῆς πολιτείας). (8:1–4, 16–17)

The slaughter of infants designated here as παράνομος had been carried out by the soldiers of Antiochus (5:13). The violation of the holy place, here called ἀνόμως, was accomplished by Antiochus and the Jewish apostate Menelaus (5:15). Thus, the author of 2 Maccabees does allow terms of νόμος-violation to be applied to the Seleucids in this instance. This, however, does not undermine the insight here noted. The latter violation described as ἀνόμως (profaning the holy place) is clearly a violation of the *Jewish* νόμος. The former violation (the "unlawful" killing of innocent children) might be regarded as a violation of the Jewish νόμος or some unmentioned Greek νόμος.[121] Because the slaughter was part-and-parcel with the violation of the temple, however, and because there is no Greek νόμος mentioned, it would seem that the whole desecration was being described as an outrage against, specifically, the Jewish νόμος. Since these evils amount to blasphemy against God's name (v. 4) and an "overthrow of the ancestral order [or, constitution; πολιτείας]" *of the Jews* (8:17), the νόμος being nullified by Antiochus must be Jewish (i.e. Torah). Thus, it remains the consistent witness of 2 Maccabees—both from the positive or negative perspectives—that the Seleucids lacked their own νόμοι. The Seleucids, for 2 Maccabees, may appoint "decrees," "oaths," and other rulings, but they never establish νόμοι. The Seleucids may even violate *Jewish* νόμοι; however, there is no indication of Seleucids ever violating (and thus affirming the existence of) their own νόμοι.

Identifying these lexical choices in 1 and 2 Maccabees does not itself answer the question, "How was Torah perceived to function for these writers?"[122] But it does show that a clear and deliberate distinction was being drawn between the Jewish view of the Hebrew law writings, and that of the Seleucids. Somehow, the distinction of Jewish law, and only

121. Or "the [laws] of civilized mankind" generally; see Goldstein, *II Maccabees*, 331.
122. For Renaud's conclusions, see Renaud, "La loi dans les Maccabées," 41–42, 67.

Jewish law, as νόμος is an important part of the pro-Jewish polemic of both parties here represented. It now needs to be discerned (in sections 2–3, following), how the Maccabean polemicists understood the Jewish law writings to function.

There is, nonetheless, another set of lexical choices in 2 Maccabees which begins to evince that writer's reason for ascribing only Jewish law as νόμοι. In 2 Maccabees, the Seleucid kings are five times called βάρβαροι ("barbarian"): 2 Macc 2:21; 4:25; 5:22; 10:1–5; 15:2. Second Maccabees demonstrates a skilled understanding of Greek vocabulary,[123] and it is evident that the term βάρβαρος was chosen with appreciation for its precision. It is used, not only as a term of cruelty, but specifically the cruelty of "tyranny sans law."

This is especially clear in the account of Nicanor's stratagem to attack Judas on the sabbath day (15:1–5). It is there reported that certain Jews (who were in Nicanor's army "under compulsion") pleaded with him not to attack the Jews on the sabbath: "Do not so cruelly and barbarously (βαρβάρως) destroy, but show reverence for the day honored...by the All-Seeing One..." (15:2). It was not the cruelty of the attack, but the violation of a day protected by law, which qualified Nicanor's plan as "barbarian." Nicanor's reply to the appellant affirms this: Nicanor asked whether there is a sovereign (δυνάστης) who has commanded (προσ-τάσσω) the keeping of the sabbath (15:2). The Jews respond that there is such a one in heaven. Nicanor concluded: "And I, I say, am a sovereign (δυνάστης) upon the earth. Here is the command (προστάσσω): take up arms and complete the king's business!" (15:5). Nicanor saw himself as sovereign by virtue of royal commission (able even to overrule the command of God). The barbarity here in view is not a matter of cruelty therefore, but disregard for any law other than the king's will. It is the violation of law which made this particular attack "blasphemous and barbarous."[124] By describing the Seleucids as both βάρβαρος and without νόμοι, the epitomist is clearly setting his case within the categories of an "anti-barbarian" stereotype.[125]

---

123.   Habicht, 2 Makkabäerbuch, 178; Nigel M. Kennell, "New Light on 2 Mac-cabees 4:7–15," JJS 56, no. 1 (2005): 17; Goldstein, II Maccabees, 20–22; Doran, Temple Propaganda, 46; "2 Maccabees," 181–82; Renaud, "La loi et les Macca-bées," 55–58.

124.   Doran, Temple Propaganda, 71; "2 Maccabees," 295.

125.   Note that in the opening lines of 2 Maccabees (2:21), the paradigm "Juda-ism"/"barbarian" is introduced as a replacement of the traditional "Hellenism"/"barbarian" paradigm.

In both 1 and 2 Maccabees, there is a discernable effort to avoid ascribing νόμοι to the Seleucids. In contrast, both works readily describe the Jewish laws as νόμοι. Second Maccabees adds clarity to the reason Seleucid rulings are denied the ascription νόμος: it is because the Seleucid rulers are βάρβαροι. Of greater importance than lexical patterns, however, is the way in which both authors actually showed Jewish and Seleucid legal instruments as operating. It must next be examined: how Seleucid "non-νόμος" rules and Jewish "νόμος" laws actually operated for these authors.

2. *The Force of Seleucid Law*

Not surprisingly, a review of Seleucid rulings in both accounts shows that Seleucid rulings are unreliable and subject to royal whim. That is, the choice *not* to call Seleucid rulings νόμοι is joined by a general portrayal of impermanence and lack of force behind Seleucid acts.

This can be illustrated from 1 Maccabees through reference to the siege of Lysias against Jerusalem (1 Macc 6:55–63). Lysias was an aspirant to the Seleucid throne after Antiochus IV's death. While attacking Jerusalem, Lysias received word that a rival claimant, Philip, was in Antioch. Desperate to return home, Lysias treated for peace. He made an "oath" (ὁρκισμός) with the Jews, the author reports, guaranteeing them "peace [and]…their laws."[126] These terms were warmly welcomed by Judas, since the Hasmoneans were always content to remain under the Seleucid crown so long as Jewish laws were allowed them (cf. especially 13:37).[127] The oath being established, the gates of Jerusalem were opened and Lysias welcomed as their king. Once inside the city walls, however, Lysias saw his opportunity; he promptly "broke the oath he had sworn and commanded to break down the wall all around" (6:62). Lysias' treaty had no actual binding force: it was an oath he readily abandoned once he had opportunity to seize control.[128]

Such "making and breaking" of legal instruments by the Seleucids is a regular feature in 1 Maccabees. "The Seleucids have already been depicted as deceitful (1:30)," Doran notes, "and the narrative will con-

---

126.   This oath reinstates the treaties of Antiochus IV (2 Macc 11:31) and Antiochus III (Josephus, *Ant.* 12.3.138–44; see Dancy, *1 Maccabees*, 117).

127.   Doran, "1 Maccabees," 91; "2 Maccabees," 287; "Independence or Co-Existence."

128.   Dancy believes the Jews misunderstood Lysias, who only promised to secure the temple (not the walls). If Dancy is correct, Lysias was not so duplicitous as 1 Maccabees presents. Moreover, if correct, this further indicates the effort of the author to re-tell history in a way that shows Seleucid decrees as unreliable; see Dancy, *1 Maccabees*, 118; cf. Goldstein, *1 Maccabees*, 325.

tinue to show them to be untrustworthy (7:10–18, 27; 11:2)."[129] There is a concerted effort to show the "non-nomistic" decrees of the Seleucids with a lack of binding force. In another context, this conclusion is explicitly stated by the text: "There is neither truth nor judgment in them, for they have violated the agreement and the oath they had sworn" (7:18; cf. 10:25–46). The Seleucids are presented in 1 Maccabees as sovereign tyrants completely above all legal enactments—even their own. It is almost certainly for this reason that the dignity of the term νόμος is never attached to their legal instruments, whatever else they might be called.

The author of 2 Maccabees paints in similar strokes. In 2 Macc 11, King Antiochus is said to have published an edict (ἐπιστολή) making peace and promising that the Jews "should be free from disturbance" (11:25). Even though this guarantee came from the king himself, district governors (τῶν κατὰ τόπον στρατηγῶν, 12:2) were not actually bound by it.[130] The city of Joppa facetiously "celebrated" this new peace treaty with a city ordinance (ψήφισμα) funding a Mediterranean cruise for the Jews. Because "they wished to be at peace and suspected nothing," the Jews went along with this peace offering. Once out to sea, however, they were ruthlessly cast overboard: "at least two hundred" drowned (12:3–4). Other local authorities are said to have been plotting similarly, but Judas intervened to block further treachery (12:5–9). Even though the king had passed an edict (ἐπιστολή) guaranteeing peace, no lower authorities were bound by it. Even though the Joppans enacted the boat cruise by city ordinance (ψήφισμα), the ordinance was a ruse. No enforcement from the king followed the violation of his edict; it fell to Judas to restore peace. The lesson is repeated in other examples.[131] "Oaths," "edicts," and "covenants" are made when it suits Seleucid purposes; they are broken when their cancellation suits better. It is surely because of this impermanence of Seleucid rulings (and the king's whimsical authority over them) that Seleucid laws are never ascribed as νόμοι.

In both 1 and 2 Maccabees, it seems that every time a Seleucid ruling is mentioned, it is introduced only to show how the Greek rulers subsequently broke it. This is clearly a polemical description. Hartog identifies this as stereotypical of barbarians: "A despot cannot restrain himself from violating the *nomoi*...whether his own or in any other society. That is clearly a Barbarian way of behaving."[132] In fact, according to James Redfield's synthesis of Herodotus, "The tyrant may even be said

129.   Doran, "1 Maccabees," 92.
130.   Goldstein, *II Maccabees*, 432.
131.   E.g. 2 Macc 4:34; 13:22–14:2; 14:19–30; 15:10.
132.   Hartog, *Memories of Odysseus*, 86.

to *prove* his authority by defying the *nomoi*."[133] It is such a portrayal of the Seleucids which one encounters in 1 and 2 Maccabees.

The real history of Seleucid rule can hardly have been so perfidious. Most likely, the Seleucid kings saw themselves as just rulers seeking to contain a troublesome region.[134] Probably in the view of Antiochus and his successors, the Jews were the unruly, law-breaking barbarians and they the law-enforcing governors.[135] (This is nearly admitted in 2 Macc 5:11.) "In contrast [to the image in the Maccabean histories]," Grabbe notes, "there is evidence that Antiochus was a very able ruler."[136] It was not characteristic of the Seleucids to undermine local laws and traditions. On the contrary, the Seleucids tended to permit local peoples their own laws and religion. It is obvious the Maccabean historians were stereotyping the Seleucids.

Furthermore, both Maccabean histories speak of Antiochus IV granting to Jerusalem πόλις status (1 Macc 1:13–14; 2 Macc 4:9–12), which likely included the granting of a new city constitution (cf. 4 Macc 4:19).[137] Both narratives focus on the introduction of the educational institution of a πόλις (i.e. the gymnasium), and 2 Maccabees speaks of the city's renaming as "Antioch"; but neither narrative gives direct attention to the city's new νόμοι. The author of 1 Maccabees does mention that the king "gave them authority to implement the ordinances (δικαιώματα) of the Gentiles" in Jerusalem (1 Macc 1:13). The author of 2 Maccabees likewise reports that the king gave approval (ἐπινεύω) to change Jerusalem "to the Greek model" (χαρακτῆρα, 4:10). This latter text is particularly significant, since the verb ἐπινεύω is a rare Greek legal term known specifically by its use in Antiochan grants of Greek law codes to subject cities. It was customary in setting up a πόλις to receive a model

133. James Redfield, "Herodotus the Tourist," in T. Harrison, ed., *Greeks and Barbarians*, 47.

134. Grabbe, *Judaism*, 1:247–55; John R. Bartlett, *1 Maccabees* (Guides to the Apocrypha and Pseudepigrapha 5; Sheffield: Sheffield Academic Press, 1998), 62–64.

135. So Tacitus, *Hist.* 5.8.

136. Grabbe, *Judaism*, 1:248. Cf. Ma, *Antiochus and the Cities*.

137. Tcherikover, *Hellenistic Civilization*, 161–69; E. Schürer, *Jewish People in the Age of Jesus Christ (175 BC–AD 135)* (ed. Geza Vermes et al.; Edinburgh: T. & T. Clark, 3 vols., 1973–87), 1:148; Hengel, *Judaism and Hellenism*, 1:278; Doran, "1 Maccabees," 32; idem, "2 Maccabees," 216–17; Grabbe, *Judaism*, 1:277–81; Schäfer, *Jews in Greco-Roman World*, 37; Kennell, "Light on 2 Macc 4:7–15." But see G. M. Cohen, "The 'Antiochenes in Jerusalem,' Again," in *Pursuing the Text: Studies in Honor of Ben Zion Wacholder on the Occasion of his Seventieth Birthday* (ed. John C. Reeves and John Kampen; JSOTSup 184; Sheffield: Sheffield Academic Press, 1994), 243–59.

law code from another πόλις for implementation.[138] Nigel Kennel has recently shown, based on the aforementioned allusions in the Maccabean narratives and the presence of law-grant terms such as ἐπινεύω, that such a borrowed law code was likely given to Jason.[139] All this is to say that the Seleucids are known to have granted law codes to subject cities, and that there is good chance that some sort of νόμος was authorized for "Jerusalem–Antioch." If this was the case, both Maccabean authors went to great lengths to overlook the presence of this Seleucid-appointed νόμος. It served their polemic better to present these overlords as being *sans* νόμοι.

What actually happened is not the focus of the present study. What is of interest is to note the obviously stylized nature of 1 and 2 Maccabees to support the aims of the authors. The stereotype employed for the Seleucid rulers, in both accounts, is that of the "lawless" barbarian despot. This is accomplished, in large measure, by showing that Seleucid legal instruments lack any prescriptive force.

3. *The Force of Jewish Law*

In contrast with the Seleucids who lack νόμοι, the Jewish laws are νόμοι. Other designations are also used for the Jewish law.[140] It is, nonetheless, the important designation νόμος which is prominent—and it is a lexical choice which is matched by a description of binding authority. The picture of Jewish law is not, however, completely uniform between the two books. The most striking difference is that 1 Maccabees expects the Hasmonean dynasty to enforce Torah; 2 Maccabees expects God himself to enforce Torah. Other differences also will be noted. Nonetheless, in contrast to the lack of force behind Seleucid instruments, Torah is shown to be a binding νόμος. Second Maccabees' view is slightly simpler, and will therefore be considered first.

The compiler of 2 Maccabees expects that Torah is the νόμος of the Jews and that God himself enforces it. This begins to become clear from the first major event of the book: the account of Heliodorus (2 Macc 3:1–40). According to the account, King Seleucus heard about "unspeakable wealth" (v. 6) held at the temple treasury in Jerusalem. In keeping with his caricature, Seleucus could hardly restrain from appropriating the funds. He appointed Heliodorus to the task. It is reported, nonetheless,

138.   Welles, *Royal Correspondence*, #3; Lloyd Jonnes, ed., *The Inscriptions of the Sultan Dağli I: Philomelion, Thymbrion/Hadrianopolis, Tyraion* (Inscriften Griechischer Städte aus Kleinasien 62; Bonn: Rudolf Habelt, 2002), #393.

139.   Kennell, "Light on 2 Macc 4:7–15," especially 16–18.

140.   See nn. 88–99, 107–19, above.

that the king gave Heliodorus explicit instructions *not* to seize temple property: the *sacrificial* deposits were to be left untouched (v. 6). Only private monies kept at the temple were to be taken. The Jews had adopted a practice common in the ancient world, whereby private individuals could bank money at the temple.[141] It was these private deposits —"deposits of both widows and orphans, and also some deposits of Hyrcanus son of Tobias" (3:10–11)[142]—which Heliodorus was to seize.

When the king's agent arrived in Jerusalem, he declared his purpose to the high priest Onias and "set a day" to take inventory of the funds (vv. 9–14). The horror that fell upon the community is extravagantly described:

> ...There was great anguish throughout the whole city. The priests in their priestly robes, casting themselves down before the altar, called to heaven... But whoever saw the appearance of the high priest was pierced to the heart, for his face and the change in his color mirrored the anguish of his soul, for terror came over the man, and bodily trembling, through which it became obvious to observers the pain lodged in his heart.
>
> Moreover, the people rushed from their houses in crowds for public supplication because the place was about to be brought to shame. The women, girt below their breasts with sackcloth, thronged the streets, and the cloistered maidens ran together unto the gates, or some upon the walls, or leaning out the windows. And everyone, stretching their hands toward heaven, made the entreaty. (vv. 14–20)

This graphic description is meant to show the universality of Jewish distress. Off-duty priests donned vestments to join the urgent prayers.[143] The laity, including women and virgins, were moved to take part. Most notable is the righteous Onias, whose visage was profoundly distorted with horror. "It was pitiable [to see]," the author concludes, "not only the varied prostration of the populace, but also the foreboding of the high priest's great anxiety" (v. 21). What Heliodorus planned to do was profoundly troubling.

What actually was Heliodorus' crime? It does not appear to have been desecration. Elsewhere the crime of sacrilege is named (ἱεροσυλία, e.g. 4:39, 42; 9:2; 13:6). The crime of Heliodorus is not so identified. There was no danger to sacred property. There is also no indication that the treasury where private funds were banked was in precincts off-limits to

141. Goldstein, *II Maccabees*, 207.

142. That Hyrcanus' money is listed with that of "widows and orphans" confirms that these are private deposits, not "tithes set aside for [widows and orphans]." Contra Doran, "2 Maccabees," 207.

143. Goldstein, *II Maccabees*, 209.

Gentiles;[144] and if they were, this may have been Heliodorus' purpose for "appointing a day" to return for the funds—to allow priests to bring them out where he could retrieve them. Heliodorus' incursion is conducted to avoid sacrilege; there is no fear of desecration in this pericope. Instead, there is a particular Torah commandment which is the stated focus of the account: "they called to heaven *upon him who had given the law about deposits* to keep them safe for those who deposited them" (v. 15). Goldstein notes, "[it] is God's protection of *private deposits* in His temple, not His protection of sacred funds or His exclusion of pagans from holy soil" that is at issue in this case.[145]

The law concerning deposits is that recorded in Exodus:

> And if anyone gives his neighbor money or goods to keep, and they are stolen from the man's house, if the thief is found he shall repay double. But if the thief is not found, the lord of the house shall appear before God and he shall swear that he surely has not done evil in regard to any of his neighbor's deposit. According to every alleged injury...and every chargeable loss (whatever it may be): the judgment of all shall be before God, and the one convicted by God shall repay double to his neighbor... (Exod 22:6–14 LXX [EV 7–15])

Torah expects that a householder keeping funds in trust for another is responsible to give account if they disappear. As applied to the Heliodorus incident, *Yahweh himself* is the householder keeping funds for others. How can it be that Yahweh would be made an accomplice to theft by permitting funds held in trust in his house to be taken? The high priest's distress, and the anxiety of the people, is that Yahweh himself is about to be made an accomplice to thievery: "They were imploring the All Powerful Lord to keep (φυλάσσω) safe, with all security, the entrusted things..." (v. 22; cf. φυλάσσω in Exod 22:6 LXX [EV v. 7]). This incident is of particular interest, because Yahweh is at once both a *party* to this case (the householder in Exod 22:7–15),[146] and the *judge* of it—the one "who executes justice for the orphan and the widow" from whom Heliodorus would steal (Deut 10:18; cf. Exod 22:23–24). Yahweh, then, is being called upon to enforce a particular Torah-νόμος in the face of injustice. Before stepping back to assess the implications of this Torah enforcement, there are details in Yahweh's response to the people's cry which ought to be observed.

144.   Ibid., 209. Contra John R. Bartlett, *The First and Second Books of the Maccabees* (Cambridge: Cambridge University Press, 1973), 239.

145.   Goldstein, *II Maccabees*, 205.

146.   Doran (*Temple Propaganda*, 49) identified this case as "a legal controversy...between Heliodorus and Onias." It is indeed a "legal controversy," but it is between Heliodorus and Yahweh.

Upon entering the treasury, Heliodorus is met by "a great manifestation, so that all those presuming to accompany him were panic stricken" (v. 24). A gold-armored warrior on horseback, attended by two others, beat Heliodorus so that he "was lying at his very last breath." Unless Onias had promptly intervened with a sacrifice, Heliodorus would have died (vv. 31–33).

There is uncertainty among commentators whether the gold-clad rider was Yahweh himself. Doran notes that the account is remarkably similar to Greek divine-intervention myths, in which the deity personally appears to protect his (or her) temple.[147] However, other divine intervention accounts in 2 Maccabees involve angels, so that Doran concludes, "…the author has so skillfully taken over the descriptions of interventions of Greek gods and heroes and used them to depict angels. This is another instance of how the author has combined his Jewish faith with his Greek style."[148]

Doran is correct that subsequent interventions involve angels from Yahweh, not Yahweh himself.[149] This is no reason to insist the present manifestation is not Yahweh. Actually, the text reports that "the Almighty Lord had appeared" (v. 30). The certainty of death which is repeatedly emphasized to have fallen upon Heliodorus—"now unable to help himself" (v. 28); who "lay silent" and "deprived of all hope and salvation" (v. 29); "lying quite at his last breath" (v. 31) until "the Lord has granted you your life" (v. 33)—further suggests the certainty of the fate of the sinner who comes face-to-face with God (cf. Exod 33:20; Judg 13:22). Heliodorus, at least, understood this to be Yahweh: he subsequently reported to the king, "the one whose dwelling is in heaven is *himself* keeping watch and is a helper (αὐτὸς…ἔχων ἐπόπτης ἐστὶν καὶ βοηθός) of that place" (v. 39). Such language could simply emphasize that God was behind the divine warriors; however, there is also a marked difference between the way this divine warrior operates and that of later angelic warriors. In 2 Maccabees, angels typically empower the Jews to fight; here the divine warrior fights for himself while the Jews look on (and must sacrifice to restrain him).[150] There are enough indicators of theophany in this account to distinguish it from later angelic epiphanies.

---

147. Ibid., 47–52, 99–100, 102–3. Cf. Goldstein, *II Maccabees*, 198, 213.
148. Doran, *Temple Propaganda*, 103.
149. Frequently called "a good angel" (2 Macc 11:6; 15:23; cf. 10:26).
150. Daniel J. Harrington, *The Maccabean Revolt: Anatomy of a Biblical Revolution* (OTS 1; Wilmington, Del.: Michael Glazier, 1988), 40.

There are two possible explanations for this theophany. On the one hand, it may be that Yahweh acts personally because he is party to this case: it is his house that is being robbed. The "law about deposits" holds Yahweh himself accountable for protecting goods banked in his house. In a later incident however, the temple is again set upon both to be robbed and desecrated (5:1–20; to be discussed on pp. 220, below), yet Yahweh does not intervene in that later incident. This points to another reason for Yahweh's personal intervention here. Because all Jerusalem was faithful to Yahweh under Onias, and the corruption of certain "lawless Jews" had not yet diluted their corporate standing before God, *God himself* intervenes on behalf of his people. After Jason's high priesthood, when many Jews began to apostatize, God's interventions are no longer direct. Even though a partial restoration begins under the Maccabees (8:5, 29), God's interventions are only mediated by angels. The theology here being employed is that of the Golden Calf story from Exodus.

Prior to Israel's sin with the Golden Calf at Sinai, God had intended to lead his people personally into the Promised Land. After the sin of the Golden Calf, however, Yahweh told Moses he could no longer go personally with Israel into the land. He would send an angel to lead them instead (Exod 32:34–33:3; cf. 23:20–22). The fact that 2 Maccabees repeatedly cites the Exodus "good angel" promise confirms the importance of that history for the interventions in 2 Maccabees.[151] At the outset of the book, when all the Jews were united in lawful living, God acted *personally* in their defense. The recovery of divine favor is a gradual process in later chapters (especially 5:17–20; 8:5, 29; 15:14–16).[152] Therefore, later interventions are mediated by angels but not (yet) executed by God directly. The implication of this representation of Yahweh's dealings with the Jews in 2 Maccabees is this: once the Jews become *united* in their (Hassidim) obedience to Torah, God will personally act

151. See discussion of "good angel" texts on pp. 221–23 (points d, e, g), below.

152. Divine favor is recovered gradually. At first, Judea was invulnerable under the ideal Torah piety of Onias (3:1). Judea fell to the Seleucids when Onias (and, with him, popular Torah piety) was lost (4:1–10). Then the Torah piety of seven martyrs became an atoning sacrifice "to bring an end to the Almighty's wrath that is upon our whole nation" (7:38). At that turning point, Judas is introduced (8:1) and victory begins because "the wrath of the Lord was turned to mercy" (8:5). Yahweh, however, is "[not yet] wholly reconciled with his servants" (8:29). It is only at the end of the book that Onias appears again (in a vision) to pronounce the Aaronic blessing on "the whole community of the Jews" (15:12), and Jeremiah indicates that the sword of Yahweh is now with his people (15:15–16). Cf. Doran, *Temple Propaganda*, 75.

on behalf of his people again and make them "invulnerable."[153] In this opening narrative, Yahweh acts in person. In later events, he will act through the agency of angels. In all cases, however, it is Yahweh who intervenes to enforce Torah. The Heliodorus account sets this pattern in motion,[154] by showing Yahweh's enforcement of a specific Torah commandment.

Significant clues concerning the Hassidim view of written law are already emerging. Torah is cited in 2 Maccabees as a source of law—a law code along the lines of Greek νόμοι. The use of Torah here is unlike the citations of Torah identified in Deuteronomic and Persian-era accounts. In those previous periods, Torah was frequently cited as a guide for cultic renewal and Yahwistic fidelity, but cases of social justice were carried out without appeals to the law book. The Heliodorus incident, however, appeals to the Torah as the grounds for securing justice in a civil case. A house is being robbed, and Yahweh, as Judge-King of Israel ("him who had given the law about deposits"), is called upon to enforce that "law about deposits" (3:15) on behalf of "widows and orphans" (3:10). Here is a judge being called to enforce *the Torah* (i.e. Exod 22:7–15, 23–24) in the midst of a crime. The Torah is being utilized as a prescriptive source of law.

It is also remarkable to find that Yahweh himself is *liable* under Torah. He is called upon as the householder accountable to answer for deposits stolen from his home. This is significant in the book's polemic: it shows that God is no barbarian despot but a civilized king who himself honors the law book. This is also significant of Hassidim legal theory: by portraying *God himself* accountable to Torah, there is no mistaking but that Torah is itself regarded as being "the law." In contrast with its portrayal of Seleucid kings as "lawless" barbarian despots, 2 Maccabees shows the Jews as having a civilized, nomistic king in Yahweh—with Torah as the law code he himself observes and enforces.[155]

Seven accounts of divine Torah enforcement appear in the book. Other references to Torah abound beyond these which cannot all be surveyed in the present study. There are seven instances in 2 Maccabees where God is said to intervene in a crisis to enforce Torah. Having examined the first of these at some length, the full series can be summarized as follow:

---

153. 2 Macc 8:34–36: "...the Jews had a Defender, and...were invulnerable, because they followed the laws ordained by him."

154. Goldstein, *II Maccabees*, 215: "The verse [3:40] closes the unit on Heliodorus but contains the Greek particle *men* to let the reader know that there will be more to come."

155. Cf. 2 Macc 1:24–25; 7:9; 13:4; *b. ʿAbod Zar.* 3b.

a. *The Heliodorus incident (2 Macc 3:7–39/Exod 22:6–14 [EV vv. 7–15])*—As already discussed, Heliodorus laid claim to funds banked at the temple. The Jews "called on him that gave the law concerning deposits" (2 Macc 3:15; citing Exod 22:6–14 [EV vv. 7–15]). Yahweh appeared (vv. 24–36) "to keep the entrusted things safe" (v. 22), showing himself to be a judge who enforces Torah.

b. *Antiochus plunders the temple (2 Macc 5:1–20/Deut 11:13–17)*—Antiochus is reported to have launched a campaign against Ptolemaic Egypt. At that time, the Jews reported visions of angelic armies over Jerusalem (2 Macc 5:1–4). The connection of heavenly armies on the move with Antiochus' march was clear, but the Jews were unsure whether the omen was good or bad (v. 4). Then Antiochus attacked and plundered Jerusalem (and the temple) on his return from Egypt. The narrator is quick to explain: if the Jews had been right with God, "this man, like Heliodorus…would have been scourged and turned back" (v. 18). The author here admits an inconsistency in God's justice: he has not dealt with Antiochus as he did Heliodorus. The author cites Deuteronomy to justify the difference:[156] "the Lord did not choose the nation because of the place, but the place because of the nation" (v. 19; cf. Deut 11:13–17).[157] Here is a primitive instance of midrash: citing one law to justify the non-enforcement of another. In earlier chapters of this project, other scholars have been criticized for *assuming* "midrash" wherever legal practices are seen to be inconsistent with Torah statements.[158] One ought not *assume* midrashic activity to explain an inconsistency. Here, however, no assumption is necessary: the narrator has frankly recorded his way of exegetically justifying an apparent inconsistency in divine justice. The writer invokes one law (Deut 11:13–17) to justify the non-application of another (e.g. Exod 22.7–15 per 2 Macc 3:15; 5:17–18). The fact that such justification is necessary, and that it is accomplished through citation of another Torah precept, suggests that Torah itself has become the basis for deciding, justifying, and exacting penalty. Torah would seem to be Judea's code of justice.

---

156.   Contra Goldstein, *II Maccabees*, 260. Goldstein only sees this Deuteronomy citation as assuring that Jerusalem is still the chosen place. The problem being set up by the writer, however, is of an inconsistent act of Yahweh which needs to be justified.

157.   Cf. also Deut 12:5–7; 32:19–30.

158.   E.g. pp. 129–31, above. Cf. Launderville, *Piety and Politics*, 34–35.

c. *The death of Antiochus (2 Macc 9:1–29/Exod 21:23–25)—*
Antiochus led one army on a campaign into Persia while sending
another into Judea. The army in Judea was defeated. When
Antiochus learned of it, he set out for Judea himself to make the
Jews suffer. In consequence of his villainous purpose, "the judgment from heaven" came upon Antiochus—the hand of God
supernaturally smote him with fatal torments (vv. 4–6, 28). The
narrator points out the remarkably precise, "eye-for-eye" nature
of God's intervention against Antiochus: "an incurable pain of
the bowels and bitter, internal torments gripped him—and that
altogether justly, for he had tormented other men's bowels...
Thus the murderer and blasphemer, having endured the worst
kinds of sufferings just as he had inflicted on others, [died]..."
(vv. 5–6, 28).[159] The *lex talionis* (Exod 21:23–25) is not named
but is clearly in view.[160] The author shows God enforcing this
Torah precept quite literally.

d. *Angelic warriors in battle with Timotheus (2 Macc 10:24–31/
Exod 23:20–22)—*In this account, the Jews receive word that
Timotheus has raised an Asian army and is approaching Jerusalem. Judas and his men approach the altar in sackcloth. They
pray that God will "be an enemy to their enemies and an adversary to their adversaries, as the law declares" (2 Macc 10:26).
The citation is from Exod 23:20–22: "And behold, I send my
angel before you... If you carefully heed my voice and do all that
I command...then I will be an enemy to your enemies and an
adversary to your adversaries" (LXX). In the subsequent battle,
five gold-arrayed horses and riders "appeared to their adversaries
from heaven" (v. 29).[161] That it was specifically "unto their
adversaries" that this vision came is probably meant to show the
precise fulfillment of the law's provision: "to be an adversary to
your adversaries." Harmony between law writings and law
practice does not in itself indicate the presence of prescriptivism;
nonetheless, a pattern of repeated interest (as is here emerging) to
document literal correspondence between the *statement* of the
law and its *enforcement* probably does indicate prescriptivism.
God is a precise enforcer of Torah's stipulations.

159. Second Maccabees records nothing of Antiochus "tormenting other men's
bowels." Such detail was probably in Jason of Cyrene's work; see Goldstein, *II
Maccabees*, 354. Cf. 4 Macc 11:19.
160. Ibid., 354: "God makes the punishment fit the sin." Cf. 2 Macc 4:38; 5:10;
8:33, 34–35; 9:13–14; 15:30–35.
161. On the five angelic warriors, see ibid., 392–93.

e.   *Angelic warrior in battle with Lysias (2 Macc 11:1–15/Exod 23:20–22)*—Another account like the previous one follows. This time it is Lysias who commands a Seleucid force against Judas. Again, all the people "prayed to the Lord to send a good angel to save Israel" (2 Macc 11:6). In light of the previous narrative, the reference here to "an angel" probably again has Exod 23.20–22 in view.[162] Indeed, "a horseman in white apparel, brandishing weapons of gold,"[163] appears at the head of the Jewish army (v. 8), leading them to victory.

f.   *Onias and Jeremiah intercede for victory (2 Macc 15:6–16/Num 6:23–27, et al.)*—On the day before what will be their final battle, Judas read to the people "from the law and the prophets" (2 Macc 15:9). That night, Judas had "a dream worthy of belief" (15:11).[164] In his dream, Onias appeared to Judas and pronounced the Aaronic blessing over all the Jews (Num 6:23–27; cf. Mal 2:5–7). Also in that dream, Judas saw Jeremiah the prophet, interceding for the city of Jerusalem. Jeremiah was restricted from interceding for Jerusalem in his own day on account of their wickedness,[165] but "now nothing impedes him from praying for the people and for the city."[166] That Jeremiah's prayers are with Judas' army is significant of their being restored to divine favor. Jeremiah also gave Judas "the holy sword...from God" (v. 16).[167] Most commentators see in the sword investiture an "assurance of victory" similar to other sword-from-the-deity visions.[168] This view overlooks the significance of *Jeremiah* (not God or an angel) as the one giving the sword. The sword of Yahweh is thematic in Jeremiah's prophecies: God's sword was turned against Israel in Jeremiah's early prophecies (e.g. Jer 12:12); then it was turned against Israel's foes when favor was restored (e.g. Jer 50:35–37).[169] By giving the sword to Judas, a turning

---

162.   Cf. also Exod 33:2; Josh 5:13–15; 2 Kgs 19:35; see Doran, "2 Maccabees," 266.

163.   On one angelic warrior: Goldstein, *II Maccabees*, 405.

164.   Or "a certain waking reality" (ὕπαρ τι), that is, a "dream so realistic that Judas thinks he is awake" (Doran, "2 Maccabees," 296).

165.   Jer 7:16–20; 11:14; 14:11–12.

166.   Goldstein, *II Maccabees*, 499. Cf. Jer 42:2–22.

167.   Based on 1 Enoch 90:34, Goldstein believes Judas displayed a literal sword, afterward stored at the Temple (Goldstein, *II Maccabees*, 499).

168.   Doran, *Temple Propaganda*, 72–74; idem, "2 Maccabees," 296; Goldstein, *II Maccabees*, 499.

169.   Bartlett, *1–2 Maccabees*, 339.

point in the restoration of the Jews to God's favor is indicated.[170] In fact, it is presented as that turning point prophesied by Jeremiah when Israel, for so long under the heel of Babylon and its successors, would throw off and achieve mastery: the sword of the Lord is now with Israel to defeat pagan nations, and is no longer with those nations to punish Israel (cf. 5:17–18; 6:12–17). Both of Jeremiah's actions (prayer and handing over of the sword) pick up on thematic indicators in his prophecy of God's restored favor. With these manifestations of Onias (manifesting the law; especially the Aaronic blessing) and Jeremiah (manifesting the prophets), the "law and the prophets" read the night before have now become "literally" active on behalf of the Jewish army. The general effort of 2 Maccabees, to show God dealing literally "by the book," finds vivid expression here.

g. *The hand of God against Nicanor (2 Macc 15:20–27/Exod 23:20–22)*—Following the preceding visions, Judas' army draws up in battle with Nicanor. Seeing the terribleness of the foe, Judas prays once again for "a good angel" (2 Macc 15:23) to lead them to victory, just as God did for Hezekiah when Jerusalem was besieged in Hezekiah's day (v. 22; cf. 2 Kgs 19:15–36). No divine visions are described; nonetheless, the troops go forward "contending with their hands and praying to God with their hearts" and everyone recognizes "the manifestation (ἐπιφάνεια) of God" among them (v. 27). Though unseen this time, God (by his good angel?) has again intervened according to Exod 23:22.[171] In celebration of a great victory, the army "blessed the Sovereign One in the language of their fathers" (v. 29).[172]

These seven incidents encompass those places in 2 Maccabees where Yahweh is explicitly said to intervene on behalf of the Jews. In each of these, a Torah basis for God's action is apparent. In distinction from previously noted narratives (e.g. in Ezra–Nehemiah) where Torah is cited as an imprecise guidebook for cultic reforms, 2 Maccabees cites Torah as a verbally precise source book by which God exacts national justice. This

170. See n. 152, above.
171. Doran, "2 Maccabees," 297; Goldstein, *II Maccabees*, 501; Bartlett, *1–2 Maccabees*, 341. Note that the author is ambivalent about the nature of God's intervention: was this epiphany visible? Was it angelic? Now that God's blessing and sword are with Israel, was it theophanic? Perhaps the author deliberately left the nature of the intervention ambivalent since he was writing at a time when the long-term success of what Judas won was still uncertain.
172. Cf. 2 Macc 7:8, 21, 27; 12:37.

distinction indicates that prescriptivism has been embraced. Of especial significance (and confirming this conclusion) is the nature of the argument in which Torah is being so portrayed. The Greeks are barbarian, ruled by a king without νόμοι; but the Jews are civilized, with νόμοι, and a νόμος-enforcing king (Yahweh). The Hassidim author *has accepted the standards of the Greeks for measuring a society*, even though he has turned those standards against the Greeks to vindicate his God and his people.

The author of 1 Maccabees similarly regards Torah fidelity as key to Judea's prosperity. In this book, however, it is the responsibility of the Hasmonean priests to enforce Torah (1 Macc 5:61–62). Rather than leaving Torah enforcement to God, the Hasmonean doctrine takes its cue from the example of Phinehas and his sons (Num 25:1–13). In Moses' day, God's wrath was against Israel for "yoking themselves" to the Moabites—until Phinehas rose up and executed justice against the apostates. For 1 Maccabees, God does not intervene unless a Phinehas arises among the priests, executes the needed justice (Exod 22:19 [EV v. 20]), and thereby turns away divine wrath. It is Mattathias who proved to be such a Phinehas when he rose up in Modein to slay an apostatizing Jew at the altar of sacrifice: "Thus [Mattathias] was zealous for the law, just as Phinehas did unto Zimri the son of Salu. And Mattathias cried out…, Whoever is zealous for the law and upholds the covenant, let him come after me!" (2:26–27).[173]

In this manner, 1 Maccabees sets the scene for its version of events. Matthias, and his sons after him (cf. Num 25:13/1 Macc 2:54, 64–68), are the priestly Torah enforcers necessary to restore Israel to God's favor.[174] With the priestly line responsible for enforcing law identified, the form which that enforcement takes can now begin to be observed. The bulk of Mattathias' subsequent story is devoted to his handling of a particularly sticky legal question: the matter of self-defense and the sabbath laws (2:29–42).[175]

173.   Just as Phinehas plunged his spear through the pagan and Jew conjoined in immorality (Num 25:8), Mattathias slew the apostacizing Jew and the king's officer together in their pagan rite (1 Macc 2:24–25).

174.   Doran, "1 Maccabees," 44–45; Goldstein, *I Maccabees*, 5–7; Nils Martola, *Capture and Liberation: A Study in the Composition of the First Book of Maccabees* (Acta Academiae Aboensis A.63.1; Åbo: Åbo Akademi, 1984), 208–21.

175.   The extensive word count devoted to this issue and its central placement within the Mattathias narrative (2:1–28 / *29–42* / 43–48) underscore its importance to the author. After introducing Mattathias (2:1–28) and before recounting his battles (2:43–48), the Hasmonean sabbath-day policy is vindicated (2:29–42).

As Mattathias' party fled to the mountains (v. 28), "many who were seeking righteousness and justice went down into the wilderness" (v. 29). These "Seekers of Justice and Vindication" may have been Jews who understood prophecies such as Zeph 2:3 as a promise of miraculous deliverance if they "sought justice and vindication" in the wilderness.[176] It was against this second party, dwelling in caves, that the king's forces came on a subsequent sabbath day.

The order given to these Seekers was to "*come out* [of the caves]—do as the king commands and you will live" (v. 33). The Seekers of Justice replied, "*We will not come out*, nor will we do what the king commands to desecrate the sabbath day" (v. 34). This conviction not to "come out" on the sabbath day derives from Exod 16:29. In that text, Moses gave instructions concerning the provision of manna in the wilderness. God would provide enough manna on the sixth day so no gathering would be necessary on the sabbath. Therefore Moses instructed, "Look, for the Lord has given you that day as the sabbath; therefore, he gives you on the sixth day bread for two days. Each of you will remain in your house. *Let no one come out of his place the seventh day*" (LXX). Evidently, the Jews of Mattathias' day understood this to be an abiding norm—not to "come out" of one's place on the sabbath.[177] Furthermore, the *Seleucids* knew about this Jewish scruple. The king knew the Jewish dietary laws and had instructed Jews to be tested by the forced eating of pork (1:47, 62). He had likewise commanded their abandonment of circumcision laws by leaving their sons uncircumcised (1:48, 60–61). This command to "come out" of the caves was knowingly crafted to force violation of the sabbath law (cf. 1:45).[178] This was the reason the king's army brought this command on the sabbath day. The question of self-defense on the sabbath was not an issue, having never been faced before now.[179]

It was probably a surprise to the Seleucids when their subsequent attack went unrepelled. Nonetheless, just as the Jews could not "come out" on the sabbath, they also would not "throw a stone...nor block up their hiding places" (2:36) when the Seleucids attacked. Presumably

---

176. Goldstein, *I Maccabees*, 235–36; Doran, "1 Maccabees," 46. Cf. also Isa 32:16; Jer 23:5; Ezek 18:27; 33:19; 45:9; *CD* 2:29 (on the latter source, see D. Harrington, *Maccabean Revolt*, 66).

177. On later Rabbinic strictures against "going out"; see E. P. Sanders, *Judaism: Practice and Belief 63 BCE–66 CE* (London: SCM Press, 1998), 367.

178. Bezalel Bar-Kochva, *Judas Maccabaeus: The Jewish Struggle Against the Seleucids* (Cambridge: Cambridge University Press, 1989), 481; Goldstein, *I Maccabees*, 237; Dancy, *I Maccabees*, 86.

179. Bar-Kochva, *Judas Maccabaeus*, 474–81; Dancy, *I Maccabees*, 86.

lifting stones would be work (cf. gathering sticks in Num 15:32–36). The inability to defend themselves was merely a consequence of the sabbatical prescriptions which restricted them from building a barricade: "And they set against them in battle on the sabbath, and they died—they, and their wives, and their children, and their livestock, to the number of a thousand persons" (2:38).[180]

It was this early confrontation which made it startlingly clear that the sabbath laws were going to be a problem. This was, on the one hand, a war to uphold the law; yet, on the other, observance of this particular law left the Jews embarrassingly vulnerable. Sabbath observance could lead to the collapse of the whole community in a few weekend wars. For the author of *Second* Maccabees, such a dilemma is no dilemma at all: since Yahweh himself defends the Jews *when they are obedient*, strict observance of the sabbath in the face of martyrdom was the key to their success.[181] For the author of *First* Maccabees, however, since it was the Hasmoneans' duty to ensure the law did not fall, such a martyr mentality would not do: "When Mattathias and his friends learned of it, they mourned greatly for them. And each man said to his neighbor: 'If we all do as our brothers have done and do not fight with the Gentiles for our lives and our ordinances, they will quickly destroy us from the earth'" (2:39–40).

Some amendment needed to be made. It is in the Hasmonean *exception* to the sabbath-day law that significant insights into their view of Torah can be discerned. The Hasmonean response to this problem is not presented in terms of a different view of Torah's use. No alternate interpretation of Exod 16:29 is offered (e.g. showing Moses' instruction as a described example rather than an abiding prescription). On the contrary, Mattathias and his party implicitly affirm the Seekers for rightly keeping the sabbath law. What was needed was an amendment to the law. For the sake of the laws as a whole, this particular law needed to be altered. The solution produced is that of a consultative, "δῆμος-approved" amendment:[182]

---

180. The 2 Maccabees parallel states that the king's army set fire to the caves (2 Macc 6:11; cf. Josephus, *Ant.* 12.6.2.274–75). Fire may have been chosen as a final test, whether they would "come out"—or remain and burn.

181. It is unclear what, if any, relationship there was between the Seekers and the Hassidim (cf. 1 Macc 2:29, 42; Paul L. Redditt, "Hasideans," in *ABD* 3:66; John Kampen, "Hasidim," in *ABD* 3:66–67). In any case, the Seekers' martyrdom, treated as an unfortunate mistake in 1 Macc 2:39–40, is commended as an exemplar in 2 Macc 6:11.

182. Cf. Doran, "1 Maccabees," 47.

And each man said to his neighbor: "If we all do as our brothers have done and do not fight with the Gentiles for our lives and our ordinances, they will quickly destroy us from the earth." So they made a determination (βουλεύω) that day, saying, "Any man whatsoever, who comes against us for battle on the sabbath day, we will fight against him; and let us not all die as our brothers died in their hiding places." (1 Macc 2:40–41)

Exodus 16:29 was accepted by the Hasmonean party as verbally binding. As enforcers of Torah, however, Mattathias' party could also propose amendments to its enforcement. There does not seem to be a sense of "canonical" inflexibility to Torah in this account. The above amendment was proposed, adopted by mutual consent, and recorded verbatim. (Whether this Hasmonean amendment would be temporary or permanent is not immediately clear.[183]) The author is quick to show that other sects (especially the Hassidim) concurred: "Then there united with them a company of Hassidim, mighty warriors of Israel, all the devout for the law. And all the fugitives from trouble joined them and became their support. They organized an army, and struck down sinners…" (2:42–44).

It was purportedly this decision to fight on the sabbath that galvanized the Jewish resistance. Rather than being a divisive matter, the new sabbath regulation is creatively presented as a (indeed, *the*) unifying doctrine behind the successful coalition army of the Maccabees. It was because of this legislative leadership of the Hasmoneans, with all other law-zealous parties falling in line, that successful resistance began:[184] "They struck down sinners…forcibly circumcised all the uncircumcised boys, as many as they found within the territory of Israel…and they rescued the law from the hands of the Gentiles and kings" (2:44–48).[185] In reality, the Hasmoneans may have had a reputation as "less loyal" to Torah than the Hassidim since the latter willingly died rather than violate the sabbath law. The Hasmonean propagandist would have wanted to show that this Hasmonean exception to Torah (1) was derived from

183. Ginsberg believes *CD* 11:15 is a continuation of Mattathias' amendment (Louis H. Ginsberg, *An Unknown Jewish Sect* [New York: The Jewish Theological Society of America, 1976], 68; cf. Josephus, *Ant.* 12.6.2.277). Marcus believes *Jub* 1:12, which opposes sabbath-day warfare, intends to repeal the Maccabean amendment (Marcus, *Law in the Apocrypha*, 78).

184. Dancy, *I Maccabees*, 86; Doran, "*1 Maccabees*," 47; Goldstein, *I Maccabees*, 237.

185. This forced circumcision of "as many as they found within the borders of Israel" may be an effort to show faithfulness to the Torah stipulation to circumcise "every male among you"; see Gen 17:14–19; Exod 12:44, 48; Lev 12:3; cf. Steven Weitzman, "Forced Circumcision and the Shifting Role of Gentiles in Hasmonean Ideology," *HTR* 92, no. 1 [1999]: 44–51).

Mattathias himself, (2) was an act of loyalty (not disloyalty) to Torah, (3) was indeed *the* instrumental decision which brought the salvation of Torah, and (4) was embraced even by the Hassidim of the day. With this description of Mattathias' zeal for Torah, the account turns to his deathbed speech (2:49–70). After the model of a dying "patriarch,"[186] he calls his sons and their followers to, "rally to yourselves all doers of the law, and exact the justice of your people. Render a recompense to the Gentiles and hold fast to the commandments of the law" (vv. 67–68).

What do these observations from the Mattathias record indicate concerning the Hasmonean attitude toward law? For one thing, the Torah is here regarded as a prescriptive code. In Exod 16:29, Moses instructed Israel not to go out to gather food on the sabbath since sufficient manna would be provided on the sixth day. This historical description of how Moses protected the sabbath in a certain setting was accepted as a prescription with binding force for all Israel for all time. This is different from the use of Torah previously observed in, for instance, Ezra–Nehemiah. As previously seen (pp. 117–19, above), Ezra also cited Torah when drawing up a sabbath-observance pact (Neh 10:29). Also like Mattathias, Ezra deemed it necessary to vary from what Torah actually stipulated. In Neh 10, however, no justification was necessary for such variation: Ezra was free to apply Torah's ideal without being bound by Torah's terms. The situation is markedly different for the author of 1 Maccabees: variation from the terms of Torah required legal justification. A legal process of justification, consensus, and pronouncement of a stated amendment was required. For 1 Maccabees, the terms of Torah (e.g. Exod 16:29) are themselves "the law," and can be varied by drafting another law.[187]

These features of Hasmonean legal thought can be further discerned through three Torah-enforcement citations in 1 Maccabees. While there are many allusions to the law book throughout 1 Maccabees, there are three instances where the expression κατὰ τὸν νόμον is employed, signaling an explicit implementation of Torah:

a. *Judas forms an army (1 Macc 3:42–60/Deut 20:1–9)*—Judas enjoyed early success regaining control of Judea from "the workers of lawlessness" (1 Macc 3:6) thereby "turn[ing] away [God's] wrath from Israel" (v. 8). King Antiochus appointed a new army, however, to re-enforce his dominion (vv. 27–41). When Judas' men learned of the army coming against them, they determined to raise an army to defend themselves (vv. 42–43).

186. Doran, "1 Maccabees," 49.
187. Cf. Westbrook, "Origins of Legislation," 202; see also p. 25, above.

The Jewish volunteers therefore gathered to pray at Mizpah, "because, in Israel's former times, a place of prayer was in Mizpah" (v. 46).[188] Because the temple was in ruins (v. 45), they could not go there to pray, so they resorted to Mizpah "facing Jerusalem" (v. 46). There the Jews laid out the temple law book (Deut 31:24–26), priestly vestments (Exod 28:40–43), firstfruits and tithes (Deut 12:6–18), and assembled the Nazirites "who had completed their days" (vv. 48–49; Num 6:13–21). The common thread that explains these objects is that they were all rites to gain God's blessing—*but they had to be brought into the temple.*[189] These were the rites which the Jews *would* have performed in order to secure blessing before warfare, but they could not: "What shall we do with these?" they cried out to God, "Where shall we take them? Your sanctuary is trampled… And behold, the Gentiles are gathered against us to destroy us… How will we be able to stand before them, if you do not help us?" (vv. 50–53). The rituals of blessing are not possible. However, based on Solomon's assurance that those "going out to battle" can pray "toward the city" and be heard even without access to the temple rites (1 Kgs 8:44–45), Judas' army prays from "Mizpah facing Jerusalem" (v. 46).

After these "ritual-less" prayers for blessing, Judas reads from the Torah to find God's answers to the practical side of their prayer—how to withstand the enemy: "And after this, Judas appointed leaders of the people, captains of thousands…hundreds…fifties…and tens. He also said to those building houses, and to those betrothed to women, and to those planting vineyards, and to the fearful, to return each to his own house, according to the law" (vv. 55–56). The acts of Judas are based on Deuteronomy. In Deut 20:2–8, the priest is to give a speech before war, releasing men with new houses, wives, vineyards, or who were fearful. This speech was, furthermore, part of the process for appointing officers before battle (Deut 20:9). Judas follows both these preparations κατὰ τὸν νόμον (v. 56). He also draws upon Deut 1:15 (cf. Exod 18:21, 25) for the detailed hierarchy of officers implemented.[190] In other words, Judas found practical answers to his prayer by reading from the law book.

188. On Mizpah, see P. R. Davies, "A Note on I Macc. III. 46," *JTS* 23 (1972): 117–21.
189. See excursus on pp. 230–32, below.
190. Doran, "1 Maccabees," 63–64.

Historically, Torah has been seen cited as an imprecise guide for cultic reforms; Judas here uses it *as a source book for divine answers to prayer* for the right military order.[191] On its own, this pericope is not conclusive evidence for a prescriptive or idyllic consultation of the law book. In conjunction with other indicators in the work, however, the depiction of Judas looking to the Torah for instructions to organize an army—and that as a quasi-oracular source of divine direction in response to prayer—is at least consistent with the prescriptivistic outlook elsewhere reflected.[192]

Excursus: The Law Book in 1 Maccabees 3:48

There is much confusion over the description of the law book unrolled for display in v. 48. The passage reads, καὶ ἐξεπέτασαν τὸ βιβλίον τοῦ νόμου περὶ ὧν ἐξηρεύνων τὰ ἔθνη τὰ ὁμοιώματα τῶν εἰδώλων αὐτῶν.

Doran translates the verse, "They unrolled the book of the Torah concerning those things about which they were inquiring, namely, the Gentiles and the likenesses of their idols" (Doran, "1 Maccabees," 64). For Doran, the Jews are reading the Torah to find passages about how to deal with Gentiles and idols. The main problem with Doran's translation is that it requires that *the Jews* be the subject of ἐξεπέτασαν. It is more natural to read τὰ ἔθνη as the subject of the inquiry. Also, dealing with Gentile idolatry is not the concern of this pericope: warding off an approaching enemy army is the problem.

Goldstein (*I Maccabees*, 262) translates the verse as follows: "They spread open the scroll of the Torah at the passages where the gentiles sought to find analogies to their idols." In Goldstein's view, the Gentiles had previously exploited "problem texts" in the Torah to pass off their idols as "biblical." The Jews are here opening the Torah to those texts "to rouse God's vengeance." This reading properly identifies the Gentiles as the subject of ἐξεπέτασαν, but in fact the Seleucids burned the scrolls and killed anyone revering them (1:57). There is no pretended reverence or use of Torah by the Seleucids in 1 Maccabees. (It seems unlikely the author would want to admit Torah contained "analogies" permissive of pagan idolatry, anyhow.) Furthermore, this identification of the Torah scroll is inconsistent with the other items which were placed on display. The other items displayed (i.e. priestly garments, gifts, and Nazirites; vv. 49–50) are not items which have been profaned; rather, they are items which, in order to be rightly used, needed to be taken into the temple—*but cannot* due to the temple's desolation.

---

191. Contrast Dan 9–10 (p. 138 n. 122, above); for Daniel, *the book prompts the question* and mantic rites bring angelic answers; here temple rites raise the question and *the book provides the answers*.

192. The Hellenistic idea that a small, νόμος-ordered army is more powerful than a large, barbarian force may also be here implied (cf. p. 138 n. 22, above).

Eduard Meyer (*Ursprung und Anfänge des Christentums* [3 vols.; Stuttgart/Berlin: J. G. Cotta'sche, 1921–23], 2:207) followed by F. M. Abel (*Les Livres des Maccabées* [Paris: Gabalda, 1949], 69–70), Dancy (*I Maccabees*, 94–95), and others, translates the passage, "The Jews unrolled their books, looking in them for the things which the Gentiles look for from their idols." According to this reading, the Jews sought oracles from the Torah in a way comparable to Greek idolatry. Though this reading grammatically allows that τὰ ἔθνη are the subject of ἐξεπέτασαν, this interpretation requires an assumption that the Jews also are conducting such inquiry (based on a comparative use of περί). But no verb of inquiry is actually applied to the Jews here. Moreover it is the *likeness* of the Gentile idol (i.e. its manifestation of the deity's presence), not its oracular use, which is the central point of comparison (τὰ ὁμοιώματα τῶν εἰδώλων αὐτῶν). Though later details indicate the Jews did, at some point, read from the book (v. 56), reading is not the reason for its being unrolled in v. 48. Furthermore, a proper understanding of the book must fit the nature of the full group of items among which it is displayed—and the other items are not tools of divination.

Each of the above interpretations overlook the specific problem which these items all represent together. Their common link is that *they are objects which must be in the temple for proper use*. The Nazirites here are those who have fulfilled their days; according to Num 6:13–21 they now need to bring their offerings and be shaved *at the temple*. The tithes and firstfruits needed to be brought *into the temple* (Deut 12:6–18). The priestly garments could only be worn and used *in the temple* (Exod 28:40–43). The problem here being raised is that *none of these ritual objects can be used outside of the temple, and the temple is in ruins* (vv. 45, 51). Note that Doran rightly recognizes that these items require use at the temple, but he mistakenly concludes that Mizpah is being presented as an alternate temple for their use (p. 64.) This misses the point: the Jews cry out because they cannot use these ritual items outside of the temple: "What shall we do with these things? Where shall we take them? Your temple [being] in ruins..." (vv. 50–51). A proper understanding of the Torah scroll must fit within this reasoning, for it is listed within this same complex of temple-dependent objects.

The point of the descriptive line, περὶ ὧν ἐξηρεύνων τὰ ἔθνη τὰ ὁμοιώματα τῶν εἰδώλων αὐτῶν, is to identify this scroll *as specifically the one which belongs in the holy place*. Just as the Gentiles looked to the likeness of the idol when beseeching their god for help, either in the temple or parading the idol from the temple for public veneration, the Jews looked to the Torah scroll housed in the holy place of their temple and may have brought it out in times of battle. Moses had appointed for a copy of Torah to be kept in the holy place next to the ark (Deut 31:9–15, 24–26; cf. Exod 25:21). The ark was probably absent from the Second Temple. Consequently, rather than looking to the ark as was customary in First Temple times (e.g. Josh 6:4; 1 Sam 4:3–6), the Jews of 1 Maccabees looked to the Torah scroll still kept there. It must have been *that* copy of the Torah which, along with the priestly vestments, had been salvaged from the temple during Antiochus' plunder. This scroll was (like those garments, offerings, and Nazirite sacrifices) considered incapable of fulfilling its ritual use unless housed in the temple (Deut 31:26). The reason for the added description in v. 48 is to indicate that the scroll which Judas unrolled was *that very scroll*—the ritual scroll which was the focal point of the Jewish temple in contrast to the idols in Gentile temples.

All the items and rituals listed are those which the Jews would use to secure divine favor for the battle ahead: prayers in proper vestments; bringing in all due gifts; special Nazirite vows; and prayer toward the Torah scroll (in lieu of the ark) in the holy place (cf. the similar list of pre-battle ritual acts in Ps 20). These items are laid out in Mizpah with the desperate cry, "How can we use them when the temple is in ruins? How can we secure God's blessing for the battle ahead?" It is in setting up this problem that the law book's unrolling participates; and it is to identify the scroll thus unrolled as *that particular scroll from the holy place* that the added description, likening it to the temple idols of Gentiles, is added.

b.   *Judas restores the temple (1 Macc 4:42–58/Exod 20:25; 29:38–42)*—Jerusalem had been left desolate by Antiochus' forces (1 Macc 3:45; 4:38–39). When Judas retook Zion, he appointed "blameless priests devoted to the law" to cleanse the holy place (4:42). The reforms are twice identified as taking place "according to the law" (vv. 47, 53). But one question arises which the priests do not know how to resolve "according to the law": what to do with the defiled stones of the old altar?[193] In handling this problem, the Hasmonean recognition that Torah is not comprehensive enough to address every circumstance becomes further evident. The priests reach a consultative decision—"they came to a good determination (βουλή)" (v. 45)—to store the defiled stones elsewhere on the mount "until a prophet should appear with the answer concerning them" (vv. 45–46; cf. 14:41).[194] The decision is similar to that previously seen in Neh 7:65 (cf. Ezra 2:63), where Levites of uncertain genealogy were barred from the priesthood until a priest with הָאוּרִים וְהַתֻּמִּים should arise (see pp. 133–34, above). Like the Ezra–Nehemiah instance already discussed, this Maccabean account poses a problem for Fishbane's thesis that Torah came to be seen as a comprehensive source for "inquiry-by-exegesis." The Hasmoneans recognize that Torah is not capable of supplying answers for all problems, nor do they see the book as a replacement for divine oracles.[195]

193.   Goldstein (*I Maccabees*, 285) sees a dilemma between Deut 12:2–3 (commanding the destruction of altars used in pagan worship) and 12:4 (commanding that the Jerusalem altar should not be treated as heathen altars). It is resolved by keeping the old altar intact but out of use. Doran ("1 Maccabees," 71) sees that the stones are being disposed of after the manner of the remnant portions of a sacrificial bull (Lev 4:11–12).

194.   Doran, "1 Maccabees," 71–72.

195.   Contra Renaud, "La loi et les Maccabées," 51–52. Renaud acknowledges this text but negates it with a misinterpretation of 1 Macc 3:48 (see the Excursus, pp. 230–32, above).

Nonetheless in those matters which Torah *does* address, its instruction is followed—in this instance: building a new altar using "whole stones according to the law" (1 Macc 4:47; Exod 20:25), and offering upon it "sacrifice according to the law" (1 Macc 4:53; Exod 29:38–42).

This account is a cultic restoration similar to those seen under Josiah and Ezra. Unlike those accounts, however, there is no indication of variations made in how the law book's pattern was applied.[196] Where significant inconsistencies between law book and practice *do* appear (as under Josiah and in Ezra–Nehemiah), the implication is that the law book is being used descriptively (the text is not *itself* "the law"). Where no inconsistencies appear (as in this account), prescriptivism or descriptivism are possible. On its own, this account does not give a clear indication of how the Torah is being used.

   c.   *Simon's judging the land (1 Macc 14:14; 15:21/Deut 17:19–20)*—Perhaps the most telling "according to the law" statement is that reported in a letter from the Romans. It is addressed to various Gentile nations concerning Simon the Hasmonean high priest (15:16–21). Declaring Roman alliance with the Jews, the letter instructs neighboring rulers, "If any troublemakers have fled from their country to you, deliver them to Simon the high priest, that he may execute justice upon them *according to their law*" (v. 21). The reason for such an order was probably to undermine any apostates conspiring to overthrow Simon from abroad.[197] It frankly declares, moreover, that Simon would enforce justice against criminals κατὰ τὸν νόμον (v. 21)—Torah as a source of justice. If authentic,[198] this letter would represent a *Roman* understanding of Judean jurisprudence. This understanding is affirmed

---

196. That is, calling on God with trumpets (1 Macc 4:40; Num 10:1–10); "unblemished priests" (1 Macc 4:42; Lev 21:17–23); decommissioning the old altar (1 Macc 4:44; Deut 12:2–4; Lev 4:11–12 [see n. 193, above]); reverence for the prophet (1 Macc 4:46; Deut 18:18); new altar with "uncut stones" (1 Macc 4:47; Exod 20:25; Deut 27:5–6); temple, vessels, curtains, etc. restored (1 Macc 4:49–51, 57; Exod 25–27; 2 Chr 3–5); burnt offerings (1 Macc 4:53; Exod 29:38–42); songs, harps, lutes, cymbals, bowing to worship (1 Macc 4:54–55; 2 Chr 5:11–14; 7:3); "dedication" festival (1 Macc 4:56; 1 Kgs 8; 2 Chr 29); priestly chambers (1 Macc 4:57; 1 Chr 9:17–27); crowns (1 Macc 4:57; Zech 6.14) and shields (1 Macc 4:54; 2 Kgs 11.10). See Dancy, *1 Maccabees*, 182–83; Doran, "1 Maccabees," 71–72; Goldstein, *1 Maccabees*, 285–87.

197. Goldstein, *1 Maccabees*, 497–98.

198. Generally accepted by such scholars as Goldstein, *1 Maccabees*, 492–94, 496–500; Bartlett, *1 Maccabees*, 92–94.

by the *Jewish* author as well, however, by a matching description in the nearby context.[199] The Hasmonean narrator writes, "and the land had rest all the days of Simon... The law he searched out, and he removed every lawless and wicked person" (14:4–14; cf. 2:68). This description derives from Deut 17:19–20. In that text, the king of Israel (after the land is secure) is said to read daily from the law book. As noted in a previous chapter (pp. 88–90, above), the actual Deuteronomic expectation is for the king to be humbled by his study of this law text. If the book is presupposed to be a law code, however, the Deuteronomic text could easily lead to the picture which here emerges, a picture of a ruler who searches the book in order to exact its judgments upon law breakers in the land. The author of 1 Maccabees (along with the Romans behind one of his source documents) plainly announces that Simon read and enforced the Torah as Israel's criminal law code.

*   *   *

The above survey of Torah's use in 1 and 2 Maccabees is not exhaustive. It is nonetheless sufficient to draw several conclusions for the present hypothesis. Whereas the Seleucids are depicted as "lawless" barbarians whose rules are arbitrary, the Jews are a civilization-under-law. For 2 Maccabees, the Torah is a complete and inflexible law code enforced by Yahweh personally.[200] For 1 Maccabees, Torah is a law code which needs supplementing at points, and which it is the duty of a Phinehas-like priest to enforce. What is of particular interest to this project is not merely *that* the Maccabean historians view Torah prescriptively, but *how* this way of understanding the Torah has been presented. It is the Jewish embrace of a prescriptive model for Torah *as part of a defense of national civility according to Greek philosophical definitions* that offers an important explanation why the Jews widely embraced the prescriptive model of law. (See the diagram opposite.)

The operation of this civilized/barbarian polemic in 1 and 2 Maccabees is far more widespread than has here been developed. Further circumstantial evidence could be multiplied. As barbarian despots are stereotypically portrayed in Greek literature as those who turn even against their own supporters when deemed advantageous,[201] so the Seleucids are

---

199.   This Roman letter probably belongs between 14:15 and 14:25 (Dancy, *I Maccabees*, 182–83; Goldstein, *I Maccabees*, 492–94).

200.   Cf. Philo, *Moses* 2.3.12–16; Josephus, *Ag. Ap.* 1.15.156.

201.   Hall, *Inventing the Barbarian*, 109–10.

Changing Indicators of National Superiority

SUPERIOR
Nation

"RIGHTEOUS"

Ruled by a king
who pleases
the gods

Israel = Superior
on claim of serving
the True God

(Torah = description
of Mosaic Yahwism)

INFERIOR
Nation

"UNRIGHTEOUS"

Ruled by a king
who is impious
and unjust

Pre-Alexander: Traditionally, ancient Near Eastern nations were measured by standards of righteousness or unrighteousness, with the righteousness of the king as a focal point.

SUPERIOR
Nation

"CIVILIZED"

Ruled by a
law code

Israel = Superior
on claim that Torah is
an ancient law code

(Torah = Mosaic
legislation)

INFERIOR
Nation

"BARBARIAN"

Ruled by a
sovereign king
(i.e., a tyrant)

Post-Alexander: The Hellenistic paradigm measured nations by standards of civilized or barbarian, with the sovereignty of a law code (not a king) as a focal point.

found executing their own.[202] As unrestrained tyrants are typified by an insatiable lust for wealth,[203] the Seleucids are found stealing even the funds of the helpless and draining the very land of its fruitfulness (although the Jews contribute toward the care of the weak).[204] As the stereotypical tyrant is one who makes decisions alone and the civilized ruler consults the people,[205] so Seleucid officers and Jewish officers are respectively portrayed.[206] As barbarian despots were stereotyped as possessing authority over the very forces of nature (see, e.g., Herodotus, *Hist.* 7.35), so the Seleucids are depicted as presuming to "command the waves of the sea, and…weigh the high mountains in a balance."[207] As barbarian military effectiveness is viewed as dependent on the presence of a feared commander but "rule of law" armies are able to operate without direct supervision,[208] the Jews are able to maintain military effectiveness without a commander present (see, e.g., 1 Macc 12:49–52). The Greeks came to expect all barbarian kings to have an insatiable hunger for expanding their boundaries,[209] just as the Maccabean authors are quick to identify the Seleucid rulers.[210] Indeed, the deathbed conversion of Antiochus IV (in 2 Macc 9:12–27; cf. 1 Macc 6:12–14) is described as a political conversion as much as a religious one. When Antiochus declared himself "subject to God" (9:12) and a "Jew" (9:17), he made Jerusalem a free πόλις of equal status to Athens (9:14–15),[211]

202.   2 Macc 5:6; 13:3. Cf. 1 Macc 9:69; 14:7.

203.   Hall, *Inventing the Barbarian*, 127–29.

204.   E.g. 1 Macc 3:29; 2 Macc 3:10; 8:28.

205.   Hall, *Inventing the Barbarian*, 193.

206.   E.g. 1 Macc 2:40–41; 4:44, 59; 5:16; 9:30; 13:7–9; 2 Macc 10:8; 14:20; 15:36.

207.   E.g. 2 Macc 9:8–12. Daniel R. Schwartz believes 2 Macc 9:8–12 is actually modeled upon Aeschylus' portrayal of Darius in Persians §§744–51; see his "On Something Biblical About 2 Maccabees," in *Biblical Perspectives: Early Use and Interpretation of the Bible in Light of the Dead Sea Scrolls—Proceedings of the First International Symposium of the Orion Center for the Study of the Dead Sea Scrolls and Associated Literature, 12–14 May, 1996* (ed. Michael E. Stone and Esther G. Chazon; STDJ 28; Leiden: Brill, 1998), 227.

208.   Hall, *Inventing the Barbarian*, 80; François Hartog, *The Mirror of Herodotus: The Representation of the Other in the Writing of History* (trans. Janet Lloyd; Berkeley: University of California Press, 1988), 334; Wilfried Nippel, "The Construction of the 'Other'" (trans. A. Nevill), in T. Harrison, ed., *Greek and Barbarian*, 289–90.

209.   Hall, *Inventing the Barbarian*, 125–26; Redfield, "Herodotus the Tourist," 43–44.

210.   E.g. 1 Macc 1:9; 11:13–14; 12:39; 13:31–32.

211.   That Antiochus chose Athens for its stereotypical value is evident, due to the fact that Athens was not part of his domain.

and he declared himself a fellow citizen thereof (9:19).[212] Doran questions whether the text really involves Antiochus becoming a *political*
Jew; Doran sees it instead as only *religious* Judaism being adopted.[213] It
is doubtful, however, that the author of 2 Maccabees distinguished
between political and religious Judaism. The appointment of Jerusalem
to a *political* status (a "'free' city" with "its own traditions and system of
government"),[214] supports the political *and* religious intent of Antiochus'
conversion (as 2 Maccabees portrays it).

Any one of these similarities between the Maccabean polemic and
civilized/barbarian stereotypes might be considered coincidental. The
appearance of so many, however, indicates a thorough adoption of
Hellenistic political ideals as the standard whereby Jewish civilization
was defended. This is significant, for it means that the argument of 1 and
2 Maccabees is not one of Jewish law vs. Seleucid law. The argument is
advanced as the defense of a law-abiding civilization against barbarian
anti-nomism. This point ought not be missed—*neither 1 nor 2 Maccabees fundamentally pit Jews against Gentiles, but nomistic societies
against barbarian societies.*

Both 1 and 2 Maccabees present the Jews as equal to stereotypically
civilized polities like Athens (2 Macc 9:15), Sparta (1 Macc 12:5–23;
14:20–23; 2 Macc 5:9),[215] and especially Rome (1 Macc 8:1–32; 12:1–4,
16; 14:16–19, 24; 15:15–24; 2 Macc 4:11; 12:1–4, 16).[216] The Hasmonean
writer goes to particular lengths to describe the Roman government in a
manner remarkably like that of the Hasmoneans (1 Macc 8:1–32).[217] On
the other hand, the Seleucids are identified with despotic and barbarian
peoples, like the Scythians (2 Macc 4:44–47) and Persians (1 Macc
1:1).[218] The Scythian comparison occurs in a juridical context of particular interest—a trial before the Seleucid king:

212. Goldstein, *II Maccabees*, 356.
213. Doran, "2 Maccabees," 254.
214. Ibid., 254.
215. In relating to Sparta, the Maccabean authors draw on the "common-
brotherhood-in-Abraham" legend previously noted in Cleodemus Malchus (p. 197,
above; Doran, "1 Maccabees," 142–43).
216. Cf. Sara R. Mandell, "Did the Maccabees Believe that They had a Valid
Treaty with Rome?," *CBQ* 53 (1991): 202–20.
217. Morton Smith, "Rome and the Maccabean Conversions: Notes on 1 Macc.
8," in *Donum Gentilicum: New Testament Studies in Honour of D. Daube* (ed. Ernst
Bammel et al.; Oxford: Oxford University Press, 1978), 3–4; Goldstein, *I Maccabees*, 347–48.
218. For the author, Alexander and his heirs merely continue the Persian oppression: "[Alexander] succeeded him [Darius] as king" and "put on crowns…caus[ing]
many evils on the earth" (vv. 1, 9).

> When the king came to Tyre, three men sent by the [Jewish] senate pre-
> sented the case before him. But [the antagonist] Menelaus, already losing,
> promised Ptolemy the son of Dorymenes a substantial bribe to persuade
> the king. Thereupon...the king acquitted [Menelaus] of the charges
> against him, while he sentenced to death those poor men who would have
> been freed uncondemned if they had pleaded even before Scythians.
> (2 Macc 4:44–47)

The Scythians were regarded as the epitome of barbarianism.[219] Such
was the Seleucid king's disregard for law that he is characterized as
worse than the worst of the barbarians. Such a description is not only
applied to the *Seleucid* king; note the international attitudes portrayed
against the *Jewish* apostate, Jason, whose downfall is described in the
following way:

> The end of his conspiracy was shame. He fled, a fugitive, back into the
> land of the Ammonites. Thus he met a miserable end: accused before
> Aretas the ruler of the Arabs; fleeing from city to city; hunted by every-
> one; despised as a rebel from the law and traitor from his country and
> countrymen; castaway into Egypt; and...having set sail to the Lacedae-
> monians—supposing to receive shelter there because they are kindred—
> he died...unmourned and without funeral of any kind, nor a place in an
> ancestral tomb. (2 Macc 5:7–10)

All the world—Ammonites, Arabians, Egyptians, and especially the
Spartans—despise Jason for two reasons: he had gained reputation as a
murderer of his own fellow citizens; and he had revolted against his own
nation's νόμοι. The civilized Spartans, though allegedly kindred to the
Jews, disowned Jason and left him to die as a stranger. In other words,
though some cultures regard "blood as thicker than water," for civilized
peoples like the Spartans, "law-abiding civility is thicker than blood."
Jason dies a barbarian disowned by his kin and refused burial in his
family tomb.

It is neither blood nor ethnicity which determines the "good guys" and
"bad guys" in these accounts. Nor is it (surprisingly) religion: the
Romans and Spartans are nowhere supposed to be worshipers of Yahweh
yet are close friends and allies of the Maccabees.[220] The framework
around which these Jewish historians are arguing their case is one of
"civilization vs. the barbarians." They do not describe "Jews vs. Gentiles,"
or even "Jewish law vs. Gentile law." These works pit "rule of law"

---

219. Goldstein, *II Maccabees*, 243; Hartog, *Mirror of Herodotus*, 12–13.
220. The Spartans are even included in the temple prayers in 1 Macc 12:11.
Contrast Ezra–Nehemiah, which must show the Yahwism of the Persian king before
including him in temple prayers (Ezra 1:2–4).

societies (Jerusalem, Rome, Athens, Sparta) on one side of a grand struggle against "lawless" tyrannies (the Seleucids, Persians, Scythians) on the other.[221]

IV. *Conclusions*

It is the presence of the civilized/barbarian polemic in both Maccabean histories which contributes to the hypothesis here being constructed. In the previous chapter, the Ptolemaic court reform was seen to provide a plausible *administrative mechanism* for Torah becoming a law code. In the present chapter, a *cultural impetus* has been identified. Through a survey of apologetic literature from diaspora and Judean Judaism, the widespread embrace of the Hellenistic civilization ethnography was noted. The civilization/barbarian polemic introduced by the Greeks was adopted by Jews (and other subject peoples) as "the right" indicators of social superiority. Inherent in accepting those indicators was the embrace of legislative uses for native law writings. Although Judaism broadly rejected Greek religion and remained faithful to Hebrew religion, it was *by the standards of Greek legal philosophy* that the Jewish Torah was to be vindicated before the world. Thus it was deemed necessary to pre-suppose that Moses was a legislator and to insist that Torah was ancient Israel's abiding law code. Scholars have long noted similar tendencies in Hellenistic-era Judaism to resist the *content* of Hellenism while adopting its *conventions.*[222] The present chapter has explored such a tendency for Jewish understandings of the Torah.

The present chapter, however, highlights a further problem. It has been seen that fidelity to Torah as a law code was a particularly polemi-cal issue. This is true not only in terms of Judaism's representation of itself to the outside world; competing views of how Torah's legislation should be enforced arose within Judaism as well. The markedly different arguments of 1 and 2 Maccabees provide a case in point. The preceding chapters have constructed a hypothesis for a *common* acceptance of Torah as a law code within Hellenistic-era Judaism; but it can also be

221. Goldstein, *I Maccabees*, 12. Cf. p. 186, above; Daniel R. Schwartz, "Israel and the Nations Roundabout: 1 Maccabees and Hasmonean Expansion," *JJS* 42 (1991): 16–38; S. Cohen, "Jewish Identity."

222. Cf. the scholarly discussion of Ben Sira's anti-Hellenistic conservatism, nonetheless presented in the manner of a Hellenistic philosopher-sage; see Martin Hengel, "The Influence of Hellenistic Civilization in Palestine down to the Maccabean Period," in Stone and Satran, eds., *Emerging Judaism*, 163. Cf. Christine Schams, *Jewish Scribes in the Second-Temple Period* (JSOTSup 291; Sheffield: Sheffield Academic Press, 1998), especially 312–21.

seen that *divisions* would emerge over how actually to practice Torah enforcement. Such complexities are already evident in the Hellenistic era (e.g. 1 and 2 Maccabees). In the next chapter, it will be seen that this complexity—how to apply Torah legislation in *practice*—continued into the Roman era.

Chapter 7

WRITTEN LAW IN GRECO-ROMAN TORAH SECTS:
A PROJECTION

The thesis of the present study has been developed in two parts. In Chapters 1–4, scholarly consensus on the "early" prescriptivization of Torah has been challenged. As a result, the timing of Torah's reconceptualization as a law code has been shifted into the Hellenistic era. In Chapters 5 and 6, evidence that Torah came to be viewed prescriptively in the Hellenistic period was produced; furthermore, a double-pronged hypothesis for how that transformation came about was offered.

By advancing two mechanisms behind Torah's reconceptualization, and broadly dating that transition in the Hellenistic period, it is not supposed that so radical a shift in legal thought occurred in a simple, smooth, or "all-at-once" manner. After all, the Torah is hardly conducive to use as a law code. Moreover, the Jerusalem community and cultus had been in continuous operation from Persian times; Hellenistic Judaism was not "built from scratch" with the Torah as a prescriptive constitution. Consequently, existing customs had to be accounted for, many of which had no textual basis. In fact, based on the evidence of Ezra–Nehemiah, it can be expected that many of the community and cultic traditions in operation were inconsistent with the actual stipulations of the Mosaic Torah. How would these inconsistencies and unmentioned (thus, "unauthorized"?) practices be accounted for, or "corrected"?

In the present chapter, a lack of "smoothness" in Torah's prescriptive handling will be observed into the Roman era. This lack of smoothness does not undermine the fact of a conceptual shift occurring in the Hellenistic period. Rather, it indicates that the shift was far more complex in practice than in principle. Theory can change rapidly; the practical implications of that theory may take many years to work out.

The present chapter will project the practical implications of Torah's Hellenistic-era reconceptualization from the late Hellenistic into the Roman period. Three of the better-known Judaic sects of the time have been chosen for this projection. The field is ripe for a more thorough examination of the many splintering branches of Judaism in relation to this shift; nonetheless, the present chapter will focus on three (and that in a merely introductory manner): Rabbinic Judaism (via the Mishnah); Qumran Judaism (via the *Community Rule* scroll); and "Nazarene" Judaism (via Matthew's portrait of Jesus).

I. *Rabbinic Judaism: The Mishnah*

Although the Mishnah was compiled around 200 CE, it is not wholly a product of that time. Sayings of roughly 150 rabbinic sages from over three centuries (ca. 50 BCE–200 CE) are preserved in its pages.[1] The years 135–200 seem to be best represented (Jacob Neusner notes that two-thirds of the sages named are post-Bar Kokhba[2]), but earlier sayings can be dated confidently as well.[3] The Mishnah's detailed treatment of the temple cultus ("at least two-thirds of Mishnaic law addressed the temple and its regular maintenance"[4]) almost certainly contains tradition from before 70 CE. When examining the Mishnah, it must be recognized that this document is primarily a witness to second-century Judaism; nonetheless, it documents a line of Judaism emerging from (and continuing) a long, ongoing dialog over legal practices.

The legal findings contained in the Mishnah are presented in two forms: *midrashic* or *mishnaic*.[5] Scholars generally define a מדרש as a ruling which gives its source text. A משנה, however, does not cite a source text for its finding. The Mishnah contains mostly משניות (hence the name), but it also contains many דרשות. It is the latter, the דרשות in the Mishnah, which will be looked at first (since their explicit citation makes their attitude toward written law somewhat more apparent). Possible implications of the משניות of the Mishnah will be considered, thereafter.

1. *Torah Use in the Mishnah's* דרשות
The task of analyzing the Mishnah's דרשות is greatly aided by the 2002 publication of Alexander Samely's *Rabbinic Interpretation of Scripture*

---

1. Roger Brooks, "Mishnah," in *ABD* 4:871. Herbert Danby (*The Mishnah* [Oxford: Clarendon, 1933], iii) asserted sources as early as 200 BCE.

2. Jacob Neusner, *The Mishnah: Introduction and Reader* (Philadelphia: Trinity Press International, 1992), 5.

3. Halivni, *Midrash*, 18–37.

4. Brooks, "Mishnah," 4:872.

5. In this chapter, the anglicized terms (*mishnaic* and *midrashic/midrash*) will be employed in reference to forms and processes; Hebrew terms (מדרש / דרשות and משניות / משנה) will be used in reference to texts; the title *Mishnah* will be capitalized when the 63-tractate collection is intended.

*in the Mishnah.*⁶ Samely's thorough analyses of all appearances of midrash in the Mishnah has produced well-grounded insights which can be drawn upon without having to reproduce the massive primary work behind them. His work will therefore be useful to set the stage for what follows, and to extend the significance here deduced from a few select examples.

Samely identifies over 600 דרשות within the Mishnah.⁷ In these דרשות, it is not difficult to discern a prescriptivistic attitude toward the Torah.⁸ This is especially evident where conclusions are drawn based on the vocabulary or grammar of a cited text (i.e. the text itself is "the law"). For example, in *m. Ber.* 1:3, the schools of Shammai and Hillel seek to determine the posture in which, and the number of times each day which, the שמע should be recited. Their determinations are based on the wording of Deut 6:7: "The School of Shammai say: In the evening all should recline when they recite [the שמע], but in the morning they should stand up, for it is written, *And when thou liest down and when thou risest up.* But the School of Hillel say: They may recite it every one in his own way, for it is written, *And when thou walkest by the way...*"⁹

It is not merely the presence of citation which indicates a text has become prescriptive. After all, the Mosaic example might be pointed to as describing the law without thereby regarding the text as *being* "the

---

6. Alexander Samely, *Rabbinic Interpretation of Scripture in the Mishnah* (Oxford: Oxford University Press, 2002). Samely's book is accompanied by his *Database of Midrashic Units in the Mishnah.* Online: www.art.man.ac.uk/mes/samely/home.php. Cf. Samely's other works: "Between Scripture and its Rewording: Towards a Classification of Rabbinic Exegesis," *JJS* 42 (1991): 39–67; "Scripture's Implicature: The Midrashic Assumptions of Relevance and Consistency," *JSS* 37, no. 2 (1992): 167–205; "Justifying Midrash: On an 'Intertextual' Interpretation of Rabbinic Interpretation," *JSS* 39, no. 1 (1994): 19–32; "Stressing Scripture's Words: Semantic Contrast as a Midrashic Technique in the Mishnah," *JJS* 46 (1995): 196–229; "Delaying the Progress from Case to Case: Redundancy in the Halakhic Discourse of the Mishnah," in *Jewish Ways of Reading the Bible* (ed. George J. Brooke; JSSSup 11; Oxford: Oxford University Press, 2000), 99–132.

7. Samely, *Rabbinic Interpretation*, 18, 81–109.

8. The Mishnah actually treats the whole Hebrew Bible as Torah, and Samely's statistics are based on the Mishnah's use of all Scripture as Torah. However, attention in this study will focus on the Mishnah's use of "actual" law texts. This distinction is not of consequence here, as it is not a question of which texts constituted the Mishnah's Torah, but Mishnaic *attitude toward written law* (whatever that included) which is of concern. Treating all Scripture as Torah would have provided more material for deducing rulings, the Torah proper being inadequate on its own. See Samely, *Rabbinic Interpretation*, 51–54.

9. Quotations from the Mishnah are from Danby, *Mishnah.*

law." It was in such a manner that Josiah and Ezra drew upon the authority of Moses for their own radical reforms, which reforms were open-
facedly contrary to many of the actual stipulations of Torah. Citation
alone is not indication that the text (*qua* text) is "the law."[10] Nonetheless,
justifying a legal ruling *on the authority of a text's vocabulary and grammar* is indication that the text *qua* text is "the law."

Samely describes the dependence on wording in Mishnaic דרשות as an
exercise in "emphasis": "what is characteristic for rabbinic interpretation
is a fusion of the movements of emphasizing on the one hand and decod-
ing emphasis on the other."[11] In other words, biblical texts are read as if
particular words are stressed, and then findings are drawn from those
stressed terms. Samely provides the following illustration—and deduces
a telling insight:

> Consider the differences in commitment which can exist even within the
> space of one sentence, if that sentence is used as a promise:
>
> (a) At six o'clock I shall come to the entrance of the park with my friends.
>   Clearly, if the person making this promise does not turn up on the
> agreed day at all, she or he has not kept the promise. But what if the per-
> son were to turn up at five past six?… Or brings only one friend? [etc.]…
> [If such detailed precision was intended,] we would in most circumstances
> expect the utterance to highlight them in some way, as when saying:
>
> (b) **At** precisely **six o'clock**, not a minute earlier or later, **I shall** *arrive* **at
> the entrance of the park**, exactly by the gate, *and bring* no less than two
> **friends.**[12]
>   …In a manner of speaking, this new utterance is not so much a promise
> as the text of a contract, since we tend to ascribe *legal* language such
> elaborate nailing down of a commitment. Mishnaic interpretation offers
> many examples of a biblical sentence of the type (a) being read as if it had
> the meaning of (b).[13]

It is this tendency to read the descriptive statements of Scripture (a) as
though they were legal contracts (b)—where the very *words* of the text
are binding—that makes clear the Mishnah's prescriptive use of written
law. As in the case of *m. Ber.* 1:3 (above), the voices in the Mishnah
often assert requirements based on the way Torah commands are worded.

10. See especially pp. 49–50, 59–63, 103–31, above.
11. Samely, *Rabbinic Interpretation*, 283.
12. "The text in bold marks words identical with (a), while italics show parts
which are modified by (near-) synonymous rephrasing…" (ibid., 308 n. 11 [empha-
sis original).
13. Ibid., 308–9. Cf. David Instone-Brewer, *Techniques and Assumptions in
Jewish Exegesis before 70 CE* (TSAJ 30; Tübingen: J. C. B. Mohr, 1992), 15, 163–71.

This concern to justify decisions by the Torah's wording led to a particular hermeneutical possibility which Samely calls "segmentation": "Mishnaic interpretations do not target *the whole* of Scripture, or any one of its larger parts, but rather segments approximately of sentence length. The hermeneutic licence to cut the text into small units which can be interpreted *as if they stood alone* creates a wide hermeneutic choice."[14]

For instance, Rabbi Aqiba reportedly used a *segment* of Deut 24:1 in his ruling on divorce: "R. Akiba says: Even if he found another fairer than she [he may divorce her], for it is written, *And it shall be if she find no favour in his eyes*" (*m. Gi*ṭ. 9:10).[15] In the Deuteronomy source text, the permissive, "if she does not find favor in his eyes," is qualified: "if she does not find favor in his eyes *because* (כי) *he has found some indecency in her*."[16] By lifting this segment from its co-text, Aqiba was able to justify divorce regardless of the condition of the wife. It is immaterial for Aqiba whether there is any indecency in the spurned wife; even if the husband only "finds another one more pleasant than her" he may divorce. By loosing the segment from its co-text, the original qualifier was removed.[17] Such segmentation would certainly raise eyebrows if employed in a modern courtroom. Nonetheless, the scholars of the Mishnah clearly appreciated the exegetical possibilities facilitated by reverent segmentation.[18] The purpose for identifying this trait of Mishnaic exegesis is not to legitimize or critique it, but only to note its witness to a prescriptivistic understanding of the Torah. It is the text *qua* text that is the source for legal rulings—the text is "the law."

Samely finds that segmentation is so widespread in the Mishnaic use of Scripture that he calls it "a silent partner in almost all hermeneutic

14. Samely, *Rabbinic Interpretation*, 31 (emphasis original). Instone-Brewer (*Jewish Exegesis*, 22) calls this feature "atomization".

15. See Samely, *Rabbinic Interpretation*, 39. Cf. his discussion of *b. Gi*ṭ. 90a (p. 39 n. 31).

16. Hence, the School of Shammai's ruling in *m. Gi*ṭ. 9:10.

17. Samely, *Rabbinic Interpretation*, 37: "The co-text's effect is…to narrow down the range of meaning available for the Lemma [the segment]: it is that effect which is being cancelled by [segmentation]… The semantic options are opened up to their full range, approximating the *plurality* of meanings given in the entry for a single word in a dictionary. At some virtual moment in the hermeneutic process the word, expression, clause, or sentence has all its potential meaning nuances available to it, has maximum ambiguity—before, that is, it is narrowed down again, to some other meaning which meets the concerns of the Mishnaic reader."

18. It was done knowingly and carefully by Samely (*Rabbinic Interpretation*, 41, 45). Samely disdains comparison of rabbinic segmentation to postmodern deconstructionism (pp. 2–5).

operations."[19] Many of the דרשות he analyzes presuppose the possibility of neutralizing a phrase from its biblical co-text in order to reinterpret it within a new context. Undoubtedly, one of the attractive features of segmentation was that it allowed the limited contents of the Scriptures to be mined for direction on an unlimited range of questions, or to find different applications of an old law for new situations. This capacity of rabbinic interpretation is well known, especially in later rabbinic literature.[20] What Samely has demonstrated is "a 'mild' version of neutralization of co-text which pervades Mishnaic interpretation."[21] For the present purposes, it is sufficient to note that one of the presuppositions evinced by this hermeneutic is that the text *is* "the law."[22]

These features are adequate, for the present, to indicate a well-developed concept of prescriptive Torah in the Mishnah's דרשות. This witness, however, is not necessarily even; and its unevenness is best seen through reference to the משניות.

2. *Torah Use in the Mishnah's* משניות

The explicit presence of citation (and the nature of those citations) in the דרשות makes their textual basis evident. The absence of citation in the משניות does not necessarily mean a lack of textual sourcing, though in cases it may. Scholars are divided as to whether mishnah and midrash are merely different forms for *presenting* legal rulings, or whether they indicate different *processes* for arriving at such rulings. David Weiss Halivni has argued the former position: mishnah and midrash are forms which *alike* depend on text-based, midrashic reasoning (משניות simply do not record the reasoning). Halivni explains:

> Such a substantial difference [between Mishnaic and Talmudic (i.e. midrashic) forms] could not have taken place accidentally. There must have been a conscious decision [in writing the Mishnah] to preserve carefully the fixed law and to neglect benignly the argumentational material. After a conclusion was reached, the means of arriving at it...seemed no longer important... This is exactly the way the authors of the Mishnah and the Braitha (ca. 50–200 C.E.) practiced transmission.

---

19. Ibid., 34.
20. Danby, *Mishnah*, xxv; Instone-Brewer, *Jewish Exegesis*, 22.
21. Samely, *Rabbinic Interpretation*, 34.
22. Goldberg speaks of the importance of the subtle rabbinic conception: "Torah is not speech which happens to be written down...but is...essentially a written thing" (Arnold Goldberg, "The Rabbinic View of Scripture," in *A Tribute to Geza Vermes: Essays on Jewish and Christian Literature and History* [ed. P. R. Davies and R. T. White; JSOTSup 100; Sheffield: JSOT Press, 1990], 157).

> The Mishnah...contain[s] very little discursive material... Apparently,
> to the authors of the Mishnah...law was to be officially transmitted only in
> the apodictic form. Arguments and discussion were necessary—indeed,
> indispensable—but only as a means of arriving at decisions, not as ends in
> themselves... [It was not] until the [time of the] redactors of the Talmud...
> [that scribes] came to the aid of the discursive material and affirmed it
> worthy to be preserved.[23]

In other words, the fact that *some* rulings in the Mishnah are midrashic
indicates the kind of reasoning which took place behind *all* the Mishnah's findings. Only as a matter of presentation—probably for ease of
memorization—the textual basis was not normally cited.[24] Halivni's
proposal is reasonable, but it is not conclusive. While accepting the likelihood that some משניות may derive from unrecorded midrash, there
might be more behind changing forms of legal statement than mere
presentation.

Note, for instance, the description in *m. Ḥag.* 1:8:

> [The rules about] release from vows hover in the air and have naught to
> support them; the rules about the Sabbath, Festal-offerings, and Sacrilege
> are as mountains hanging by a hair, for [teaching of] Scripture [thereon] is
> scanty and the rules many; the [rules about] cases [concerning property]
> and the [Temple]Service, and the rules about what is clean and unclean
> and the forbidden degrees, they have that which supports them, and it is
> they that are the essentials of the Law.

The lack of textual support for certain customs is here regarded as problematic—*but the phenomenon is admitted.* Received rulings that lack
textual support are described as precarious due to the felt need for legislative backing.

Later rabbis, commenting on this משנה, invoked the doctrine of an
"oral Torah" to resolve the problem. For example, in the Jerusalem Talmud on this passage: "R. Zeira [said] in the name of R. Yohanan: 'If a
law [*halakah*] comes to hand and you do not know its nature [or, source],
do not discard it for another one, for lo, many laws were stated [orally] to
Moses at Sinai, and all of them have been embedded in the Mishnah'"
(*y. Ḥag.* 1:8).[25] Actually, the statement in the Mishnah does not seem
to share the confidence of the Talmud. For the Mishnah, traditions lacking written תורות "hang by a hair" and "hover in the air." There is no

---

23. Halivni, *Midrash*, 2–3. Cf. Daniel Patte, *Early Jewish Hermeneutic in
Palestine* (SBLDS 22; Missoula, Mont.: Scholars, 1975), 90–93.

24. Halivni, *Midrash*, 19, 40.

25. Trans., Jacob Neusner, *The Oral Torah: The Sacred Books of Judaism—An
Introduction* (San Francisco: Harper & Row, 1986), 184.

(clear) concept here of an alternative, unwritten legislative code equally as solid as the written code. On the contrary, the lack of written sources for certain מֹשְׁנָיוֹת seems troublesome for the Mishnah, but it is admitted as a fact.[26]

It might be suspected that the Mishnah contains, therefore, a combination of both textually sourced traditions *and* living traditions for which little (or no) textual basis was known. The Mishnah may be a window into the midst of an ongoing struggle to reckon with a heritage of traditions for which no verbal bases were known.[27] Only over many generations would adequate exegetical methods (i.e. complex midrash), and alternative sources of Sinai legislation (i.e. the oral Torah[28]) be devised to supply legislative grounding for traditions which had previously "hung as mountains by a hair."

The Mishnah provides adequate evidence that the Torah was, indeed, regarded as a prescriptive law code for Judaism. *Conceptually*, Torah was legislation. *Practically*, however, it would take time and debate (and the development of new exegetical tools) to reckon this principle with the existing customs of the community.

II. *Qumran:* Community Rule *(1QS)*

Among the first stash of scrolls unsealed and published from Qumran was a document called, "The Rule of the Community" (סֶרֶךְ הַיַּחַד), a text commonly referred to as 1QS, and generally dated to the first century BCE.[29] The fact that thirteen copies of the *Community Rule* were located in the caves (being one of the more frequent materials found) probably

---

26. Cf. *m. Pesaḥ.* 4:1–5; *m. ʿOr.* 3:9; *m. ʾAbot.* 1:1–18; Martin S. Jaffee, *Torah in the Mouth: Writing and Oral Tradition in Palestinian Judaism 200 BCE–400 CE* (Oxford: Oxford University Press, 2001), 85–87.

27. Samely, *Rabbinic Interpretation*, 51. Cf. P. Davies, "'Law' in Judaism," 17; Westbrook, *Studies*, 7.

28. See Mayer I. Gruber, "The Mishnah as Oral Torah: A Reconsideration," *JSJ* 15 (1984): 112–22; Alan J. Avery-Peck, "Oral Tradition: Early Judaism," in *ABD*, 5.34–5; Bernard S. Jackson, "The Original Oral Law," in Brooke, ed., *Ways of Reading*, 3–19.

29. Frank Moore Cross ("Introduction," in *Scrolls from Qumrân Cave I: The Great Isaiah Scroll, The Order of the Community, The Pesher to Habakkuk from Photographs by John C. Trever* [ed. Frank Moore Cross et al.; Jerusalem: Albright Institute of Archaeological Research and the Shrine of the Book, 1972], 1–5) dates 1QS between 100–75 BCE. George J. Brooke ("1Q28b: 1QSerekh ha-Yaḥad b (fragment)," in *Qumran Cave 4.XIX: 4QSerekh ha-Yaḥad*" [ed. Philip H. Alexander and Geza Vermes; DJD 26; Oxford: Clarendon, 1998], 229) places it between 125 and 75 BCE.

indicates something of its importance as a witness to the community that formed it.[30] It is the witness of the *Community Rule* which will here be used as a (limited) window into Qumran law.

The *Community Rule* is arranged along the pattern of Greco-Roman guild or religious association charters.[31] It describes matters such as terms of membership, ranking within the community (היחד), and governance. Community decisions (including at least some court cases) were made by majority vote. Within the *Community Rule* there are collections of written statutes. There is also a strong commitment to the Law of Moses throughout. Two questions therefore are of interest in considering the theory of written law practiced in the community: (1) How were the laws which were compiled and inscribed in the scroll itself used? And: (2) What was the relationship between those statutes inscribed in the *Community Rule* and the Mosaic Torah?

The answer to the first question would seem to be simpler than the second. The charter introduces its own precepts saying, "These are the rules by which cases are to be decided at a community inquiry" (1QS 6.24; cf. 5.1; 6.2).[32] It is impossible to conclude how strictly the subsequent provisions were followed; nevertheless, that the *Community Rule* laws were *addressed to the court* as penalty instructions *the court was charged to implement in adjudication* is an explicit statement of a written law collection as prescription.[33] How closely the community followed this form of jurisprudence is another question, but here is an indication that the *Community Rule* was composed with a prescriptive use of written law in view.

The answer to the second question is not so straightforward. The Qumran community may have possessed a legislative view of its own written laws, but was the Mosaic Torah also regarded as prescriptive, or was Torah an "academic treatise" on law? The *Community Rule* places great importance on the community's constant study of Moses' law book

30. Michael Wise et al. eds, *The Dead Sea Scrolls: A New Translation* (New York: Harper Collins, 1996), 123.

31. Moshe Weinfeld, *The Organizational Pattern and the Penal Code of the Qumran Sect: A Comparison with Guilds and Religious Associations of the Hellenis-tic–Roman Period* (NTOA 2; Fribourg: Éditions Universitaires, 1986); Matthias Klinghardt, "The Manual of Discipline in the Light of Statutes of Hellenistic Associations," in *Methods of Investigation of the Dead Sea Scrolls and the Khirbet Qumran Site* (ed. Michael Wise; New York: New York Academy of Sciences, 1994), 251–70.

32. Translations of the Qumran Scrolls are from Wise et al., eds., *Dead Sea Scrolls*.

33. Westbrook, "Origins of Legislation," 202; cf. p. 25, above.

(6.6–8),[34] with one of the reasons being to train the men of the assembly for participation in legal deliberations (6.18–24).[35] This document also seems to expect that the community would be governed by what is learned from Torah (1.13–15; 4.2–3; 5.8–13; 6.2–8; 8.1–2, 15–16, 21; 9.9–10, 12–16, 20, 23–25; cf. 10.5–11.21). Nevertheless, those community precepts which are actually recorded in the *Community Rule* show "virtually no explicit dependence on scripture."[36] Is the Torah the unstated source of community legislation? Is the Torah a superior code of laws to which community legislation is added? Or is the Torah an "academic treatise" on law, but only community law is statutory? The first two possibilities are currently debated (and unresolved).[37] The last may have yet to be considered.

No solution to these questions will here be ventured, although one scholar's assessment is intriguing in relation to the present thesis. Sarianna Metso has studied the redaction of the *Community Rule* (by reference to 1QS with 4QS[b,d] and 4QS[e]). Her conclusion is thought provoking:

> One of the main results of my study of the redaction history of the Community Rule was that the need to find scriptural legitimization for the regulations of the community arose only at a later stage, presumably in a situation in which the community's strict rules had been questioned. Thus, the process appears to have been the reverse of what has been presumed, at least in some cases. The laws regulating…community life seem not to have emerged as a result of scriptural exegesis, but scriptural quotations or allusions were added because of the need to justify the rules already in effect.[38]

Is it possible that the *Community Rule* sect had inherited legal commitments which were not exegetically derived, and for which it was later felt that verbal grounding in Torah was needed?[39] It can only here be raised

---

34. Also 1QS 1.12–15; 2.25–3.1, 9–11; 4.2–5; 5.21; 6.18; 9.15.

35. Also 1QS 7.21; 8.24–25.

36. George J. Brooke, "Reading the Plain Meaning of Scripture in the Dead Sea Scrolls," in Brooke, ed., *Ways of Reading*, 68.

37. On equating community law with Torah, see Sarianna Metso, *The Textual Development of the Qumran Community Rule* (STDJ 21; Leiden: Brill, 1997), 127; Lawrence H. Schiffman, *The Halakhah at Qumran* (SJLA 16; Leiden: Brill, 1975), 19–20. On distinguishing community law from Torah, see Weinfeld, *Organization of Qumran*, 71–73.

38. Sarianna Metso, "Constitutional Rules at Qumran," in *The Dead Sea Scrolls After Fifty Years: A Comprehensive Assessment* (ed. Peter W. Flint and James C. VanderKam; 2 vols.; Leiden: Brill, 1998), 1:200.

39. Joseph M. Baumgarten's insight ("The Disqualification of Priests in 4Q Fragments of the 'Damascus Document': A Specimen of the Recovery of Pre-Rabbinic

as a question. The relationship between the Qumran community rules and the Torah remains unclear. Comparison with other Qumran legal texts (4QMMT, *CD*, the *Temple Scroll*, etc.) further demonstrates the development of a strong sense of connection between community laws and Torah, but the nature of that connection "continues to intrigue scholars."[40]

This much seems clear: the *Community Rule* demonstrates an embracing of legislative ideals for community regulation. That community law writings were legislative is explicit (6.24). The present study merely raises the possibility that the relationship between community law and Torah at Qumran may be a sticky question for modern scholars because it may have been a sticky problem for the community itself. Though a legislative model was adopted, how (and, indeed, whether) to relate the Torah to that model may have been a gradual and complex process. It seems that the community did have written legislation, but whether *Torah* was regarded legislatively in the Qumran sect needs yet to be demonstrated and explained.

III. *"Nazarene" Judaism: Matthew's Jesus*

A third sect emerging in the period is that of Jesus of Nazareth. This "Nazarene" Judaism (which became the Christian Church) is interesting because it raises the possibility that some Judaic sects may have tried to reverse the process of regarding Torah as a source of law. Dale Patrick has already pointed this way:

> Jews hold the actual text of laws in great esteem, meditating upon it, seeking guidance from it, and praising God for having given it. Christians are generally impatient with a body of rules of vast multiplicity. They

Halakha," in *Madrid Qumran Congress: Proceedings of the International Congress on the Dead Sea Scrolls, Madrid, 18–21 March, 1991* [ed. Julio Trebolle Barrera and Luis Vegas Montaner; 2 vols.; STDJ 11; Leiden: Brill, 1992], 513) into the similarity of the received law across sects is interesting: "There is a large, very significant body of halakha which apparently was not limited to any...[sect], but represents the common traditional law of the Second Temple Period." Cf. Lawrence H. Schiffman, "The *Temple Scroll* and the Nature of Its Law: The Status of the Question," in *The Community of the Renewed Covenant: The Notre Dame Symposium on the Dead Sea Scrolls* [ed. Eugene Ulrich and James C. VanderKam; Christianity and Judaism in Antiquity Series 10; Notre Dame: University of Notre Dame Press, 1994], 51–53).

40. Hannah K. Harrington, "Biblical Law at Qumran," in Flint and VanderKam, eds., *Dead Sea Scrolls After Fifty Years*, 1:183–84. Brooke ("Reading in the Dead Sea Scrolls," 89) has recently stated that "a new model is required" for assessing the exegetical assumptions at Qumran. Sensitivity to Torah's "recent" prescriptivization may open one avenue for new insights.

> want them reduced to a manageable size—an essential core, like the Ten
> Commandments, or a single overriding principles, like the law of love...
> In this commandment [the "law of love"], I believe, the New Testament
> has revived the understanding of divine law as an unwritten law.[41]

It is probably not necessary (or accurate) to contrast "Jews and Christians" in the present discussion. Jesus himself taught as a Jew within Judaism. His followers were, initially, another Judaic sect. Furthermore, almost as soon as the followers of Jesus did became a faith distinct from Judaism, that faith system incorporated a prescriptivistic view of the Torah. If not as early as Paul, at least by the time of Justin Martyr's *Dialogue with Trypho* (second century CE), the Christian Church espoused that Torah was legislation for ancient Israel.[42] For most (if not all) of the Church's history as a distinct faith, Christianity has held that Torah was originally legislation for Israel and has sought to justify discontinuing its enforcement.[43] Ironically therefore, *as distinct faiths*, Judaism and Christianity *share a common view* of Torah as legislative. Consequently, the question here considered is of little help for comparing the views of Torah held by Judaism and Christianity today. However, the question of Torah's prescriptive or descriptive nature may be extremely helpful for understanding how the Judaism of Jesus arrived at its distinctive attitude toward the Torah. Was Jesus' complex devotion to, yet freedom with, the Torah indicative of his effort to assert a descriptivistic role to the Mosaic law collection in opposition to the prescriptivism of other Judaic movements? A few, provocative lines of evidence from Matthew's portrait of Jesus will here serve to open the question.

First of all, there is a seeming "double-mindedness" in Matthew's handling of the Torah which scholars have often noted. Roger Mohrlang describes it this way:

> ...When we inquire more specifically into Matthew's understanding of
> the law, we find ourselves confronted by a problem of considerable
> complexity. For side by side lie statements that appear to assert both the

41. Patrick, *Old Testament Law*, 204–7.

42. Theodore G. Stylianopoulos, *Justin Martyr and the Mosaic Law* (SBLDS 20; Missoula, Mont.: Scholars Press, 1975), especially 65–68.

43. E.g. ibid., 45–130, and various works by Thomas Aquinas: *Summa Theologiæ* (trans. Thomas Gilby; Cambridge: Blackfriars, 1966), 1.2.98.5, 99.4, 104.1–4; *Catechism of the Catholic Church: Revised Edition* (London: Geoffrey Chapman, 1999), paras. 1950–74; *Westminster Confession*, 19.1–7; *Second Helvetic Confession*, 12.1–4; *Thirty-nine Articles*, §7 (cf. Edgar C. S. Gibson, *The Thirty-Nine Articles of the Church of England: Explained with an Introduction* [London: Methuen, 1902], 280–82, 294).

continuing validity of the law and its abrogation, that express both rigorous conservative and radically progressive interpretations. How do we reconcile such seemingly disparate statements?[44]

Mohrlang further identifies five possible kinds of solution to this problem so far advanced by scholars:

> ...We may (1) treat the contradictory elements as different but equally viable strands of Christian tradition...; (2) regard one as tradition, the other as redaction...; (3) consider them as the results of separate redactions representing different viewpoints; (4) treat one as of negligible importance in its context, and give priority to the other; (5) consider both as viewpoints of a single author, held in either reconcilable or irreconcilable tension: if the former, attempts may be made to explain them in terms of their contexts, as addressed to different issues; if the latter, they may be assumed to represent some degree of inconsistency in the thoughts of the writer himself.[45]

Mohrlang himself prefers a version of (5), with Matthew giving different emphases to counter two different groups: "on the one side, against some unspecified antinomian threat or charge; and on the other, against the misplaced priorities of the Pharisees."[46] It is difficult to be sure, however, that such an effort would not backfire. What is to keep Matthew's statements upholding the Torah from being picked up by the "pharisee-like" party, and his statements loosening the Torah being championed by the "unspecified antinomian" party? Perhaps a sixth possibility should be added to the above list: for Matthew, Jesus was a conservative Jew who sought to restore the use of Torah as a moral and cultic ideal; for Matthew, the "scribes and pharisees" were the innovators by their efforts to make Torah a legislative code of conduct. In this case, the difference between this Judaic sect and that of Jesus' opponents was not a matter of Torah's validity, *but a difference over how the law book was to function.*[47]

"Sharply set over against the strictly legalistic interpretation of Pharisaic Judaism," Mohrlang writes, "Jesus' interpretation focuses not on the letter of the law, but on radical obedience to its deepest intent..."[48] This

---

44. Roger Mohrlang, *Matthew and Paul: A Comparison of Ethical Perspectives* (Cambridge: Cambridge University Press, 1984), 7.

45. Ibid., 22. Cf. William R. G. Loader, *Jesus' Attitude Towards the Law: A Study of the Gospels* (Grand Rapids: Eerdmans, 2002), 150–51.

46. Mohrlang, *Matthew and Paul*, 22. Cf. Gerhard Barth, "Matthew's Understanding of the Law," in *Tradition and Interpretation in Matthew* (ed. Gunther Bornkamm et al.; trans. Percy Scott; London: SCM Press, 1963), 58–164.

47. Cf. R. T. France, *Matthew: Evangelist and Teacher* (Downer's Grove, Ill.: InterVarsity, 1989), 196.

48. Mohrlang, *Matthew and Paul*, 25.

fundamental distinction between Jesus and his opponents is well recognized. However, scholars have generally *assumed* that Jesus was "radically progressive" for using Torah in this way: "express[ing] both rigorous conservat[ism]" by his claims to uphold Torah "and radically progressive interpretations" by his emphasizing the spirit rather than the letter of the law.[49] Perhaps this is a false dichotomy, since Matthew does not seem to feel such a contradiction. Matthew may have perceived the reverse: that Jesus was conservative both in his claims *and* in his use of Torah. Jesus was restoring the "ancient use" of Torah in resistance to "Hellenistic legalism." The claims of "rigorous conservat[ism]" by the Matthean Christ were not contradicted, but proven, by his overruling legislative interpretations of Torah in order to bring Torah's tacit ideal to bear on his audience.

This possibility can be explored through Jesus' much-discussed handling of the Mosaic divorce law (Matt 5:31–32; 19:3–12/Deut 24:1–4). In the words of Hans Dieter Betz, Jesus' divorce prohibition "has been— and still is—one of the most hotly contested passages of the New Testament."[50] What is said here certainly will not resolve the debate, but may open a new perspective on it.

Jesus' ruling on divorce in 5:31–32 is particularly complicated because, in that passage, Jesus "contradicted Deut 24:1–4"[51] directly after insisting "not an iota, not a dot, will pass from the law" (5:18) and after condemning to hell fire any who teach contrary to "the least of these commandments" (5:19–20). How can Jesus claim to uphold the whole Torah (5:18–20) while ruling against (5:31–32) that which is legitimated in it (Deut 24:1–4)? Mohrlang seeks resolution by asserting that Jesus did not remove anything from Torah in his divorce ruling—he simply made the law more strict.[52] Other scholars aptly insist that removing a legalized "permission" to divorce is still a contradiction of it.[53] The whole question, however, *presupposes* that Deut 24 is legislation. It is only when the Torah is presupposed to be legislation that the rather cryptic description in Deut 24 can be understood to legalize divorce.[54] But Matthew's Jesus may not have considered Moses' ruling to be legislation; he apparently regarded Deut 24:1–4 as a record of Mosaic efforts to

49. Ibid., 7.
50. Hans Dieter Betz, *The Sermon on the Mount* (Minneapolis: Fortress, 1995), 243. (Betz's comment is particularly aimed at Matt 5:31–32.)
51. Ibid., 255.
52. Mohrlang, *Matthew and Paul*, 12.
53. E.g. France, *Matthew*, 193.
54. Betz, *Sermon on the Mount*, 246–47.

set controls on remarriage after divorce (divorce being a fact Moses could not stop) without thereby legalizing it.[55] Matthew may see Jesus as a Torah conservative by the very act of his overthrowing the "new" legislative interpretation of his opponents. For Matthew, Jesus was restoring the true law which was tacitly behind (not verbally within) Moses' example.

The parallel divorce dialog in Matt 19 offers further clues. In that passage, the pharisees set Deut 24:1–4 before Jesus as "the Mosaic command" on divorce. Jesus answered them by citing instead Gen 2:22–24. This text, Jesus said, is the Mosaic command on the matter (not Deut 24). According to Jesus, Deut 24 merely describes how Moses dealt with the fact of divorce: "Because of your hardness of heart, Moses allowed you to divorce your wives…" (19:8). This was a historical description, not a legislative precept. Instead, *it is the divine, creational order itself* that is "the law" and thus authoritative: "…Moses allowed you to divorce your wives, but from the beginning it was not so" (19:8). Scholars have often understood Jesus to have invoked a hierarchy of laws, placing creation law over Mosaic law.[56] Jesus, however, is probably not setting a law hierarchy; he is citing *divine order* as "the law" and *Mosaic example* as an illustration of Moses' effort to implement that order in a certain "hard-hearted" society.

In other words, for Matthew's Jesus, the Mosaic law writings are another kind of history text. Though the pharisees regarded Moses as having *legislatively* "commanded" (ἐνετείλατο) divorce, Jesus sees Moses as having *historically* "suffered" (ἐπέτρεψεν) divorce while wrestling to lead a "hard-hearted" people (vv. 7–8).[57] Thus the Mosaic precepts function as "condensed narrations," recording Moses' efforts to order the stiff-necked Hebrews of his day. *Both the narratives of Torah and the precepts of Torah are therefore history about law; neither are "the law."* For Jesus, "the law" remains a metaphysical reality embodied in the creation order—not in texts. Matthew may see Jesus as a defender of Torah within a traditional, ancient Near Eastern concept of law in contest with novel, legislative approaches.

There is another facet of Matthew's portrait of Jesus which emerges from these texts. Jesus not only claims absolute fidelity to the Torah, but he also identifies himself as the one responsible for the fulfillment of the

55. Ibid., 255.

56. E.g. Marcus Bockmuehl, *Jewish Law in Gentile Churches: Halakhah and the Beginning of Christian Public Ethics* (Edinburgh: T. & T. Clark, 2000), 6.

57. Donald A. Hagner, *Matthew 14–28* (WBC 33B; Dallas: Word, 1995), 548; Betz, *Sermon on the Mount*, 255–56.

Torah's ideal: "Do not think that I have come to abolish the Law or the Prophets; I have not come to abolish them but to fulfill them" (5:17). This claim is matched, then, by his frequent expression, "You have heard…but I tell you (λέγω ὑμῖν)."[58] Is Matthew painting Jesus after the likeness of the traditional ancient Near Eastern sovereign (disparaged by Hellenism under the stereotype of "barbarian")? Is Matthew promoting a return to the rule of an absolute king (i.e. a "despot") who is personally responsible to know God and implement the divine law to which a written collection merely bears witness? Matthew obviously places great weight on Jesus' lineage from David and his claim to be "the King of the Jews."[59] Of course, Matthew would avoid using the loaded terminology of "barbarianism" to describe Jesus. Nonetheless, he does speak of Jesus as a sovereign who personally mediates divine justice (e.g. 11:27; 17:5; 28:18–20). He describes Jesus as one who (to repeat Aristotle's definitions of barbarianism) treats the Torah as "enunciat[ing] general principles" but not "directions for dealing with circumstances as they arise"[60] (e.g. 12:1–8; 19:4–8; 22:34–40; 23:23–24). Unlike sects which sought to reckon Torah with received traditions, Matthew's Jesus possesses authority to change traditions and the "stipulations" of Torah too (e.g. 5:21–48; 7:28–29; 15:1–2, 10–11; 19:8–9; 26:28; 28:19). He does so without any sense that this somehow "violates" true law. The appearance is like that of a barbarian sovereign. Moreover, in keeping with the traditional ancient Near Eastern ideal (and contrary to Hellenistic stereotypes), Jesus is presented as a sovereign who employs his absolute power, not for self-aggrandizement, but to care for the poor and needy (e.g. 11:27–29; 12:15–21).

It might even be wondered whether a decisive issue for sectarian approaches to law writings was just this: a Judaic sect which had a divine king (i.e. a messianic sect) would tend to recover a traditional role for the law book; a Judaic sect which lacked a king required an alternate sovereign which "rule of law" theory offered through legal exegesis of the prescriptivized Torah.

It was Jesus' claim to be the Davidic heir, combined with his "free" handling of the Torah, that contributed to the ultimate break between ἐκκλησία and συναγωγή. The full dynamics of that break, and the legitimacy or illegitimacy of Jesus' royal claims, are not the issue here. Furthermore, as earlier noted, the emerging Church itself soon came to

58. Matt 5:20, 21–22, 27–28, 31–32, 33–34, 38–39, 43–44 (cf. 19:9).
59. Matt 1:1–16, 23; 2:1–6, etc.
60. Aristotle, *Pol.* 3.10.4. (See p. 187, above.)

regard Torah as innately prescriptivistic, leading to the perpetually vexing problem of Torah's inclusion in the Christian Bible while "abrogating" its "legislative force." Matthew's Jesus may have had a simpler view of Torah which explains his insistence on its continued observance (albeit not after the manner in which other Judaisms were observing Torah). Was a return to traditional, ancient Near Eastern ideals of king and law collection (with Jesus as that king) behind the Nazarene sect? To state the question is to suggest the possibility that some sects, as late as the Roman period, may have yet resisted Torah's re-characterization as a law code.

IV. *Conclusions*

The three sects given cursory attention in this chapter might be regarded as indicative of the complexity following in the wake of the new, Hellenistic legal climate. The received law writings may have been widely reconceived as legislation *in principle* in connection with the Ptolemaic court reforms (Chapter 5) and Hellenistic ethnology (Chapter 6). This does not mean the embrace was universal. Some sects may have continued to use Torah in traditional ways longer than others. Furthermore, once a group did come to treat Torah as a legislative text, the *practical* implications would have been long and controversial to work out. The refining of exegetical tools, and the contests between interpretative schools over how received traditions might be accounted for, would take time— and exacerbate the sectarian divisions of Judaism.[61]

The mechanisms earlier identified are therefore "triggering" mechanisms. The process itself would prove far more complex and varied, taking place community-by-community, generation-by-generation, tradition-by-tradition.

---

61. Cf. Joseph Blenkinsopp, "Interpretation and the Tendency to Sectarianism," in *Jewish and Christian Self-Definition*. Vol. 2, *Two Aspects of Judaism in the Greco-Roman Period* (ed. E. P. Sanders; London: SCM Press, 1981), 1–26.

Chapter 8

CONCLUSION: THE RE-CHARACTERIZATION
OF ISRAEL'S WRITTEN LAW

Why were the laws of Moses written down?

It is too often taken for granted that laws are written down to regulate society. This cannot be assumed in reference to ancient law collections such as the Pentateuch. Other ancient Near Eastern societies inscribed laws as memorial or didactic texts, but ancient Near Eastern peoples did not typically prepare written decisions ahead of time for judges to implement (prescriptions). Law writings in Mesopotamia and Asia Minor (and likely Egypt as well) do not appear to have been legislative. What about the Hebrew law writings? Clarity is more difficult in relation to biblical law due to the lack of law-practice materials. Nonetheless, most scholars believe that Israel also wrote laws for idyllic reasons. They are descriptions of Yahwistic ideals, not prescriptions binding upon institutions. Though no Hebrew contracts, court dockets, or case records have yet emerged, the witness of juridical narratives in the biblical literature supports this conclusion.

But somehow, over the course of time, the Mosaic law writings did come to be viewed as ancient legislation. Later Judaism came to regard the inherited law writings as the constitutional law code by which Israel had once been ruled. Consequently, it came to be held that the restoration of Israel (and fidelity to Yahweh) required "continued" enforcement of Torah's precepts as verbally binding upon society and worship. How did this re-characterization of Israel's written law come about? That is the question addressed by this project: *What process brought the people of Torah to use this "law collection" as a "law code"?*

The conclusions drawn in this study can be summarized in two parts. First, law-practice evidence from two key periods was analyzed (Chapters 3 and 4), leading to the conclusion: *Torah was not regarded as a legislative text prior to the Hellenistic era.* Second, administrative and cultural forces in that era were examined (Chapters 5 and 6), leading to the hypothesis of two mechanisms for "triggering" the prescriptivization of Torah: *the court system of Ptolemy II introduced Jews to the use of Torah as a law code; the new ethnography brought by Hellenism gave impetus to the claim that Torah always was legislation.* The nature of this project requires that its findings be accepted as, to some extent, provisional. Far too broad a sweep of history has been covered, and far too much literature and other evidence from the relevant periods left untouched, to suppose that the model here constructed is comprehensive. Nevertheless, the focal points of this study have been carefully chosen to ensure the development of reliable results.[1]

Key conclusions arising from this project, as well as potential implications and areas for further study, can now be indicated.

I. *Main Project Conclusions*

The primary contributions produced in the course of this project can be summarized under the following four points.

1. *A New Dating for Torah's Re-characterization*
This study has introduced a new dating for Torah's re-characterization as legislation, breaking with the current consensus which focuses on the Persian era. Raymond Westbrook is typical in this regard:

> Described as a priest and a "scribe skilled in the *torah* of Moses," [Ezra] may be credited with laying the jurisprudential foundations of Jewish Law as we understand it today. For he and his fellow priests read "from the book, from the *torah* of God, with interpretation" before the assembled people (*Neh.* 8:1–8). Thus the legal system became based upon the idea of a written code of law interpreted and applied by religious authorities.[2]

To date, however, no one has tested this conclusion against the actual practice-material in Ezra–Nehemiah. It is clear that the law book did play some kind of practical role in the post-exilic reforms. The assumption that this "practical role" was, specifically, *legislative* has never been adequately tested. In this study, therefore, the practice-material from Ezra–Nehemiah (and from Josiah, who is sometimes credited with an earlier movement toward prescriptivism) has been tested. It emerged from that examination that Josiah and Ezra/Nehemiah were more traditional than innovative in their legal methods. They cannot be credited with legal innovations so radical as to recast Torah as a law code. This project has therefore pushed the window for Torah's re-characterization into the Hellenistic period.

1. See pp. 29–30, above.
2. Westbrook, "Biblical Law," 3–4.

In offering this revised dating, however, two qualifications need to be noted. First, the paucity of Ptolemaic-era evidence has required the utilization of materials from as far afield as Egypt and from as late as the Seleucid era. It is therefore impossible to state more precisely "when" in the Hellenistic period the legislative views demonstrated in these materials "took hold" in Judea. It is not possible to determine whether both mechanisms identified were equally or disproportionately influential on Jewish legal thinking, or other details of their relationship as "coordinate" forces. Both of the identified mechanisms were present as early as Ptolemy II; but how quickly the intellectual climate of Judean law adapted to these influences cannot be established with any more precision than "the Hellenistic era." No precise date, only a general era, of transition can here be asserted. Second, it has also been shown that the recasting of Torah as a law code was not so neat a process as to be completely restricted to the Hellenistic period. As a *conceptual* shift, the Hellenistic era can be regarded as the period of Torah's re-characterization; as a *practical* development, however, the legislative use of Torah evolved in different ways in different branches of Judaism over a much longer and more complicated process—stretching into the Roman era and beyond.

The present study has, therefore, advanced a case for re-dating the prescriptivization of Torah to the Hellenistic period as a corrective to the current consensus.

2. A Complex Model for Torah's Development

The aforementioned break with current scholarship, however, is not an absolute break. It rather calls for a re-appropriation of the scholarly data around a more complex model of Torah development than is generally allowed. In other words, scholars are correct to find a "new esteem" for law writings in the reforms of Josiah and Ezra. However, this study introduces a more complex model of Torah development to account for these insights without mistaking them for "new functions" (e.g. legislation).

It seems that scholars generally recognize two faces of Torah's growth over time: (1) the development of its *content*, and (2) the enhancement of its *authority*. Problems arise, however, when Torah's increasing authority is confused with a change in Torah's *function*. The development of legislative uses for Torah needs to be accounted for along a third line of development distinct from the other two: (3) the adaptation of its *functions*. This study clarifies the importance of distinguishing evidence for Torah's changing functions from evidence indicating its rising authority.

These three, distinct planes of Torah's development can be summarized as follows:

1. *Torah's changing content*—It is generally held that the content of Israel's "official" law book was expanded in the periods of Josiah and Ezra. BC was, it is generally believed, the oldest law collection in ancient Israel. Josiah is credited with appointment of a BC-expansion (Deuteronomy) as Judah's "official" law book.[3] Post-exile, the purportedly Yahwistic king of Persia appointed Ezra to teach his law book in Yehud—a law book close to the present Pentateuch. On one plane, it is possible to trace development in the *content* of Torah.

2. *Torah's rising authority*—It would appear that the earliest law writings were texts for instructing *the people*.[4] Their authority was particularly that of popular guidance. The Deuteronomic school, however, expected Israel's *kings* to be "like their brothers" and to learn under the Levitical law writings. This was intended to humble the king (not so much to exalt the law book to a new level of authority). There nonetheless emerges in DtrH an identification of the law book as a symbol of kingship.[5] Ezra's reforms (re-)assert the authority of Torah (under Levitical translation/ instruction) for both leaders *and* commoners alike.[6] Though subtle, there does seem to be a rising gradation of authority attached to Israel's law writings in these events. However, development in a law book's authority is not necessarily the same thing as a change in its practical function.[7]

3. *Changing Torah functions*—Examination of the law-practice materials from periods connected with Torah's rising authority showed an absence of *legislative function*. These results have confirmed the need to distinguish this third facet of Torah's evolution from the previous one. What a law book is, and thus how it is used, does not necessarily change on account of new authority accorded to it (any more than ascribing household proverbs to Solomon's court made them legislative). This is an important corrective (or clarification) offered by the present project for current scholarship. Within the biblical literature, there are indications of multiple functions for law writings: memorial inscription; ritual

---

3. Dating Deuteronomy (either its composition or its royal sanction) to the Josianic reform is, of course, a matter of controversy (see pp. 56–57, above).

4. See pp. 46–47, above.

5. See p. 93, above.

6. See, pp. 131–32, above.

7. See especially pp. 141–43, above.

reading; archival deposit; private and public pedagogy; and per-haps others.[8] These are, nonetheless, all functions which essen-tially regard the law book as an ideal but not itself as "the law." The radical re-characterization of Torah as itself the source of law has been placed in the Hellenistic era based on assessments of the law book's use. It is in this third plane—changes in the *functions* (or uses) of law writings—that the identification of Torah as description or prescription is to be discerned. Develop-ments on this level must therefore be carefully distinguished from changes in content or increasing authority.

At the risk of oversimplification, these three lines of Torah's develop-ment point can be displayed in the diagram opposite.

3. *Analyses of the Law-Practice Materials of Josiah and Ezra–Nehemiah*
Josiah's reforms and those of Ezra and Nehemiah are central to the ques-tion of the law book's use in the late monarchy and post-exilic period. To date, however, a systematic examination of the relevant law-practice materials for those reforms has been lacking. The completion of such an examination (in Chapters 3 and 4) has been an important feature of this project.

4. *A Hypothesis for Two Mechanisms behind Torah's Re-characterization*
Since the prescriptivization of Torah has not previously been dated to the Hellenistic period, it was necessary to explore the possible forces of *that era* which brought it about "then." Scholars have sometimes connected Torah's re-conception as a law code with other mechanisms, especially the dynamics of an oral society becoming a literate society.[9] The present study does not contradict the presence of such forces behind *generic* cognitive shifts in Hebrew society, or their likely "contributing influ-ence" on changes in Jewish legal thought. But this project has introduced two key mechanisms effecting *legal institutions specifically* which can be dated to the *Hellenistic* period (when Torah begins to take on a legislative character): the court reform of Ptolemy II (Chapter 5) and the polemical force of Hellenistic, "rule of law"-centered ethnography (Chapter 6).

---

8   See pp. 37–38, above. This study has not attempted to identify whether these *various* descriptivistic functions were co-operative or each reflective of different layers of development.

9. Fitzpatrick-McKinley, *Transformation*, 152–55; Jackson, *Studies*, 70–75; Grabbe, *Ezra–Nehemiah*, 194–95. Cf. Niditch, *Oral World*.

Distinguishing Three Aspects of Torah's Development

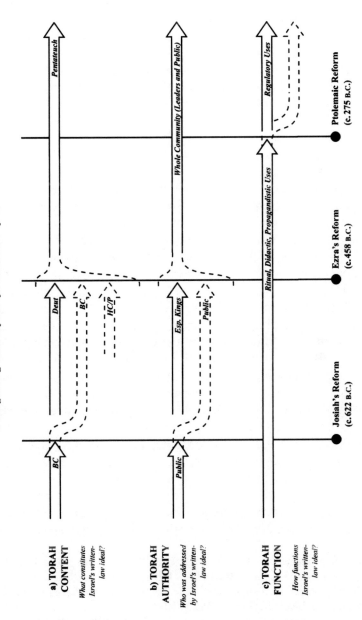

a) TORAH CONTENT

What constitutes Israel's written-law ideal?

b) TORAH AUTHORITY

Who was addressed by Israel's written-law ideal?

c) TORAH FUNCTION

How functions Israel's written-law ideal?

BC

Deut

BC

HC/P

Pentateuch

Public

Esp. Kings

Public

Whole Community (Leaders and Public)

Ritual, Didactic, Propagandistic Uses

Regulatory Uses

Josiah's Reform
(c. 622 B.C.)

Ezra's Reform
(c. 458 B.C.)

Ptolemaic Reform
(c. 275 B.C.)

II. *Projected Implications/Further Research*

As noted at the head of this chapter, the literary and historical breadth of
the model constructed in this project leaves it open to further study and
potential revision. Nevertheless, the significance of the whole idea of law
for virtually every department of biblical (and related) studies indicates
the value of pursuing it—and the potential for ramifications as it is
developed and utilized. Some of the ramifications (and areas for further
study) opened up by this project can be indicated below.

1. *Hebrew Bible Studies*

Few concepts are as pervasive in the biblical literature as "law."[10] Sensitivity to what law is, and how the written law works, for a given text
has important implications for how it is understood. For instance, what is
to be made of the "happy man" in Ps 1 meditating upon Torah? Why is
Torah his day-and-night delight? What, indeed, is he *doing* with the
Torah he studies? Psalm 1 is an interesting illustration since it is a text
which likely emerges from post-exilic Yehud. If Torah was by that time
a law code, then Ps 1 conveys legalistic assumptions. If, as has here been
argued, "the law" continued to be conceived as an unwritten order
described (but not embodied) in the written Torah, Ps 1 would need to be
approached accordingly.[11] A model for Torah's reconceptualization
offers an important framework for approaching texts involving law/law
books. This point is double-sided, of course. Ultimately, it is not the
framework that decides how texts are read; it is the evidence of biblical
texts that define the model. Where texts are clearly prescriptive in their
handling of the law book, either that text's provenance or the model will
need to be accommodated. In any case, the idea of law is too important to
the biblical literature to be left to assumption: a model for shifting ideas
about law (and law writings) is critical to Hebrew Bible studies.

2. *Judaic Studies*

One of the most far-reaching implications of the present study is that, by
pushing the period of Torah's prescriptivization into the Hellenistic era

10. Kaiser regards תורה as the sought-after "center" of the Hebrew Bible (Otto
Kaiser, "The Law as Center of the Hebrew Bible," in *"Shaʿarei Talmon": Studies in
the Bible, Qumran, and the Ancient Near East Presented to Shemaryahu Talmon*
[Winona Lake, Ind.: Eisenbrauns, 1992], 93–103).

11. Cf. these observations with those of Michael LeFebvre, "Torah-Meditation
and the Psalms: The Invitation of Psalm 1," in *Interpreting the Psalms: Issues and
Approaches* (ed. Philip S. Johnston and David G. Firth; Leicester: InterVarsity,
2005), 213–25.

(with practical ramifications continuing to reverberate into later generations), the issue has been opened up to a much wider sphere of scholarship. The matter of Torah's originally descriptive function, and its re-characterization as legislation, has generally been treated as a curiosity of Hebrew Bible studies. It has now been laid at the front doorstep of Early Judaic and New Testament studies. Chapter 7 has shown, in a preliminary fashion, the way in which this concern could have a bearing on how early Judaic sects are understood. Sectarian developments may involve more than competing interpretations of Torah prescriptions, but different views of what Torah is, how it functions, and how (or whether) received traditions need to be harmonized with received texts. Though the re-characterization of Torah was evidently widespread from the Hellenistic period, it cannot be assumed that all Judaic circles embraced it. The actual history of Torah's recasting as a legal source remains to be worked out on a case-by-case, sect-by-sect basis. By offering an answer to one question (How did this transition come about?), this study has set the stage for posing yet others (How did this transition work out in one sect or another?).

3. *New Testament Studies*

Making sense of the various sentiments toward the Mosaic law displayed in the New Testament literature is one of the perpetual dilemmas of New Testament studies. Current debates over Paul's doctrine of justification, for instance—the so-called "New Perspective on Paul"—include questions about the legal attitudes of Paul and those of his stereotyped adversaries.[12] By bringing the re-characterization of Torah into the Greco-Roman era, this study exposes a previously unnoticed aspect of the legal conflicts of Paul's time. It consequently offers an important new framework for assessing New Testament views on Torah.

4. *Christian Theology*

As noted in an earlier chapter, the theology of the Christian Church has long interpreted Jesus as advocating the abrogation of Torah. His (and Paul's) perplexing statements, at once upholding and then overruling, the Torah have led to the classical construct: the ceremonial law is abolished; the civil law is repealed; only the moral law (i.e. the Ten Commandments) remains in force.[13] If the interpretation of Jesus suggested in

12. Stephen Westerholm, *Perspectives Old and New on Paul: The "Lutheran" Paul and his Critics* (Grand Rapids: Eerdmans, 2004), especially 297–340.

13. See p. 252, above. Many theologians have endeavored to move beyond the classical, tripartite division of biblical law. Nevertheless, new approaches still

Chapter 7 were to be further developed and found correct, a re-assessment of this point of longstanding Christian theology would be required. The present study has barely introduced a possible window into Jesus' approach to Torah, and thus cannot be considered as having demonstrated it. Nonetheless, the model which has been constructed in this project, and the question of its intersection with Christian theology, requires further attention..

5. *Contemporary Ethics*

Though the "law code" of an ancient and extinct society, the Torah of Moses (especially the Ten Commandments) has enjoyed considerable influence on Western ethics.[14] Not only in regard to enduring ethical matters (such as honesty and sexual fidelity), but also with respect to current "front page news" debates (such as homosexual marriage, stem-cell research, and just-war theory), the voices of the church, synagogue (and mosque) have exercised important influence. The appropriateness and methodology for drawing upon the Torah for addressing current ethical dilemmas remains controversial.[15] The question is far outside the scope of anything touched on directly by this project; nevertheless, the issues here raised should prompt exploration of potential ramifications for the field of ethics. For instance, the simplistic assumption—Moses enjoined stoning adulterers (Deut 22:24) *therefore* God-fearing judges in ancient Israel always stoned adulterers—is not only historically inaccurate,[16] it introduces a potentially catastrophic expectation on biblically

---

frequently reflect a presupposition that Torah was a civil law code for ancient Israel leading to a theological construct to justify its "abrogation" today (e.g. J. Daniel Hays, "Applying the Old Testament Law Today," *BS* 158.629 [2001]: 30). Other modern approaches still reflect the influence of the classical construct (see Jonathan F. Bayes, *The Weakness of the Law: God's Law and the Christian in New Testament Perspective* [Paternoster Biblical and Theological Monographs; Carlisle: Paternoster, 2000], 44–52).

14. E.g. Paul Grimely Kuntz, *The Ten Commandments in History: Mosaic Paradigms for a Well-Ordered Society* (Grand Rapids: Eerdmans, 2004).

15. See Christopher J. H. Wright, "The Ethical Authority of the Old Testament: A Survey of Approaches. Part I," *TynBul* 43, no. 1 (1992): 101–20, and "The Ethical Authority of the Old Testament: A Survey of Approaches. Part II," *TynBul* 43, no. 2 (1992): 203–31.

16. "We have no instance of the biblical [sanctions] on adultery actually being put into effect... Public humiliation (and presumably divorce), was sometimes practiced... The wisdom writings imply that the main sanctions to be feared were loss of reputation and the wrath of the offended husband" (McKeating, "Sanctions," 59, 62).

trained ethicists dealing with the same issue today.[17] A sharpened understanding of how the law writings were used by Israel's leadership (here
modeled in its basic contours from Moses to the Maccabees, and projected
forward from there) introduces an important framework for Christian and
Jewish ethicists seeking to consider their own appropriation of biblical
law.

*   *   *

Reverence for the Mosaic law writings are a common theme running
through each of the aforementioned fields, and others besides. It is hard
to overstate the importance of properly assessing Torah's function and
bringing that to bear on these fields. At risk of seeming "over bold," the
above areas of implication are here indicated to highlight the importance
of modeling the use of Torah. Drafting such a model has been the task
begun by this project.

17. See Tremper Longman III critique of contemporary arguments (with cita-
tions) for enforcing Mosaic penology, in his "God's Law and Mosaic Punishments
Today," in *Theonomy: A Reformed Critique* (ed. William S. Barker and W. Robert
Godfrey; Grand Rapids: Zondervan, 1990), 41–54.

BIBLIOGRAPHY

Abel, F. M. *Les Livres des Maccabées.* Paris: Gabalda, 1949.

Adang, Camilla. *Muslim Writers on Judaism and the Hebrew Bible: From Ibn Rabban to Ibn Hazm.* Leiden: Brill, 1996.

Aeschylus. *The Persians.* Pages 107–207 in *Aeschylus.* Translated by Herbert Weir Smyth. 2 vols. LCL. London: Heinemann, 1922.

Albertz, Rainer. *A History of Israelite Religion in the Old Testament Period.* Translated by John Bowden. 2 vols. OTL. Louisville, Ky.: Westminster John Knox, 1994.

Allam, S. "Egyptian Law Courts in Pharaonic and Hellenistic Times." *JEA* 77 (1991): 109–27.

Allen, Leslie C., and Timothy S. Laniak. *Ezra, Nehemiah, Esther.* NIBC 9. Carlisle: Paternoster Press, 2003.

Alt, Albrecht. *Essays in Old Testament History and Religion.* Oxford: Blackwell, 1966.

Andocides. *On the Mysteries.* Pages 323–451 in *Minor Attic Orators I: Antiphon; Andocides.* Translated by K. J. Maidment. LCL. London: Heinemann, 1941.

Aquinas, Thomas. *Summa Theologiæ.* Translated by Thomas Gilby. Cambridge: Blackfriars, 1966.

Aristotle. *The Athenian Constitution; The Eudemian Ethics; On Virtues and Vices.* Translated by H. Rackham. LCL. London: Heinemann, 1935.

—*The Politics.* Translated by H. Rackham. LCL. London: Heinemann, 1932.

Arrian. *Anabasis Alexandri.* Translated by P. A. Blunt. LCL. London: Heinemann, 1983.

Avery-Peck, Alan J. "The Mishnah, Tosefta, and the Talmuds." Pages 173–216 in *Judaism in Late Antiquity.* Vol. 1, *The Literary and Archaeological Sources.* Edited by Jacob Neusner. HO 16. Leiden: Brill, 1995.

—"Oral Tradition: Early Judaism." *ABD* 5:34–35.

Bagnall, Roger S. *The Administration of the Ptolemaic Possessions Outside Egypt.* Columbia Studies in the Classical Tradition 4. Leiden: Brill, 1976.

—"Ptolemaic Administration." Appendix I, pages 253–55 in Bagnall and Derow, eds., *Greek Documents.*

Bagnall, Roger S., and Peter Derow, eds. *Greek Historical Documents: The Hellenistic Period.* Edited by Roger S. Bagnall and Peter Derow. SBLSBS 16. Chico, Calif.: Scholars Press, 1981.

Bammel, Ernst, et al., eds. *Donum Gentilicium: New Testament Studies in Honour of D. Daube.* Oxford: Oxford University Press, 1978.

Barmash, Pamela. "The Narrative Quandry: Cases of Law in Literature." *VT* 54, no. 1 (2004): 1–16.

Bar-Kochva, Bezalel. *Judas Maccabaeus: The Jewish Struggle Against the Seleucids.* Cambridge: Cambridge University Press, 1989.

Barrick, W. Boyd. *The King and the Cemeteries: Toward a New Understanding of Josiah's Reform.* VTSup 88. Leiden: Brill, 2002.

Barth, Gerhard. "Matthew's Understanding of the Law." Pages 58–164 in *Tradition and Interpretation in Matthew*. Edited by Gunther Bornkamm et al. Translated by Percy Scott. London: SCM Press, 1963.

Bartlett, John R. *1 Maccabees*. Guides to the Apocrypha and Pseudepigrapha 5. Sheffield: Sheffield Academic Press, 1998.

—*The First and Second Books of the Maccabees*. Cambridge: Cambridge University Press, 1973.

Baumgarten, Joseph M. "The Disqualification of Priests in 4Q Fragments of the 'Damascus Document': A Specimen of the Recovery of Pre-Rabbinic Halakha." Pages 503–13 in *Madrid Qumran Congress: Proceedings of the International Congress on the Dead Sea Scrolls, Madrid, 18–21 March, 1991*. Edited by Julio Trebolle Barrera and Luis Vegas Montaner. 2 vols. STDJ 11. Leiden: Brill, 1992.

—*Studies in Qumran Law*. SJLA 24. Leiden: Brill, 1977.

Bayes, Jonathan F. *The Weakness of the Law: God's Law and the Christian in New Testament Perspective*. Paternoster Biblical and Theological Monographs. Carlisle: Paternoster, 2000.

Berlin, Adele, et al. *1 & 2 Maccabees, Job, Psalms*. New Interpreter's Bible 4. Nashville: Abingdon, 1996.

Berquist, Jon L. *Judaism in Persia's Shadow: A Social and Historical Approach*. Minneapolis: Fortress Press, 1995.

Betz, Hans Dieter. *The Sermon on the Mount*. Minneapolis: Fortress, 1995.

Bickerman, Elias. "La Charte séleucide de Jérusalem." Pages 44–85 in vol. 2 of *Studies in Jewish and Christian History*. 3 vols. AGJU 9. Leiden: Brill, 1980. Repr. from *Revue des Études Juives* 100 (1935): 4–35.

—*The God of the Maccabees: Studies on the Meaning and Origin of the Maccabean Revolt*. SJLA 32. Leiden: Brill, 1979.

—"Ein jüdischer Festbrief vom Jahre 124 v. Chr. (II Macc. 1.1–9)." *ZNW* 32 (1933): 233–54.

—*The Jews in the Greek Age*. London: Harvard University Press, 1988.

—"Makkabäerbücher: Buch I–III." In PW, 14.1.779–805.

—"Une proclamation séleucide relative au temple de Jérusalem." Pages 86–104 in vol. 2 of *Studies in Jewish and Christian History*. 3 vols. AGJU 9. Leiden: Brill, 1980. Repr. from *Syria* 25 (1946–48): 67–85.

—*Studies in Jewish and Christian History*. 3 vols. AGJU 9. Leiden: Brill, 1976–86.

Blenkinsopp, Joseph. *Ezra–Nehemiah: A Commentary*. London: SCM Press, 1988.

—"Interpretation and the Tendency to Sectarianism." Pages 1–26 in *Jewish and Christian Self-Definition*. Vol. 2, *Two Aspects of Judaism in the Greco-Roman Period*. Edited by E. P. Sanders. London: SCM Press, 1981.

—"The Mission of Udjahorresnet and Those of Ezra and Nehemiah." *JBL* 106, no. 3 (1987): 409–21.

—*The Pentateuch: An Introduction to the First Five Books of the Bible*. New York: Doubleday, 1992.

—"Was the Pentateuch the Civic and Religious Constitution of the Jewish Ethnos in the Persian Period?" Pages 41–62 in Watts, ed., *Persia and Torah*.

Bockmuehl, Marcus. *Jewish Law in Gentile Churches: Halakhah and the Beginning of Christian Public Ethics*. Edinburgh: T. & T. Clark, 2000.

Boecker, Hans Jochen. *Law and the Administration of Justice in the Old Testament and Ancient East*. Translated by J. Moiser. London: SPCK, 1980.

Boling, Robert G. *Joshua: A New Translation and Commentary.* AB 6. Garden City, N.Y.: Doubleday, 1988.

Borgen, Peder. "Philo of Alexandria." *ABD* 5:333–42.

Bottéro, Jean. "Le 'Code' de Hammurabi." *Annali della Scuola Normale Superiore di Pisa classe di lettere e filosofia* 12. no. 3 (1982): 409–44.

—*Mesopotamia: Writing, Reasoning, and the Gods.* Translated by Zainab Bahrani and Marc van de Mieroop. London: University of Chicago, 1992.

Braulik, Greg. "The Sequence of the Laws in Deuteronomy 12–26 and the Decalogue." Pages 313–35 in Christensen, ed., *Song of Power.* Trans. of "Die Aberfolge der Gesetze in Deuteronomium 12–26 und der Dekalog." Pages 252–72 in Lohfink, ed., *Deuteronomium.*

Breneman, Mervin. *Ezra, Nehemiah, Esther.* NAC 10. Nashville: Broadman & Holman. 1993.

Brockington, L. H., ed. *Ezra, Nehemiah and Esther.* The Century Bible. London: Thomas Nelson, 1969.

Brooke, George, ed. "1Q28b: 1QSerekh ha-Yaḥad b (fragment)." Pages 227–34 in *Qumran Cave 4.XIX: 4QSerekh Ha-Yaḥad.* Edited by P. H. Alexander and G. Vermes. DJD 26. Oxford: Clarendon, 1998.

—ed. *Jewish Ways of Reading the Bible.* JSSSup 11. Oxford: Oxford University Press, 2000.

—"Reading the Plain Meaning of Scripture in the Dead Sea Scrolls." Pages 67–90 in Brooke, ed., *Ways of Reading.*

Brooks, Roger. "Mishnah." *ABD* 4:871–73.

Brunt, Peter A. "The Aims of Alexander." Pages 45–53 in *Alexander the Great: A Reader.* Edited by Ian Worthington. London: Routledge, 2003.

Budd, Philip J. *Numbers.* WBC 5. Waco, Tex.: Word, 1984.

Butler, Trent C. *Joshua.* WBC 7. Waco, Tex.: Word, 1983.

Cagni, Luigi. *The Poem of Erra.* Sources and Monographs: Sources from the Ancient Near East 1/3. Malibu, Calif.: Undena, 1977.

Campbell, Anthony F., and Mark A. O'Brien. *Unfolding the Deuteronomistic History: Origins, Upgrades, Present Text.* Minneapolis: Fortress, 2000.

Carmichael, Calum. *Law and Narrative in the Bible: The Evidence of the Deuteronomic Laws and the Decalogue.* London: Cornell University Press, 1985.

—*The Laws of Deuteronomy.* London: Cornell University Press, 1974.

—"Laws of Leviticus 19." *HTR* 87, no. 3 (1994): 239–56.

—*The Origins of Biblical Law: The Decalog and the Book of the Covenant.* London: Cornell University Press, 1992.

—*The Spirit of the Law.* Athens, Ga.: University of Georgia Press, 1996.

Carpenter, Eugene E. "Exodus 18: Its Structure, Style, Motifs and Function in the Book of Exodus." Pages 91–108 in *A Biblical Itinerary: In Search of Method, Form and Content. Essays in Honor of George W. Coats.* Edited by Eugene E. Carpenter. JSOTSup 240. Sheffield: Sheffield Academic Press, 1997.

Carr, David M. *Reading the Fractures of Genesis: Historical and Literary Approaches.* Louisville, Ky.: Westminster John Knox, 1996.

Carroll, Robert P. *Jeremiah: A Commentary.* OTL. London: SCM Press, 1986.

Catechism of the Catholic Church: Revised Edition. London: Chapman, 1999.

Chamberlain, Gary Alan. "Exodus 21–23 and Deuteronomy 12–26: A Form-Critical Study." Ph.D. diss., Boston University Graduate School, 1977.

Childs, Brevard S. *Exodus: A Commentary*. OTL. London: SCM Press, 1974.

—Review of Michael Fishbane, *Biblical Interpretation in Ancient Israel*. *JBL* 106, no. 3 (1987): 511–63.

Chirichigno, Gregory C. *Debt-Slavery in Israel and the Ancient Near East*. JSOTSup 141. Sheffield: JSOT Press, 1993.

Christensen, Duane, ed. *A Song of Power and the Power of Song: Essays on the Book of Deuteronomy*. Sources for Biblical and Theological Study 3. Winona Lake, Ind.: Eisenbrauns, 1993.

Civil, Miguel. "New Sumerian Law Fragments." Pages 1–12 in Güterbock and Jacobsen, eds., *Studies in Honor of Benno Landsberger*.

Clifford, Richard J. *Proverbs: A Commentary*. OTL. Louisville, Ky.: Westminster John Knox, 1999.

Clines, D. J. A. *Ezra, Nehemiah, Esther*. NCB. Grand Rapids: Eerdmans, 1984.

—"Nehemiah 10 as an Example of Early Jewish Biblical Exegesis." *JSOT* 21 (1981): 111–17.

Clinton, Kevin. "The Nature of the Late Fifth-Century Revision of the Athenian Law Code." Pages 27–37 in *Studies in Attic Epigraphy, History and Topography: Presented to Eugene Vanderpool*. *Hesperia* Supplement 19. Princeton: American School of Classical Studies in Athens, 1982.

Coats, George W. *Exodus 1–18*. FOTL 2A. Grand Rapids: Eerdmans, 1999.

Cogan, Mordechai, and Hayim Tadmor. *II Kings: A New Translation with Introduction and Commentary*. AB 11. Garden City, N.Y.: Doubleday, 1988.

Cohen, G. M. "The 'Antiochenes in Jerusalem', Again." Pages 243–59 in *Pursuing the Text: Studies in Honor of Ben Zion Wacholder on the Occasion of his Seventieth Birthday*. Edited by John C. Reeves and John Kampen. JSOTSup 184. Sheffield: Sheffield Academic Press.

Cohen, Mark E. *The Cultic Calendars of the Ancient Near East*. Bethesda, Md.: CDL Press, 1993.

Cohen, Shayne J. D. "Religion, Ethnicity, and 'Hellenism' in the Emergence of Jewish Identity in Maccabean Palestine." Pages 204–23 in *Religion and Religious Practice in the Seleucid Kingdom*. Studies in Hellenistic Civilization 1. Edited by Per Bilde et al. Arhaus: Arhaus University Press, 1990.

Collins, John J. "Artapanus." *OTP* 2:889–903.

—*Between Athens and Jerusalem: Jewish Identity in the Hellenistic Diaspora*. Grand Rapids: Eerdmans, 2000.

Cook, J. M. *The Persian Empire*. London: Dent, 1983.

Cook, S. L. "The Tradition of Mosaic Judges: Past Approaches and New Directions." Pages 286–315 in *On the Way to Nineveh: Studies in Honor of George M. Landes*. Edited by Stephen L. Cook and Sara C. Winter. Atlanta: Scholars Press, 1999.

Corbett, Richard. *The Treaty of Maastrich—From Conception to Ratification: A Comprehensive Reference Guide*. Essex: Longman, 1994.

Craigie, Peter C. *The Book of Deuteronomy*. NICOT. London: Hodder & Stoughton, 1976. Reprint, Grand Rapids: Eerdmans, 1994.

Cross, Frank Moore. "Introduction." Pages 1–5 in *Scrolls from Qumrân Cave I: The Great Isaiah Scroll, The Order of the Community, The Pesher to Habakkuk from Photographs by John C. Trever*. Edited by Frank Moore Cross et al. Jerusalem: Albright Institute of Archaeological Research and the Shrine of the Book, 1972.

Crüsemann, Frank. *The Torah: Theology and Social History of Old Testament Law.* Translated by A. W. Mahnke. Edinburgh: T. & T. Clark, 1996. Trans. of *Die Tora: Theologie und Sozialgeschichte des alttestamentlichen Gesetzes.* Munich: Kaiser, 1992.

Dam, Cornelis van. *The Urim and Thummim: A Means of Revelation in Ancient Israel.* Winona Lake, Ind.: Eisenbrauns, 1997.

Danby, Herbert. *The Mishnah.* Oxford: Clarendon, 1933.

Dancy, J. C. *A Commentary on I Maccabees.* Oxford: Blackwell, 1954.

Daube, David. "Rabbinic Methods of Interpretation and Hellenistic Rhetoric." *HUCA* 22 (1949): 239–64.

Davies, Philip R. "Halakhah at Qumran." Pages 37–50 in Davis and White, eds., *A Tribute to Geza Vermes.*

—*In Search of "Ancient Israel."* JSOTSup 148. Sheffield: Sheffield Academic Press, 1992.

—"'Law' in Early Judaism." Pages 13–33 in Neusner and Avery-Peck, eds., *Judaism in Late Antiquity III.*

—"A Note on I Macc. III. 46." *JTS* 23 (1972): 117–21.

Davies, Philip R., and Richard T. White, eds. *A Tribute to Geza Vermes: Essays on Jewish and Christian Literature and History.* JSOTSup 100. Sheffield: JSOT Press, 1990.

Davies, Norman de Garis. *The Tomb of Rekh-mi-rēʿ at Thebes.* 2 vols. The Metropolitan Museum of Art, Egyptian Expedition 11. New York: Plantum, 1943.

Démare (-Lafont), Sofie. "Le valeur de la loi dans les droits cunéiformes." *Archives des philosophie du droit* 32 (1987): 337–46.

Diodoros. *History.* Translated by C. H. Oldfather. LCL. London: Heinemann, 1933.

Diogenes. *Lives of the Philosophers.* Translated by R. D. Hicks. LCL. London: Heinemann, 1925.

Doran, Robert. "1 Maccabees." Pages 1–178 in Berlin et al., eds., *1 & 2 Maccabees.*

—"2 Maccabees." Pages 179–299 in Berlin et al., eds., *1 & 2 Maccabees.*

—"Cleodemus Malchus." *OTP* 2:883–87.

—"Independence or Co-Existence: The Responses of 1 and 2 Maccabees to Seleucid Hegemony." *SBLSP* 38 (1999): 94–103.

—"Pseudo-Eupolemus." *OTP* 2:873–82.

—"Pseudo-Hecataeus." *OTP* 2:905–19.

—*Temple Propaganda: The Purpose and Character of 2 Maccabees.* CBQMS 12. Washington, D.C.: Catholic Biblical Association of America, 1981.

Driver, G. R., and J. C. Miles. *The Babylonian Laws.* Oxford: Clarendon, 1952.

Duggan, Michael W. *The Covenant Renewal in Ezra–Nehemiah (Neh 7:72b–10:40): An Exegetical, Literary, and Theological Study.* SBLDS 164. Atlanta: Society of Biblical Literature, 2001.

Durham, John I. *Exodus.* WBC 3. Waco, Tex.: Word, 1987.

Eaton, J. H. *Psalms of the Way and the Kingdom: A Conference with the Commentators.* JSOTSup 199. Sheffield: Sheffield Academic Press, 1995.

Edgar, C. C. *Catalogue Général des Antiquités Égyptiennes du Musée du Caire: Zenon Papyri.* 5 vols. Cairo: Imprimerie de l'Institut Français d'Archéologie Orientale, 1925–28.

Enns, Peter E. *Exodus.* NIVAC. Grand Rapids: Zondervan, 2000.

Eusebius. *Praeparatio evangelica.* Oxonii: E Typographeo Academico, 1903.

Eynikel, Erik. *The Reform of King Josiah and the Composition of the Deuteronomistic History.* OTS 33. Leiden: Brill, 1996.

Fallon, Francis T. "Eupolemus." *OTP* 2:861–72.

Feinberg, Charles L. *Jeremiah: A Commentary.* Grand Rapids: Zondervan, 1982.

Feldman, Louis H. "Hengel's Judaism and Hellenism in Retrospect." *JBL* 96, no. 3 (1977): 371–82.

—"How Much Hellenism in the Land of Israel?" *JSJ* 33, no. 3 (2002): 290–313.

—"Torah and Secular Culture: Challenge and Response in the Hellenistic Period." Pages 487–503 in *Studies in Hellenistic Judaism.* Edited by Louis H. Feldman. Leiden: Brill, 1996.

Fensham, F. Charles. *The Books of Ezra and Nehemiah.* NICOT. Grand Rapids: Eerdmans, 1982.

Finkelstein, J. J. "Ammi-Ṣaduqa's Edict and the Babylonian 'Law Codes.'" *JCS* 15 (1961): 91–104.

—*The Ox That Gored.* Transactions of the American Philosophical Society 71/2. Philadelphia: American Philosophical Society, 1981.

—"Some New *Misharum* Material and its Implications." Pages 233–46 in Güterbock and Jacobsen, eds., *Studies in Honor of Benno Landsberger.*

Fischel, Henry A. *The First Book of Maccabees.* New York: Schocken, 1948.

Fishbane, Michael. *Biblical Interpretation in Ancient Israel.* Oxford: Clarendon, 1985.

—*The Exegetical Imagination: On Jewish Thought and Theology.* Cambridge, Mass.: Harvard University Press, 1998.

—"From Scribalism to Rabbinism: Perspectives on the Emergence of Classical Judaism." Pages 439–56 in *The Sage in Israel and the Ancient Near East.* Edited by John G. Gammie and Leo G. Perdue. Winona Lake, Ind.: Eisenbrauns, 1990.

—*The Garments of Torah.* Indianapolis: Indiana University Press, 1989.

—"Midrash and the Meaning of Scripture." Pages 549–63 in *The Interpretation of the Bible: The International Symposium in Slovenia.* Edited by Joze Krašovec. JSOTSup 289. Sheffield: Sheffield Academic Press, 1998.

—"*Varia Deuteronomica.*" *ZAW* 84 (1972): 349–52.

Fitzpatrick-McKinley, Anne. *The Transformation of Torah from Scribal Advice to Law.* JSOTSup 287. Sheffield: Sheffield Academic Press, 1999.

Flint, Peter W., and James C. VanderKam, eds. *The Dead Sea Scrolls After Fifty Years: A Comprehensive Assessment.* 2 vols. Leiden: Brill, 1998.

Fox, Michael V. *The Song of Songs and the Ancient Egyptian Love Songs.* Madison: University of Wisconsin Press, 1985.

France, R. T. *Matthew: Evangelist and Teacher.* Downer's Grove, Ill.: InterVarsity, 1989.

Frankfort, Henri. *Kingship and the Gods: A Study of Ancient Near Eastern Religion as the Integration of Society and Nature.* Chicago: University of Chicago Press, 1978.

Fraser, P. M. *Cities of Alexander the Great.* Oxford: Clarendon, 1996.

Frei, Peter, and Klaus Koch. *Reichsidee und Reichsorganisation im Perserreich.* OBO 55. Fribourg: Universitätsverlag, 1984.

Frei, Peter. "Persian Imperial Authorization: A Summary." Pages 5–40 in Watts, ed., *Persia and Torah.* Trans. of "Die persische Reichsautorisation: Ein Überblick." *ZABR* 1 (1995): 1–35.

Fried, Lisbeth S. "'You Shall Appoint Judges': Ezra's Mission and the Rescript of Artaxerxes." Pages 63–89 in Watts, ed., *Persia and Torah.*

Fritz, Volkmar. *1 & 2 Kings*. Translated by Anselm Hagedorn. Continental Commentary. Minneapolis: Fortress, 2003.

Gagarin, Michael. *Early Greek Law*. Berkeley: University of California Press, 1986.

Garner, Richard. *Law and Society in Classical Athens*. London: Croom Helm, 1987.

Garrett, Duane A. "Song of Songs." Pages 1–265 in Duane A. Garrett and Paul R. House, *Song of Songs/Lamentations*. WBC 23B. Nashville: Thomas Nelson, 2004.

Gaster, Moses. *Samaritan Eschatology: The Belief of the Samaritans in Immortality, Resurrection, Future Punishment and Reward, the Taheb and the Second Kingdom*. The Samaritan Oral Law and Ancient Traditions 1. London: Search, 1932.

Gauger, Jörg-Dieter. *Beiträge zur jüdischen Apologetik: Untersuchungen zur Authentizität von Urkunden bei Flavius Josephus und im I. Makkabäerbuch*. BBB 49. Cologne: Hannstein, 1977.

—"Formalien und Authentizitätsfrage: noch einmal zum Schreiben Antiochus III. an Zeuxis. (Jos. Ant. Jud. 12: 148–53) und zu den Antiochos-Urkunden bei Josephus." *Hermes* 121 (1993): 63–69.

Georgi, Dieter. *The Opponents of Paul in Second Corinthians*. Edinburgh: T. & T. Clark, 1987.

Gerbrandt, Gerald E. *Kingship According to the Deuteronomistic History*. SBLDS 87. Atlanta: Scholars Press, 1986.

Gibson, Edgar C. S. *The Thirty-Nine Articles of the Church of England: Explained with an Introduction*. London: Methuen, 1902.

Ginsberg, Louis H. *An Unknown Jewish Sect*. New York: The Jewish Theological Society of America, 1976.

Glatt-Gilad, David A. "Reflections on the Structure and Significance of the *ʾămānāh* (Neh 10,29–40)." *ZAW* 112, no. 3 (2000): 386–95.

Goldberg, Arnold. "The Rabbinic View of Scripture." Pages 153–66 in Davies and White, eds., *A Tribute to Geza Vermes*.

Goldhill, Simon. "Battle Narrative and Politics in Aeschylus' *Persae*." Pages 50–61 in Harrison, ed., *Greeks and Barbarians*.

Goldstein, Jonathan A. *I Maccabees: A New Translation with Introduction and Commentary*. AB 41. New York: Doubleday, 1976.

—*II Maccabees: A New Translation with Introduction and Commentary*. AB 41A. New York: Doubleday, 1984.

Goody, Jack. *The Logic of Writing and the Organization of Society*. Cambridge: Cambridge University Press, 1986.

—*The Oriental, the Ancient, and the Primitive: Systems of Marriage and the Family in the Pre-Industrial Societies of Eurasia*. Cambridge: Cambridge University Press, 1990.

Gordon, Cyrus H. "Sabbatical Cycle or Seasonal Pattern? Reflections on a New Book." *Or* 22 (1953): 79–81.

—*Ugaritic Literature: A Comprehensive Translation of the Poetic and Prose Texts*. Rome: Pontifical Institute, 1949.

Grabbe, Lester L. *Ezra–Nehemiah*. London: Routledge, 1998.

—*Judaism From Cyrus to Hadrian*. Vol. 1, *The Persian and Greek Periods*. Minneapolis: Fortress, 1992.

Grainger, John D. *A Seleukid Prosopography and Gazetteer*. Leiden: Brill, 1997.

—*Seleukos Nikator: Constructing a Hellenistic Kingdom*. London: Routledge, 1990.

Graupner, Axel. "Exodus 18,13–27—Ätiologie einer Justizreform in Israel?" Pages 11–26 in *Recht und Ethos im Alten Testament—Gestalt und Wirkung: Festschrift für Horst Seebass zum 65 Geburstag.* Edited by Stefan Beyerle et al. Neukirchen–Vluyn: Neukirchener Verlag, 1999.

Gray, John. *I & II Kings: A Commentary.* OTL. London: SCM Press, 1977.

—*Joshua, Judges, Ruth.* NCBC. Grand Rapids: Eerdmans, 1986.

Greenberg, Moshe. Review of Anthony Phillips, *Ancient Israel's Criminal Law: A New Approach to the Decalogue. JBL* 91, no. 4 (1972): 535–38.

—"Some Postulates of Biblical Criminal Law." Pages 25–41 in Moshe Greenberg, *Studies in the Bible and Jewish Thought.* Philadelphia: The Jewish Publication Society of America, 1995. Repr. from "Some Postulates of Biblical Criminal Law." Pages 5–28 in *Yehezkel Kaufmann Jubilee Volume.* Edited by Menahem Haran. Jerusalem: Magnes, 1960.

—*Studies in the Bible and Jewish Thought.* Philadelphia: The Jewish Publication Society of America, 1995.

Greengus, Samuel. "Law in the Old Testament." *IDBSup* 532–37.

—"Some Issues Relating to the Comparability of Laws and the Coherence of the Legal Tradition." Pages 60–90 in Levinson, ed., *Theory and Method.*

Grimal, Nicolas C. *A History of Ancient Egypt.* Translated by Ian Shaw. Oxford: Blackwell, 1992.

Gruber, Mayer I. "The Mishnah as Oral Torah: A Reconsideration." *JSJ* 15 (1984): 112–22.

Güterbock, Hans Gustav. "Mursili's Accounts of Suppiluliuma's Dealings with Egypt." *RHA* 18.66 (1960): 57–63.

Güterbock, Hans Gustav, and Thorkild Jacobsen, eds. *Studies in Honor of Benno Landsberger on his Seventy-Fifth Birthday, April 21, 1965.* AS 16. Chicago: University of Chicago Press, 1965.

Habicht, Christian. *2. Makkabäerbuch.* JSHRZ 1/3. Gütersloher: Gerd Mohn, 1979.

Hagner, Donald A. *Matthew 14–28.* WBC 33B. Dallas: Word, 1995.

Halivni, David Weiss. *Midrash, Mishnah, and Gemara: The Jewish Predilection for Justified Law.* Cambridge, Mass.: Harvard University Press, 1986.

—*Peshat and Derash: Plain and Applied Meaning in Rabbinic Exegesis.* Oxford: Oxford University Press, 1991.

Hall, Edith. *Inventing the Barbarian: Greek Self-Definition through Tragedy.* Oxford: Clarendon, 1989.

Hallo, William W., and Hayim Tadmor. "A Lawsuit from Hazor." *IEJ* 27 (1977): 1–11.

Hamilton, Jeffries M. *Social Justice and Deuteronomy: The Case of Deuteronomy 15.* SBLDS 136. Atlanta: Scholars Press, 1992.

Hamilton, Victor P. "מָזוֹר" (#4927). *NIDOTTE* 2:971.

Hamlin, E. John. *Inheriting the Land: A Commentary on the Book of Joshua.* ITC. Grand Rapids: Eerdmans, 1983.

Hammond, N. G. L. *Philip of Macedon.* London: Duckworth, 1994.

Handy, Lowell K. "Historical Probability and the Narrative of Josiah's Reform in 2 Kings." Pages 252–75 in *The Pitcher is Broken: Memorial Essays for Gösta W. Ahlström.* Edited by Steven W. Holloway and Lowell K. Handy. JSOTSup 190. Sheffield: Sheffield Academic Press, 1995.

—"The Role of Huldah in Josiah's Cult Reform." *ZAW* 106 (1994): 40–53.

Hansen, Mogens Herman. *The Athenian Ecclesia: A Collection of Articles 1976–1983.* Opuscula Graecolatina 26. Copenhagen: Museum Tusculanum Press, 1983.

—"Did the Athenian *Ecclesia* Legislate after 403/2?" Pages 179–206 in *The Athenian Ecclesia.* Repr. from *GRBS* 20 (1979): 27–53.

—"*Nomos* and *Psephisma* in Fourth-Century Athens." Pages 161–77 in *The Athenian Ecclesia.* Repr. from *GRBS* 19 (1978): 315–30.

Haran, Menahem. "Behind the Scenes of History: Determining the Date of the Priestly Source." *JBL* 100 (1981): 321–33.

Harper, R. F. *Assyrian and Babylonian Letters Belonging to the Kouyunjik Collections of the British Museum.* Decennial Publications, University of Chicago 2/4. Chicago: University of Chicago Press, 1892–1914.

Harrington, Daniel J. *The Maccabean Revolt: Anatomy of a Biblical Revolution.* OTS 1. Wilmington, Del.: Glazier, 1988.

Harrington, Hannah K. "Biblical Law at Qumran." Pages 160–85 in vol. 1 of Flint and VanderKam, eds., *Dead Sea Scrolls After Fifty Years.*

Harrison, A. R. W. "Law-Making at Athens at the End of the Fifth Century B.C." *JHS* 75 (1955): 26–35.

Harrison, Thomas. *The Emptiness of Asia: Aeschylus' Persians and the History of the Fifth Century.* London: Duckworth, 2000.

—ed. *Greeks and Barbarians.* Edinburgh: Edinburgh University Press, 2002.

Hartog, François. *Memories of Odysseus: Frontier Tales from Ancient Greece.* Translated by Janet Lloyd. Edinburgh: Edinburgh University Press, 2001.

—*The Mirror of Herodotus: The Representation of the Other in the Writing of History.* Translated by Janet Lloyd. Berkeley: University of California Press, 1988.

Hauge, Martin Ravndal. *The Descent from the Mountain: Narrative Patterns in Exodus 19–40.* JSOTSup 323. Sheffield: Sheffield Academic Press, 2001.

Hays, J. Daniel. "Applying the Old Testament Law Today." *BS* 158.629 (2001): 21–35.

Hecht, N. S., et al., eds. *An Introduction to the History and Sources of Jewish Law.* Oxford: Clarendon, 1996.

Heel, K. Donker van, ed. *The Legal Manual of Hermopolis (P. Mattha): Text and Translation.* Uitgaven vanwege de Stichting Het Leids Papyrologische Instituut 11. Leiden: Papyrologisch Instituut, 1990.

Hengel, Martin. "The Influence of Hellenistic Civilization in Palestine down to the Maccabean Period." Pages 147–66 in Stone and Satran, eds., *Emerging Judaism.*

—*Judaism and Hellenism: Studies in their Encounter in Palestine During the Early Hellenistic Period.* Translated by John Bowden. 2 vols. London: SCM Press, 1974.

Hentschke, Richard van. *Satzung und Setzender: Ein Beitrag zur israelitischen Rechtsterminologie.* Beiträge zur Wissenschaft vom Alten und Neuen Testament 83/3. Stuttgart: Kohlhammer, 1963.

Herodotus. *Histories.* Translated by A. D. Godley. LCL. London: Heinemann, 1922.

Hobbs, T. R. *2 Kings.* WBC 13. Waco, Tex.: Word, 1985.

Hoftijzer, J. "Description or Categorical Rule? Some Remarks on Ex. 18:16." Pages 193–96 in *Veenhof Anniversary Volume: Studies Presented to Klaas R. Veenhof on the Occasion of his Sixty-Fifth Birthday.* Edited by W. H. Van Soldt et al. Leiden: Nederlands Instituut voor het Nabije Oosten, 2001.

Hoglund, Kenneth G. *Achaemenid Imperial Administration in Syria–Palestine and the Missions of Ezra and Nehemiah.* SBLDS 125. Atlanta: Scholars Press, 1992.

Holladay, Carl R. *Fragments from Hellenistic Jewish Authors.* Vol. 3, *Aristobulus.* SBLTT 39. SBLPS 13. Atlanta: Scholars Press, 1995.

Holladay, William L. *Jeremiah 2: A Commentary on the Book of the Prophet Jeremiah Chapters 26–52.* Hermeneia. Minneapolis: Fortress, 1989.

Holmgren, Fredrick Carlson. *Israel Alive Again: A Commentary on the Books of Ezra and Nehemiah.* ITC. Grand Rapids: Eerdmans, 1987.

Honigman, Sylvie. "The Birth of a Diaspora: The Emergence of a Jewish Self-Definition in Ptolemaic Egypt in the Light of Onomastics." Pages 93–127 in *Diasporas in Antiquity.* Edited by Shayne J. D. Cohen and Ernest S. Frerichs. Atlanta: Scholars Press, 1993.

House, Paul R. *1, 2 Kings.* NAC 8. Nashville: Broadman & Holman, 1995.

Houtman, Cornelis. *Exodus: Volume 2 (Chapters 7:14–19:25).* Historical Commentary on the Old Testament. Translated by S. Woudstra. Kampen: Kok, 1996.

—*Exodus: Volume 3 (Chapters 20–40).* Historical Commentary on the Old Testament. Translated by S. Woudstra. Leuven: Peeters, 1999.

—"Ezra and the Law: Observations on the Supposed Relation Between Ezra and the Pentateuch." Pages 91–115 in *Remembering all the Way.: A Collection of Old Testament Studies Published on the Occasion of the Fortieth Anniversary of the Oudtestamentisch Werkgezelschap in Nederland.* Edited by Bertril Albrektson. OTS 21. Leiden: Brill, 1981.

Instone-Brewer, David. *Techniques and Assumptions in Jewish Exegesis before 70 CE.* TSAJ 30. Tübingen: J. C. B. Mohr, 1992.

Jackson, Bernard S. *Essays in Jewish and Comparative Legal History.* SJLA 10. Leiden: Brill, 1975.

—"From Dharma to Law." *American Journal of Comparative Law* 23 (1975): 490–512.

—"Ideas of Law and Legal Administration: A Semiotic Approach." Pages 185–202 in *The World of Ancient Israel: Sociological, Anthropological and Political Perspectives—Essays by Members of the Society for Old Testament Study.* Edited by Ronald E. Clements. Winona Lake, Ind.: Eisenbrauns, 1989.

—"'Law' and 'Justice' in the Bible." *JJS* 49 (1998): 218–29.

—"Legalism and Spirituality: Historical, Philosophical, and Semiotic Notes on Legislators, Adjudicators, and Subjects." Pages 243–61 in *Religion and Law, Biblical-Judaic and Islamic Perspectives.* Edited by Edwin B. Firmage et al. Winona Lake, Ind.: Eisenbrauns, 1990.

—"Modelling Biblical Law: The Covenant Code." *Chicago-Kent Law Review* 70 (1995): 1745–1827.

—"Models in Legal History: The Case of Biblical Law." *JLR* 18, no. 1 (2002): 1–30.

—"The Original Oral Law." Pages 3–19 in Brooke, ed., *Ways of Reading.*

—Review of Anne Fitzpatrick-McKinley, *The Transformation of Torah from Scribal Advice to Law. JSS* 47, no. 2 (2002): 327–33.

—*Studies in the Semiotics of Biblical Law.* JSOTSup 314. Sheffield: Sheffield Academic Press, 2000.

Jaffee, Martin S. *Torah in the Mouth: Writing and Oral Tradition in Palestinian Judaism 200 BCE–400 CE.* Oxford: Oxford University Press, 2001.

Japhet, Sara. "From the King's Sanctuary to the Chosen City." Pages 3–15 in *Judaism and Hellenism in Antiquity: Conflict or Confluence.* Edited by Lee I. Levine. Peabody, Mass.: Hendrickson, 1999.

Jones, A. H. M. *The Cities of the Eastern Roman Provinces.* Oxford: Clarendon, 1937.

—*The Greek City from Alexander to Justinian.* Oxford: Clarendon, 1979.

278   *Collections, Codes, and Torah*

Jones, J. W. *The Law and Legal Theory of the Greeks: An Introduction.* London: Oxford University Press, 1956.

Jonnes, Lloyd, ed. *The Inscriptions of the Sultan Dağli I: Philomelion, Thymbrion/Hadrianopolis, Tyraion. Inschriften Griechischer Städte aus Kleinasien* 62. Bonn: Rudolf Habelt, 2002.

Josephus. *Josephus.* Translated by H. St. J. Thackeray et al. 13 vols. LCL. London: Heinemann, 1958–65.

Kaiser, Otto. "The Law as Center of the Hebrew Bible." Pages 93–103 in *"Sha'arei Talmon": Studies in the Bible, Qumran, and the Ancient Near East Presented to Shemaryahu Talmon.* Edited by Michael Fishbane and Emmanuel Tov. Winona Lake, Ind.: Eisenbrauns, 1992.

Kampen, John. 1992. "Hasidim." *ABD* 3:66–67.

Kaufman, S. A. Review of Anthony Phillips, *Ancient Israel's Criminal Law: A New Approach to the Decalogue. JNES* 32, no. 1–2 (1971): 279.

Kaufmann, Yehezkel. *History of the Religion of Israel.* Vol. 9, *From the Babylonian Captivity to the End of Prophecy.* Dallas: Institute for Jewish Studies, 1977.

Keil, C. F. *The Books of the Kings.* Translated by James Martin. Volume 3 in C. F. Keil and Franz Delitzsch, *Commentary on the Old Testament.* 10 vols. Grand Rapids: Eerdmans, 1978.

Kennell, Nigel M. "New Light on 2 Maccabees 4:7–15." *JJS* 56, no. 1 (2005): 10–24.

Keown, Gerald C., et al, eds. *Jeremiah 26–52.* WBC 27. Waco, Tex.: Word, 1995.

King, L. W., and R. C. Thompson. *The Sculptures and Inscription of Darius the Great on the Rock of Behistûn in Persia: A New Collation of the Persian, Susian, and Babylonian Texts, with English Translations, Etc.* London: British Museum, 1907.

Klíma, Josef. "La perspective historique des lois hammourabiennes." *CRAI* (1972): 297–317.

Klinghardt, Matthias. "The Manual of Discipline in the Light of Statutes of Hellenistic Associations." Pages 251–70 in *Methods of Investigation of the Dead Sea Scrolls and the Khirbet Qumran Site.* Edited by Michael Wise et al. New York: New York Academy of Sciences, 1994.

Knierim, Rolf P. "The Composition of the Pentateuch." *SBLSP* 24 (1985): 393–415.

—"Exodus 18 und die Neuordnung der Mosaischen Gerichtsbarkeit." *ZAW* 73 (1961): 146–71.

Knoppers, Gary N. "Rethinking the Relationship between Deuteronomy and the Deuteronomistic History: The Case of Kings." *CBQ* 63 (2001): 393–415.

Köhler, Ludwig. *Hebrew Man: Lectures Delivered at the Invitation of the University of Tübingen December 1–16, 1952, with an Appendix on "Justice in the Gate."* Translated by P. R. Ackroyd. London: SCM Press, 1956.

Kooij, A. van der, and K. van der Toorn, eds. *Canonization and Decanonization: Papers Presented to the International Conference of the Leiden Institute for the Study of Religions (LISOR), Held at Leiden 9–10 January 1997.* Leiden: Brill, 1998.

Kraus, F. R. "Ein zentrales Problem des altmesopotamischen Rechtes: Was ist der Codex Hammu-rabi?" *Aspects du contact suméro-akkadien, Geneva* NS 8 (1960): 283–96.

—*Königliche Verfügungen in altbabylonischer Zeit.* Studia et documenta ad iura orientis antiqui pertinentia 11. Leiden: Brill, 1984.

Kruchten, Jean-Marie. "Law." Pages 277–82 in vol. 2 of *The Oxford Encyclopedia of Ancient Egypt.* Edited by Donald B. Redford. New York: Oxford University Press, 2001.

Kugel, James L. "The Need for Interpretation." Pages 27–39 in *Early Biblical Interpretation*. By James L. Kugel and Rowan A. Greer. Edited by Wayne A. Meeks. Philadelphia: Westminster, 1986.

—*Studies in Ancient Midrash*. Cambridge, Mass.: Harvard University Press, 2001.

Kuntz, Paul Grimley. *The Ten Commandments in History: Mosaic Paradigms for a Well-Ordered Society*. Grand Rapids: Eerdmans, 2004.

Lafont, Sophie (Démare-). "Ancient Near Eastern Laws: Continuity and Pluralism." Pages 91–118 in Levinson, ed., *Theory and Method*.

—"Codification et subsidiarité dans les droits du Proche-Orient ancien." Pages 49–64 in Lévy, ed., *Codification*.

Lambert, W. G. *Babylonian Wisdom Literature*. Oxford: Clarendon, 1960.

Landau, Y. H. "A Greek Inscription Found near Hefzibah." *IEJ* 16 (1966): 54–70.

Launderville, Dale. *Piety and Politics*. Grand Rapids: Eerdmans, 2003.

Leemans, W. F. "Quelques considérations à propos d'une étude récente du droit du Proche-Orient ancien." *BO* 48 (1991): 409–37.

LeFebvre, Michael. "Torah-Meditation and the Psalms: The Invitation of Psalm 1." Pages 213–25 in *Interpreting the Psalms: Issues and Approaches*. Edited by Philip S. Johnston and David G. Firth. Leicester: InterVarsity, 2005.

Leichty, E. "The Colophon." Pages 147–54 in *Studies Presented to A. Leo Oppenheim: June 7, 1964*. Edited by Robert D. Biggs et al. Chicago: University of Chicago Press, 1964.

Lemche, Niels Peter. "The Manumission of Slaves—The Fallow Year—The Sabbatical Year—The Jobel Year." *VT* 26 (1976): 38–59.

Levine, Lee I., ed. *Jerusalem: Its Sanctity and Centrality to Judaism, Christianity, and Islam*. New York: Continuum, 1999.

Levinson, Bernard M. "Calum M. Carmichael's Approach to the Laws of Deuteronomy." *HTR* 83, no. 3 (1990): 227–57.

—*Deuteronomy and the Hermeneutics of Legal Innovation*. Oxford: Oxford University Press, 1998.

—"The Reconceptualization of Kingship in Deuteronomy and the Deuteronomistic History's Transformation of Torah." *VT* 51 (2001): 511–34.

—ed. *Theory and Method in Biblical and Cuneiform Law: Revision, Interpolations and Development*. JSOTSup 181. Sheffield: Sheffield Academic Press, 1994.

Lévy, Edmond, ed. *La codification des lois dans l'antiquité: actes du colloque de Strasbourg 27–29 novembre 1997*. Travaux du centre de recherche sur le Proche-Orient et la Grèce antiques 16. Paris: De Boccard, 2000.

Liebesney, Herbert J. "Ein Erlass des Königs Ptolemaios II Philadelphos über die Deklaration von Vieh und Sklaven in Syrien und Phönikien (PER Inv. Nr. 24.552 gr.)" *Aeg* 16 (1936): 257–91.

Lingat, Robert. *The Classical Law of India*. Berkeley: University of California Press, 1973.

Liver, Jacob. "The Half-Shekel Offering in Biblical and Post-Biblical Literature." *HTR* 56 (1963): 173–98.

Loader, William R. G. *Jesus' Attitude towards the Law: A Study of the Gospels*. Grand Rapids: Eerdmans, 2002.

Lohfink, Norbert. "Die deuteronomistische Darstellung des Übergangs der Fëhrung Israels von Moses auf Josue: Ein Beitrag zur alttestamentliche Theologie des Amtes." *Schol* 37 (1962): 32–44.

280   *Collections, Codes, and Torah*

—*Das Deuteronomium: Entstehung, Gestalt und Botschaft.* Edited by Norbert Lohfink. BETL 68. Leuven: Uitgeverij Peeters, 1985.
—"Distribution of the Functions of Power: The Laws Concerning Public Offices in Deuteronomy 16:18–18:22." Pages 336–52 in Christensen, ed., *Song of Power.* Trans. of "Die Sicherung der Wirksamkeit des Gotteswortes durch das Prinzip der Schriftlichkeit der Tora und durch das Prinzip der Gewaltenteilung nach den Ämtergesetzen des Buches Deuteronomium (Dt 16,18–18,22)." Repr. from pages 55–75 in *Great Themes from the Old Testament.* Chicago: Franciscan Herald, 1981.
—"Zur neueren Diskussion über 2 Kön 22–23." Pages 24–48 in *Deuteronomium.* Repr. in "Recent Discussion on 2 Kings 22-23: The State of the Question." Pages 36–61 in Christensen, ed., *Song of Power.*
Long, Burke O. *2 Kings.* FOTL 10. Grand Rapids: Eerdmans, 1991.
Longman, Tremper, III. "God's Law and Mosaic Punishments Today." Pages 41–54 in *Theonomy: A Reformed Critique.* Edited by William S. Barker and W. Robert Godfrey. Grand Rapids: Zondervan, 1990.
Lundbom, Jack R. *Jeremiah 1–20: A New Translation with Introduction and Commentary.* AB 21A. New York: Doubleday, 1999.
—*Jeremiah 21–36: A New Translation with Introduction and Commentary.* AB 21B. New York: Doubleday, 2004.
—"The Lawbook of the Josianic Reform" *CBQ* 38 (1976): 293–302.
Ma, John. *Antiochus III and the Cities of Western Asia Minor.* Oxford: Oxford University Press, 1999.
MacDowell, Douglas M. *The Law in Classical Athens: Aspects of Greek and Roman Life.* London: Thames & Hudson, 1978.
Maine, Henry S. *Ancient Law: Its Connection with the Early History of Society and its Relation to Modern Ideas.* The World Classics. London: Oxford University Press, 1950.
Malul, Meil. *The Comparative Method in Ancient Near Eastern and Biblical Legal Studies.* AOAT 227. Kevelaer: Butzon & Bercker, 1990.
Mandell, Sara R. "Did the Maccabees Believe that They had a Valid Treaty with Rome?" *CBQ* 53 (1991): 202–20.
Marcus, Ralph. "Antiochus III and the Jews (Ant. XII. 129–153)." Appendix D on pages 743–66 in vol. 7 of Josephus, *Josephus.* Translated by H. St. J. Thackeray et al. 13 vols. LCL. London: Heinemann, 1941.
—*Law in the Apocrypha.* New York: Columbia University Press, 1927.
Martola, Nils. *Capture and Liberation: A Study in the Composition of the First Book of Maccabees.* Acta Academiae Aboensis A.63.1. Åbo: Åbo Akademi, 1984.
Mayes, A. D. H. *Deuteronomy.* NCB. London: Marshall, Morgan & Scott, 1981.
McBride, S. Dean, Jr. "Polity of the Covenant People: The Book of Deuteronomy." Pages 62–77 in Christensen, ed., *Song of Power.* Repr. from *Int* 41 (1987): 229–44.
McCarthy, Dennis J. "Covenant and Law in Chronicles–Nehemiah." *CBQ* 44 (1982): 25–44.
—"An Installation Genre?" *JBL* 90 (1971): 31–41.
McConville, J. G. *Deuteronomy.* Apollos Old Testament Commentary 5. Leicester: Apollos, 2002.
—"Deuteronomy, Book of." Pages 182–93 in *Dictionary of the Old Testament: Pentateuch.* Edited by T. Desmond Alexander and David W. Baker. Downers Grove, Ill.: InterVarsity, 2003.

—*Grace in the End: A Study in Deuteronomic Theology.* Grand Rapids: Zondervan, 1993.

—*Law and Theology in Deuteronomy.* JSOTSup 33. Sheffield: JSOT Press, 1986.

McKeating, Henry. "A Response to Dr Phillips by Henry McKeating." *JSOT* 20 (1981): 25–56.

—"Sanctions Against Adultery in Ancient Israelite Society, with Some Reflections on Methodology in the Study of Old Testament Ethics." *JSOT* 11(1979): 57–72.

McNamara, Martin. *Intertestamental Literature.* Wilmington, Del.: Glazier, 1983.

Meier, Christian. *The Greek Discovery of Politics.* Translated by David McLintock. Cambridge, Mass.: Harvard University Press, 1990. Trans. of *Entstehung des Politischen bei den Griechen.* Frankfurt: Suhrkamp, 1980.

Meier, Samuel A. "Hammurapi." *ABD* 3:39–42.

Mendenhall, G. E., and G. A. Herion. "Covenant." *ABD* 1:1179–1202.

Merrill, Eugene H. *Deuteronomy.* NAC 4. Nashville: Broadman & Holman, 1994.

Metso, Sarianna. "Constitutional Rules at Qumran." Pages 186–210 in vol. 1 of Flint and VanderKam, eds., *The Dead Sea Scrolls After Fifty Years.*

—*The Textual Development of the Qumran Community Rule.* STDJ 21. Leiden: Brill, 1997.

Meyer, Eduard. *Ursprung und Anfänge des Christentums.* Stuttgart: J. G. Cotta'sche Buchhandlung Nachfolger, 1921–23.

Miller, Margaret C. *Athens and Persia in the Fifth Century B.C.: A Study in Cultural Receptivity.* Cambridge: Cambridge University Press, 1997.

Modrzejewski, Joseph Mélèze. "Jewish Law and Hellenistic Legal Practice in the Light of Greek Papyri from Egypt." Pages 75–99 in Hecht et al., eds., *An Introduction to the History.*

—*The Jews of Egypt: From Ramses II to Emperor Hadrian.* Translated by R. Cornman. Edinburgh: T. & T. Clark, 1995.

—"Law and Justice in Ptolemaic Egypt." Pages 1–19 in *Legal Documents of the Hellenistic World: Papers from a Seminar arranged by the Institute of Classical Studies, the Institute of Jewish Studies and the Warburg Institute, University of London, February to May 1986.* Edited by Markham J. Geller and Herwig Maehler in collaboration with A. D. E. Lewis. London: The Warburg Institute, 1995.

—"The Septuagint as *Nomos:* How the Torah Became a 'Civil Law' for the Jews of Egypt." Pages 183–99 in *Critical Studies in Ancient Law, Comparative Law and Legal History.* Edited by John W. Cairns and Olivia F. Robinson. Oxford: Hart, 2001.

Mohrlang, Roger. *Matthew and Paul: A Comparison of Ethical Perspectives.* Cambridge: Cambridge University Press, 1984.

Momigliano, Arnaldo D. *Alien Wisdom: The Limits of Hellenization.* Cambridge: Cambridge University Press, 1975.

—"*Beiträge zur jüdischen Apologetik: Untersuchungen zur Authentizität von Urkunden bei Flavius Josephus und im I. Maccabäerbuch.* By Jörg-Dieter Gauger." *CP* 77 (1982): 258–61.

—"The Hellenistic Discovery of Judaism." Pages 129–46 in Stone and Satran, eds., *Emerging Judaism.*

Müller, Manfred. "Sozial- und wirtschaftspolitische Rechtserlässe im Lande Arrapḫa." Pages 53–60 in *Beitrage zur sozialen Struktur des alten Vordersien.* Edited by Horst Klengel. Schriften zur Geschichte und Kultur des alten Orients 1. Berlin: Akademie-Verlag, 1971.

Murphy, Roland. *Proverbs.* WBC 22. Nashville: Thomas Nelson, 1998.

Musaph-Andriesse, R. C. *From Torah to Kabbalah: A Basic Introduction to the Writings of Judaism.* Translated by John Bowden. London: SCM Press, 1981.

Myers, Jacob M. *Ezra–Nehemiah.* AB 14. Garden City, N.Y.: Doubleday, 1965.

Na'aman, Nadav. "Royal Inscriptions and the Histories of Joash and Ahaz, Kings of Judah." *VT* 48 (1998): 333–49.

Najman, Hindy. "Torah of Moses: Pseudonymous Attribution in Second Temple Writings." Pages 202–16 in *The Interpretation of Scripture in Early Judaism and Christianity: Studies in Language and Tradition.* Edited by Craig A. Evans. JSPSup 33. Studies in Scripture in Early Judaism and Christianity 7. Sheffield: Sheffield Academic Press, 2000.

Naville, Eduard. "Egyptian Writings in Foundation Walls, and the Age of the Book of Deuteronomy." *Proceedings of the Society of Biblical Archaeology* 29 (1907): 232–42.

Nelson, Richard D. *Deuteronomy: A Commentary.* OTL. Louisville, Ky.: Westminster John Knox, 2002.

—*First and Second Kings.* Int. Louisville, Ky.: John Knox, 1987.

Nestle, Eberhard. "Das Deuteronomium und 2 Könige 22." *ZAW* 22 (1902): 170–71, 312–13.

Neufeld, Edward. "The Rate of Interest and the Text of Nehemiah 5.11." *JQR* 44 (1953–54): 194–202.

—"Socio-Economic Background of Yōbēl and Šemiṭṭa." *RSO* 33 (1958): 53–124.

Neusner, Jacob, ed. *Four Stages of Rabbinic Judaism.* London: Routledge, 1999.

—*Judaism in Late Antiquity I: The Literary and Archaeological Sources.* HO 16. Leiden: Brill, 1995.

—*Judaism: The Evidence of the Mishnah.* Chicago: University of Chicago Press, 1981.

—*The Oral Torah: The Sacred Books of Judaism—An Introduction.* San Francisco: Harper & Row, 1986.

—"The Mishnah in Philosophical Context." *JBL* 112, no. 2 (1993): 291–304.

—*The Mishnah: Introduction and Reader.* Philadelphia: Trinity, 1992.

—*The Mishnah: Social Perspectives.* Leiden: Brill, 1999.

—*The Modern Study of the Mishnah.* Leiden: Brill, 1973.

Neusner, Jacob, and Alan J. Avery-Peck, eds. *Judaism in Late Antiquity III: Where We Stand: Issues and Debates in Ancient Judaism.* 2 vols. HO 40. Leiden: Brill, 1999.

Niditch, Susan. *Oral World and Written Word: Ancient Israelite Literature.* Library of Ancient Israel. London: SPCK, 1997.

Nicholson, Ernest W. *Deuteronomy and Tradition.* Oxford: Blackwell, 1967.

—Review of Anthony Phillips, *Ancient Israel's Criminal Law: A New Approach to the Decalogue. Theology* 75 (1972): 154–55.

Nims, Charles F. "The Term *Hp,* 'Law, Right,' in Demotic." *JNES* 7 (1948): 243–60.

Nippel, Wilfried. "The Construction of the 'Other.'" Translated by A. Nevill. Pages 278–310 in Harrison, ed., *Greeks and Barbarians.*

North, Robert. *Sociology of the Biblical Jubilee.* AnBib 4. Rome: Pontifical Biblical Institute, 1954.

Noth, Martin. *Exodus: A Commentary.* OTL. London: SCM Press, 1962.

Ober, Josiah. *The Athenian Revolution: Essays on Ancient Greek Democracy and Political Theory.* Princeton: Princeton University Press, 1996.

—*Mass and Elite in Democratic Athens: Rhetoric, Ideology, and the Power of the People.* Princeton: Princeton University Press, 1989.

O'Brien, Mark A. "The Book of Deuteronomy." *CurBS* 3 (1995): 95–128.

—*The Deuteronomistic History Hypothesis: A Reassessment.* OBO 92. Göttingen: Vandenhoeck & Ruprecht, 1989.

Oppenheim, A. L. *Ancient Mesopotamia: Portrait of a Dead Civilization.* Chicago: University of Chicago Press, 1977.

Östborn, Gunnar. *Tōrā in the Old Testament: A Semantic Study.* Lund: Håkan Ohlssons Boktryckeri, 1945.

Ostwald, Martin. *From Popular Sovereignty to the Sovereignty of Law: Law, Society, and Politics in Fifth-Century Athens.* Berkeley: University of California Press, 1986.

—*Nomos and the Beginnings of the Athenian Democracy.* London: Oxford University Press, 1969.

—"Was There a Concept of ἄγραφος νόμος in Classical Greece?" Pages 70–103 in *Exegesis and Argument: Studies in Greek Philosophy Presented to Gregory Vlastos.* Edited by E. N. Lee et al. Phronesis Supplement 1. Assen: Van Gorcum, 1973.

Otto, Eckart. "Aspects of Legal Reforms and Reformulations in Ancient Cuneiform and Israelite Law." Pages 160–96 in Levinson, ed., *Theory and Method.*

—"Town and Rural Countryside in Ancient Israelite Law: Reception and Redaction in Cuneiform and Israelite Law." *JSOT* 57 (1993): 3–22.

Pagán, Samuel. "Ezra, Nehemiah, and Chronicles." Pages 119–33 in Steussy, ed., *Chalice.*

Paton, L. B. "The Case for the Post-Exilic Origin of Deuteronomy." *JBL* 47 (1928): 322–57.

Patrick, Dale. "Deuteronomy." Pages 63–78 in Steussy, ed., *Chalice.*

—"God's Commandment." Pages 93–111 in *God in the Fray: A Tribute to Walter Brueggemann.* Edited by Tod Linafelt and Timothy K. Beale. Minneapolis: Fortress, 1998.

—*Old Testament Law.* London: SCM Press, 1986.

—Review of Bernard S. Jackson, *Studies in the Semiotics of Biblical Law. CBQ* 64, no. 2 (2002): 353–54.

Patte, Daniel. *Early Jewish Hermeneutic in Palestine.* SBLDS 22. Missoula, Mont.: Scholars Press, 1975.

Paul, M. J. "Hilkiah and the Law (2 Kings 22) in the 17th and 18th Centuries: Some Influences on W.M.L. de Wette." Pages 9–12 in Lohfink, ed., *Deuteronomium.*

Paul, Shalom M. *Studies in the Book of the Covenant in the Light of Cuneiform and Biblical Law.* VTSup 18. Leiden: Brill, 1970.

Person, Raymond F., Jr. *The Deuteronomic School: History, Social Setting, and Literature.* SBL Studies in Biblical Literature 2. Atlanta: Society of Biblical Literature, 2002.

Petschow, H. P. H. "Die §§45 und 46 des Codex Ḫammurapi. Ein Beitrag zum altbabylonischen Bodenpachtrecht und zum Problem: Was ist der Codex Ḫammurapi?" *ZA* 74 (1984): 181–212.

Phillips, Anthony. *Ancient Israel's Criminal Law: A New Approach to the Decalogue.* Oxford: Blackwell, 1970.

—*Essays on Biblical Law.* JSOTSup 344. London: Sheffield Academic Press, 2002.

—"Prophecy and Law." Pages 164–78 in *Essays on Biblical Law.* Repr. from pages 217–32 in *Israel's Prophetic Tradition: Essays in Honour of Peter Ackroyd.* Edited by Richard Coggins et al. Cambridge: Cambridge University Press, 1982.

Philo. *The Works of Philo: Complete and Unabridged.* Translated by C. D. Yonge. Peabody, Mass.: Hendrickson, 1993.

Plato. *Laws.* Translated by R.G. Bury. LCL. London: Heinemann, 1926.

—*The Republic.* Translated by P. Shorey. LCL. London: Heinemann, 1935.

Porter, J. Roy. "The Succession of Joshua." Pages 102–32 in *Proclamation and Presence: Old Testament Essays in Honour of Gwynne Henton Davies.* Edited by John I. Durham and J. Roy Porter. London: SCM Press, 1970.

Propp, W. H. C. *Exodus 1–18.* AB 2. New York: Doubleday, 1999.

Rad, Gerhard von. *Deuteronomy: A Commentary.* Translated by D. Barton. OTL. London: SCM Press, 1973.

Rappaport, Uriel. "The First Judean Coinage." *JJS* 32 (1981): 1–17.

Ray, J. D. *The Archive of Hor.* Texts from Excavations, Memoirs 2. Excavations at North Seqqâra, Documentary Series 4. London: Egypt Exploration Society, 1976.

Redditt, Paul L. "Hasideans." *ABD* 3:66.

Redfield, James. "Herodotus the Tourist." Pages 24–49 in Harrison, ed., *Greeks and Barbarians.*

Redford, Donald B. "The So-Called Codification of Egyptian Law under Darius I." Pages 135–59 in Watts, ed., *Persia and Torah.*

Renaud, B. "La loi et les lois dans les livres des Maccabées." *RB* 68 (1961): 39–67.

Reuter, E. *Kultzentralisation: Zur Entstehung und Theologie von Dtn 12.* BBB 87. Frankfurt: Anton Hain, 1993.

—" 'Nimm nichts davon weg und füge nichts hinzu!' Dtn 13,1 seine alttestamentlichen Parallelen und seine altorientalischen Vorbilder." *BN* 47 (1989): 107–14.

Reviv, Hanoch. "The Traditions Concerning the Inception of the Legal System in Israel: Significance and Dating." *ZAW* 94 (1982): 566–75.

Rofé, Alexander. "The Covenant in the Land of Moab (Deuteronomy 28:69–30:20): Historico-Literary, Comparative, and Form-Critical Considerations." Pages 269–80 in Christensen, ed., *Song of Power.*

—"The Organization of the Judiciary in Deuteronomy (Deut. 16.18–20; 17.8–13; 19.15; 21.22–23; 24.16; 25.1–3)." Translated by H. N. Bock. Pages 92–112 in *The World of the Arameans I: Biblical Studies in Honour of Paul-Eugène Dion.* Edited by P. M. M. Daviau et al. JSOTSup 324. Sheffield: Sheffield Academic Press, 2001.

Rogerson, J. W. Review of Anthony Phillips, *Ancient Israel's Criminal Law: A New Approach to the Decalogue. PEQ* 104 (1972): 157.

Römer, Thomas C. "Transformations in Deuteronomistic and Biblical Historiography: On 'Book-Finding' and other Literary Strategies." *ZAW* 109 (1997): 1–11.

Rostovtzeff, Michael I. *The Social and Economic History of the Hellenistic World.* 3 vols. Oxford: Clarendon, 1941.

Roth, Martha T. "Hammurabi's Wronged Man." *JAOS* 122, no. 1 (2002): 38–45.

—*Law Collections from Mesopotamia and Asia Minor.* SBLWAW 6. Atlanta: Scholars Press, 1995.

—"The Law Collection of King Hammurabi: Toward an Understanding of Codification and Text." Pages 9–31 in Lévy, ed., *Codification.*

Rowlett, Lori L. *Joshua and the Rhetoric of Violence: A New Historicist Analysis.* JSOTSup 226. Sheffield: Sheffield Academic Press, 1996.

Sailhamer, John H. *The Pentateuch as Narrative: A Biblical-Theological Commentary.* Grand Rapids: Zondervan, 1992.

Samely, Alexander. "Between Scripture and Its Rewording: Towards a Classification of Rabbinic Exegesis." *JJS* 42 (1991): 39–67.

—"Delaying the Progress from Case to Case: Redundancy in the Halakhic Discourse of the Mishnah." Pages 99–132 in Brooke, ed., *Ways of Reading*.

—"Justifying Midrash: On an 'Intertextual' Interpretation of Rabbinic Interpretation." *JSS* 39, no. 1 (1994): 19–32.

—Online Database of Midrashic Units in the Mishnah. Online: www.art.man.ac.uk/mes/samely/home.php.

—*Rabbinic Interpretation of Scripture in the Mishnah*. Oxford: Oxford University Press, 2002.

—"Scripture's Implicature: The Midrashic Assumptions of Relevance and Consistency." *JSS* 37, no. 2 (1992): 167–205.

—"Stressing Scripture's Words: Semantic Contrast as a Midrashic Technique in the Mishnah." *JJS* 46 (1995): 196–229.

Sanders, E. P. *Jewish Law from Jesus to the Mishnah: Five Studies*. London: SCM Press, 1990.

—*Judaism: Practice and Belief 63 BCE–66 CE*. London: SCM Press, 1998.

Sanders, J. A. Review of Michael Fishbane, *Biblical Interpretation in Ancient Israel*. *CBQ* 49 (1987): 302–5.

Sarna, Nahum M. *Exodus*. JPS Commentary. Philadelphia: The Jewish Publication Society of America, 1991.

—*Exploring Exodus: The Heritage of Biblical Israel*. New York: Schocken, 1986.

—"Zedekiah's Emancipation of Slaves and the Sabbatical Year." Pages 143–49 in *Orient and Occident: Essays Presented to Cyrus H. Gordon on the Occasion of his Sixty-Fifth Birthday*. Edited by Harry A. Hoffner. AOAT 22. Neukirchen–Vluyn: Neukirchener Verlag, 1973.

Schäfer, Peter. *The History of the Jews in the Greco-Roman World*. London: Routledge, 2003.

Schams, Christine. *Jewish Scribes in the Second-Temple Period*. JSOTSup 291. Sheffield: Sheffield Academic Press, 1998.

Scheil, Jean-Vincent. "Code des lois de Hammurabi." *Mémoires dé la Délégation en Perse, Textes Sémitiques* 4.11–162 (1902) (+ plates 3–15).

Schiffman, Lawrence H. *The Halakhah at Qumran*. SJLA 16. Leiden: Brill, 1975.

—"The *Temple Scroll* and the Nature of Its Law: The Status of the Question." Pages 37–55 in *The Community of the Renewed Covenant: The Notre Dame Symposium on the Dead Sea Scrolls*. Edited by Eugene Ulrich and James C. VanderKam. Christianity and Judaism in Antiquity Series 10. Notre Dame: University of Notre Dame Press, 1994.

Schniedewind, William M. *The Word of God in Transition: From Prophet to Exegete in the Second Temple Period*. JSOTSup 197. Sheffield: Sheffield Academic Press, 1995.

Schürer, E. *Jewish People in the Age of Jesus Christ (175 BC—AD 135)*. Edited by Geza Vermes et al. 3 vols. Edinburgh: T. & T. Clark. 1973–87.

Schwartz, Daniel R. "Israel and the Nations Roundabout: 1 Maccabees and Hasmonean Expansion." *JJS* 42 (1991): 16–38.

—"On Something Biblical About 2 Maccabees." Pages 223–32 in *Biblical Perspectives: Early Use and Interpretation of the Bible in Light of the Dead Sea Scrolls—Proceedings of the First International Symposium of the Orion Center for the Study of the Dead Sea Scrolls and Associated Literature, 12–14 May, 1996*. Edited by Michael E. Stone and Esther G. Chazon. STDJ 28. Leiden: Brill, 1998.

—"The Other in 1 and 2 Maccabees." Pages 30–37 in *Tolerance and Intolerance in Early Judaism and Christianity*. Edited by Graham N. Stanton and Guy G. Stroumsa. Cambridge: Cambridge University Press, 1998.

Sealey, Raphael. *The Athenian Republic: Democracy or the Rule of Law?* London: Pennsylvania State University Press, 1987.

—*The Justice of the Greeks*. Ann Arbor: University of Michigan Press, 1994.

—"On the Athenian Concept of Law." *CJ* 77 (1982): 289–302.

Shaver, Judson R. *Torah and the Chronicler's History Work: An Inquiry into the Chronicler's References to Laws, Festivals, and Cultic Institutions in Relationship to Pentateuchal Legislation*. BJS 196. Atlanta: Scholars Press, 1989.

Shavit, Jacob. *Athens in Jerusalem: Classical Antiquity and Hellenism in the Making of the Modern Secular Jew*. Translated by C. Naor and N. Werner. London: Littman Library of Jewish Civilization, 1997.

Shutt, R. J. H. "Letter of Aristeas." *OTP* 2:7–34.

Sievers, Joseph. *The Hasmoneans and their Supporters: From Mattathias to the Death of John Hyrcanus I*. South Florida Studies in the History of Judaism 6. Atlanta: Scholars Press, 1990.

Sigal, Phillip. *The Emergence of Contemporary Judaism*. Vol. 1, *The Foundations of Judaism from Biblical Origins to the Sixth Century A.D.* Part 1, *From the Origins to the Separation of Christianity*. PTMS 29. Pittsburgh: Pickwick, 1980.

Smith, Morton. "Hellenization." In Stone and Satran, eds., *Emerging Judaism*.

—*Palestinian Parties and Politics that Shaped the Old Testament*. New York: Columbia University Press, 1971.

—"Rome and the Maccabean Conversions: Notes on 1 Macc. 8." In *Donum Gentilicum: New Testament Studies in Honour of D. Daube*. Edited by Ernst Bammel et al. Oxford: Oxford University Press, 1978.

Sonnet, Jean-Pierre. *The Book within the Book: Writing in Deuteronomy*. BibInt 14. Leiden: Brill, 1997.

Speyer, Wolfgang. *Bücherfunde in der Glaubenswerbung der Antike: Mit einem Ausblick auf Mittelalter und Neuzeit*. Hypomnemata 24. Göttingen: Vandenhoeck & Ruprecht, 1970.

Sprinkle, Joe M. Review of Bernard M. Levinson, *Deuteronomy and the Hermeneutics of Legal Innovation*. *JETS* 42, no. 4 (1999): 720–21.

Steinkeller, Piotr. "Studies in Third Millennium Paleography, 2: Signs ŠEN and ALAL." *OrAnt* 20 (1981): 243–49.

Steussy, Marti J., ed. *Chalice Introduction to the Old Testament*. St. Louis, Miss.: Chalice, 2003.

Stone, Michael E., and David Satran, eds. *Emerging Judaism: Studies on the Fourth and Third Centuries B.C.E.* Minneapolis: Fortress, 1989.

Stylianopoulos, Theodore G. *Justin Martyr and the Mosaic Law*. SBLDS 20. Missoula, Mont.: Scholars Press, 1975.

Tacitus. Translated by William Peterson et al. 6 vols. LCL. London: Heinemann, 1963–81.

Taubenschlag, Raphael. *The Law of Greco-Roman Egypt in the Light of the Papyri: 332 B.C.–640 A.D.* Milan: Cisalpino-Goliardica, 1972.

Tcherikover, Victor A. *Hellenistic Civilization and the Jews*. Translated by S. Applebaum. Philadelphia: The Jewish Publication Society of America, 1961.

Theil, Winfried. *Die deuteronomistische Redaktion von Jeremia 26–45: Mit einer Gesamtbeurteilung der deuteronomistischen Redaktion des Buches Jeremia.* WMANT 52. Neukirchen–Vluyn: Neukirchener Verlag, 1981.

Théodoridès, Aristides. "The Concept of Law in Ancient Egypt." Pages 291–322 in *The Legacy of Egypt.* Edited by J. R. Harris. Oxford: Clarendon, 1971.

Thomas, Rosalind. "Written in Stone? Liberty, Equality, Orality and the Codification of Law." Pages 9–31 in *Greek Law in Its Political Setting: Justifications not Justice.* Edited by L. Foxhall and A. D. E. Lewis. Oxford: Clarendon, 1996.

Thompson, Herbert. *A Family Archive from Siut: From Papyri in the British Museum, Including an account of a Trial Before the Laocritae in the Year B.C. 170.* Oxford: Oxford University Press, 1934.

Throntveit, Mark A. *Ezra–Nehemiah.* IBC. Louisville, Ky.: John Knox, 1992.

Tigay, Jeffrey H. *Deuteronomy. JPS Torah Commentary.* Jerusalem: The Jewish Publication Society of America, 1996.

Tod, Marcus. N. *A Selection of Greek Historical Inscriptions.* Vol. 2, *From 403 to 323 BC.* Oxford: Clarendon, 1948.

Tuplin, Christopher. *Achaemenid Studies.* Stuttgart: Steiner, 1996.

Van Selms, Adrianus. "The Goring Ox in Babylonian and Biblical Law." *ArOr* 18, no. 4 (1950): 321–30.

Van Seters, John. "Etiology in the Moses Tradition: The Case of Exodus 18." *HAR* 9 (1985): 355–61.

—*A Law Book for the Diaspora: Revision in the Study of the Covenant Code.* Oxford: Oxford University Press, 2003.

—*The Life of Moses: The Yahwist as Historian in Exodus–Numbers.* Louisville, Ky.: Westminster John Knox, 1994.

Veenhof, Klaus R. "'In Accordance with the Words of the Stele': Evidence for Old Assyrian Legislation." *Chicago-Kent Law Review* 70 (1995): 1717–44.

Venema, G. J. *Reading Scripture in the Old Testament: Deuteronomy 9–10; 31—2 Kings 22–23—Jeremiah 36—Nehemiah 8.* OTS 48. Leiden: Brill, 2004.

VerSteeg, Russ. *Law in Ancient Egypt.* Durham, N.C.: Carolina Academic Press, 2002.

Vidal-Naquet, Pierre. *Le Bordereau d'ensemencement dans l'Egypte ptolémaique.* Papyrologica Bruxellensia 5. Brussels: Foundation égyptologique Reine Elisabeth, 1981.

Vogelsang, Willem J. *The Rise and Organisation of the Achaemenid Empire: The Eastern Iranian Evidence.* SHANE 3. Leiden: Brill, 1992.

Wacholder, Ben Zion. *Eupolemus: A Study of Judaeo-Greek Literature.* Monographs of the Hebrew Union College 3. New York: Hebrew Union College—Jewish Institute of Religion, 1974.

Watson, Alan. *The Evolution of Law.* Oxford: Blackwell, 1985.

—*Legal Transplants: An Approach to Comparative Law.* Edinburgh: Scottish Academic Press, 1974.

—*Society and Legal Change.* Edinburgh: Scottish Academic Press, 1977.

Watts, James W., ed. *Persia and Torah: The Theory of Imperial Authorization of the Pentateuch.* SBLSymS 17. Atlanta: Society of Biblical Literature, 2001.

—*Reading Law: The Rhetorical Shaping of the Pentateuch.* Sheffield: Sheffield Academic Press, 1999.

—Review of Bernard S. Jackson, *Studies in the Semiotics of Biblical Law. Review of Biblical Literature.* RBL 02/2003. No pages. Online: http://bookreviews.org/pdf/1404_3083.pdf.

Weems, Renita J. "Huldah, the Prophet: Reading a (Deuteronomistic) Woman's Identity." Pages 321–39 in *A God So Near: Essays on Old Testament Theology in Honor of Patrick D. Miller*. Edited by Brent A. Strawn and Nancy R. Bowen. Winona Lake, Ind.: Eisenbrauns, 2003.

Weidner, E. F. "Das Alter der mittelassyrischen Gesetzestexte: Studien im Anschluss an Driver and Miles, The Assyrian Laws." *AfO* 12 (1937): 46–54.

Weinfeld, Moshe. *Deuteronomy and the Deuteronomic School*. Oxford: Oxford University Press, 1983.

——*The Organizational Pattern and the Penal Code of the Qumran Sect: A Comparison with Guilds and Religious Associations of the Hellenistic–Roman Period*. NTOA 2. Fribourg, Switzerland: Éditions Universitaires, 1986.

——*Social Justice in Ancient Israel and in the Ancient Near East*. Jerusalem: Magnes, the Hebrew University Press, 1995.

Weippert, Helga. *Die Prosareden des Jeremiabuches*. BZAW 132. Berlin: de Gruyter, 1973.

Weitzman, Steven. "Forced Circumcision and the Shifting Role of Gentiles in Hasmonean Ideology." *HTR* 92, no. 1 (1999): 37–59.

Welles, Charles Bradford. *Royal Correspondence in the Hellenistic Period: A Study in Greek Epigraphy*. Chicago: Ares, 1934.

——"New Texts from the Chancery of Philip V of Macedonia and the Problem of the 'Diagramma,'" *AJA* 42 (1938): 245–60.

Wellhausen, Julius. *Prolegomena to the History of Israel*. Edinburgh: A. & C. Black, 1885.

Westbrook, Raymond.

——"Biblical and Cuneiform Law Codes." *RB* 92, no. 2 (1985): 247–64.

——"Biblical Law." Pages 1–17 in Hecht et al. eds., *An Introduction to the History*.

——Review of Moshe Weinfeld, *Justice and Righteousness in Israel and the Nations: Equality and Freedom in Ancient Israel in the Light of Social Justice in The Ancient Near East*. *RB* 93 (1986): 602–5.

——"The Character of Ancient Near Eastern Law." Introduction on pages 1–90 in vol. 1 of *A History of Ancient Near Eastern Law*. Edited by Raymond Westbrook. 2 vols. Leiden: Brill, 2003.

——"Codification and Canonization." Pages 33–47 in Lévy, ed., *Codification*.

——"Cuneiform Law Codes and the Origins of Legislation." *ZA* 79 (1989): 201–22.

——"Jubilee Laws." *Israel Law Review* 6 (1971): 209–26.

——*Property and the Family in Biblical Law*. JSOTSup 113. Sheffield: JSOT Press, 1991.

——"Social Justice in the Ancient Near East." Pages 149–63 in *Social Justice in the Ancient World*. Edited by Morris Silver and K. D. Irani. Westport, Conn.: Greenwood, 1995.

——*Studies in Biblical and Cuneiform Law*. CahRB 26. Paris: Gabalda, 1988.

——"What is the Covenant Code?" Pages 15–36 in Levinson, ed., *Theory and Method*.

Westbrook, Raymond, and Roger D. Woodard. "The Edict of Tudhaliya IV." *JAOS* 110, no. 4 (1990): 641–59.

Westenholz, Joan G. "Writing for Posterity: Naram-Sin and Enmerkar." Pages 205–18 in *Kinattūtu ša dārâti: Raphael Kutscher Memorial Volume*. Edited by A. F. Rainey. Tel Aviv: Tel Aviv University Press, 1993.

Westerholm, Stephen. *Perspectives Old and New on Paul: The "Lutheran" Paul and his Critics*. Grand Rapids: Eerdmans, 2004.

Wette, W. M. L. de. "Dissertatio critica qua a prioribus Deuteronomium Pentateuchi Libris Diversum alius cuiusdam recentioris auctoris opus esse monstratur." Thesis. 1805.

Whitehead, David. *The Demes of Attica—508/7–CA. 250 B.C.: A Political and Social Study*. Princeton: Princeton University Press, 1986.

Whitelam, Keith W. *The Just King: Monarchical Judicial Authority in Ancient Israel*. JSOTSup 12. Sheffield: Sheffield Academic Press, 1979.

Wiesehöfer, Josef. *Ancient Persia: From 550 BC to 650 AD*. Translated by Azizeh Azodi. New York: I.B. Tauris, 2001.

Wilcken, Ulrich. *Urkunden der Ptolemäerzeit: Älter Funde*. 2 vols. Papyri aus Oberägypten 2. Berlin: de Gruyter, 1957.

Williams, David. "Recent Research in 1 Maccabees." *CurBS* 9 (2001): 169–84.

—"Recent Research in 2 Maccabees." *CBR* 2, no. 1 (2003): 69–83.

Williamson, H. G. M. *Ezra, Nehemiah*. WBC 16. Waco, Tex.: Word, 1985.

Wilson, R. R. "Israel's Judicial System in the Preexilic Period." *JQR* 74, no. 2 (1983): 229–48.

Wilson, J. A. *Authority and Law in the Ancient Orient*. *JAOS* Supplement 17. Baltimore: American Oriental Society, 1954.

Wise, Michael, ed. *Methods of Investigation of the Dead Sea Scrolls and the Khirbet Qumran Site*. New York: New York Academy of Sciences, 1994.

Wise, Michael, et al., eds. *The Dead Sea Scrolls: A New Translation*. New York: Harper Collins, 1996.

Wiseman, Donald J. "The Laws of Hammurabi Again." *JSS* 7 (1962): 161–72.

—"A Gilgamesh Epic Fragment from Nimrud." *Iraq* 37 (1975): 157–63.

Wolff, Hans Julius. "Faktoren der Rechtsbildung im Hellenistisch-Römischen Aegypten." *Zeitschrift der Savigny-Stifung für Rechtsgeschichte romanistiche Abteilung* 70 (1953): 20–57.

—*Das Justizwesen der Ptolemäer*. MBPF 44. Munich: Beck, 1962.

—"Plurality of Laws in Ptolemaic Egypt." *RIDA* (3d Series) 7 (1960): 191–223.

—*Das Recht des griechischen Papyri agyptens in der Zeit der Ptolemaeer und des Prinzipats*. Vol. 1, *Bedingungen und Triebkräfte der Rechtsentwicklung*. Munich: Beck, 2002.

—*Das Recht des griechischen Papyri agyptens in der Zeit der Ptolemaeer und des Prinzipats*. Vol. 2, *Organisation und Kontrolle des privaten Rechtverkehrs*. Munich: Beck, 1978.

Wright, Christopher J. H. "The Ethical Authority of the Old Testament: A Survey of Approaches. Part I." *TynBul* 43, no. 1 (1992): 101–20.

—"The Ethical Authority of the Old Testament: A Survey of Approaches. Part II." *TynBul* 43, no. 2 (1992): 203–31.

—"What Happened Every Seven Years in Israel? Old Testament Sabbatical Institutions for Land, Debt and Slaves." *EvQ* 56 (1984): 129–38, 193–201.

Yaron, Reuven. *Laws of Eshnunna*. Jerusalem: Magnes, 1988.

Yonge, C. D. *The Works of Philo: Complete and Unabridged*. Peabody, Mass.: Hendrickson, 1993.

INDEXES

INDEX OF REFERENCES

13:31–32	236	3:10	219, 236	5:18	220
13:35	207	3:13	208	5:19	220
13:37	211	3:14–20	215	5:22	210
13:48	207	3:15	206, 208,	6:1–6	206
14:4–14	234		216, 219,	6:1	208
14:7	236		220	6:5	208
14:14	207, 208,	3:21	215	6:8	208
	233	3:22	216, 220	6:11	205, 226
14:15	234	3:24–40	206	6:12–17	223
14:16–19	237	3:24–36	220	6:21	208
14:20–23	237	3:24	217	6:23	208
14:20	207	3:28	217	6:28	206, 208
14:24	237	3:29	217	7:2	206, 208
14:25	234	3:30	217	7:8	223
14:29	206, 207	3:31–33	217	7:9	206, 208,
14:41	232	3:31	217		219
15:1	207	3:33	217	7:11	206, 208
15:15–24	237	3:39	217	7:21	223
15:15	207	3:40	219	7:23	206, 208
15:16–21	233	4:1–10	218	7:24	206, 208
15:21	207, 233	4:2	206, 208	7:27	223
16:19	207	4:9–12	213	7:30	206, 208
16:23–24	203	4:10	213	7:37	206, 208
16:24	207	4:11	206, 208	7:38	204, 208
		4:14	206, 208	7:39	218
2 Maccabees		4:16–17	206	8:1–4	209
1:1	205	4:17	206, 208	8:1	218
1:4	208	4:25	208, 210	8:4	209
1:10	205	4:34	208, 212	8:5	204, 218
1:24–25	219	4:38	221	8:16–17	209
2:2	208	4:39	215	8:21	206, 208
2:3	208	4:42	215	8:23	206
2:13	208	4:44–47	237, 238	8:26–27	205
2:18	208	5:1–20	218, 220	8:28	236
2:20–22	206	5:1–4	220	8:29	218
2:21	210	5:4	220	8:33	221
2:22	208	5:6	236	8:34–36	219
2:23	203	5:7–10	238	8:34–35	221
3:1–40	214	5:8	208	8:36	206, 208
3:1	206, 208,	5:9	237	9:1–29	221
	218	5:10	221	9:2	215
3:6	214, 215	5:11	213	9:4–6	221
3:7–39	220	5:13	209	9:5–6	221
3:7	208	5:15	208, 209	9:5	208
3:9–14	215	5:17–30	218	9:8–12	236
3:10–11	215	5:17–18	220, 223	9:12–27	236

INDEX OF AUTHORS